MAKING HISTORY

MAKING HISTORY

RAY MUNCY IN HIS TIME

ELOISE MUNCY WITH JOHN WILLIAMS

New
Leaf
Books

MAKING HISTORY: Ray Muncy in His Time
published by New Leaf Books

ISBN 0-9714289-5-6
Printed in the United States of America

For information:
New Leaf Books, 12542 S. Fairmont, Orange, CA 92869
1-877-634-6004 (toll free)

Visit our website: www.newleafbooks.org

Lovingly dedicated to
David, Marc, and Zac
and their wives

to the memory of
our beloved Kandy

to my precious granddaughters
and grandsons

For they refreshed my spirit and yours also. Such men deserve recognition.

Apostle Paul
I Corinthians 16:18, *NIV*

History is not a science through which we banish the incalculable but rather an analysis of...the surprising hand of Providence.

Let us then praise God for the unexpected, for the untimely, for the crooked, the uneven and the unpredicted. No doubt our existences will grow knotty... as a piece of wood filled with the perplexities of grain and growth. The time will come when a better hand than ours will plane us off and reveal the beauty that irregularity has made.

Raymond Lee Muncy,
"Some Reflections on the
Accidental in History, Personal
and Otherwise"

TABLE OF CONTENTS

FOREWORD

Ray Muncy appears prominently in several of my happiest memories from college days. He was bright, with a healthy balance between seriousness and humor. One never worried that he would be part of an activity that would stray from Christian principles. His later accomplishments—especially as a teacher and writer of history—only increased my admiration for him.

The announcement of his biography kindled my anticipation. I had known only a hint of his early life as an orphan. His love for Eloise was apparent early in their relationship, but their experiences in ministry, their joys and sorrows in family life, even his scholarly work, I had known only from a distance.

The portrait that emerges in *Making History* is endearing. "Consecrated, capable, courageous, compassionate, cooperative"—traits he ascribed to leadership—are clearly and consistently evident in Ray's life.

If Carlyle is correct that "the history of the world is but the biography of great men," it is equally true that the history of families and of institutions is the biography of unique individuals. Ray's life story gives insights into the history of churches of Christ, of Harding University, and of the challenges of life in a Christian family during the last half of the twentieth century.

I feel a debt of gratitude to Ray for his "long obedience in one direction" (borrowing a Peterson title), and to Eloise Muncy and John Williams for making this story accessible!

Harold Hazelip, Chancellor
Lipscomb University
Nashville, Tennessee

ACKNOWLEDGEMENTS

Our effort to bring Ray Muncy's story to the public has been helped by many people. The listing of their names is meager enough thanks, but we hope that the finished book will be a reward of sorts for them.

Gary Swaim and Don Umphrey provided early support and advice, and Al Haley helped us find a publisher. All three men are writers whose example helped in more ways than one.

Along the way Rod Brewer, Patty Barrett, Marvin Robertson, Eugene Underwood, Travis Thompson, Buddy Rowan, and Ken Hammes offered useful suggestions, added information, or made available research material. Ann Dixon and her library staff at Brackett Library aided in research.

Even with our intention to write more a memoir than a biography, we interviewed many people, and they were without exception gracious and helpful, starting with these Harding colleagues of Ray's: Rachel Roberson, Joe Segraves, Mark Elrod, Tom Statom, Paul Haynie, Fred Jewell, Virgil Lawyer, Tom Howard, Don England, Gary Elliott, Dennis Organ, Evan Ulrey, Winfred Wright, Ed Higginbotham, Larry Long, Cecilia and Rowan McCleod, Betty and Ken Davis.

Doug Shields and his wife, Cora Beale, were helpful in filling in details of Ray's time in Mississippi. Woody Loden and Morris Womack, two Freed-Hardeman classmates of Ray's, sent material or shared memories. Connie Peck Selbe of West Virginia reminded us of events from Ray's childhood. Former students Richard Hughes, Kevin Klein and Darlene Rivas provided detailed and useful memories.

Dr. Neale Pryor and his secretary, Martha Hodges, cooperated above and beyond the call of duty in loaning office space and material for research. In addition to encouraging the project, John and Phyllis Clayton read pertinent sections of the manuscript and John granted permission to use material from his books. Tom and Mary Formby sat for an interview, read portions of the manuscript, and encouraged us along the way.

Other generous readers of the manuscript include Mark McInteer, Dean Priest, Larry Long, Alice and Fred Jewell, Mike Cope (also an interviewee and encourager), Harold Hazelip, James Atteberry, Carisse Berryhill, and Dennis Organ, who took on the arduous task of reading page proofs.

The Harding Administration granted a reduced teaching load to John during the spring semester of 2001, a period of time crucial to completing the book. We want to make special mention of Clifton Ganus, who granted an interview, read the manuscript twice, and whose support of the book made it much easier to finish.

Needless to say, we depended on the understanding and cooperation of Eloise's three sons, whose lives are portrayed in the book, even to undertake, much less finish, this project. David, Marc, and Zac shared essential memories and supported their mother's desire to tell an honest story. We are also grateful to their wives, Paula, Tina, and Connie for their support and patience as well.

Speaking of wives, Pam Williams was her usual tolerant self during the project, fulfilling roles of typist, reader, and listener enough times to write the book herself.

We realize that we could have tapped the memories of many more equally willing friends of Ray Muncy, and the book would have been richer for their input. In fact, writing the book has reminded Eloise and shown John just how rich in friends Ray Muncy was. Speaking to them and reliving their memories of Ray during the past few years has been one of the best things about the process.

Thanks to all of those friends listed here and to all those who have blessed the lives of the Muncy family.

Eloise Muncy
John Williams

The Man He Became

Ray's decline and death came too quickly for me. For forty-six years he had been the central human focus of my life, and while we were planning our trip to Greece, one more journey into the unknown, he got sick. Amazingly he had to enter the hospital, but even then I didn't fear the worst. Deluded by his optimism, I thought for a brief moment that he would recover from the heart surgery. However, after coming home from the hospital, he quickly regressed until that night when I knew he would never make it to Greece.

In many ways those days remain vivid. Our anxiety, then grief, seemed to slow down time. I can still remember the dedicated paramedics who worked feverishly to resuscitate him at home before rushing him to the hospital. I recall clearly the kindness of friends and fellow Christians in our home of Searcy, Arkansas, some of whom joined us at White County Medical Center. These precious friends heard with me the terrible words uttered by Dr. Leon Blue.

The memorial service in Searcy was attended by nearly a thousand people and featured Bruce McLarty, minister for the College Church of Christ; Clifton Ganus, Chancellor of Harding University, where Ray had taught for thirty years; and Mike Cope, our former preacher and acclaimed brotherhood speaker. They all said nice things, of course, about Ray's accomplishments: his teaching, his leadership, his devotion to us, and his spiritual maturity. These things are mandatory at a service like that, even when they may not be entirely true. Forgive my bias, but in Ray Muncy's case, they were entirely true.

We all basked in the glow of the official sentiments at Ray's memorial service, but they could not tell the entire story—no eulogy ever can. As I reflect on my time with Ray, I think of Mike's comparison of him to Mr. Valiant in *Pilgrim's Progress*. Mike emphasized the triumphant crossing of the dark river of death, with the trumpets sounding his arrival in the Celestial City. That seems right to me, for life is a journey and Ray made his way valiantly, not in action-movie fashion, but with missteps and real human fears along the way. What needs to be told—what I'd like to tell—are the stories leading up to that triumphant crossing.

Ray's life ended with him a different man than the one I first met. Like all of us, he changed during his journey. It was not a melodramatic change. Our life together had its ups and downs, but Ray was never a profligate and his evolution was a gradual one, the kind of progress, so Christians believe, resulting from God's providence. While life challenges all of us to grow up, God promises spiritual maturity for those who can accept Him as a caring father over time. In that sense my husband's life was unremarkable because he followed so many in the faith who have let God mold them. Still, not everyone grows up, and not everyone was my husband. One of the joys I have now that he is gone is this observation: I liked the man Ray became even more than I liked the man I married.

Don't misunderstand. The guy I married was wonderful: witty, ambitious, and dedicated to the Lord. His dark hair and eyes and small, lithe body attracted me from the first. I was proud to stand beside him on our wedding day, feeling I had the catch of the year among the Freed-Hardeman males. Yet he needed more; he was unfinished and both of us knew it. The sense of unfinished business was exciting to me, I think; it gave me a sense of going somewhere. For if Ray was bound to have himself "perfected," I would be there to see it. Further, I felt a part of him early on, and that meant I would also be changed.

Maybe that's why weddings are so exciting—as we stand there, brand new husbands and wives, we sense life's possibilities in each other, the unfulfilled promise of the human race residing in seed form within us. It is a giddy feeling all right and not all mere romance. Or maybe that's what romance is, in its fullest sense, an overpowering whiff of potential perfection. New lives, children, careers. New churches. New hopes for humanity. I don't mean that I was conscious of any such grand ideas, only that their hidden presence explains some of the excitement I felt, the pride in simply being with Ray. New beginnings, with their hope, remain among God's great gifts to His children.

On December 17th, 1993, after forty-six years on the journey of hope with Ray, I saw it coming to an end. We were in Eureka Springs when Ray became ill. I drove him to the local hospital, and the next day he was air-lifted to Springdale, where he had open-heart surgery on December 20. We returned to Searcy on December 30. In our home at 1002 Hayes we wel-comed what proved to be the last of many new years together. I had lived with Ray Muncy for the second half of the twentieth century. Gracious enough to give me that much time with my husband, God also gave me the strength to face the twenty-first century without him.

Ray was a man of his times, so I'm interested in saying some things about those times—not as a historian of course—but as a participant. Ray's life and mine have seen changes in the world at large as well as the two other "worlds" most important to us: the church and Christian education. It's not that we were at the center of the most dramatic moments or change. Ray did not join the charismatic movement or engage in Vietnam war polemics or debate communism or advocate new roles for women. But he did journey from the more narrow concerns of a post-war brotherhood to the tensions of what I've heard some writers call the postmodern church. Along the way we had many small adventures, some funny, some sad, most quiet—as adventures of the spirit usually are.

I am not presumptuous enough to say that Ray was an Everyman, but his life does represent what many lived, members of a generation that just missed coming of age in the depression, just missed service in World War II, and just missed the certainty of a simpler America. If that slightly older group can be called, as one observer has done, "the greatest generation," Ray's life falls into the category of greatest generation, peace-time division. Reaching adulthood at the end of the 1940s, Ray and his Christian peers faced a much more amorphous foe than Hitler or poverty. They had to fight the anonymous, intense battles—conflicts of the heart and intellect—for meaning in a culture where the old values were increasingly questioned and the old answers seemed less and less satisfactory.

In this "good fight," not all the battles were, at first glance, worth head-lines, but on closer inspection the fate of families and churches hinged on their outcome. Not all of them ended in victory, but all yielded fruit of the Spirit. In light of that reality, Ray Muncy's achievements represent the quiet victories of God in the lives of those who try to live for Him.

I should make clear that as a participant in the events of Ray's life, I do

not pretend to be objective or comprehensive or complete. I have recorded the events the way I remember them, with help from friends and family and written documents. Some readers might be bothered by an occasionally reconstructed conversation, but I resort to inventing particular words or
content only when I could not discover the actual content of what was said
or done, and when I feel confident that those approximate words or descriptions will not distort the truth of what happened. Of course, in one sense,
any telling of a story is a distortion because of the limitations or bias of the
teller. Sometimes more than one witness or participant can clarify the picture, sometimes muddle it. In the process of talking to others about the
events described in this book, I have learned the frustrating lesson that few
things will be recalled exactly the same way by any two people who were
involved. Thus I apologize in advance for episodes that seem to any reader
inaccurate or incomplete. As Ray knew, the past is hard to subdue using
mere words.

As part of my desire to capture the past, I have tried to make this an
honest record of both the strengths and weaknesses of my family. In some
cases, I offer opinions on events or people with whom Ray and I came in
contact. My guideline here has been truth in love. If I thought that some
information or opinion would do more harm than good, I have not included it. This doctrine of honesty starts with how I portray myself. As I write
this book, I realize it will show my weaknesses perhaps more than those of
anyone else. I am content to face the judgment of readers because I'd like to
feel that life has taught me to "rise above" any bad thoughts and deeds, as
Ray might put it.

Besides, Ray's story would mean much less if I were to withhold too
much. Ignoring flaws, trouble or conflict only robs any story of its power. The
Bible is my chief model here. It unflinchingly depicts the sins of its main
characters, but only to have us appreciate the salvation they found in God.
The struggle makes the prize all the sweeter. Our life has had its struggles and
revealed flaws in us and in our family and friends. Now, near the top of the
mountain, I can see more clearly how those struggles have fit in with God's
plan. The pain in my life, whether it involved my own weakness, my children, friends, or Ray, has been used by God to get us up the mountain. I'd like
to think of my life with Ray as an upward journey that readers of this book
will find familiar and encouraging.

ONE

Little Raymond with the Musical Feet

Rand, West Virginia (1928-1946)

SON OF A COALMINER'S DAUGHTER

Ray Muncy was born in a place that no longer exists. Before it died of attrition, Eunice was not far from Cabin Creek, off Route 60 which went through nearby Charleston, the largest city in West Virginia, a state better known for its natural beauty and coal mining than for its cities. A few years ago some government-hired ad agency contrived the slogan "wild and won-derful" to describe the state. In 1928, the adjective "wild" applied a good deal more than "wonderful."

On June 26 of that year Lona Muncy Jack gave birth to her fifth child. She called him Raymond Lee, and though I suppose she loved him as much as she did the previous four, his arrival probably did not seem wonderful to her. After all, her husband, John E. Jack, was having trouble finding steady work. He tried a little coal mining with his father and with Lona's dad, Lotus Muncy, and later worked on the railroads, but times were hard and nothing seemed to last long. In between births she tried to deal with the men who made life tough for women: the bosses who would not hire, the slovenly cronies who took John away from home. And she tried to pay attention to the five children who crowded in the little house in a place called Eunice that, like so many of the small towns in West Virginia, had been carved out of a mountainside and seemed to begrudge a living, or even human comfort, to its inhabitants.

Before Ray came along there had been Audra, then Thelma, then Charlotte. Out came annual babies, as if it was Lona's duty to add a new life for each year of marriage. The three sisters saw their first brother, Paul, as a bearable intrusion. Then Lona took a year off and didn't have a child. Two years later Ray fell into the world, though, demanding much of Lona's time and adding to his sisters' chores. Maybe in Ray they caught a glimpse of how hard life was going to be. They could see their mother going from sunrise to dark without rest. In the months after Ray's birth they saw her change. The thin lips rarely broke into a smile. The smooth round face peered at the world through sad almond eyes set above a slightly flattened nose. She kept her dark braided hair swept back from her forehead, but strands of it broke loose as each hard day wore on. Her child's body shrank. John Jack seemed different too. The brightness of his eyes flickered; his tall frame—six feet two inches— filled the house on days he did not work. Both of them, dark-haired and dark-eyed, moved as if weighed down. Lona started spending time in the bathroom; the girls (Audra was six) heard veiled references to pregnancy. The husband and wife exchanged long, meaningful glances when the subject of babies came up. Lona was surrounded by the bittersweet fruit of her womb.

I try to imagine what it must have been like for a woman in those circumstances. Men were different then, rougher, closer to the frontier mentality, especially in a place where life itself was coarser. My instinct is that Lona must have felt isolated in the midst of harsh male reality. She was the only female survivor in Lotus Muncy's family. Several girls died, leaving her alone with the eleven brothers. To illustrate the rough masculine world of that day, Ray would tell stories and point to a sepia photograph of a nameless saloon in Kanawha county. The vertical gray boards of the building look weather-beaten. Sitting and standing on the ramshackle front porch are twenty men in various poses with beer bottles. They wear hats and vests and handlebar mustaches. Ray would isolate with his finger the central figure in the group, a tall, strong man turned sideways, swilling a bottle of beer: "That, no doubt, is a Muncy!" he would laugh.

Whoever it might have been, it was not John Jack. Ray's father was not around much. If things had not turned out as they did, Lona would have faced a tough decision; she had too many children and not enough life to give them. It was not uncommon for parents in those days to give up children to extended family. Grandmothers turned into de facto parents. Lona could have considered such a move in those stretches of time when John was away looking for work, or when he did get a temporary job with the railroad. Surrounded by four dirty children and new baby Raymond in a coal camp

shack, she would be tempted. The camps were collections of two-room houses with plank floors, erected originally by the coal company but after some
time and evictions likely to be inhabited by any poor worker. In some camps
the shelters were no more than tents. Transients often outnumbered resi-
dents. Life was improvisational and often dangerous.

One night when the children were all asleep, Lona's neighbors heard a
shot. Gunshots that close meant either a quarrel or a raid by company detectives, so they rushed to see what had happened. They found Lona dead, the
floor bloody, and a weapon nearby. No one remembers how many of the children had been awakened by the shot. Barely 10 months old, Ray was too young
to know what was going on. I can only imagine the effect the sight would have
had on his three older sisters and toddler Paul. Did the neighbors find him crying over his mother's body? And John Jack was there, somewhere. Did he greet
the neighbors with the news? The investigation, if it can be called that, turned
up nothing conclusive. People talked, of course. They wondered who in the
world would have left a gun there, or why John had so little to say. He had
always been an evasive sort of man; after his wife's death he faded into the
landscape even more. Officially the cause of death was unnamed; privately it

*Ray's mother, Lona Muncy, at about the time she married
John Jack.*

was judged suicide or domestic murder. One of them, Lona Jack or John Jack, had decided Lona's future—and the future of the unborn baby, if there was one.

The children were divided three ways. John Jack and his three daughters went to live with Grandma Schoolcraft, his mother, at Sissonville. Paul went to Uncle Tony and Delia Jack's place in Logan County. Ray was adopted in spirit the night of his mother's death by his great-uncle, John D. Muncy, and his wife Flara. Muncy was a hard-working, hard-living man of some size and strength, who had in his younger years worked in the mines. Sometime around 1930—by the time the Muncys had moved to Rand—he got on at DuPont, which meant that the family could get by, but Flara was obsessed with saving money. Maybe it was the memory of how they had lost everything in a flash flood a few years before Ray came to live with them. When the solid earth itself turns to raging water, you would take nothing for granted. Flara seemed to have a perpetual anxiety about financial security. A stocky, buxom woman, she walked the hills around Charleston looking for work—mostly as a restaurant cook. It wasn't much, but it enabled her to pinch a few more pennies, which she hoarded and doled out to John D at her pleasure. More than once he begged for his allowance in front of their foster son.

When Ray came along, Flara had a new male to bring into line. Since she and John D were childless, control of the boy proved to be a new and sometimes difficult experience.

Ray remembered a trip to Kresge's five and dime when he was four. It was a glorious day in the big city of Charleston and a chance to eat at the famous lunch counter. A piece of pie spoiled lunch. Ray didn't like it, or maybe he wanted a piece that Flara wouldn't let him have. Anyway, Ray threw a fit, probably screamed and pounded the counter. Her first reaction was to ask a nearby stranger, "What do you do with a child who acts like that?" Maybe she meant it rhetorically, but based on what happened next, I'm not so sure. If she did mean the question as a way to express her own exasperation, she was surprised to hear the man to whom she posed it answer quickly and bluntly. He said, "You do something that you haven't done enough of with this one!" He needed to say no more. Flara grabbed Ray from the counter and began to spank him with the flat of her right hand, holding the squirming child with her left. Ray remembered hating that stranger who had brought down such wrath upon his tender behind.

In spite of occasional whippings like this, Flara let Ray run free most of the time and harped on his faults when he was at home. Criticism was part of the child's education, but the strongest teaching John D and Flara did involved Ray's father. They were convinced that John Jack had murdered their niece. As soon as Ray was old enough, they inculcated the hateful lesson in him. Poisoned by the indoctrination of John D and Flara, Ray found it hard to accept his real father. They met when Ray was entering adolescence, after the Muncys had moved to Rand. The tears shed by John Jack on that first reunion did little to melt Ray's heart. It took time for him to love his father. But eventually it happened. He saw, for one thing, that his foster parents were so much better off financially and that splitting up the family allowed him and the others to survive. Who knows what privations they would have endured had they stayed together? Looking back from the vantage point of adulthood, Ray could even see love in those tears, a father agonizing over how to save his family. As an adolescent, however, he saw John Jack as another hard-living, apathetic railroad man and part-time miner who had killed his mother by gunshot or indirectly by neglect. The man possessed only one redeeming trait back then, as far as Ray could see: he was a teetotaler, which made him unique in his crowd.

If the men drank too much and stayed away from the women too much, it was because of the mines. The coal mining industry presided over the southern half of the state like a perverse god. The men looked to it with hope of a decent living but got mostly blackened souls to go with blackened faces. South of Charleston in Matewan, in 1920, eight years before Ray's birth, the miners shot it out with company detectives because they could no longer abide the scabs sent in to take their jobs, and because Albert C. Felts, head of the strike-breaking group known as the Baldwin-Felts Detective Agency, shot the mayor of Matewan in broad daylight for having the audacity to side with the miners. The agency also brought in Italian and African-American workers to replace striking locals, a tactic designed to play on the racial and xenophobic hatreds of the hill people. The coal company was banking on anti-scab emotion to be bolstered by bigotry.

In 1920 labor relations were palpably raw, with no federal regulations to control the passions of either side. Capitalism itself was raw, with owners often unwilling to provide basic safety for their workers. The company owned the very houses its employees lived in and paid in tokens redeemable only at company stores. It charged the workers for every conceivable item or service that could be labeled as extra—even the work of timbering the mine shafts had to be done at the miner's expense, if he wanted any safety at all down below. The union men, the socialists, and the communists rallied workers with cries of the system's heartlessness: "To the company, you're not a man; you're just another piece of machinery to be used and then thrown away!" All that sounds one way in classroom debate; it had a different ring to a wide-eyed five-year-old who listened to stories about the battles fought on West Virginia soil for the dignity of its workers. It got very personal for the Muncy family.

A year after the Matewan massacre, the union tried to expand to Logan over in Mingo County. Over 2,500 of them marched toward town but were met by company detectives carrying machine guns. Droning ominously above them, company planes—rumored to have guns, even bombs aboard—removed any doubt about whether or not this was a war. The miners and union organizers retreated in the face of such firepower to a little town called Blair, where they held out for four days, reinforced by volunteers from northern West Virginia, Kentucky, and Ohio. The state government pressured President Harding to issue an order for the miners to disperse to their homes. The problem was that most of them had no homes—having been evicted when the protests began. Finally Harding gave in to further state demands and sent 2,000 federal troops as well as a squadron of bombers. When skirmishes left several members dead, the union retreated completely. After the carnage, 543 miners were arrested and twenty-two charged with treason. John D. Muncy, Ray's great uncle and adoptive father, was one of the twenty-two. A jury found all of them innocent, but Ray, hearing the story at the feet of John D, the man who raised him, absorbed the legacy of what it's like to be an enemy of your own country. Though he never got very close to a mine, Ray grew up union.

THE OLD FARM HOUR: MUNCY ON STAGE

Protest against the government was part of life for the Muncy's social class. It even got into the cowboy and country music taking hold in the state. The depression had created a lot of restless men who traveled the country in search of work. Buddy Starcher was one of them. Born in Ripley, West Virginia, he learned Appalachian music from his grandfather and took it with him to Charleston, then out of state to Baltimore and Washington, D.C., where he saw and joined a protest group called the Bonus Army. Buddy sang the "Bonus Blues" on the streets while his fellow "soldiers" passed out the lyrics on leaflets. The song expressed the same anger that could be seen in the eyes of coal men as they emerged from the mines:

> When we were in France, boys, fightin' for our lives,
> And thinkin' of our mothers, our sweethearts, and wives;
> Hoover was at home, boys, and he made himself rich—
> Now we fight for our bonus and sleep in a ditch.

Anti-government sentiment attracted small audiences, and Buddy's career as protest singer was short-lived. Soon he wandered back to Charleston, about the time radio had come into its own as a vehicle for country music, and blended into a host of other performers trying to make a living. Country music was more entertainment than protest as audiences demanded escape from the harsh reality of depression. By 1933, when Buddy got back to town, WCHS had begun to do live shows. It had hired Frank Welling to emcee the *Old Farm Hour* in the persona of Uncle Si, a rambunctious codger who joked with hillbilly comics and introduced the acts. Soon Buddy Starcher joined the station's favorite country music show. The owners of stations like WCHS were not entirely comfortable with country music; it was lowbrow; it did not help the image of the state. But the people had loved it ever since Wheeling started broadcasting it a few years earlier. They loved not only the visiting acts like Grandpa Jones but the local boys and girls who would drive from Ripley or Sissonville or Belle to audition for Uncle Si. These were folks just like them—their own relatives on the magic airwaves singing about hard times or lost love.

Old Farm Hour ran from six to eight in the morning, so you would have to load up the Model T early —if you lived in Nicholas County you might have to leave at 4 A.M. The roads were not good and the sharp mountain curves made travel slow and dangerous, especially when the fog and factory smoke rose up from the valleys. But it would be worth it if your favorite niece could sing "The Good Ship Lollipop," or if Uncle Joe got a chance to fiddle for a radio audience. He might even win a spot in the big shindig Frank Welling was putting together: "West Virginia String Band, Fiddlers, and Yodelers Championship Contests." Eventually the station got its own auditorium and the people could come see as well as listen. They came to glimpse some reflections of their happier selves in those depression days of the 1930s.

On one Saturday in 1933, a five-year-old boy arrived in the company of his great-aunt and -uncle. He had dark hair slicked down with Vitalis. He wore a poor family's version of knickers, black shorts actually, and a wide-lapelled tan jacket. His yellow tie was short and fat, with a cartoon wolf adorning the middle of its broadest part. He looked up at Aunt Flara, the only mother he had ever known, with eyes brown and bright, his left hand holding her right in the small crowd backstage so as not to get swept away—like he might in the Kanawha River she always warned him about, painting terrible, vivid pictures of boys drowning in its dirty expanse. But he wasn't really afraid, either. He wanted to show the big people he could dance.

Ray as a child in an outfit that was one of Flara's favorites.

He stared down at the tap shoes Flara had bought him. I wonder if she could afford lessons for him in those days. When she returned Raymond's gaze, she felt pride in his outfit though the coat was baggy and the shorts did not really match anything else. Still, she loved to dress the boy; in summer she clothed him all in white, a Victorian dream of masculine purity. But the shoes had been her extravagance, her final touch in this public display. They were black with metal studs gleaming at the edges where shoe met floor. She smiled down at Raymond. He was so excited that in spite of her sense of dislocation in this place she felt part of something grand.

Ray smiled back at her and swiveled his head around and up to Dad Muncy. Dad Muncy had helped him lace up the shoes back at home in the darkness of 5 A.M.; the strings felt thick to Ray's little fingers. It was winter and the stove was not yet going, so grasping the strings was almost like tying rope. But Uncle John D. Muncy, the only daddy he had ever known, calmly pulled Ray's hands away and found the strings. Ray felt the sharp tightening of the whole shoe and then the firm knot on top of his foot. The old man never looked at Ray, but he murmured softly in the darkness as he cinched up the shoes until Ray's feet felt secure.

He loved the stiff new feel of the shoes. In the car he glanced down at them repeatedly as from the front seat he heard the voices of his aunt and uncle. Aunt Flara sounded worked up, but John D kept talking to her in the same murmuring tones with which he had soothed Ray back at the house. Ray could not really understand the words, but the rhythm was familiar: a burst of tense, rapid female sound followed by slow male monosyllables, and maybe a pause, followed by the screech of a handle being turned, and the moist thud of John D's lips spitting tobacco out the open window. Ray didn't worry about the habit in February, but in summer he would have to duck because often as not, the juice would blow back in the open rear window and seek him out. This morning he just noted it dreamily as punctuation in the drama played out in the predawn world of the moving car. John D was calming her down, but she needed to spit out a few doubts, or complaints, or accusations before she could swallow her anxiety. Then the only sounds would be the engine, the screech of the handle, and the soft explosion of the tobacco flying into the air. The familiar rhythm of their lives comforted the little boy even as the car swerved around mountain curves in the dark.

Even without light he looked at the shoes. They were beautiful. They offered evidence of grace beyond the limits imposed by life as he lived it then. He didn't really get sick until later, but he lived in the valley of smoke and mines and industry. The grime stained everything and the smoke was part of the air. Sickness was a way of life. He had heard Flara say, "Why, none of those Hatfield boys survived childhood." If it wasn't illness it was the machinery. Years later, his older brother Paul would take a screw in the chest one day in the mine; it would be spat out by an ornery machine and he would be in the way, so he would die at twenty-four. In West Virginia, kids were taught by experience to grab for pleasure when they had a chance. And dancing for the radio people was a chance.

I don't know where Ray got the idea he could dance, maybe from the street performers he saw on the tobacco-stained sidewalks of Charleston on trips with Dad Muncy. But there he was, backstage at the WCHS auditorium waiting to perform. He had come in earlier in the week with his foster parents. Old Uncle Si himself had greeted them. He did not sound the same there in the empty auditorium as he had on the radio. On radio he talked loud about the healing powers of Pow-a-Tan Tonic and cackled when he laughed at the jokes of others. Ray could almost imagine him in a clown suit. But at the audition he spoke quietly and crisply, with hardly a trace of hillbilly accent. People walking by even called him by a different name—Frank.

"So you dance, do you, little man?" He smiled down at Ray. Flara had to nudge Ray twice to get him to respond. "Well, I want you to dance for me right now a little bit. We just love little boys who can dance—I see you got tap shoes on. Can you show me some steps?"

It had been pretty quick. Ray shuffled on the stage floor without music for about thirty seconds while Uncle Si/Frank watched. Then he called some-one named Buddy over to sit at the piano. "I'll tell you what," he said. "Since you're a fine little man, why don't you do your dance on this great big piano? I think our crowd would just love to see that." For some reason, I don't think Ray would have been daunted by this new wrinkle. He was already becom-ing an adventurer of sorts, being left pretty much to his own devices during long summer days. Anyway, John D lifted him up on the piano where he did his steps while Buddy played a tinkly tune.

Frank Welling was satisfied. Now they must name this new local act. Whether it was suggested by Ray's family or Welling, the eventual name might have been borrowed from a Charleston native with the stage moniker of Orville Q. Miller, who called himself the "boy with the musical feet." The "Q" stood for "quickstep," and Miller was enough of a local celebrity in the early '30s to have inspired listeners like Ray. The three of them—Ray, Flara, and John D—had returned to Rand in a state of excitement. Little Raymond was going to be on radio.

By the time Ray sat on a wooden bench in the crowded WCHS audito-rium on Saturday morning, waiting to perform again on the piano top, he was known as Little Raymond with the musical feet. Adult performers towered over him. John D and Flara sat on either side, rigid and quiet in the general melee. Storming back and forth as the Muncys watched, Uncle Si had revert-ed to more of his radio personality. He was energetic and jovial, directing stagehands and musicians alike out of pre-show chaos into some semblance of order. He even stopped to reassure the amateurs like Ray and his parents: "Your boy's gonna do fine! Now don't you worry. He'll do the same thing as the other day—just two minutes, same tune, everything. It'll be fine." He said this to John D. Flara sat almost trance-like on the backless bench. She locked her knees and teeth together in this strange environment, from time to time admonishing Ray to sit straight or not to ask too many questions. John D nod-ded to Uncle Si, who added quickly before sashaying over to another act, "Now remember, Little Raymond here is first up after the op'nin' chorus and mah tête-à-tête with Slim Clere and Nimrod."

Ray listened to the crackle of microphones being tested, stared at the welter of wires, inhaled the cigarette smoke that hung over the backstage, and tried to take in all the people gathering, shifting, leaving, and arriving. Finally everyone started shushing each other. Some people disappeared into the dark hallway behind the stage and those who stayed organized themselves around the various benches in the space behind and to the left of the stage. These were the other amateurs, the locals who could not be fitted into the dressing rooms. Ray saw clusters of two or three men and women that included some young girls but no other children his age. He was the only little boy there, a realization that awed him.

The people began to get wavy in his sight and something alive gnawed at his stomach. He sought Flara's hand and she squeezed it without a word. He was not sure he could stand up, though. He heard music and suddenly men and women emerged from the hallway and stampeded past the amateurs as the heavy dark curtain parted. From his seat, Ray could see only the backs of dozens of these giants, but mingled with the fiddles and guitars he heard the stirring of hundreds of others beyond the stage. At the precise moment the chorus of performers erupted into song, Ray felt a surge of true terror through his already weakened legs.

Quickly the song was over and the stampede reversed direction. Uncle Si stayed on the stage with two other men dressed in colorful clothes. As they yelled at each other, Ray's vision cleared enough to realize one of the giants had stopped in front of him. It was a lanky boy dressed in powder blue, fringed shirt and big hat, smiling not a foot from Ray's face. "Hey there, partner, you look a little peaked." John D agreed that he sure enough did and told the young man that it was Raymond's first time at the show. "Oh, so you're little Raymond! I been wantin' to meet you, son. I can't wait to see you step lively on that piano!" Ray nodded, but his face did not signify eagerness at the prospect.

The cowboy, who was on his haunches, grabbed Ray's knee. "Let me tell you somethin, young'un. There's no need to be nervous cause these people love you. I know, 'cause I've been all around these parts—to Cincinnati even—and that's the way folks are." He winked at Flara and gave Ray's knee one more squeeze before rising: "Go get'em, son!" he said over his shoulder, where a guitar was slung. Then the sound of applause broke the spell. A man came up to where John D, Flara, and Ray sat and told them Ray was on. He took Ray's hand and led him to a point just out of the audience's sight. Ray could hear Uncle Si talking about him before the man gently pushed Ray onto the stage.

The lights shone down brilliantly and reduced the people in the audience to a dark mass. To his right, Ray saw Uncle Si beckoning, his form outlined in a thin bright halo. With the desperation of Peter seeing Jesus standing on the water, Ray rushed for his old friend, who reached down to shake his hand with much pomp and circumstance.

"And where are you from, Li'l Raymond?"

"Rand."

"Well, Ra-aand! That thrivin' metropolis just down the road! We are proud to have you! What say you show these folks how they dance in Rand?" With that he swept Ray up to the piano, told the pianist to hit it, and Ray heard the same tinkly music he had danced to at the audition. For two minutes he tapped and pirouetted on the tiny stage. Flara and John D took up a vantage point backstage where they could see Ray from behind.

"Oh my Lord," Flara cried twice, "he's comin' too close to the edge! He's gonna fall!" John D just murmured that he would be all right. With seconds to go Ray went into his big finish, kicking his feet out behind him and thrusting his arms in the same direction, like Bill Bojangles Robinson. When the music stopped he bowed and someone else, not Si, scooped him up and guided him backstage, where for just a moment he could not see Uncle John D or Flara. He felt flushed, dizzy, lost. Then they hurried up to embrace him. They both seemed very happy, even Flara. To his surprise, she hugged him tightly and, like the best show business mom, declared how proud she was of her little Raymond.

Before they left, some other people talked to John D and Flara about Ray coming back, then invited them to watch the rest of the show from backstage, which they did. After Ray got a cool drink and went to the bathroom, he fell asleep in Flara's lap and missed most of the show. He woke up in time to see a tall, pale blue ghost cross his line of vision. Then he heard Uncle Si announce, "Ladees and gentlemen, *The Farm Hour* is proud to conclude this great show with a true singing star, all the way from Cincinnati, the one and only Cowboy Copas!" Fully awake now, Ray strained to see this familiar figure. Although from the rear he could make out only the big hat and blue fringe trailing from the arms of the singer, Ray knew: "Mother, we know him. We know Cowboy Copas!" And maybe somewhere in his little boy's head, he realized how right his friend Cowboy had been. In show business, everybody loves everyone. The stage must have seemed like the best place in the world.

LIFE ON THE KANAWHA

No one can remember how many times Ray went back to the station, and no one knows how long his stardom lasted, but it lived like a meteor in his memory. He told the story often. It was the most modern event of his childhood; otherwise he lived as if in the 19th century. Oh, he was Tom

Sawyer all right, to hear him tell it, living on West Virginia's version of the Mississippi River: the Kanawha.

Aunt Flara supervised him about like Aunt Polly kept track of Tom. As severe as she could be, Ray's adventures imply that she pretty much let him run free during the summer. The family lived in a small white clapboard house on a dirt service road. Its covered porch rested on three rows of concrete blocks, with steps up to the front door and a black wrought-iron rail to hold on to. The house sat on a ledge. Behind it rose a sheer, wooded mountain, so that it felt closed in, the end of the line. Each summer day of his childhood, it seemed, Ray would go out the door and down the steps in the morning, past the barn and the family cow, and not come back until dark.

While he was out he found his friends and took off for the river, where they swam, fought, and courted death. Ray and his buddies acted out their own version of the Hatfields and McCoys on the banks of the Kanawha River that separates North from South Charleston, winding through the hills and valleys where factories still send out smoke that lies like fog over the city. They cultivated an opposing army of boys on the other side of the river. The two groups taunted each other, then escalated into hurling bricks across the river, and would have been shocked if they ever hit anybody. As far as I know, there were no casualties in the skirmishes, but lots of glory to go around.

Ray's childhood home in Rand, West Virginia.

Far more dangerous than the brick battles was the sport of chasing the paddle steamboats that went by. The idea was to get as close to the churning paddle wheel as possible. To feel the exhilarating wake, with its violent waves pulling you under then bouncing you back up again. It was an exhaust-ing game that began with a swim of at least fifty yards to the center of the river and then another few minutes of furious stroking to find the wake. It all proved to the boys their own bravery. During Ray's childhood, one boy had bad luck, though; he got too close to the wheel and went under, hit his head on the bottom, and never came up. Undaunted, Ray swam strong in his childhood, proud of his ability to get close enough to feel the pull of the big paddle without letting it take him under.

When Ray did not go with boys his age, he might take off with some of the gypsy families that passed through the area in the summers, trying to sell their willow furniture and scam old ladies when they could. They even used little Raymond a few times to distract potential victims.

I'm not sure how many times he went with these wanderers, but the fact that he did is significant. Like them, the child was in a sense drifting. Separated from his siblings, without experienced parents, he was a candidate for trouble or tragedy. Before John D and Flara became religious, for exam-ple, they, like so many of the hill people, made, drank, and sold their own brew. Prohibition gave them one more way to make some money. They mixed the stuff in their bathtub and entertained others until the wee hours of the morning. Ray had vivid memories of himself as a child of no more than five or six, awaking early in the morning and meandering among the remains of the previous night's party while the adults slept it off in the base-ment. It was a ragtag group of relatives and hangers-on, dead to the world by sun up, their inert forms the object of Ray's scrutiny. The small house was strewn with bottles and glasses and unwashed plates. When Ray found some liquid left in a glass, he would gladly drain it. After helping himself to sever-al such dregs on one occasion, he felt his head spin and had to sit down. So little Raymond with the musical feet got drunk, after a fashion, in his own house one quiet morning.

John D and Flara had a lot to learn as parents, though they did their best. At times they treated their new child more like a hired man than as a son. The family cow had to be driven into the barn during thunderstorms. It was always Ray's job. I can still see, from Ray's descriptions, that frail lit-tle boy chasing a cow on a West Virginia mountainside with lightning flash-ing all around, while John D was at work and Flara watched apprehensively from inside.

If danger didn't come from the sky, it came from his friends. One of Ray's cousins, Bill Gardner, remembers when some of Ray's friends tried to hang him. They were about twelve years old and playing at Bill's house. For some reason the rest of them talked Ray into putting a noose around his neck and standing on a flower pot. Someone kicked the pot out from under Ray's feet. If Dave, Bill's dad, had not entered at that point, who knows what would have happened? Years later when Ray was preaching at Belle, he stopped in the middle of his lesson when he saw Bill and Uncle Dave walk in: "But by the grace of God that man would have killed me!" he told the startled congregation. While the embarrassed Gardners smiled uncomfortably, Ray then related the story.

He spent a lot of time with the Marshalls, a nearby Italian family that took to Ray. Mr. Marshall had shortened his Italian name for the benefit of West Virginians who could not pronounce it. He tried to provide for a big family, and came to John D once on behalf of his son, knowing that Ray's father worked for DuPont. He spoke in broken English: "I want that you should getta my son Sammy a job. He a gooda pipe fitta but he no speaka English!" The musical intonations, so different from the flat drawl of his own people, delighted the young Ray. Despite John D's inability to help him in that case, Mr. Marshall showed no resentment. The Marshalls always welcomed Ray, often asking "little Ramone" to stay for supper in their big kitchen where they served warm, buttered slices of bread and passed around a block of Parmesan cheese. The Marshalls influenced him considerably in those years by providing a more joyous, loving atmosphere and by allowing a glimpse of an ethnic world beyond West Virginia.

That larger world turned dangerous in 1941, when the Japanese bombed Pearl Harbor and brought America into World War II. The Muncys were relatively untouched by the war, really, but Ray learned the news in traumatic fashion for a thirteen-year-old. He had been outside when he noticed how quiet things seemed. In the house he discovered John D and Flara gathered around a radio—there may have been others in the house too—listening with somber faces to the words, "The Japanese have bombed West Virginia!" Ray gasped and ran outside, searching the sky for planes and straining to hear the explosions. He knew next to nothing about Japan and failed to realize that the announcer was referring not to his home state, but to the U.S.S. West Virginia, a ship stationed in Pearl Harbor.

With no enemy planes above, Ray was about to give up on hearing the sounds of war when he was startled by the shattering of something behind him. He saw Aunt Flara astride shards of pottery. After learning about the attack over the radio, she had flown into a patriotic rage, ransacking the house for any item made in Japan. What Ray saw at her feet were the remains of a cheap bowl. For the next few frantic minutes, he watched her repeat the process, finding an enemy product and then taking it outside to smash it into the ground or against a tree. With Flara's compulsive shopping habits, there may have been quite a few things to smash. As a teacher at Harding College years later, Ray told the story in chapel of the day his mother declared war on the Japanese and bombed them with their own merchandise in retaliation for Pearl Harbor.

The war did not greatly disturb life for this restless child. It only made him more aware of the world out there. Ray liked to recall the biggest, bluest ridge that towered over the town: "I could see this mountain from my school room window. I'd stare at it every day, it seemed, and think, 'If I could just climb that mountain I could find China on the other side!'" Illness almost kept him from making it out of adolescence. He missed a year of school in junior high when he got rheumatic fever. Flara worried about her foster son. The mortality rate for the fever was high and the Muncy family's medical history spelled trouble too. She told me later, "I said to myself, 'Even if it doesn't kill him now he won't live past thirty.'" Thankfully she was wrong, but the fever did seem to drain away part of Ray's stamina, leaving a hint of frailty beneath the youthful vigor. Spending much of the year in a hospital, Ray had time to dream of China.

His combination of curiosity about the world but indifference to school made Ray a typical adolescent. Of course, he was not typical in his family situation, but he did not know that for a long time. He did not realize that some of the children he called cousins were really his sisters and brother. Oh, he had inklings. There were the family reunions, held down at Cabin Creek in the coal fields. Flara used to dress him in his white sailor suit and march him into the bleak and barely green clearing where the rest of the Muncy family was gathered. Around them the dust of the coal industry seemed to settle even on picnics and games. Ray's outfit got him teased, I'm sure, so when his cousins said what they did, he considered it one more minor affliction to be suffered. Audra and Thelma would flit up to him, giggling, and whisper, "We're your sisters, Raymond." Ray would run to Flara yelling, and she would scurry over to the girls, who hid their faces behind cupped hands, and lecture them about upsetting things. "Don't you know you're not supposed to talk about that? Now hush or Grandma Schoolcraft is going to know about this! And some silly little girls I know are going to regret their words on the seat of their pants!" Shadowed by Flara's giant form and frightened by her tone, Audra and Thelma would run off crying. At the time, I suppose, little Raymond was left shaking his head about the strange ways of cousins—especially female cousins.

One day, when Ray was about twelve, John D and Flara woke him too late for school. "We're going on a trip," they explained. This deviation from routine meant either a rare treat or an impending disaster. The solemn look on their faces told Ray it was not a pleasure outing. They traveled several miles into the hills in the old car. In answer to Ray's questions, Flara spoke only of going to meet some family. The trees loomed large and dark, the flaming colors of earlier autumn having recently faded, but the ruts in the dirt road had not yet taken on winter depth. Still, it must have been a bumpy ride for the boy. Soon he realized that they were headed to cousin Paul's and Aunt Delia's. Their garden would be pretty much gone by now, though, and Paul would be in school. He liked Paul, but the boys didn't get to see each other much; the two sides of the family had little in common and travel was hard.

Finally the jalopy pulled up to an old country school with gray boards and a high-pitched roof missing a few of its worn shingles. A school, Ray thought. Could it be that he was being placed in a new school? Aunt Delia was waiting by a car. The adults, all of them, seemed to shuffle and hesitate, but after a few awkward hello-and-how-are-you's, John D went inside the school. He reemerged with Paul, like Ray dark-haired, but taller. Maybe Paul is going to spend the day with us after all, Ray thought. John D brought the older boy to where Ray stood, while Aunt Flara and Aunt Delia, their long print dresses rustling in a slight breeze, watched with folded arms.

"Raymond," said the man he thought was his father, "this is your brother, Paul." Ray could not absorb this news. His mind reeled with vague implications. Then he heard John D explaining how Ray's family had been split up when their real mother died. "Her name was Lona," he said. Ray looked up at Flara, who continued to grip her elbows. She and Aunt Delia looked like worried bookends. John D did not say anything about sisters, but Ray could not help but remember with sudden vividness his cousins' whispered taunt: "We're your sisters." The whole place seemed strange to Ray—the schoolhouse, the dark hills, the stolid, gawking adults trying to reassure him. But the fact remained that Ray Muncy was not who he thought he was.

Who knows why the family decided to break the news to him in this manner? Or why they didn't mention his three cousins who were really his sisters? Of course, they didn't mention John Jack at that point because they detested him so (The Muncys' campaign against him as the murderer of Lona was still to come). Well, Ray coped with the shock as young people have a

way of doing. He went on with the life he had been given, only occasionally fighting back bitterness over the loss of his siblings. He and Paul never did
get close. Separated by about thirty mountainous miles, they might as well
have been a world apart. Paul grew up, married into a family thought by the
Muncys to be weird, and was killed in the mines at age twenty-four, when
that screw slammed into his heart, causing cardiac arrest. He was buried in a
small cemetery on top of a West Virginia mountain and rests there, then and
forever a dark older shadow of Ray's self.

Although Ray took pride in DuPont High School, he never talked much
about his friends and experiences there. He most likely got involved in
smoking and drinking and preferred not to bring it up to me or to his
Christian college friends. When we lived in Belle among some of his old
acquaintances during the first year of our marriage, I could detect an under-
current of those bad old times. Nothing of substance, but offhand remarks
from friends, little jokes with indirect references to wilder days.

Whatever he did that was out of bounds, Ray also seemed to enjoy the
legitimate pleasures of high school. He made the cheerleading squad (his junior high fever disqualified him from varsity athletics) and was in school plays,
or at least he had one dramatic role for sure—he played Li'l Abner in a school
skit predating the Broadway version of Al Capp's comic strip. Apparently he
liked to perform, a holdover from the days of his musical feet, even to the
point of being class clown. One classmate remembers Ray on stage, sporting
a huge red bow tie and singing the following words to the tune of "Let Me
Call You Sweetheart":

> Let me call you Lizzie, I'm in debt for you—
> Let me hear you rattle like you used to do—
> Keep your taillights burning, and your headlights too—
> Let me call you Lizzie—I'm in debt to you!

He was also in the school marching band. A friend recalls the bass bleating of
Ray's trombone echoing in the Kanawha valley on autumn evenings, as he
stood out on the hill beside the house in Rand, practicing in front of old Bossy.

I wish I knew more about Ray's life at this crucial point, but I have little
more than bits and pieces. He overcame a lot in those years: the family's
poverty, its affinity for homemade liquor, the trauma of being an orphan, and
his own attraction to the wild side of life. He reunited first with sister Thelma
and then Charlotte during high school. Thelma and her husband lived only
a few blocks from the Muncys' home, and Ray could go there to smoke, something which, of course, Flara did not permit. Whatever bad habits Thelma

Ray upon graduation from high school.

may have tolerated, she loved and accepted Ray. It was also her apartment where Ray first reunited with John Jack, beginning the slow, sporadic process of establishing some kind of father-son relationship.

The most important event may have taken place long before Ray entered high school. In July of 1937, Flara Muncy started attending the Belle Church of Christ. Belle was a suburb of Charleston not far from Rand, where the Muncys had lived ever since Ray was small. Flara's sister was a member there. A year later John D joined her in attending the little congregation where he would later serve as an elder. Very few folks in rural America in those days grew up without some religion, and going to church was a return to their roots, in a way. Choosing the Church of Christ meant giving up the gin parties and the bootlegging of liquor, but John D and Flara were ready to do that. It seemed the right thing for their foster child too. Flara saw child raising in terms of discipline, and having a child in church was a way to get the help she needed.

Besides, Ray himself had helped shame the foster parents into thinking about religion. Once back in the bad old days of Ray's unsupervised wanderings, he showed up in at the Rand Church of God on Sunday morning. Some of the good brethren in the throes of revival week might not have noticed his small face pressed against a window, but he saw them singing and praying. Then he just walked in and sat down among the strangers in the congregation. The little boy came back again too, and began to go on a semi-regular basis with some of his friends. Apparently he made the switch to the Church of Christ with no problem.

It turned out to be exactly what Ray needed to focus his energy. Although the Muncys could provide only rudimentary guidance for Ray's spiritual growth, the Belle congregation had some men who served as role models and inspiration. Two men in particular stood out to Ray: W. C. Sawyer and Hubert Peck. Sawyer was the preacher, probably a notch above many in the area because he had been trained at one of the Church of Christ colleges, Freed-Hardeman, in Henderson, Tennessee. This tiny school would have instilled in Sawyer a respect for the Bible and a formula for using it as the center of every sermon. No doubt Ray heard more scripture in one Sawyer sermon than he had his entire life before going to church. Peck was an elder who took an interest in the young people of the congregation. By the time I met Ray, he regarded Brother Peck as his "father in the faith."

Ray credits Sawyer with sparking his desire to preach. The minister realized that the boy felt relatively comfortable in front of people and that he was smart. He probably talked to Ray about Freed-Hardeman and how he could study the Bible there. More than anything else, I believe, both men, the preacher and the elder, talked to Ray in positive tones. I don't know how much a role their encouragement played in Ray's decision to become a Christian, but it had to a have been worth a dozen doctrinal sermons to feel accepted and valued. Not very long after starting to attend at Belle, in 1939, Ray was baptized by J. W. Bankes. Soon afterwards he began thinking about becoming a preacher.

He was twelve years old.

Ray did not attain spiritual maturity right away, of course. In high school, the temptations of Belle's "roadhouse mentality" took him down a reckless road that he simply never talked much about. Until his junior year he was still sowing those wild oats. It must have been a rough time for Flara and John D, a man who did not seem to have any desire to discipline his foster child. But Ray was absorbing more than the worried adults could know.

The turning point may have come when Ray started leading in worship services. Hubert Peck and the other elders believed strongly that young men should be trained to conduct a service, so every three months, the male teens were put in charge of the Sunday evening song leading, prayer, and sermon. In these services Ray first preached. He must have been a senior because his main memory of the occasion was Flara's complaint that he kept twisting his class ring as he spoke. Brother Sawyer was more positive, however, and on the whole Ray was exhilarated by the experience. Before his senior year was over, he announced his intention to attend Freed-Hardeman College as a Bible major.

There are no records of what the very first sermon attempt might have been, but on August 23, 1946, a few weeks before he was scheduled to leave for college, Ray preached at Belle. The title of the sermon was "Fall and Restoration of Man." His text was Hebrews 1:1-4. All that remains is the outline, which smacks of the prevailing subject matter and style of the day. Ray began with a discussion of God's nature; then he moved to a description of man's fall and the need to be justified by the process of "H-B-O," as the outline puts it, or "Hear, Believe, Obey." The rest of the sermon takes the audience through Old Testament prophecy, the nature and career of Christ, and the establishment of the church on Pentecost. And according to his records, Ray covered all that ground in just twenty minutes! The lesson obviously emphasized what the brethren liked to call "first principles"; no doubt Brother Sawyer modeled such an approach for his students. In an era that saw the Church of Christ competing with the larger and more established denominational churches, the cry throughout the brotherhood was for a distinctive fundamentalism. If this sermon is any indication, Raymond Muncy had learned to respond to that call.

The sobering content of this early sermon is a long way from tap dancing on top of a piano. The near-orphan had found a niche, a place to perform the serious business of leading others to Christ. Oh, Ray was so young then! I'm not sure how much boys like him really understand what being a preacher means. Thank God they don't, or fewer would try. This small, trim high schooler knew only that he had at last seen a way to get to the other side of the mountain. As a boy he had wanted to find China on the other side. In a few weeks, he would find Freed-Hardeman, a place about as unlike the exotic promise of the Orient as anywhere on earth. And he would find me.

TWO

Rise and Fall of the Bull-Bat Club

The Freed-Hardeman Years (1946-48)

THE ROLLING TERRACES OF FREED-HARDEMAN COLLEGE

Henderson, Tennessee, was a clean but skimpy-looking town in 1946 when Ray arrived as a college freshman. He came in raw and excited, got terribly homesick the first week, survived to get mediocre grades while cultivating a great social life, and even preached faithfully and passably well on weekends. That year he joined the small band of Freed-Hardeman students, as I would in the fall of 1947, as consumers of the town's delights and critics of its shortcomings.

The town had enough stores and shops for all 3,000 citizens as well as inhabitants of the outlying area. A New York store promised sophistication, but the rest of the businesses sounded more familiar. There was a hardware store and a Rexall drugstore, where medicine, toiletries and sodas could be bought cheap. For those who preferred a little more atmosphere with their sundries, the Sweet Shoppe beckoned a mere two blocks over. The town had an ice and cola company, a Ben Franklin and a Firestone. First State Bank stood solidly on Main Street, and Bolton's Ford advertised not only cars but also Esso products. There were jewelry stores and shoe stores and clothing stores like McCall-Hughes, which had "ready-to-wear" suits. There was the People's Cleaners where students took those suits in preparation for special school functions, and a funeral home where suits would never have to be cleaned again. There was The Grill on Highway 45 that shimmered unattainably in the distance for students without cars. It lured us with its newfangled short orders and curb service. For most of us, the City Cafe and City Drug had to do because they were a short walk from campus.

In brief, Henderson was small town America, riding the post-war boom but not yet changed into the chain-dominated service economy of the future. It was enough like any other town in Tennessee to produce benign contempt on the part of college students but different enough to warrant a casual glance or two. We immediately declared it dull beyond endurance but were secretly thrilled to find it so recognizable.

The buildings that housed all these fine businesses, all of which graciously bought ads for the *Treasure Chest,* FHC's yearbook, clustered on a few streets—Main, Cason, and White. In this pre-interstate era, the town was dependent on the highway to Jackson for a lifeline to the larger world. On Saturdays during the school year, FHC girls could get special permission to take a bus over and shop, if at least three rode together. In those days, though, not as many people needed to get to the "big city." Henderson was remote, a place where college students could go for an unmolested education in a Christian atmosphere. The town's one movie house, the State Theater, was in the early years off limits to students, and the administration never felt entirely comfortable with its images of glamorous stars smoking and drinking.

For visitors the campus appeared suddenly in the midst of town, a tree-bowered nest of colonial buildings that stood in sharp contrast to the functional one or two-story offices or stores surrounding it. The administration building was a massive, two-story red brick edifice with stately columns at the front entrance. In the spring the oak trees all but concealed it from some angles. Men were housed in Paul Gray Hall—looking like a plantation house with its white rail balconies and Doric columns— and the women in a more modest building called simply, when we were there, "Girls' Dorm." There was also a gym, but these three structures, along with the cafeteria and home economics building, formed the main campus. Its geography symbolized the aim of Christian education: men on one side, women on the other, and knowledge, both secular and spiritual, in between.

Freed-Hardeman was not large but was easy on the eye, although on my first visit there, accompanied by my parents, I was deeply disappointed in the discrepancy between the advertisement for the school and the reality. One of the most appealing things in the brochure was the description of the luxurious rolling terraced lawns. It sounded grand to me—akin to the ivy-covered walls we associated with Harvard. When we arrived on campus, however, the lawn proved to be tiny and the terraces minuscule ridges. Freed-Hardeman was not grand in the sense I had been thinking. In fact, the entire campus was such a small patch of ground within Henderson that Ray's parents drove right past it on their first visit.

On our family's first visit in the summer of 1947, my father had no problems finding the campus or with its appearance. Nor did he mind that Freed-Hardeman was a two-year college. Back then any college experience was relatively valuable. He wanted a place that was sound doctrinally. No Harding for him, even though a boyfriend of mine, Wilburn Bullington, was headed there. All Daddy could see was the taint attached to its former president, J. N. Armstrong, a reputed supporter of premillennialism. Besides, Daddy did not necessarily envision a degree for me. What he did covet was two years of protection. He originally wanted to send me to Athens (Alabama) Female College to keep a closer eye on my education. When he met Brother Hardeman, however, he was sold. Hardeman was a man after Daddy's own heart: girls should be segregated from boys, especially after dark. That was right up Daddy's alley. Whatever misgivings he may have had about money or distance paled to insignificance in the conservative aura of Freed-Hardeman's leader.

My own misgivings about the way things looked were only momentary. In fact, they began to dissipate as soon as the students talked to me. Months later, at the start of school, I remember how willingly they helped us move in, especially Dudy Walker, looking like a well-fed Van Johnson as he carried my things up the steps. The warmth of these young people proved much more grand than a large or stately campus could have ever been. After overcoming his initial homesickness, Ray felt completely at ease there, and when I came a year later in 1947, so did I.

For so many of us in the postwar generation, college was a door opened on a broader world. Despite the provincial aspects of the town and school, Freed-Hardeman allowed me to meet and live with people from other regions. And in the era before television, that kind of interaction excited a girl who had known only a few square miles of Alabama soil.

Sweet Home Alabama

While Ray was living the life of a young Tom Sawyer on the river, I was growing up a grocer's daughter in landlocked Cross Key, five long miles from Athens. The eldest child among four, I was Daddy's first employee as well as his first child. In both capacities I felt his strong disciplinary hand. My father, J. Barney Griffin, purchased the store from his father and had in his sharp blue eyes the tunnel vision of a good merchant. Located next door to our house, the business took all his energy during the week, with its filling station, grease rack, and grist mill on the side, not to mention a small patch of peanuts and a big vegetable garden. In fact, it took all of us to make the business go. My mother, Elizabeth, worked at the counter. My brother Bill eventually handled the mechanic's work, but in his earliest days on the job as a seven-year-old, he helped me stock the shelves. As I got older, my after-school hours and Saturdays were spent working at the counter in relief of mother: taking money, filling out tickets, impaling them on the sharp spindle, and, at the end of business hours, recording each transaction in our ledger.

I got paid every week, but Daddy marched me down to the bank where we children were "encouraged" to put most of our earnings in a savings account. He believed in saving. I suppose it paid off, because by the time Ray and I got married I still had a small amount of money—more than he did, in fact. Daddy worked us hard and worked himself harder. He juggled all parts of his business like he was born to it. I can still see him with farmers at our grist mill, his slender form gesturing and his loud voice booming as he ground the corn they had brought in to trade for needed supplies. From the store I would shrivel in embarrassment at the sound of that voice. But it was just Daddy doing business, talking big and teasing his customers. And they didn't seem to mind his loudness; they kept coming back. We were never really affluent in the modern sense of the term, but we always had something.

One thing we had was a radio, which provided much of our outside entertainment. As a child, I loved a program called *The Story Hour*, which, as its name implies, featured classic stories for a young audience. What I really remember about the Saturday morning show was the commercial for its sponsor, Cream of Wheat cereal. The ad featured a catchy sing-song tune calculated to capture the attention of kids and drive parents crazy. I sang it so much that I remember it to this day:

> Cream of Wheat is so good to eat, we eat it every day!
> It makes us strong as we go along; it makes us shout hoo-ray!
> Its good for growing children and grown-ups too to eat.
> For all your family's breakfast, you can't beat Cream of Wheat!

Cream of Wheat was one of the foods rationed when the war intruded on my family's secure world. Like the rest of the country, Cross Key was soon involved in the war effort. Adults talked in grave voices about all the things the government would call upon us to do, and soon we were rationing our food and planting victory gardens.

By the time victory came, my brother Frank had been born, and I had graduated to chief babysitter, a job which I resented at first. What I didn't understand at the time (I was thirteen then) was Mother's need to work at the store. With Daddy's total commitment to the business, she rarely saw him. Their work together allowed her more of a relationship than some wives of businessmen could have. I could not see then how important such closeness was for her. As a matter of fact, the babysitting proved a pleasant enough task, and Frank and I survived with only a few fights and one set of burned fingers, courtesy of a heated pan of fudge that I unwittingly left on a table. Exercising the normal curiosity of a toddler, he stuck his fingers into the hot brown confection and shrieked in pain. I sat with him in my lap, both of us crying until mother got home. Though I feared her anger, she rushed to us and put her arms around Frank and me, comforting, not scolding. It was a lesson I would take to heart. I was twelve when Frank was born—on my birthday. By the time of Nancy's birth I was past fifteen and able to resume duties at the store while Mother took over at home. With two little ones, she wanted to be there.

Elizabeth Griffin, born Elizabeth Legg, was giving us what she never had as a child, I suppose. Her own mother left the family when Elizabeth was a girl. At the age of six, she heard her mother telling the family that she could no longer stand the alcoholic behavior of her husband. She walked out the door to a car where a stranger waited. When Elizabeth saw her mother poised at the door on the passenger side, she and her brother, three-year-old Ed, ran to the car calling for her not to go. Kathryn Colbert Legg pushed her children aside and got in. As her car drove off, Kathryn, looking very stylish in a new cloche hat, did not look back to see them weeping.

Elizabeth's memories after that include standing on a chair to wash dishes and cook while her father was off drinking with his pals. For all practical purposes she raised Ed. By the time she was sixteen, life had become unbearable. When she met Barney, she kept most of it—the neglect, the violence—to herself. But my dad gradually realized what a burden this girl carried at home. His attraction to her developed quickly and blossomed into love because of a piano, as he tells it. Remarkably, Elizabeth had learned to play the piano on an old upright left behind by her mother. After a few dates, Elizabeth asked Barney over to her house, and the evening sealed their future together.

It was his first time to hear her play, and it was beautiful. So was she, J. Barney thought, with her dark, braided hair, brown eyes, high cheekbones, and delicious southern drawl. But in the middle of a song, her drunken father barged into the room, along with some of his buddies. He began to carp that she should play a tune he wanted to hear. Elizabeth did so, but the old man was loud and abusive for the benefit of his drinking companions. J. Barney, eighteen at the time and ready to take the part of a man, trembled in anger and frustration as he watched his girlfriend try to concentrate on the keys while the drunk berated her. "I had to leave," Daddy said when he told me the story, "because I knew if I stayed I would have hit the old man." Later, as he walked home alone in the cold air, J. Barney Griffin resolved to marry his sixteen-year-old girlfriend: "I had to take her away from that," he would say. That very year, he carried her off like a knight in shining armor. Until the day she died, Daddy could never hear mother play the piano without a flood of memories overtaking him.

I loved my mother and have always felt sorry for the hard life she led. After we were married, Ray and I, our baby David in tow, drove to New Orleans where Elizabeth's absentee mom had built her new life. We thought she might want to see her great-grandson, and we also thought we could encourage her to take an interest in her daughter. On the contrary, the woman was unrepentant and cared only about protecting her current life.

She had told her new husband that she was childless and almost got hysterical at the thought of his finding out about Elizabeth: "If anyone comes down here and ruins things for me, I'll just walk in front of a car!" My husband listened to her selfish prattle with no sign of impatience. Though his presence kept me outwardly calm, I let him say our goodbyes—I was too angry.

"Why, she could have cared no less about David had he been a rag doll in the back seat!" I cried. Then through clenched teeth I told Ray, "I have no maternal grandmother." He, who lost his own mother, let me vent my anger and advised me on what to say to mine about our trip. Maybe one of the things that brought Ray and me together and kept us strong was our sense of how very devastating it is to miss maternal love. He experienced it first hand; I had seen it in my mother's sad eyes. It was just like him to use his bitter childhood experience to help me in my moment of bitterness.

Thankfully, our family remained intact as I grew up, so life was never all bad. As a result of my necessary involvement in the family business, my social life suffered. But in those days very few enjoyed what we now think of as a social life, meaning possession of a car and lots of leisure time. In our little communities, two institutions made up the life of a child: school and church.

I remember little Cross Key Elementary School—all of two blocks from our house. It featured three rooms and six grades. Each of my teachers— Irene Clanton, Beulah Byram, and Lula Staton—taught two grades with a captivating discipline and style. I saw in them elegant models of womanhood. I remember them retiring after a lesson to a personal cabinet, which opened onto a basin, a pitcher of water, a cake of soap, towels, and a jar of hand lotion. At this sanctified station, after removing the long white smocks that protected their dresses and hanging them carefully on a hook, they would wash their hands—we had no running water—and dry them crisply, with backs straight and faces delicately composed. Then, while we were reading or writing, they applied lotion in long deft strokes to their lovely hands. Finally the smock would be draped back in place, their shoulders pulled back and hands focused in the small of their backs as they retied the strings. Each movement seemed so right, so graceful. With the fragrance of lotion in my nostrils and the grace of their ablutions in my memory, they seemed such excellent, such wise, and such beautiful teachers.

After attending Elkmont Junior High, I switched to Athens Bible School, the new Christian academy for which Daddy served as board member. The good experience begun at Cross Key and at Elkmont continued there. I sang in the chorus, watched ball games, and dated a handsome boy named Wilburn Bullington pretty regularly, along with a few other guys tolerated by Daddy.

The other dominant institution in my life was the church, of course. Daddy and mother had come into the Church of Christ from the Methodist congregation where she had played piano. Barney and Elizabeth were baptized in 1935 at the New Hope Church of Christ. I was six years old. Seven years later, at the age of thirteen, I followed their example and went forward to be immersed for the forgiveness of my sins. It felt good to be saved and to be a part of the body that had become so important to my parents, but my early memories of church life are mixed. What I remember most was the negative attitude our congregation emitted toward other groups. The Methodists and Baptists and others made up the bad denominational world and the Church of Christ (or Campbellites, as some derisively called us) contained the true Christians who would be the only ones going to heaven. Not only did I sense resentment in the community over our attitude, but I also felt uncomfortable with it. However sincere this idea of exclusivity was, and as true as our claims about the importance of baptism were, we were bred to be narrow-minded and legalistic. It was a shadow over the church—over me—as I grew up.

The other thing I recall about my early Christian life was the seemingly constant attendance required. In the early 1940s church meant going not only on Sunday mornings and Sunday nights but also to Wednesday night class and to all the revival meetings that might take place in the region. In Limestone County we held summer revivals because travel was easier.

People would come from miles away—I remember some coming in wagons—and the meeting would last two weeks. It was a social as well as religious occasion.

I could not sit still for the long sermons, squirming in my seat and wishing I had the nerve to sneak out—Daddy would always refuse my requests to leave. It was hard on adolescents to sit through interminable sermons on baptism and instrumental music and salvation based on faith and the five steps to salvation, but somehow the closeness of family life, fellow Christians my age, and a spirit of finding fun in the boredom kept me from moving from frustration to rebellion. Still, I can sympathize with a story told about Carrie Neal Hardeman, daughter of one of the founders of Freed-Hardeman College. Obviously her father's life consisted, in large part, of church activities, and as a preacher's kid, she went to her share of services. On one occasion when she was a child, her father, N. B. Hardeman, stopped by Carrie's room to light a fire under her and her sister: "Come on, girls, we have to get to the meeting!" Carrie Neal whined, "But daddy, I have heard sound doctrine until I am sick of sound doctrine!"

I came close to that feeling during those July meetings, but I don't ever remember any real bitterness on my part toward the church. In my own way I was legalistic too, I suppose. I liked the certainty of "speaking where the Bible speaks and being silent where the Bible is silent." As a young girl, I knew I believed in God and in His son Jesus—and felt secure in the church. If at times it seemed a boring lifestyle, I didn't see anything better on the horizon. I felt intimations of a more exciting faith, but I didn't think too deeply on the matter. As in the case of home and school, life in the Lord's body suited me. I don't ever remember chafing at going to a Christian college. It seemed the natural thing to do.

Even when church or school got to be unbearable, good friends like Willodean Campbell and Mary Greenhaw helped me get through the rough times. We never really did anything special, just sat together at church, wrote notes, visited each other, went for walks, and of course talked about boys. Willodean asked me if I was going to follow Wilburn Bullington to Harding. "No," I said. "Wilburn is a nice boy, but we're just friends" (and as I said, Daddy was suspicious of Harding anyway). Eventually Willodean and I decided to attend Freed-Hardeman and be roommates. I cannot deny that the cliché about women and Christian education was at least a little true in our case: we were thinking about the possibility of an MRS. degree.

Thus on my first visit to Henderson, Tennessee, after I could tell that Daddy was ready to let me go to Freed-Hardeman, I was excited about the prospect of getting away from Cross Key and Elkmont. Away from the store and the routine of my life.

When I left for FHC, my mother drove me. Both of us wore dresses—everyone dressed up to travel in those days. When I arrived at college, I owned no pants, and they were permitted at FHC only for rigorous outings anyway. The whole trip was an emotional one for Mother. She cried a good part of the time. As for me, I felt a twinge of regret at seeing our home disappear from the car window, but I thought mostly of the freedom that lay ahead. Goodbye, little Cross Key, Alabama, and hello, broader horizons. Although I was headed for another small town and a tiny campus, I felt I was entering a spacious new world that would also be a new home.

Life at FHC

Despite the homeyness of Henderson and the Freed-Hardeman campus, their small size led inevitably to a struggle for eighteen-year-olds looking to find variety in recreational experience. Even today Christian colleges are famous—or infamous—for their rules. In 1947 when I arrived, I soon found out what Ray, who was starting his second year, already knew. FHC had plenty of rules. As was common in those days, men and women had curfews—ten o'clock at night for men. Women had to be in their rooms by seven o'clock to study except on Wednesday and Sunday evenings, which were reserved for church. Naturally no alcohol or tobacco was permitted. Like all church-related colleges and many secular institutions, FHC conducted daily chapel. And church attendance was pretty much mandatory. These big items were so much a given that most of us had little trouble adjusting to them (though curfew provoked its share of transgressions).

The devil, as they say, was in the details. It was how much we were chaperoned that made FHC distinctive and frustrating at times. Of course, young men and women were chaperoned to a much greater extent in those days, but culturally the move toward greater freedom had been underway for some time. In contrast, FHC seemed to commit itself to the segregation of men and women at all possible levels—the philosophy that had brightened Daddy's day so much on his visit. Years after Ray and I left Freed-Hardeman, he still enjoyed saying that our relationship "couldn't have been infatuation. They didn't let us get close enough for that. It had to be love."

It all started in chapel. Every day we marched into the auditorium to the accompaniment of a piano played by none other than Miss Carrie Neal Hardeman, daughter of N. B. If she grew tired of "sound doctrine" as a girl,

imagine how she must have suffered through daily chapel. She cut quite a figure at the piano, a feisty woman who played with her whole ample body. Of
course, the boys would notice her gyrations and often made her the butt of
their humor. Nevertheless, she always played with a smart rhythm that insin-
uated a certain joy into our marching.

But a simple marching plan carried us into our daily devotional. We
marched in with boys in one line and girls in another. Moreover, each gender was organized into two groups according to singing parts: boys into bass
and tenor; girls into soprano and alto. As Miss Carrie played, boys would
proceed to fill the seats on one side of the center aisle and the girls the seats
on the other side. In we came, 350 strong, until all seats were full and we
were arranged like the choir eternal, ready to sing praises to God. The
singing was glorious, of course. Most of us had been raised in Church of
Christ congregations where a cappella style conditioned us to sing parts.

Then N. B. Hardeman, who presided over most of the chapels, would
mount the dais to signal the beginning of our program. He was a formidable
figure with his pinstripe suits and crisp white shirts decorated with dark ties.
His close-cut but wavy gray hair almost suggested mildness, but through his
wire-rimmed glasses a pair of steely brown eyes peered knowingly into the
souls of everyone seated before him. He spoke with the exaggerated dignity
characteristic of the era's most famous preachers. His customary demeanor
communicated a gravity that set the tone for chapel as serious business. It was
a gathering of all students and faculty aimed at expressing devotion to God.

Ray was over there somewhere with the other boys, but for the first two
months of school he was only a public presence. The first significant sight-
ing may have been, not among the crowd of basses on the other side of the
aisle, but up front at the podium. Ray was known for his chapel programs on
John L. Lewis, the famous labor leader. As a product of a mining family, Ray
was pro-union, and he was not shy about proclaiming the virtues of Lewis. I
mentioned the seriousness of chapel, and when it came to worshiping God
this was so. But FHC was not so strict as to deny its students fun. As a result,
devotionals were sometimes followed by secular talks or even group activities. In such programs Hardeman relaxed the atmosphere and encouraged a
rough-and-tumble wit. And he would set the tone there too.

Ray was fully prepared to discuss Lewis in that fashion—precisely
because he knew his praise of the labor leader would irritate the conservative
students and faculty. Lewis had fought his way up from the mines in the
1920s to become the leader of the United Mine Workers and in the 1930s
had founded the Congress of Industrial Organizations. His career had been

stormy. Just the summer before Ray came to FHC, Lewis had defied a court order when he led his miners out on a work stoppage to protest dangerous job conditions, especially "black lung disease." Such actions made the bushy-browed labor leader a hero to many poor working people and a villain to some in the middle class.

In the summer of 1947, the Taft-Hartley Act passed, a blow to labor because it limited the power of unions by outlawing, for example, all-union or "closed shop" operations. I don't really recall, but when Ray spoke that autumn, maybe he railed against the new law and praised Lewis as the man who would fight against its "slave-labor" mentality. I can see Ray closing with some rhetoric along these lines:

> In the history of this great country, the working man has always had to fight the special interests, the fat cats who want to keep him down. That's why God places men like John L. Lewis on this earth! Well, John L. has led us out of the mines before, and this time he'll take the fight all the way to the halls of Congress to get Taft-Hartley repealed. All those senators in their white shirts had better get ready—because before he's through, John L. might sprinkle a little coal dust on that fine silk!

It was some such rhetoric that provoked the leader of FHC to respond. According to legend, Hardeman reclaimed the podium, and, fixing his eyes on Ray, pointed a finger at him to deliver this thunderous proclamation: "You say Congress had better be ready for a fight. I hope that they are. I hope they take John L. Lewis and wear him to a FRA-AZZLE!" The student body responded with loud approval as Ray looked up into Hardeman's red, tri-umphant face, with those steely eyes twinkling just enough to take the sting out of this last uproarious word.

Ray could take it, though, as well as dish it out. He was a cute boy and whether that chapel was the first dramatic impression he made or not, I spot-ted him early. He had dark hair and penetrating brown eyes. They attracted me most, blazing with competitiveness on the playing field and with earnest-ness in debate, but not often in anger. His energy emanated from them even more than from his slender form that carried only 128 pounds on five feet ten inches. He was loose, always in motion, and even though I discovered later that he was almost as shy as I was, he never seemed ill at ease around people. When his name came up in late-night gabfests, I found my ears perking up.

We performed the ritual mating dance of Christian education. Always close, never in contact. Circling each other, confiding in friends the attraction but not daring to bring it into the open. At night three or four of us would talk about the future. To my surprise, several girls considered the prospect of marrying a preacher the loftiest of female goals. I have to confess that my high school scheming with Willodean about marriage did not feature this goal. Daddy had instilled in me the belief that "preachers never have anything." He made more lucrative plans for my wedded bliss. Certainly none of us had a clue as to what being a preacher's wife would really mean. Ray Muncy was studying to be a preacher, so at some point the fantasy of being his wife may have flashed in my mind: sitting in the front pew smiling with pride as my brown-eyed man delivered a powerful (and doctrinally sound) sermon to an enthralled congregation.

My fantasies were complicated by Ray's other professed interest: history. He would sometimes speak of pursuing a degree in it after Freed. History! I couldn't believe it—my worst subject. If I had thought much about those two strikes against Ray—he aspired to be a poor preacher and a boring history teacher—I might never have hooked up with him. Fortunately, my long-range plans were not that calculated. More often I just played out the possibilities of dating him. Life was full that first semester, and Ray competed for time in my thoughts with course work, new friends, occasional homesickness, and the wonder of being out of Cross Key, Alabama. Yet in the crowded landscape of my mind, he circled ever closer.

That circling was complicated, as I say, by the segregationist policies of FHC. Not only did the college separate the genders at chapel, but it did its best to keep us apart during meals. The cafeteria had two entrances, and after dark boys and girls each had to leave through a separate designated door. In addition, excursions off campus without chaperones were limited, and no hand-holding on dates was allowed. For example, students traveled to the movie theater in unique fashion. Since the State was not far, we walked, but in single file—girls to the front, boys to the rear, with a chaperone in front and behind. Once inside the theater, the boys had to sit behind the girls, and we used to plot to be on the last row of females so that the boys would be immediately behind us, just for the chance to flirt when a chaperone relaxed her guard. These attempts to control our movie-going were part of the battle waged to keep us wholesome. The secret is, the administration needn't have worried, at least not in our case. Those exotic screen images may have fired our lust a bit, or our rebellion, but the world of Freed was too solid, and our real-life desires for academic success overpowered any celluloid glamour.

Frankly, with its rules FHC could have been a horrible place; for some perhaps it was. Certainly time has taught that such complete control of young people is neither possible nor desirable. Yet FHC was not horrible, was in fact endearing, because the people there did love life and the Lord. The spirit of joy came through even the sillier rules.

Despite all the barriers, Ray and I got together. He was very active in one of the four social clubs, the Philomathians (lovers of learning). He played sports, of course, but like me he also led cheers. Those days on the playing fields and in the gym are mostly lost to me, but I do remember the camaraderie. Ray was a good "Philo, right down to his toes," who earned the affection of his fellow club members. They would all tease each other unmercifully. Once, when Ray and I were talking early in our relationship, before any date, Joe Hope came up to us on the sidelines and blurted out, "Muncy, you ran the bases like you were being pushed around in a wheelbarrow. The BBC would be proud!" And he was gone with a sly wink. What was the BBC, I wondered, but if the remark about the running was intended to embarrass Ray in front of me, it didn't work. I loved to watch him run. On another occasion, someone yelled at Ray, "Remember old Hammerhead!"

"Who is that?" I asked.

Reluctantly he told me, "Uh, it was a girl I knew last year."

"Oh! Was she your girlfriend?" I sort of blurted that out.

"Well... I guess so, but, you know."

"She was your girlfriend and you called her 'Hammerhead'"?

Ray was embarrassed, so I let him off the hook. Besides, it couldn't have been all that serious. Can you imagine the two sitting in the moonlight and Ray saying, "I love you, Hammerhead."?

I would also hear stories about him based on his allure as a second year student. When his name came up some girls would laugh with secret knowledge. On the other hand, school officials praised his involvement in the preacher's club. Despite being a mediocre student the year before, he was a pet of several teachers, including Mary Nell Powers, the French teacher. Ray sat next to the door in her room, and it became a ritual for Sister Powers to begin class by saying to him, "*Je t'adore*, Muncy." In French this means "I love you, Muncy," but she would lay on the phony accent so heavily that it came out more like, "*Jhut-a-door*, Muncy, *jhut-a-door*." And Ray would get up and close the door.

He was not always on the receiving end of such gamesmanship, though. In another famous chapel program, Ray sang to Miss Powers from the podium a little song called "I'll Be Glad When You Are Dead, You Rascal You." It was a hit with the students. Paul Randoff wrote in Ray's yearbook, "I'll never forget your chapel program where you really fixed sister Powers, which is the way you always did her." For her part, Mary Nell Powers—another daughter of N. B. Hardeman—loved this sort of thing. She laughed the hardest at Ray's crooning, which was accompanied, between stanzas, by his own trombone playing.

That trombone, first taken up in the hills of West Virginia, had passed into legendary status by the time I arrived at Freed-Hardeman. When Ray wasn't playing it in chapel his freshman year, he was practicing on it in the dorm, at all hours. His poorly-timed rehearsals became a sore point with Joe Hope, his roommate, and others close enough to hear its deep blasts. On some nights the offended included most of the boys in Paul Gray Hall. Finally, after his concert for Miss Powers, his buddies could take no more. They sneaked into Ray's room and made off with the dented but prized instrument, burying it behind the Hall. Ray soon received an invitation to a memorial service held in the back yard, attended by several students who paid tribute to the fallen horn. The school newspaper reported on the event in words that probably capture the spirit of the memorial service: "All is quiet—that is as far as Muncy's trombone is concerned. After an eventful life, the trusty instrument developed an acute ailment and died. Its loss is keenly felt and only memories such as this remain…. The following 'Lament For My Trombone' expresses the feeling of Muncy over the death."

> Dearest trombone there you lie,
>   so silent in your case;
> You've been a good ole trombone,
>   A real asset to your race.
> But now dear horn, you've come
>   to the end of your way.
> You've sounded your last note—
>   no more shall you play.
> You're a sweet pile of brass,
>   all dirty and worn,
> But the stars and planets
>   sang the day you were born.
> Oh pal, I hate to see you go—
>   it grieves me way down deep,
> But brass thou art, to brass thou must return.
> So go on, dear horn, to your sleep.
> If there's such a thing as musical heaven
>   with days so bright and fair,

I know you'll go there dearest one,
and be given first chair.

Regaled by stories such as these in the autumn of 1947, I felt comfortable with life at Freed-Hardeman and with Raymond Muncy of West Virginia. As the woman in this friendship, however, I had to do something to move it along. I asked him out on a date.

First Date

Well, technically it was a party, and it came in November of my freshman year. The cafeteria, site of the segregated exits at mealtime, did serve to bring men and women together every day. As I recall, the women were divided alphabetically into four groups, each of which could use the home economics room (a floor above the cafeteria) one Saturday night a month for a party. Each girl in the group could invite a date and bring food and records to enjoy under the friendly gaze of chaperones.

The room was about the size of a small church auditorium. The tables may have been rearranged into a more party-like setting, but nothing could disguise the drab walls and lab-kitchen look. Still, it was our date night and we fussed with plates of food and pots of coffee. And we had our records, thick black vinyl containing treasures like Cole Porter's "Night and Day" or "Autumn Leaves." We might have played Benny Goodman's "In the Mood" although it was pretty racy for Freed-Hardeman. In the mood for what? Not devotionals. We girls were in the mood for the romance implied in the rich texture of the clarinet, the rising intensity of the chord changes. For two months we had lived so closely with, yet so remotely from these men, had been marched in with them then herded away from them. Had flirted in class and watched them on the fields of athletic glory. My boyfriends in high school hadn't exactly been a bunch of Clark Gables, but at least they were always there. I missed the fun and security of dating. I came. I saw. I was ready to conquer or be conquered. I was ready for Muncy, the swell kid from West Virginia who shambled folksily around campus but somehow commanded attention. I don't remember one bit of embarrassment about asking him to come to the mixer. I stopped him after a Philo meeting and asked as nonchalantly as possible. He accepted readily.

I have called the evening's activity a party, but for those uninitiated in the ways of Christian colleges that term might need explanation. There was no dancing, of course, and no alcohol, but relatively few colleges in those days openly permitted drinking. Card games were forbidden too, so what remained was Monopoly. I guess it was pretty sedate by some standards. At least, we told ourselves, we dressed fashionably. In November, sweaters were almost obliga-tory for both men and women. We girls would wear our pleated skirts, with their hemlines plunging back down to mid-calf after the shortening brought on by the war. And we had to complete the outfit with bobby socks and sad-dle oxfords. I did my long blonde hair loosely curled with the sides pulled back and tied with a ribbon at the back of my head. When Ray came for me, he wore a yellow V-neck pullover sweater with dark slacks. I thought he looked dreamy.

But as even a celebrity bon vivant like Hedda Hopper would have admit-ted, it's the conversation and food that make any party, and we shared enough of both to make these evenings a success. We girls brought fudge, cookies, and drinks along with paper plates and cups. As for conversation, I cannot recall many words spoken that evening, but I'm sure it was enchanting, filled with compliments about the food and news of the latest coup pulled off by Muncy and the Bull-Bat Club. Betty Blue would come to tell me that my cake was "grand." She might add breathlessly, with a quick look in Ray's direction, "It was so much fun cooking with you! And your sweater is so cute!" And Murphy might come up, slap Ray on the back and say, "Muncy, you old fod-dler! You are outstandingly handsome tonight—now give me that dime you promised!" Ray would be persuaded to recount how he had befuddled W. C. Hall in preacher's grammar class by asking about a conjugation that the teacher had never heard of. While the *bon mots* fell from our lips, in the back-ground we could hear "The Saint Louis Blues" on the Victrola.

We had to stop the festivities at 9:45 in order to meet the 10 P. M. cur-few. Even in 1947 that seemed too early to part. At least the boys were allowed to escort us to our dorm. Ordinarily such a walk might have provid-ed romantic memories of a long and dreamy stroll, hand in hand perhaps, arriving just in time for a quick kiss before Miss Sophie shooed us inside. Unfortunately, Girl's Dorm was a scant fifty feet from the cafeteria, so it was-n't much of a walk. And Ray was not much for romance on this occasion. It was illegal, after all! As we stopped in front of the dorm, he looked at me and said something softly that I heard as "May I have a date for church tomorrow?" As my heart accelerated ever so slightly, I struggled not to sound too eager. Still, it came out much more ebulliently than I wanted: "Why yes!" He looked past me: "That's what I thought," he said curtly, wheeled around, and walked quickly in the direction of Paul Gray Hall. For a moment I could not comprehend the gulf between my positive answer and his negative reaction. Was this a stunt for buddies in the mysterious BBC? Did I miss a punchline somewhere? But no, even in the dark, those Muncy eyes shone too icily for a joke.

"What did you say?" I had to raise my voice to make sure he heard. He stopped and turned back to me, now about a dozen paces away.

"I said, 'Do you have a date for church tomorrow?'" In those days he tended to mumble when he was ill at ease. Maybe that's why I did not hear the question correctly the first time. It came through perfectly the second time, however, and my relief was mixed with laughter. "I thought you said 'May I have a date...?'" I could feel the tension escape in the chill night air.

"Well, do you have a date for church tomorrow?"

"No."

"May I have a date for church tomorrow?"

"Yes."

We both laughed and said good night, standing twenty feet apart in our sweaters, seeing our laughter explode in white clouds above our heads. November in Henderson, Tennessee, surrounded by the three stately buildings of Freed-Hardeman College. The cold air felt good on my face as I watched Muncy walk away.

The next morning we sat through old Brother Mitchell's Bible class and a sermon by Jim Cope. We would never date anyone else after that. In June of the next year we would be married. I sometimes wonder what would have happened if I had not called out to Ray and asked him to repeat his question. I have a feeling that love would have found a way.

TALES OF THE BBC

If I was going to date Ray Muncy, I was going to be a part of the BBC. Before I really got to know Ray I knew of the BBC. The sophomore men would refer to it in conspiratorial tones and sophomore girls would hear the initials and smile. What was the BBC? Oh, they said, it was a very private organization—exclusive, you know. And they would smile more broadly still. Not everyone had heard of it—the married students and dedicated, pious preacher boys couldn't have told you about it—but those who knew seemed to regard it with a combination of amusement and respect. It was an inside joke setting them apart from the crowd.

After I got to know Ray, I pieced together the history of this exclusive club. It was the creation of several returning sophs, including Dudy and Richard Walker, Harold Hazelip, and Raymond Muncy. The initials stood for "Bull-Bat Club," a label originated by no one in particular to evoke the tall-tale-telling, jocular violence of its membership. Not that they were violent in deed, exactly, though they did chafe under the restrictions of a small, rule-bound campus. More accurately, there was a kind of violence in their talk—irony, sarcasm, irreverence. It was as if they took the "bat" of their wit to the hind-end of any perceived "bull" in the air. Oh, they weren't above shooting the bull themselves. The club was predicated more than anything, I think, on a common delight in language. The members loved to invent nicknames for each other: cobhead or foddler. As I had learned, one girlfriend was anointed "Hammerhead." I don't remember what she may have done or looked like to earn that nickname. Thankfully the worst name Ray called me was "Weezie."

The Bull-Bat members may have been immature, but their love of laughter was infectious. They gave priority to puncturing any pretense they detected—whether it was in the dorm or in chapel. They pulled thoughtless pranks or they attended bull sessions in which elaborate plans were hatched for the comic ruin of faculty, staff, and the rest of the civilized world. Such high spirits were dangerous, I suppose, and at times the boys went too far. They relished playing rebel on campus. Yet a geniality prevailed, the basic goodness of each member acting as natural restraint most of the time. Ray himself had acted out darker adventures in high school, and in the atmosphere of a Christian college it would have taken a lot to tempt him down that broad way again. In truth, much of what they said and did became a healthy outlet for them and a vicarious and safe rebellion for the rest of us. After I was "initiated" into their highjinks, I usually just kept quiet when they said or did some outrageous thing, but as Harold once told Ray, "Eloise approved our meanest tricks." Part of me did, I suppose, because they were my outlet too. And they weren't really mean by most standards.

One specialty of the group was sneaking out after the school's rigidly imposed ten o'clock curfew. Ray lived on the first floor of Paul Gray Hall, and anyone who made it to his room—creeping down halls and past the doors of more law-abiding preacher-students—could then easily slip out the window to nocturnal freedom. This freedom consisted mainly of skulking about town, trying to avoid Henderson's few policemen. Or maybe walking to the closest cemetery for an official meeting of the BBC: Dudy Walker, Joe Hope, Harold Hazelip, and Richard Walker. Ray liked to tell of a typical session at the graveyard, where various members emoted in sarcastic fashion. Joe Hope, a lanky, brown-haired boy from Alabama, might chide Muncy in the persona of one of their absent classmates, known for a delicate constitution: "You know,

Ramona," Joe would say, playing his role to the hilt, "I was provoked at you when you referred to me in the feminine gender right out in the broad open public." He pranced among the gravestones before continuing. "But deep down in my heart I just loved it."

"Hey, Joe!" someone called. "I guess Muncy shouldn't have brought that snake to you, huh?"

Joe shook his head in mock-seriousness and turned to Ray: "You tried to put that snake on me and I grew faint!"

"But ain't that just like a woman," a voice called out. Joe bowed graciously, ending his impersonation.

Ray smiled and returned the bow: "Cobheads everywhere are proud of you, Josephine, for being such a sport. You do the belly drag as well as anyone I know." Laughter followed all around.

Meanwhile, "Lip" had wandered over to a marker with the name "Harold" stenciled into the stone. He slumped against it and put his hand to his forehead a la Lawrence Olivier in *Hamlet*: "Alas, poor Harold! I knew him, Horatio. A fine fellow, full of infinite jest!"

"And a foddling preacher, too!"

Hazelip ignored the interruption to deliver a eulogy worthy of his namesake, moaning at the loss and sparing no praise for the departed Harold.

And so their meetings went—friendly battles of cleverness, self-indulgence and camaraderie. Their after-hours sojourns did not always go smoothly, however. Once they were chased by police. Fearing President Hardeman's swift justice, they ran until a fence stopped them. They jumped over it into a yard full of dogs, who, as Mark Twain would say, "made it warm for them." But they managed to escape capture. Not so another time when an off-duty Henderson policeman spotted three or four furtive figures on a town street at about 11 P. M. He approached them.

"What are you boys doing out so late?"

A tall dark-haired youngster responded with a definite edge in his voice. "Who wants to know?"

"Well, son, I'm a police officer. Could I ask you where you all belong?"

The tall boy seemed undaunted. "How do we know you're a policeman? Let's see your badge!"

By this time, Ray and the other BBC'ers were extremely nervous, wishing that their buddy "Lip" would just zip his. This attitude he was displaying could mean even bigger trouble. Showing no sign of irritation, the man slowly reached into his coat pocket and produced a badge that gleamed in the moonlight. The boys stared at it for a second; then Lip conceded with a low whistle: "Man, you gotta whole hand full a badge there, all right!"

Having gotten their attention, the policeman said, "If I catch you boys out here again at this hour, I'll have to tell Hardeman." The group mumbled their cooperation, but I wonder if the local police would have done it—turn them in. They knew how bottled up FHC kids were, and they could tell the difference between real troublemakers and these silly, imaginative boys who were neatly dressed and closely shaved and coiffed. The BBC was far more adventurous in their repartee than in their night life.

The Bull-Batters had many other minor adventures like that in 1947-48. They made life more interesting for us all. In fact, life in the Bull-Bat Club was good. Life at Freed-Hardeman was good. Surrounded by good friends, Ray and I quickly grew closer. Heading into the second semester of my freshman year, I felt life was only going to get better.

LIFE IS A SWEETHEART BANQUET

On February 13, 1948, Ray and I both awoke early. It was the day before the Sweetheart Banquet, and he and I thought maybe we would be among the couples considered by the faculty committee as king and queen of the event. The Administration Building would be decorated tomorrow night in red, blue, and silver; the tables would sport fine linen and real glassware. Ray and I did not usually get excited about banquets, but something besides frost hung in the air this winter.

After entering through our gender-appropriate doors, we met in the cafeteria for breakfast. Up most of the night studying for a Bible test, Ray was very tired. After we ate some powdered eggs and toast, he yawned, then laid his head on my arm, which rested on the table. Miss Mary, the cook, saw this and grabbed immediately for her bell. She held it out in front of her face, letting the wide end droop from her hand before shaking it furiously. Ray's head shot up from my arm as if the clanging had been a blast from the last trumpet. As we looked at her behind the counter, she continued to ring with her right hand and pointed at Ray with her left. Ray's pals, the few who were up, hooted and mimicked Mary's pointing: "Shame, shame, Mr. Cobhead."

"Don't you realize that head-arm contact must be saved for marriage?"

Ray said something like, "Boy, she must be in a foul mood this morning."

"Haven't you heard?" Willodean, my roommate, said. "Miss Mary is mad at the boys for dressing so sloppy. She's announced new dress codes for Sunday noon—boys have to have wear coat and tie."

"Well, I'll cut off her ears for that one."

"She must be out of her mind. I bet I know some who won't take kindly to that rule."

"You'll find out day after tomorrow. The rule starts this Sunday."

By this time Mary's attention had been diverted elsewhere. Ray plopped his head back down on my arm.

In chemistry, Joanne Powers and I couldn't decide whether or not to sneak out of Brother Insley's lab. To us he was rather dull. If we didn't sneak out during lab, we talked instead of conducting experiments. Joanne, daughter of Mary Nell and a Philomathian, used to spill her troubles to me as often as she spilled chemicals, and I would tell her about Ray. Once or twice, after Insley started the experiment, we would sidle toward the back to the large window, push it up, and, with some admirable dexterity, climb onto the ledge and be outside before he knew. I'm not sure if he ever missed us. On this day it was cold outside, so we decided to stay.

After chapel, as the boys and girls filed out, Ray and I fought through the traffic to meet each other briefly. We both had classes coming up, but we met long enough to hand each other the day's letter. Our spring semester schedules proved to be so different that the only solution to the long periods of separation was to write letters. It was actually fun to slip the envelope into his hand while he passed his to me. It made us feel like conspirators. On the outside, meek and mild FHC students. On the inside, passionate, secret lovers carrying on an affair under the noses of the regime. Those letters were my lifeline to Ray, and I kept them for years, until a flooded basement in Bloomington, Indiana, destroyed them. Although I would probably be embarrassed by their intimacy and corniness, they were part of a special time when Ray and I walked on air, when we could look into that crowd of 350 students rolling out of the building and find each other as if with radar.

At any rate, my next struggle would be in English, for which I was totally unprepared because I had been with Ray the night before (he had postponed studying until after our date; I had canceled it altogether). Should I go? And if I did, should I dare read his letter in class and risk the wrath of Brother Willie Claude Hall? Once I sat down in the classroom, I couldn't resist peeking at Ray's letter. Ironically, I had just noticed how he spelled the word "naturally," when I got in trouble. Ray was a terrible speller and in the letter tried to write the word phonetically: "natcherly." I was amusing myself with thoughts of my own superiority in the art of spelling—and thinking how much trouble Ray would have passing the spelling class taught by Brother Hall, when I heard the professor calling my name.

Brother Hall retained the old-fashioned method of requiring students to stand as they answered or recited. He was calling on me. I put the letter under my notebook and stood up, my face no doubt a deep shade of crimson. Professor Hall, who managed to make his short pudgy figure, clothed in a suit and vest, intimidating, looked at me through his thick glasses in roughly the same manner as an entomologist regards a specimen before pinning it to the board.

"Miss Griffin, would you please recite today's lesson?"

"Mr. Hall, I'm sorry, but I don't have today's lesson." He let me stand there in silence for a few seconds, all eyes in the class on me, before he burst into this mock-lament:

"Oh, Eloise, if I had known that you went to that ball game with Muncy last night, I wouldn't have embarrassed you in front of all these people by asking you to know your lesson. Or if I had known that after you got home you had to write Muncy that letter...."

I had to stand there until he finished hamming it up, a gold pocketwatch chain sparkling against his wool suit. For a moment I hated FHC for being such a small campus. Why did everyone have to know so much about my love life?

When Ray and I met for lunch, the cafeteria was buzzing with news of Miss Mary's dress code for men: coats and ties required on Sunday noon. Naturally the boys were mad and were whispering revenge. Somebody asked if we were nervous about tomorrow night. Ray said, "It can't be any worse than my Bible test today." But he knew he had aced that test; Ray was in the process of turning around academically. Although the semester was only a month old, I could tell he was applying himself more. I, on the other hand, could hardly stand to go to class. Ironically, my grades did not suffer a bit. Our relationship seemed to make classes easier. Ray's only worry was the spelling test that he would have to pass to get a degree.

Amid the furor over the new dress code, people still found time to anticipate the banquet. We were sitting with Charles Gibson and Willodean. Interrupting our general chatter, Charles, the man who would later perform our wedding ceremony, said forthrightly, "I think you two will be voted king and queen of the banquet." Willodean agreed. I blushed. Ray laughed. He loved Charles but had fallen into the Bull-Bat habit of wordplay with his friend's last name, Gibson. To hide his pleasure at the compliment, Ray turned it into a joke: "And you, Nosbig [pronounced "nose-big"], will be crowned both king and queen of the Foddler's Ball."

"Ha ha! Well, all I know is that you two make a swell couple."

"Thank you, Charles," I said, "and don't pay any attention to my witty moron, I mean man, here."

Somehow I made it through my last two classes in the afternoon. I wanted to hurry with supper, leave Ray to his Bull-Bat buddies, and plan for tomorrow night. The girls on my wing were going to compare notes on wardrobe. We had fun, of course, laughing and reassuring each other that everything matched as we conducted our own fashion show—a preview of the banquet itself. With curfew looming and our planning unfinished, some of us decided to head down the hall to talk to other girls about the banquet. Marie, Jeanne, and I were restless, thinking of anything else but the strict dorm rules forbidding anyone to be out of her own room after ten o'clock.

I've forgotten whose room we were in or how many of us were in it. At some point, however, a girl said, "Oh dear, it's past curfew—we're not supposed to be here." Marie laughed at the unintentional rhyme: "Oh dear," she mimicked, "I fear we are here. Is that clear?" Every one joined in the laughter; then someone else whispered in a panicky voice, "Miss Sophie's coming down the hall!" At that point the merriment turned to terror. We did not want to be found in that room after curfew. Marie beat us to the closet and closed the door. Jeanne and I dove under one of the beds. It was crowded enough to make us giggle at the closeness. Sure enough, a knock on the door signaled the arrival of Miss Sophie, our matron, whose voice we heard questioning one of the girls. We tried to remain calm and quiet while we looked at Miss Sophie's legs. She wore silk stockings with a seam up the back and black open-toed pumps. We could see a few threads dangling from the bottom edge of her dress. As I lay there trying to breathe as quietly as possible, I remembered that this was Friday the 13th—about to be an extremely unlucky day for me if we got caught. My fantasies of doom were cut short by a pressure on my arm. Jeanne was squeezing it, her eyes wildly communicating some fear. Then I remembered. When she got into stressful situations, Jeanne had trouble controlling her bladder. Her grip on my arm and her wide eyes told me that she was in danger of losing the battle.

Since I couldn't see Miss Sophie's face, I can only imagine its expression as her interrogation of the roommates was interrupted by a disturbing sight: a pool of liquid oozing slowly from under one of the beds. She recovered from the mild shock of this sight and called out, "Jeanne, come out from under there right now!" Jeanne and I both crawled out to face the matron. Marie, too, though she might have been able to remain undetected, emerged from the closet to make it a trio. I was absolutely sick when I heard Miss Sophie say that our punishment would be to sit in the lobby for four hours tomorrow evening.

"But tomorrow is the Sweetheart Banquet!" someone cried.

Miss Sophie paused, then added evenly, "As I said, you will sit in the lobby without visitors from two to six tomorrow evening. Jeanne, you'd better clean yourself up. I'm sure the others will help. When you're finished, I will escort you back to your wing. Please report to me on time tomorrow, and please, girls, obey the rules. They are for your own good."

We all tried not to react to the times she gave, but inside the relief was noisy. Good old Miss Sophie. We would still have time to get ready for the banquet—barely.

Finally Saturday evening came. I served my time in the lobby and rushed to get ready. Ray called for me at five until seven, wearing the same dark suit he preached in. He was smart enough to compliment me on my white formal with its lace bodice and taffeta skirt. I slipped my arm under his and we joined the small procession from "Girl's Dorm" to the Administration Building. It was lovely: a dozen or so couples promenading by Paul Gray Hall, the colors of the girls' dresses like moving lights in the dark. The men looking stiff but

Ray and Eloise dress up for a FHC formal affair.

beautiful in their J. C. Penney's suits. They shouted witticisms at each other while we girls radiated smiles and clung to our dates to keep warm in the cold February night.

Inside, tables set with glowing candles awaited the couples—in all over one hundred of us. I remember two things about the evening, really. The first is that Ray and I were nominated as one of the sweetheart couples but did not win king and queen. Nevertheless, we joined the honored royalty as first runners-up, and with rest of the court marched across the Administration stage in front of the faculty reviewing stand, to the applause of the other students. Second, I remember the look in Ray's eyes and the tone in his voice. He was affected by the ambience. He joked less than usual. Normally, I could never tell when he might spring a joke on me. On one of our walks to the City Cafe, he had looked up at the quarter moon and said, "Oh, how rheumatic! It reminds me—I need to cut my toenails!" No such silliness this evening. He held my hand, and when he said good night, he lingered over his kisses. I didn't think he was ever going to let me go in, and when he did, he hemmed and hawed as if he were going to say something. All he said, however, was "Good night, sweetheart."

The next day at lunch began the new men's dress code in the cafeteria. Miss Mary got more than she bargained for, however. As students drifted into the room after church, she went about her usual business of managing the cafeteria line, directing the helpers as needed, and preparing to serve the larger Sunday crowd. After a few minutes of routine traffic, she looked up from the steaming food to find before her a crowd of boys in coats and ties, in accordance with her new rule, but all the coats had been put on backwards. With the back collar up against the front of their necks, the boys looked like some bizarre group of priests. As they had arranged, the young men said or did nothing to betray any emotion.

"All right, if you boys want to act a-fool, then go ahead. But I'll speak to Brother Hardeman about this." It was Sunday, and on the Lord's day, this was the best fight Mary could muster. Her subdued reaction spoiled the rebellion some. The boys had to be satisfied with the snickers and gasps of a few peers. Ray and I just watched, happy to be alive.

On Sunday evenings the men and women who sat together in the parlor of Paul Gray Hall were allowed to walk, one couple at a time, to the Sweet Shoppe on the corner, about five minutes from campus. The time limit was thirty minutes. It was what we did on dates every Sunday night. This Sunday, after the excitement of the Sweetheart Banquet, Ray and I took our turn. We drank coffee—Ray had put me on to coffee—then walked back. I felt a bit of a letdown after the excitement of the night before. Ray was tired, I could tell. The momentous something that had hung in the air the night before had vanished. Instead, we made small talk until we reached the steps of Paul Gray. Ray leaned against the base of one of the broad marble balustrades. Behind him rose the huge white columns of the antebellum structure. The contrast to his slumped form made him look pretty puny there in the dusk. I thought I'd better remind him of our situation.

"Ray, we've been gone about 30 minutes. She'll be wondering about us."

"I know. We should go in." But he didn't move. Then he said something so low I wasn't sure I'd heard it. My mind flashed back to the conversation leading up to our first church date almost three months earlier.

"Weezie, will you wait for me?"

""Will I what?" I asked. I knew immediately what he was asking so indirectly, and I had a quick vision of him reading that line in a book. The import of the question caught me totally off guard.

"I meant, will you be my wife?"

"Well ..." I did not mean to make him wait; I was just absorbing the full meaning of the question. My hesitation did not last long: "Yes. I will." The kiss that followed, there under the silhouettes of the bare winter trees and in the shadow of the three-story columns of Paul Gray Hall, seemed the most natural of my life.

BULL-BATTERS HAIL AND FAREWELL

As the year wore on, the BBC and Philomathians and chapel talks gave way to other concerns. For Ray and me it was the approach of marriage and a preaching job in his hometown of Belle; we spent hours planning. I dropped chemistry for home economics immediately after our engagement. I told everybody that I had better learn to boil an egg. Professor Insley, perhaps not sad to see me leave his lab permanently, sent me on my way with this sage commentary: "Eloise, a bird in the hand is worth two in the bush." Friends wished us well and teased us as usual. "You're a heart-stealer, Eloise." Or people might try out the latest fashionable pun or joke: "Been having trouble with Eloise lately, Muncy? Then try Carter's Little Lover Pills! Ha ha!"

"Hey, Muncy! Weezie told us about your date last night. She said you told her that every time you kissed her it made you a better man. And she said, 'Yes, Raymond, but do you have to try to get to heaven in one night?' What about it, Muncy?"

That was a very special time. It seemed as if our friends, in their happiness for us, placed us on a pedestal. Our coming marriage ratified our decisions to come to Freed-Hardeman and colored every mundane school activity with excitement.

Of course, we were not the only engaged couple, and other friends anticipated transfer to senior colleges. For all of us the prospect of something bigger than life at FHC beckoned. It was frightening and exhilarating at the same time. Less than a year earlier I had arrived in Henderson thrilled at its newness and larger scope of living. I had been alternately nourished and frustrated by its intimate atmosphere. Now I was leaving the states of Alabama and Tennessee behind for remote West Virginia, with the scary image of John L. Lewis staring from its terrain, and the infinitely larger state of matrimony, the most exhilarating state of all. My partner in this journey would be a boy whose main claim to fame was his ever-ready wit.

Yet I knew the silly Bull-Batter had much more in him than the nonsense of pranks and jokes. Regretably I didn't get to attend any of the preacher's club meetings that year, and it's too bad that Ray did not get the same opportunities to preach as he had his freshman year. But even with things getting in the way of his calling, it was understood that his future lay in the Lord's work. His good friend Lip, Harold Hazelip, who within two decades of leaving FHC would be one of the most well-known preachers in Churches of Christ, never forgot it. In the FHC yearbook he wrote, "Muncy, there is a lot of mischief in you, but I never heard a more sincere talk at the preacher's club."

The Bull-Bat Club joked about its "progressive" activities, meaning of course its pranks and subversive rhetoric, not "giving a hank" about the mainstream, the pious ones. I now think that at some level they did see themselves as progressive. They had a joy in living not to be contained by the outdated rules of college, and they saw possibilities in the scriptures unnoticed by some of their mentors. It was all unformed in those days, but many of them turned out to be progressive in the best sense of the word. I'd like to think my husband ended up all right, an old Bull-Batter who grew up.

THREE

Going Home Again

Belle, West Virginia (1948-49)

THURSDAY WEDDING

In summer, factory smoke billows over Charleston, West Virginia, in huge white clouds that from a distance seem as natural in the sky as cotton in the fields of Alabama. To travelers approaching on Highway 60, it looks almost tranquil. Once they are in the city, the pollution, trapped as it is in the valley, no longer looks fluffy and white. It makes everything look gray. When Ray and I stepped off the bus in Charleston, I felt queasy with the grayness. Arriving in Belle, Ray's home town, did not help my faint sense of dislocation and dizziness. Crowded against mountains a few miles east of Charleston proper, Belle's small frame houses did not escape the stain of the smoke either. And Greyhound had lost part of my luggage. I stood still but everything seemed to spin.

There, in one of those houses, number 321 on 6th Street, Ray and I had come to live. We were moving in with John D and Flara Muncy. Flara smiled and nervously promised us a good supper, but her eye was fixed upon me like a searchlight. Her solicitude at supper only put me more on edge. I needed desperately to lie down in a dark, quiet place. As I excused myself from the table, I dared not confide my apprehensions to Ray. He was talking to John D, happy to be in his childhood home. Soon he would be preoccupied with finding a temporary job and preparing for his preaching duties. That night he didn't know how miserable I felt lying there on a strange bed hundreds of miles away from my home.

Before I drifted off to sleep, scenes from our engagement and wedding played like a movie preview in my reeling mind. Drowsily, I longed for the romance of those scenes, realizing that the previews, which had shown two lovers, were over, and the real movie, crowded with other characters, had begun.

Our last semester at FHC had gone by like a dream, all soft and fuzzy in my memory. In April Ray had persuaded Mrs. Hammon, the matron at Paul Gray Hall, or "Hammie," as he called her, to let him borrow her sitting room. He then led me in, made me sit down and close my eyes. When I opened them he was holding an engagement ring, a solitaire, a single diamond in a yellow-gold setting. Of course I thought it was absolutely beautiful, and it was made more so because Ray had used most of his savings from his summer job at DuPont—working, in of all things, the formaldehyde division—to buy it. In the solitude of the sitting room, away from the busy lobby, we enjoyed one of our most romantic evenings. Soon afterwards we called our parents and set an August date for the wedding.

We were so anxious to get on with our lives that Ray chose not to attend graduation despite his glowing 4.0 grade point average (he passed the spelling test!). He wanted to go home before the wedding. I, too, was anxious to see my parents. The delicious nights in the dorm talking about china and silver patterns had run their course. In fact, the more we talked, the more Ray bewailed how impossible it seemed to wait until August. As soon as we could pack we headed for Alabama, arriving with the news that we wanted to move the wedding up to June. My mother immediately started crying and begging us not to do it. She was thinking of preparation time, since the ceremony was to be held in Alabama. She also reminded us that we would lose an opportunity to earn any money before the marriage. We didn't care. Love is truly blind—and deaf too—for her common-sense pleas could not sway us.

Our wedding was set for June 3, 1948, at 6 P.M. in the old Market Street Church of Christ in Athens, Alabama. Although a small affair, only about a hundred people in all, it still became a major event for our family. The local newspaper headlined the announcement this way: "Church Rites Solemnized Thursday." We scrapped plans for a Saturday when we realized that we would have to take Daddy's car on whatever honeymoon we had, and he needed it back first thing Sunday to go to church. At any rate, the affair was more chaotic than solemn. My uncle brought his big family from

New York several days before the wedding and filled up our house. As a result, Ray's parents and his grandfather, Lotus Muncy, who also arrived early, had to stay in the lone hotel in Athens. Thankfully, our few friends and members of the wedding party from FHC did not arrive until the day before the actual ceremony.

Lotus, whom Ray called "Grand Lotie," from the way the grandchildren pronounced the name years ago, had never been to the South before. For that matter, John D and Flara probably hadn't either. I met them all for the first time when Ray drove them to our house from the hotel. John D was aging gracefully, keeping weight off his medium frame and a smile on his kind face. Flara was even more imposing than Ray had described, or so she seemed to me. She was tall and stocky. She spoke in clipped phrases and showed no outward signs of discomfort at being among a strange family.

As the week wore on, I understood more of what Ray had told me about Flara. She talked a lot about the cost of things, for example, reminding me of a question Ray asked one day in college as we discussed our upcoming marriage.

"Are you frugal?"

"Probably not. Why do you ask? Preparing me for the worst, darling?"

Ray laughed but told a story that obviously showed his mixed feelings about Flara: "Right before I went to college, mother found this fabric on sale. It was sort of blue, or purply looking. She cut it up and made it into underwear for me to take to Freed."

He stopped without further comment. I waited, then said, "I'm not that frugal."

Ray broke into a loud laugh. "Good," he said.

Yet because she was the only mother he had known, he bowed to her wishes in matters of clothing. One of my biggest disappointments during the wedding week came when Ray showed me his suit. He and I had discussed the matter of his wedding attire back at Freed and agreed that he should buy a dark suit. In those days people of our economic level did not rent tuxedos. The groomsmen were told the same thing: bring a navy or black suit. After I met his parents and things settled down some, I asked him to show me his suit. He proudly pulled from his bag a Palm Beach tropical tan jacket and pants. Surely my jaw dropped, but he didn't seem to notice. As I tried to determine how to express my disappointment, Flara appeared. She said, "Raymond and I had so much trouble deciding on that one, but don't you love it? It was on sale." Suddenly I realized why he had disregarded my wishes. "Well," I thought, "it's his mother and we are going to be living with her for at least awhile when we first move to Belle." I bit my tongue and chirped some vague praises of the purchase. I never did let Ray know how I felt about that suit, and, by the way, it did clash with the groomsmen's dark clothes. The only good news was that the photographer's camera broke before he could take a picture of all the men together. Wouldn't it have made a nice photograph for our wall: Ray in the middle of his four friends, looking like the center of a huge Oreo cookie?

The week leading up to the actual ceremony went about as smoothly as can be expected. Flara, however, managed to create a scene one day. Betty Witty, a family friend a few years younger than I, came by at some point, maybe to confirm her family's little dinner planned in honor of the wedding. It was June but already July hot in Athens, so Betty came in wearing shorts—pretty short shorts for 1948, as I recall. When Flara saw her, she marched right up to Betty—the two had never met, of course—and said, "Young lady, you need to go home and put on some clothes!" The first person I looked at when Flara said this was my father. Though he too abhorred the wearing of shorts, he was upset and I knew why. Betty was a friend but also a customer—the last class of people a merchant wanted to insult. Fortunately, Betty had the grace to leave without making a scene, but the picture of what it would be like to live with Flara was becoming all too clear.

When Ray's friends arrived, he became instantly useless to me. Friends of the groom are dedicated to making those last single days as silly and without purpose as possible. The exception to that rule was Charles Gibson, old "Nosbig," who was to perform the ceremony.

The rehearsal turned out to be a series of headaches. We were ready to start and Ray was nowhere to be found. Finally, Ray and Joe Hope and the others came in laughing and clowning around. They had been goofing off somewhere, oblivious to the need to be on time. I looked Ray in the eye and asked with enough passion to get his attention: "Where were you? Did you forget?" It was the first time in my life that I was really angry with him. He took me aside, away from others, and apologized quickly and sincerely: "I'm so sorry, Weezie, we just lost track of the time. I am sorry." As he spoke, his voice sounded raspy, reminding me of the sinus infection he'd fought for a week. He obviously wasn't feeling well. One part of me said, "So what? That's no excuse!" The other side pitied him in his remorse.

What could I say? My mother, who had observed my growing irritation, stopped me as Ray left to join the wedding party. She put her arm around me and handed out some vintage Southern belle advice: "Honey, I know it's hard sometimes, but if you're married to a man, there's gonna be lots of times your biscuits will get cold."

The next day the ceremony went off smoothly, with one exception. Nancy and Frank, scheduled to march as junior bride and groom, missed the wedding with a sudden case of chicken pox. Their absence was very disappointing. Nevertheless, I walked down the aisle, wearing a ballerina-length white satin dress with a bustle, a bow in the back, and long, buttoned sleeves. A local trio of girls performed traditional songs, including "O Promise Me." I held a white Bible with an orchid on top along with streamers and split carnations. My beloved looked conventionally grave, but something occurred to me when our eyes met: "I think he's glad to see me!" As we stood before Charles Gibson, my maid of honor, dear friend Willodean Campbell, was beside me, and Joe Hope guarded Ray's flank. When my father let go of my arm to present me to the wedding party, Charles asked, "Who giveth this woman to be married?" I guess I should have expected it, since Daddy was not above showing emotion, but it still shook me a little to hear his voice tremble in response: "I do."

I don't remember much else about the actual ceremony, just how pleasant it was to have the deed done and to be surrounded by family and friends. I do recall joking at the reception that when Ray repeated the words "with all my worldly goods," he could have said, "There goes the bicycle." We drove to Monteagle, Tennessee, in Daddy's Pontiac to enjoy caves and other scenic beauty. It was interesting, cheap, and within two hours of our home in Alabama. Looking back on those three days, I see two children playing at being a married couple. We were fresh-faced kids without a clue, but it was a sweet, happy honeymoon, made all the better because for the first time in awhile we were together without distractions. We returned to Athens on a Saturday to rest up for our long bus ride to Charleston, West Virginia, on Monday morning.

Before that trip, we had our first tiff as a married couple. My mother had laid out several things for me to take to West Virginia. Among them was my high school yearbook. On Sunday as we all relaxed after church, Ray saw the yearbook and started browsing through it. As I said earlier, I dated regularly in high school, and one boyfriend had signed my yearbook. I don't recall much of anything written there, but we all know how high school sweethearts can go on. Ray read what must have been a pretty juicy part and immediately slammed the book down before walking out of the house. When I heard the commotion and saw the discarded book, I rushed out after him. Catching him about halfway up a rather long hill near our house, I

Ray leaves the church building in a new Palm Beach suit and with a new bride.

finally talked him back down, telling him again and again how little the boy had meant to me even then, much less in college, or now.

"Ray, I had forgotten him before I crossed the Alabama-Tennessee line. It was high school!" But he was quite unreasonable about it. The more I tried to soothe his feelings, the more sullen he got. I finally cajoled him into revealing the source of his anger. A friend had advised him to tear out all the comments made in the FHC yearbook by his ex-girlfriend. He assumed that I would have the discretion to reciprocate. He felt betrayed. I was incredulous.

"Hammerhead?" I exclaimed. What made him think I could be jealous of a girl called Hammerhead? But his male vanity had been wounded by seeing tender words written by another man. I ended the discussion by saying, "Well, it's not important to me." I grabbed the yearbook and threw it in the trash, right in front of him. It took awhile, but Ray apologized for his reaction. Men are remarkable. They can fight over a woman even when no one is there to fight. I suppose that women are remarkable too; they can see a husband fight with a ghost rival and be flattered in spite of the absurdity of it all. By the time we boarded that bus for West Virginia, Ray and I had laid these ghosts to rest.

THE FIRST JOURNEY IS THE HARDEST

I had never traveled by bus before and the trip was dreadful. We made dozens of stops in places so small that their only buildings were the sleazy cafes which doubled as bus stations.

Inevitably, there was no good food to be found at these stops, at least none we could afford. We bought snack items and shared soft drinks. It had been a long time since our last bite when Ray found one sugar cookie in a pack bought a hundred miles ago. He offered it to me. "No, you can have it," I said. My new husband was determined to be gallant, however, and insisted that I take it. We were both hungry but neither of us wanted to appear selfish. Ray tried a new tactic. He held the cookie in his right hand, moving it toward my mouth slowly while he murmured words of encouragement to take it. When I refused, he would withdraw the cookie, as if his hand were a part of a vending machine. Our polite argument continued for some seconds, but about the third time Ray withdrew the rejected cookie, the old man in the seat across the aisle shouted, "Well, just let me have it!" Then he reached up and grabbed the wafer out of Ray's hand. Without another word, he wolfed it down and resumed his sleep.

Ray and I just laughed. "Be my guest," said Ray.

By the time I stepped off that bus in Charleston, I felt very strange and dislocated: greeting John D and Flara weakly, being driven to their home, eating a supper of chicken and apple pie and hoping that a good night's rest would relieve the churning in the pit of my stomach. The trip was a giant step for me, and at that point only Ray's reassurance kept it from seeming too big.

After a fitful first night in Belle, West Virginia, my life as Mrs. Ray Muncy began.

We lived with John D and Flara from early June through early December. Until his preaching job began at the first of the year, Ray went to work for Kroger's. During his first week at work I came to Ray with a plan to get a job myself. I justified it by telling him how much we needed money; my real motive was to get away from the house. I was already convinced that it would be a lonely life, in spite of Flara's and John D's best intentions. When daily life began in earnest, my fears were realized. The three of us could make only so much small talk. Besides, the couple had friends and routines—and they were old! John D, who was Ray's blood relative, exuded warmth and optimism, and Flara acted with our best interests at heart, but

A younger John D. and Flara Muncy in a photo taken some time in the early 1940s.

my plan seemed crucial to my emotional survival. Getting a job was the solution to my problem.

It didn't fly. Ray would not hear of my going to work. It was another triumph of male ego over common sense. The man must support the wife. He thought he had a scriptural basis for his feeling and therefore would simply not discuss the matter. He kept this attitude until years later when we had all four children living at home and were working for Harding. Then his view of scripture changed. In Belle, I stayed at home and did housework, wrote letters to my parents and friends, and read everything I could find.

Flara and I were at odds from the first, maybe because we were suspicious of each other. I was immature; I would have handled our relationship much differently later, of course, been more understanding of the stress of having long-term house guests, more sympathetic to her apparently unbending personality. But I didn't try as hard as I should have. For her part, Flara seemed determined to have the neighbors think we all four basked in the glow of a harmonious relationship even if in reality we did not. She wanted Ray and me to sit on the porch every evening with her and John D. If we ever wanted to go out, she expressed her resentment, usually indirectly. One night when we told her about an invitation to visit friends, Flara exploded. She began to scream at us about our ingratitude. John D just sat there, and Ray took my hand, "Come on, let's go." As we left, she let her hurt feelings out in one more tirade: "You always want to go someplace else; you never want to stay here! Well, go on! Go on!"

John D followed us out to the street where, as usual, he acted as the peacemaker: "Now, Flara doesn't mean what she says. She talks a lot but don't let her rile you. It's a hard thing for her. Now go and have a good time." I was almost shaking from the fury of her outburst, but when I looked at Ray, he shrugged. Later, he talked to her about our coming and going, assuring her we meant no disrespect. We all made efforts, but resentment on both sides smoldered.

In fact, it was almost an impossible situation: a woman who wanted to be friends but had no idea of how to relate to others, especially young adults, and who wanted to control us as if we were still teenagers—and a young couple with no experience in living together, much less with surrogate parents in a new place not their own, with one tiny room to themselves.

When cabin fever became unbearable, we could visit Ray's sisters, who lived close by. Separated from them in childhood after his real mother's death, Ray learned their true identity shortly after the Muncys took him to see his brother Paul. He cherished their company and visited all three as often as possible. Audra, the oldest, lived in Seth, too far away for more than one or two visits while we lived in Belle, but Charlotte, the youngest, and Thelma lived close by, so we became good friends with both families. I think Ray tried during our eighteen-month stay in Belle to make up for the decade he had missed with his siblings.

The Belle congregation also made things easier by embracing us. Ray and I ran around with some of his old high school friends. One of the elders and his wife, Hubert and Mae Peck, became confidantes for me. They supported Ray too because they understood his home situation. They had two daughters about Ray's age, and we used to go en masse to DuPont High School football games. It was almost like being back in high school, including the occasional attempts at flirtation by young single girls who remembered Ray from two years ago.

Such occasions made life fun, but we still had to deal with the routine of married life back at the Muncys.

Without a kitchen or other normal material signs of matrimony, I felt limited in my role as a wife. I wanted to be able to cook for my husband, for example, so when Ray started working at the grocery, I was glad when Flara did not make an issue of who prepared breakfast. I'm not sure if it was the first breakfast I cooked up in Belle, but one time was especially memorable. Not because of the menu, that's for sure. All we had was Cream of Wheat—as in the old Alabama days. I had never seen Ray eat the stuff and silently hoped he could endure it. "Here's the specialty of the house," I said as I set a steaming bowl in front of him. "Eat hearty." I had turned back to wash up some dishes when I heard him singing: "Cream of Wheat is so good to eat, we eat it every day!"

I burst out laughing: "Why Ray, you never told me you knew that song!" He looked a bit confused, as if he had been unaware of his own singing. He probably was also trying to figure out the expression on my face. It was the song I'd heard hundreds of times on radio as a little girl. If I looked transported, it was because I felt a sudden connection to my childhood and to Ray, and as strange as it sounds, to the world—to think that years ago such a silly, pleasurable song was being sung by both of us at the same time, hundreds of miles apart: Ray in his little house in the mountains, I in the Alabama home I missed so much! I hadn't felt this happy in weeks, so I sang the next line: "It makes us strong as we go along—" and then Ray came back in with me: "It makes us shout HOO-RAY!" We belted out the last two syllables like the kids we remembered ourselves to be. Flara came to the doorway for a moment, drawn by the commotion, then disappeared. We held our breaths until she withdrew then giggled some more and hummed our new song in a conspiracy of nostalgia.

My biggest problem with Flara came in September or October after I got pregnant with David. I did not want to tell her, and Ray understood. By this time I suspected her of snooping in my room. One day I overheard her on the phone telling someone, "Well, I think she started her period but I'm not sure." I was shocked, primarily at the principle of decorum being violated. I didn't connect the conversation to myself right away. She was discussing someone else's privacy over the phone, something my mother would never do. As I continued to listen, it dawned on me that I was the subject of her investigation.

Shortly afterward, when I did confirm my pregnancy, I went to an obstetrician in Charleston—as far away from Flara's connections as possible. To fool her, I saved old Kotex boxes and put them out in the garbage. If she was going to snoop, I would give her something to find. Let her tell her friends all about how I was starting my period if she wanted to. Flara proved too thorough, however, and soon I discovered that she had gone through a drawer containing some medicine for my pregnancy. Eventually another event brought me in contact with the family doctor to whom I had first gone to consult about the pregnancy. Sure enough, he told me that Flara had called him inquiring about my medicine. "What did you tell her?" I asked him. Smart enough to put two and two together, the doctor's answer showed he was on my side in this little battle: "I told her I didn't know a damn thing!" I couldn't avoid feeling a twinge of triumph at having an ally: "Good for you!" I told him. Only later did I realize that he had cursed—right in front of a lady!

I'm sure Flara deduced my pregnancy at some point before I wanted her to, but my war with her receded in importance as time passed. I was consumed with preparing for our first child. Reading the latest health information made the time go faster, but the best tonic for me was a Christmas visit to Alabama, where we were to receive an important present—a car of our own.

That previous August we had been forced to borrow John D's car to get to Alabama, where Ray held a revival meeting for two weeks in my home church of New Hope. He preached every weekday evening and twice on Sundays. At night I kept busy washing and ironing his white shirts (at least two a day), which would be absolutely soaked after a sermon. It was great experience for him and wonderful for me to be back home. Ray used the cool mornings to polish lessons while I shared stories of life in Belle with my family and friends. My husband was exhausted at the end of the two weeks, but he had a paycheck and the promise from Daddy to search for an affordable car that we could pick up when we returned at Christmas. When December rolled around I was an expectant mom, and Ray was within a few weeks of being the located man for the Belle Church of Christ. I don't even remember how we got back to Alabama to get the vehicle, but I do know that on the return trip it felt good to be riding in our beat-up new car—a '47 Chevy for which daddy had cosigned. It sported a new two-toned green and cream paint job that made it look like an Easter egg rolling into the Kanawha valley toward Belle.

PREACHER FOR THE BELLE CHURCH OF CHRIST

The time in Alabama had been good for both of us. For me it provided needed emotional nourishment. For Ray it meant an opportunity to practice preaching before assuming full-time duties at Belle. Ray had been offered the job back in the spring (soon after our engagement) when the previous minister resigned. Though he would fill in during the summer and fall, his official starting date was to be January 2, 1949. The elders needed a replacement and Ray needed a job, so the timing was right. Both parties knew that the favorite son, the first Christian college preacher from Belle, would not stay long, and the temporary nature of the ministry was mutually appealing. As elder Hubert Peck said, "Ray needs priming."

When the first of the year finally dawned we rejoiced. Time to pack up the Chevy and my maternity clothes and live on our own. Of course, Ray had been preparing sermon material for weeks in his spare time, working at a badly lit little table in the Muncy living room, so he was excited. My excitement stemmed not so much from escaping Flara, though that was attractive, as it did with actually having a home I could call ours. The elders provided a small apartment attached to the church building, and this connection made for strange living quarters. A door from the auditorium opened onto a hallway, to the left of which was our bathroom. Unfortunately it was not just ours but the public's as well during worship services. To the right was a front room which Ray used as his study. Once again, unfortunately, it doubled as a classroom during services, which meant that it could be entered from the auditorium. Adjacent to it and connected by a door was a living area. Farther down the hall were a bedroom and a kitchen. Since no door separated the hall from our living room, it was visible to anyone going to or coming from a visit to the lavatory, and of course our study could be entered without warning.

As for furniture, we gathered mostly the discards of others, and the off-the-floor stove looked 19th-century. I was thrilled nonetheless and spent many hours decorating with cheap knicknacks. When some elders' wives told me the apartment was "fixed up cuter" by us than by any of the previous occupants, I was as proud as if I had been named queen of the Sweetheart Banquet. Most of the time we had the entire building to ourselves, so despite the inconvenience of the arrangement, we experienced a sense of freedom for which we had thirsted after six months as boarders.

At other times, the shared nature of the apartment required vigilance, as my husband learned. Ray had pretty much disciplined himself to be very careful how he dressed on Sundays or Wednesdays, in case of unexpected visitors. At other times he relaxed. One Friday, as he exited the bathroom after showering, the outer door from the auditorium opened and in walked a woman carrying a container. Such an intrusion would have been cause for only minor concern except that Ray was standing there completely nude. No robe. No towel. The woman said nothing, nor did she look away. Ray scrambled into our bedroom like one of those cartoon animals who can find no footing. I was in the kitchen when I heard a muffled cry and a loud thud. "Ray? Is something wrong?" I stuck my head in the bedroom, where I saw my husband, still naked, holding one foot and hopping on the other. On the floor was an overturned space heater. Ray forgot his pain long enough to jerk his thumb toward the hallway and hiss, "There's a woman in there!" I found her in the front room/classroom. Very calmly she gestured to the container, which was resting on the desk: "Would you please see that the wedding party gets these candles? I wasn't sure where to put them, and they'll be needed tomorrow—at the ceremony."

When I returned to the bedroom, Ray had finally put on some clothes but had not yet recovered from the shock. Even so, he managed what would become a typical comic assessment of a weird situation as he yelled, "Weezie, she saw me—and I didn't even have on my socks!"

Strange women seeing my husband naked was only one challenge of being a preacher's wife. There were the constant phone calls, the many social events, the necessary public role of greeter and hostess. I loved it; I felt useful. Of course, we did not escape Flara completely. She attended church faithfully and never kept an opinion to herself. One Sunday I walked in the front of the auditorium wearing a new dress. Maybe it was after Ray's first paycheck. I sat down in front of her and she couldn't resist: "That a new dress?" It was back to the battle of wills between us. Her question was really an accusation: "You are not frugal! Like me." But I was ready for the attack. "Yes, it is," I said, "and I didn't pay a penny for it." This rejoinder put an end to her questions. I didn't want to add that my parents had bought it for me. Even as I relished shutting her up, I knew this was not a good way to live, always tense around her, feeling judged. And I was blameworthy, too, for playing one-upmanship in the shadow of the podium from which my husband would in a few minutes proclaim the gospel.

Ray's sermons in those days leaned in the direction of legalism almost to the point of sounding like a different gospel than he came to preach later. Although he was more open than many, his concept of preaching rested on the bedrock of sound doctrine, which meant for some a set of unexamined prejudices. One of his early sermons stands out as legalistic. It was called "After Baptism, What?" Ray went through a long list of qualities modeled by faithful Jews and Christians. He reminded the congregation of the necessity of prayer and teaching and unity and charity and praise. He extolled the need of adding virtues, giving diligence, taking heed, examining self, assembling, worshiping in spirit and truth. Maybe I'm not being fair to him, but to me it sounded like a list of rules. He did talk about joy, but his example of the eunuch was drowned out by the constant reminders of what we had to do to please God. Ray preached that sermon a lot in those days, and in fairness, many in his audience had not been Christians very long and needed to hear about responsibility, about leading a life worthy of their calling. I could tell, however, that Ray was not yet comfortable in the pulpit.

As a young preacher, Ray lacked strong independence and as a result either echoed the opinions of others or was caught awkwardly in the middle on knotty issues or nitpicking debates. For example, a church janitor, Johnny Shiftlet, questioned him once on Paul's famous dictum that women should be silent in the assembly. "I think," Johnny ventured, "the scripture means that wives should be silent in Bible classes too. What do you think, Brother Muncy?" This question was put to Ray not in a class, but in an otherwise empty building during a week-long meeting Ray held in January of 1949. The revival (though we did not call it that) was to inaugurate his work with the Belle congregation. Ray had been sticking to basics, steering clear of controversy, he thought.

Two nights before his conversation with Johnny, he had used the "Fall and Restoration" sermon from his pre-college days. The night before he had preached on "The Gospel Wheel," complete with a diagram of the wheel, with its divine and human halves combining to make salvation possible. The sermon itself was a series of proof texts on, for example, the need to obey the gospel without waiting. In fact, Ray was pleased to hear one of the elders compliment him after the sermon on his use of scripture, which meant that Ray had quoted chapter and verse after nearly every sentence.

Ray's mind was on his next lesson, and he really did not want to debate someone who didn't even worship at Belle (Johnny was helping during the meeting). But to be polite to a brother in Christ, Ray tried to deal with the touchy subject of women in the assembly. He knew that some men at Belle, very uncomfortable with the more emancipated woman emerging from World War II, took I Corinthians 14:35 as a divine sanction to keep them barefoot and pregnant, and he also knew, even as a young preacher, that Paul's comments must be taken in the context of a particular problem in a particular congregation. His ability to articulate all these nuances was a different matter, however.

"Well..." Ray said slowly while he gathered his thoughts. "I certainly think the passage means women are not to preach, Johnny, not to usurp authority over the elders, you know."

"Yes, preacher, but Paul says 'it is a shame for women to speak in church.' Doesn't church include Bible class?"

"Well, that's the question. If you look at what Paul is saying about orderly worship, and since we don't know that the early church had a separate time set aside as we do...."

"What are you saying, exactly?"

"I guess I'm saying that I would like to study that issue more, but right now I wouldn't want to say that a woman cannot ask questions and participate in a Bible class. After all, the church started Bible classes so people could ask questions."

"That's all well and good, Brother Muncy, but I worry that we're too quick to take on modern ways just because they're modern. We have to be careful not to add to the Word."

"But did we add to the Word when we started having Bible class?"

"The 'antis' say we did; maybe they're right."

"Well, Johnny, what's important is that the gospel gets preached and people get saved. Let's hope that's what happens at this meeting. The other things will get sorted out, I'm sure."

Johnny Shiftlet was probably not so sure they would with wishy-washy preachers like this. That night Ray preached another standard sermon to an auditorium about two-thirds full: it was called "Broad Man at a Narrow Gate." In it Ray compared life to a journey in which we all begin as innocent, without sin. Then at the age of accountability, we all choose which of the two roads to take. The broad way, leading from the wide gate, has no caution signs or speed limits, and its end is destruction. The narrow way, proceeding from the strait gate, costs us to enter: our time, energy, and money. It's easy to miss and uphill most of the way. Since it cannot be made wider, it must be run with patience, but its end is a glorious cessation of suffering, a reunion of man and God: "And God shall wipe away all tears from their eyes, and there shall be no more death, neither sorrow, nor crying, neither shall there be any more pain: for the former things are passed away" (Rev. 21:4).

Ray closed with that scripture. He issued the invitation for all those who needed to respond to the narrow way: "The man who has taken the broad way has too much girth to enter the narrow gate—too much sin has bloated him. Don't be a broad man at the narrow gate. Lay down your sins tonight. God is calling you to a place where suffering and sin are no more. He awaits to help you through that narrow gate. Won't you come as we stand and sing?"

The congregation rose to the strains of "Just as I Am." Before the first verse was over, a dark, slender young woman slipped out of the pew, helped by the gentle squeeze of her mother's hand, and hurried down the aisle. Her name was Margaret Weaver, a young bride from Coalburg, West Virginia. She told Ray that she wanted to be baptized. Ray did not know her or her family. Somewhere in her background was a miner—either a father, brother, or husband—and probably poverty. Unlike the Belle people in the auditorium, many of whom worked for DuPont, her clothes were plain and worn. As he watched her take a seat on the front pew, Ray wondered why she had come. Did she really love Jesus and want to be with Him in heaven? Behind her young, anxious eyes Ray felt the mystery of human and divine will—the mystery of the gospel. And he quaked inwardly at the power of it vested in his words, his voice. Whatever the confluence of reasons that brought her to Belle and down that aisle, belief in one person and one person only could take her from this point. As she sat before him on the pew, everyone knew that she would be asked to name Him in a confession of faith.

Some of the women took her behind the baptistry to prepare. Ray went back, took off his coat, and pulled on a pair of huge rubber waders. As he entered the water behind the curtain, Johnny Shiftlet was there, ready to pull back the curtain when Margaret, dressed now in a white robe, met Ray in the center of the baptistry. As the curtain parted and the congregation watched, Ray took her hand. He asked her if she believed that Jesus was the Son of God. She squeaked out a "yes," and Ray told her what a wonderful day this was because of her confession. "And because you have acknowledged Jesus as your Lord and Savior, I, by the authority of the Father, the

Son, and the Holy Ghost, baptize you for the remission of your sins and so that you might receive the gift of the Holy Spirit."

He directed her to pinch her nose with the fingers of her left hand and to grasp her left wrist with her right hand. He then placed his left hand on the back of her neck and held her right elbow with his other hand, using this leverage to help her torso sink slowly under the water. He supported her head with his left hand as she became totally submerged. In that instant, he felt her grip tighten instinctively, sensed her whole body go rigid in the dark water. Ray pushed her head back to the surface and Margaret rose sputtering a little, squeezing her eyes tightly shut until she was sure they were safe from the chlorine in the little pool. Johnny drew the curtains shut again as Margaret, a bit dazed by the rapidity of it all, waded back to the women on the other side, a group which included her tearfully smiling mother. Those of us in the audience sat in respectful silence, many perhaps, like me, wondering if there wasn't something awkward in this custom of betraying no joy over the event. Except for the song. We did have the song, something like "Nothing But the Blood of Jesus" that started haltingly as the curtain closed and swelled in volume and enthusiasm.

As Johnny helped him from the pool, Ray realized that Margaret was his first baptism as a located preacher. He told me later he thought of the conversation he had with Johnny about women in Bible class. We both wondered how many men at Coalburg thought like Johnny and how young Margaret Weaver would fare in her Christian life.

The meeting had no other baptisms, but it was considered by the elders to be successful, with several responses for prayer. Ray was learning fast; he had to. He was showing an ability to deal with people, but I wished he would loosen up in the pulpit. His delivery was often stiff and lifeless. His sermons tended to sound the same notes. The best thing about them, then and always, was their clear organization. His listeners could never accuse Ray Muncy of confusing them or losing them with meaningless digressions. He was easy to follow and made his points crystal clear.

As Ray's experience began to "prime" him for his calling, he was anxious for me to embody the ideal preacher's wife. When we scheduled a walking tour and mountain climb with the young people, I told him I wanted to wear slacks. He was afraid, however, that the older church members might disapprove, so he had me carry the slacks in a small bag with other things for the outing. Thus to all the prying eyes at the outset of our walking tour, Mrs. Muncy looked very becoming in her flower print dress. Once we tramped across Route 60 away from any parent who might see, Ray let me change into the slacks. We counted on the young people to keep our secret, a doubtful proposition at best, though they were on the side of greater comfort too. It was a silly situation to be in, but Ray could not have stood up to the criticism he might have received. It was easier for him to make me jump through hoops.

I could sense his insecurity in other ways too. He was very secretive about his sermon preparation. If I intruded on his work in the front room study, he would seem uncomfortable. I might ask what he was going to preach about, and he would joke, "Oh, about forty-five minutes." If asked again he would say with forced nonchalance, "Well, I just don't want to talk about it." It seemed strange because he was otherwise so open with me. Maybe he didn't trust me on that level yet—to be his intellectual equal, or maybe he didn't trust his own ability enough to risk criticism.

When I look at Ray's filing cabinet full of five-by-seven cards with carefully typed notes, including color-coded points, I think back to those early days when he probably struggled more than I knew to have something to say. The filing cabinet contains more than seventy sermons composed during our year in Belle—the equivalent in spoken words of a novel as long as *War and Peace*. Granted, Ray's sermons were not literary masterpieces, but the work that went into them was Tolstoyesque. Beyond composing sermons,

1949 studio picture of Ray & Eloise, taken during their tenure with the Belle Church of Christ.

Ray was responsible for the weekly bulletin, which was distributed to the members on Sunday mornings. Serving as writer, typist, and compositor, he ran off copies on an old mimeograph machine. Even when the thing worked, it was laborious and messy. If it smeared copy, as it often did, the effect was maddening. One of the strongest images I retain from Belle is of Ray on a Saturday night, hands and face stained with purple ink, kicking the daylights out of the inoperable mimeograph machine.

As I think back on his reluctance to talk about his preparation, I feel a respect for my husband and the trial by fire he underwent as a twenty-one-year-old preacher. Whatever self-doubt he lived with during that year, he never let it keep him from going to the study, with his handful of commentaries, his pad and pencils, and crafting the best sermon he could for the Christians at Belle.

His self-confidence was not helped by his status as the hometown boy returned to the fold. The folks who had watched him grow up felt free to give advice. He was not that much older than some of the young people to whom he was supposed to act as mentor, and the same ones we went out with on Fridays sometimes did not respect him enough on Sundays. And, of course, Flara usually hurt him with advice she thought would help. She rarely criticized the content of Ray's sermons, but she almost always chastised him for some trait or gesture. After her sharp instruction, all I could think was "Bless John D's easy-going silence!" I resolved to do my best to make it easy for Ray, so I hid my slacks and did not pry into his work. I loved him and carried his child into our second summer in West Virginia. As the month of June began, I was reaching full term. Alabama seemed far away. I remember a sense of waiting. Waiting for our first child. Waiting for changes that would take us from Belle. I felt as if the whole world was pregnant with me.

MOTHERHOOD, FATHERHOOD, AND A NEW BEGINNING

In 1949 young mothers did not know as much as they do now—the literature and professional services simply did not exist to the same degree. I was not quite ready on the night of June 8, as Ray and I settled in for an evening alone, for the birth to begin. My back ached, so when we decided to play Rook, we used our three-pillow couch creatively. I leaned against one huge pillow; Ray used another for his backing. The third pillow was set between us to serve as a card table. We drank lime Kool-Aid as we played. Ray, not his pregnant wife, ate pickles too. The game went on until we got sleepy—another quiet evening at home. At about 2 A.M. I awoke with severe pain, which at first I thought was my back acting up again. It was labor beginning.

Ray drove me to the Charleston hospital, where at dawn I was admitted. Soon I was in a bed, sedated for the pain. No Lamaze techniques in those days. And the fathers gathered in one of those stereotypical waiting rooms, although Ray was allowed to visit me up until actual delivery, which was not until early afternoon. I was drifting in and out of the sedative, moaning and talking, but felt no pain. When Ray returned from lunch, he asked how things were going.

"Well," said one man, "green is trump now."

"What?" asked Ray. "Oh, she's replaying our Rook game from last night." Apparently I put on quite a show for the expectant fathers.

When David Raymond Muncy finally arrived, all nine pounds, six ounces of him, it was Ray's turn to put on a show. I don't remember anything particular that he did; but he was hilarious. For one thing, he was alarmed by the bruises he saw on David's head shortly after the birth. The doctor assured him that they were caused by the forceps and would go away. Ray was unconvinced at first. His body language amused me, as tired as I was: a combination of joy and terror at being in the presence of new life—one that he helped create. The name, David, incidentally, came about from a promise Ray and one of his high school friends had made to each other. The first child would be named after the old school buddy. I wasn't thrilled at this stipulation, but was happy enough with "David Raymond."

With David's arrival, our own parenthood inevitably nudged our parents to the periphery of our attention. After a brief visit to see David, J. Barney and Elizabeth returned to Alabama, and we saw less of Flara and John D as I mothered and Ray preached.

Life as a preacher was rewarding for Ray but not always easy financially. The elders paid him $200 a month and gave him rent and utilities. Still, with our debt to Daddy (for the car) added to the cost of necessities, there was more month than money much of the time. Our last Christmas in Belle, for example, we had completely run out of funds. It promised to be a grim holiday. At that point we experienced a Charles Dickens moment. In addition to preaching for Belle, Ray several times spoke for even smaller congregations, especially to one designated as Ward #9, so-called after the number of the mine that created the community. He had preached there a few weeks before, and since the people at Ward were often out of work, we assumed that this time, as had been the case previously, Ray's sermon was gratis. In fact, when the man from Ward showed up on our doorstep a few days before Christmas, Ray feared he might be called on for some emergency matter. Instead, the man presented Ray with a check for $25—in 1949 that was like getting $100.

"Who was that?" I asked Ray when he returned to the living room. I was holding David.

"That, Weezie, was Providence." We then had a prayer right there, with Ray holding my hand and the check while I held our baby.

It turned out to be a merry Christmas, after all. God had taken care of us. Eighteen months before, I had stepped off that bus feeling like a stranger in a strange land—cut off from my parents. Now I was celebrating the holidays as a parent, feeling more at home with Ray and his work than ever. And by the time Christmas came, we had been blessed in another important way—a new work.

Several weeks before, W. C. Sawyer, Ray's preacher from his high school days, had been in the area for a meeting. Originally from Kentucky, Sawyer told Ray that the Lancaster congregation was looking for a new preacher. Ray had actually preached there once, early in his work at Belle, and had made a favorable impression. Sawyer urged Ray to get in touch with them. With complete cooperation from the elders at Belle, Ray contacted Lancaster. In a matter of weeks the move was set. On Christmas Day, 1949, Ray preached his last sermon for the hometown folks. Then, on January 8, 1950, Ray began a new decade by delivering his first lesson for Lancaster.

It was an exciting time for us with Ray advancing in his vocation of preaching and with our family growing. I must remember Flara and John D here, though. Despite our stormy relationship with Flara, the two of them did exhibit Christian caring and outreach. They helped us in an hour of need. And time away from them softened the rough edges of the personality clash between me and Flara. Years afterward, when Ray was flourishing in Bloomington, Flara came up to me at some family gathering and said, "Ray has done well, but he couldn't have done it by himself." I was moved by this compliment: "Why, thank you, Flara; he is a good man. You can take some of the credit for that."

She thought for a moment, as if considering the merit of my return compliment. "You know, I guess I was pretty hard on you...." She trailed off, not explaining whether she meant me or both Ray and me. But it didn't matter. She was apologizing in her way. And I owed her an apology for my lack of sympathy, but like her I offered it only indirectly in small talk. As we stood there she seemed lost in thought, as if all the years with Ray had suddenly caught up with her. Maybe she was remembering her unexpected mother-hood, her decision to go back to church, the difficulty of disciplining a rest-less child, or the journey her little Raymond had taken away from her and toward a life of Christian service. I hope she could see in those reminis-cences, as I do now, how God used her life, even her weaknesses, as he has used my weaknesses, to work His will in the lives of others. In 1969, when her work on earth was finished, Flara Muncy died and was buried in Oak Hill, West Virginia.

FOUR

The Arch of Experience

Lancaster, Kentucky (1950-51)

ADVENTURES IN DRY CLEANING

We moved to Lancaster, Kentucky, in January 1950. Ray preached for the Maple Avenue Church of Christ, a congregation of about sixty which paid very little for a family with a six-month-old-child. To be precise, the salary was $50 a week. As a result, Ray was forced to look for other work to supplement his preaching income. Fortunately, we lived across the street from one of the owners of the Garrod County Dry Cleaners. His name was Clay Huffman and his daughter babysat for us when we first arrived. With that connection established, it didn't take Clay long to see our need and Ray's potential. Within months of our move, he and the other owners hired Ray to manage the business in spite of his youth (he was twenty-two) and inexperience. Thus Ray had two jobs, both almost full-time.

That workload made our year and a half in Lancaster hectic but rewarding because we came into contact with so many different kinds of people, all of whom made an impact on us. Like Belle, Lancaster could be only a temporary place for us, but as Tennyson says in a poem that Ray liked, "I am a part of all that I have met." Life is a process of absorbing the experience of others and growing in the process. As brief as our time was in this little Kentucky town, several people became precious parts of us.

Clay and the other owners kept an eye on Ray, especially at first, until he learned the business. In a town like Lancaster, however, it was not that complicated. Ray's job consisted of keeping the books, making sure the other employees cleaned and pressed competently, and picking up clothes from customers when necessary.

The job allowed him freedom to come and go. He always opened the shop and was in and out during the day, but in the meantime he made calls and studied for his sermons. He had to rely on the three full-time employees to keep the place going in his absence. The male presser did the dry cleaning while two female assistants took care of the washing, ironing, and sorting. One of the women, Bessie, was uneducated and unpolished in her speech. When customers came in, she embarrassed Ray with her poor grammar: "Well, I knowed I seed that order somewhere; I set it down myself" (meaning she wrote it down). Since the other girl, Doris, was a little better schooled in English fundamentals, he devised ways to make sure she met the public as often as possible. Or he would jump up from his desk to intercept the customer himself.

Ironically, though, most of the customers talked more like Bessie than like Ray. Once, Ray popped up quickly to greet an old man carrying a wadded-up garment: "Good morning! How can we help you this morning?" And the customer, whom he had been so diligent to protect from Bessie's assault of bad grammar, replied, "I done near ruint this here shirt workin' up in the attic this mornin'. What you reckon you'll charge to clean it? I be needin' it right away." As Ray formulated an answer, Bessie yelled from the back, "Ain't no way it be ready before Tuesday!"

As a would-be guardian of linguistic purity, Ray accepted the lesson in humility. Besides, his duties went beyond office management.

Most weeks, Ray would use the company van to pick up clothes. The most memorable pick-up he ever made sounds like a scene from a movie, but it really happened. After a few months on the job, the customers grew comfortable with Ray, knowing him to be trustworthy and dependable. When it came to house calls, this relaxed atmosphere meant that Ray would sometimes open the door himself if no one answered, then slip inside to grab the clothes. It was part of small town life to trust your dry cleaning man to do that.

Early one Monday morning, Ray knocked on the door of a rather ritzy two-story home that belonged to one of the three owners of the dry cleaning store—the Arnolds. He got no answer. Rather than have to come back again, he opened the door, planning to find the laundry and leave quickly. While waiting, however, he failed to notice a neighborhood dog snooping around the premises, a frisky little terrier poking his nose into bushes and flowers at the front of the Arnold house. By the time Ray opened the door, the terrier was right behind him. In stepped Ray; in trotted the strange dog. Ray saw the creature just as he heard the clatter of its paws on the tile entryway. "Come here, boy," he whispered, although why he would whisper is not clear, since no one seemed to be at home. The dog stopped to acknowledge his voice.

Forgetting all about any laundry that might have awaited him, Ray extended his right arm to the dog, talking in a calm, friendly tone: "That's a good boy. Come see Uncle Ray. We need to get you back outside." Dogs have a wonderfully alert, bright-eyed way of regarding an approaching stranger. It promises their delight to make your acquaintance. Their tongues loll smilingly, their ears are pointed up, their paws tremble, their tails wag. But that pose, at least in this case, was a big tease. The terrier really wanted to avoid Ray in direct proportion to his desire, which the pooch sensed, to lay hands on him. So the dog listened to Ray's soothing come-on in the middle of the entryway of a house which belonged to neither of them, let him get within an inch or two with his beckoning hands, then trotted away toward what looked like a dining room, where he began to tear apart a newspaper.

Ray decided to abandon pleading and take action, but when he lunged to grab the dog, his prey avoided him easily and scurried back to the entryway. He made a sharp right and scampered up the stairs. All this time the house was deathly quiet save for the scrape of the dog's feet on the tile and Ray's breathing as he bounded up the stairs in pursuit. When he got to the second floor hallway, he saw the terrier briefly, waiting in the doorway to what looked like a bedroom. As soon as the canine tease saw Ray, he darted back into the bedroom and straight under the queen-sized bed. Feeling slightly desperate now, Ray dove under the bed and again grabbed for his tormentor. This time the dog licked his hand and seemed to be yielding. Ray was on his stomach, feet sticking out from under the bed, ready to clutch the terrier. Now, he thought, get out of this room, down the stairs, and out of here. At this point of relative quiet, Ray realized that he heard the distant sound of running water. It stopped even as he became aware of it but was followed by the click of a door closing. A shower! Someone was in an adjacent bathroom getting out of what sounded like a shower stall! Then he saw the door connecting bedroom to bathroom. Its knob was turning.

Paralyzed with fear, Ray did not move for a second, while the pooch squirmed in his grasp. At last the fear energized his body and he scrambled to his feet in time to call out: "Mrs. Arnold! This is Ray Muncy—"

By the time he got this much out, the bathroom door opened and Mrs. Arnold, her head swathed in towels and her body wrapped in a bathrobe, stepped out. Her eyes met Ray's, his a little wild as he finished his sentence. "—Do you have any laundry today?" He waited with his captive squirming in his arms.

"Oh, yes, I'll think you'll find it downstairs where it always is. Don't worry, Ray, but I am glad you called out. Otherwise we both could have gotten quite a scare! Thank you for coming by."

Once outside, Ray resisted the temptation to toss the dog, who was now trying to get at his face with its tongue, into the bushes. Instead he set it down and hurried to the van, vowing never again to enter a house without permission. While under that bed, he had seen his entire career as a preacher flash before his eyes.

Needless to say, word got around that Ray had been found under the bed of one of his dry cleaning customers—an owner no less, and he suffered through a week or so of teasing, even from the owners. Leading the charge was the young presser at the cleaners, George Tevis, also a friend of Ray's. George was clever and incorrigible when it came to his humor. Standing in the back working the handle on a press, with the steam hissing, he would practically yell out to Doris and Bessie, "Yeah, the Rev was working some overtime, all right! He was goin' that extra mile." Or he would say, "Don't let them get on you none, Rev. The customer is always right; that's our motto!"

Or George might have repeated the story circulating in town that week. "Hey, Bessie, did you hear about Mr. Arnold? Yeah, he came home early the other day and surprised his wife. She was bendin' over the stove or something and Mr. Arnold he come up behind her and slaps her on the rump, real romantic like, and she giggles and says, 'Just leave the cleanin' on the bed; I'll be right up.'" True to his mild nature, Ray acted the good sport, though he was chagrined to suffer at the hands of his own employees.

The fact that George could say such things without really bothering Ray, and the fact that he was a black man saying those things in 1951, make for an interesting chapter from our time in Lancaster.

GEORGE THE PRESSER

We lived in a house with another couple, the Currys, who had come to Lancaster a few years before from Georgia. They rented out one side of their rather stately old house to us. The back room of the duplex, which we made into a den, was a special source of pride for the Currys. When Mrs. Curry told us about the renovation, she talked in a near whisper that characterized all her conversation, as if she and her auditor were seated at an elegant dinner party: "Now we bought this paint, this Cascade Blue, and don't you know, it wasn't real expensive and we think it looks rather pretty—did I say that it is called 'Cascade Blue'?—and we bought a large enough quantity to do our bedroom and this room too!" She and her husband smiled and smiled as they walked us around the entire room, which was an overpowering shade of blue somewhere between sky and navy. We detested the color—Ray called it "Casket Blue."

The Currys were interesting people. And as landlords go they weren't too bad. The worst thing that happened while we lived there showed their blind spot and opened up one of America's ugly wounds for us. It involved Ray's chief presser, the young man named George Tevis. His teasing of Ray about getting caught in a customer's house was typical banter for George. His sharp wit might well have produced a professional comedian. This lean, goateed young man with a faint resemblance to Sammy Davis, Jr., loved to talk, and his penchant for embellished tales of his own life was balanced by a genuine curiosity about others. A few years older than Ray, George instantly won my husband over.

He belonged to the St. Peter and Paul's Predestinarian Baptist Church, where he was a member of a quartet. This group was really good. Early on, when he found out Ray was a Church of Christ preacher, he started goading him about the narrowness of his spiritual experience. He would say, "You need to come to our Baptist church to see how we do it. I'm tellin' you, you get more for your nickel at St. Pete and Paul's." Ray listened with interest but at first did not take George's friendly taunts as a real invitation. When his employee told him about the singing group, Ray got more interested. And it did appeal to him to find out how Baptists—even this unique group—worshipped. The risk of going to a denominational service was great; Ray could even get fired for it—attending would be like consorting with the enemy.

George continued to invite Ray, all the while kidding him about the Church of Christ's lack of enthusiasm in its worship: "Yeah, I know why you talk so soft on Sunday mornin's. You don't want to wake up old Angle Sanders!" Sanders was a rich farmer who contributed heavily at Maple Street. George went on, "Now if you want to wake somebody up, you ought to come to our singin' next week." Ray asked him if his quartet would perform. Yes, George said, the group would sing. When he found out the singing was on a Saturday, Ray decided on impulse to go. I had to watch David, so I stayed home, worrying about what might happen if word got out that Ray had gone to such a performance. Fearlessly, Ray slipped out of our duplex early and spent part of Saturday evening at the Predestinarian Baptist Church hearing a variety of gospel groups.

He came home thrilled with what he heard. So entranced was he with their talent that he invited the members of the quartet to come by our apartment a few nights later to sing for me. The four young men came at about 7, dressed in suits no less. Ray had asked me to make some dessert for them, so we began by eating apple pie and talking. George was the life of the party, of course, telling stories about places the group had performed. Next he began teasing Ray about the Church of Christ's refusal to use the term reverend for its preachers. He said, "Rev, what is this mess that wife of yours made—it's good stuff." Noticing my reaction, he explained, "Now, I know you white folks in the Church of Christ get all nervous when somebody brings a reverend around. You don't want no holy men around your women! Well, I understand that, I respect that, but we got to have a title for your preacher man there; otherwise he don't get respect in the colored community. So I call him 'Rev' for short; that way the white folks don't get so offended and the black folks will know that he ain't no dry cleaner!"

Ray was a good sport, but quickly requested a song. George and his group sang about three or four spirituals. And they were wonderful. I had not seen Ray so relaxed and happy around others since Freed-Hardeman days. We laughed and carried on until about 10 o'clock. When the group left, Ray said, "George is a handful, but he has a good heart. I think tonight might be the start of us turning him around for the Lord. We'll have to have him over again, and maybe we can get him serious about things in the church."

The next morning Mr. Curry knocked on our door. He came in without any of the usual amenities. Before we could ask what was on his mind, he told us in blunt terms, "I want you to know that I can't have my renters entertaining Negroes." We were stunned, frankly. We were hardly progressive enough to be unaware of racial differences or barriers. Ray simply liked George so much that he did not anticipate our fellowship causing any problems. I didn't say a word. Ray, by this time becoming more experienced at dealing with people, apologized quickly and sincerely: "I'm sorry, Mr. Curry, but this boy works for me and I didn't think anything about it. Now that I know, we will abide by your rules." Even Ray's apology did not entirely diffuse Curry's anger. He seemed to be trembling a bit. It took a moment for him to acknowledge Ray's words. This was the only time we ever saw him other than pleasant and deferential.

His reaction to our integrated party should not have surprised us, I guess, especially me. Ray grew up in Belle, West Virginia, where he saw very few black people. When he went home with me before we were married, he was completely fascinated by the black children who ran in and out of our grocery store to buy two cents' worth of candy. They delighted him! He was also fascinated by my father's relationship with them, the way they depended on Daddy for everything. He was their banker, their advisor, in a way their law. When they were sick he drove them to Birmingham, answering their loyalty with his own determined devotion to their needs. Yet my parents had strong feelings about "race mixing," as it was called. My mother would not let blacks come to the front door. She made them eat on the back porch off pieces of tin or pottery that we never used. She never let us eat after them. We didn't have running water then, and I can remember my mother heating water in the tea kettle and absolutely scalding dishes used by those workers, as if black people were animals with something contagious.

Though it would take the Civil Rights movement of the 1960s to fully sensitize us to racism, Ray didn't agree with Curry's sentiments in 1950 either. He felt, however, as did I, that it was a battle he could not win. The irony was grim: only the night before Ray had hoped to use our home to befriend and perhaps convert George, but this incident threw cold water on the idea, limiting what Ray as a minister of the gospel could do to reach a person who needed Jesus. George's attachment to his Baptist roots was tenuous, but chances of getting him to attend a rival group would be slim. Ray felt deflated. To be honest, his evangelistic urge, at least in this case, needed the supportive environment of our little home. It was harder for him to visit George in the black neighborhood called the "Chute," with its forbidding poverty and racial segregation. To bring him to Maple Avenue Church of Christ was out of the question, of course.

The only other turf to engage George in religious discussion might have been at the dry cleaners, but that was not conducive to evangelism either. Later in life Ray would have perhaps figured out a way to do more. Back then he was hamstrung by his youth and the circumstances. This store was his first experience at managing people, and though he did well enough, he may have become too friendly with George. The banter between boss and employee proved unprofessional. At the same time, Ray's tacit encouragement of George's humor made it harder for the pair to have serious discussions.

After Curry's flareup, things went on as usual, with George as comically insolent as ever. He might stop working, turn to the others, and say, "Well, it's Wednesday, and we finally got all the Rev's cleaning done—guess we can start on the stuff that pays us now." He was alluding to the free cleaning available to our family. Not meant as anything but humor, such remarks kept us entertained but off balance, as I was when George asked me a question during one of my stints as helper: "Mrs. Rev, is you nosy?" By the way, George could make subjects and verbs agree when he wanted to, but he often assumed the more stereotypical black dialect when he teased us.

"What do you mean, George?"

"I mean is you nosy about what Rev does?" I said I didn't think so. He exploded: "Well, I went off to Richmond after work Friday and when I come in, that Helen Cecil, she wanted to know where I done been, and what I been doin'."

Realizing his intent in asking the question, I stopped him: "Just a minute, George, I'm pretty nosy too, if that's what you're talkin' about by nosy."

I stopped him also because I did not like hearing about the wilder side of George's life. The more comfortable he got around us, the more he talked about his problems. Helen Cecil was his girl friend when we first arrived in Lancaster. He'd get drunk and fool around on her, and as his question to me indicated, he did not want to be called to account for his behavior. Eventually George married her, but was abusive when he drank. She called the police more than once. Faced with a hearing on the matter, George asked Ray to be a character witness. Ray could not desert his friend and employee, so he provided an honest assessment of George's strengths and weaknesses. George had always been a good worker, never drinking on the job. Eventually, however, character witnesses could not protect George from his own volatile temper. He was good natured about things in general, but about women, his woman, he possessed an irritating arrogance and short fuse. Ray recalls the judge asking George on what grounds he treated his wife that way: "Grounds?" George said, "I don't need no grounds. I just can't stand the woman!"

George escaped with a few days in jail and a warning on that occasion, but the combination of alcohol and an explosive relationship led to more serious trouble. He drifted away from us emotionally. At some point after we left Lancaster, George shot a relative of Helen's who tried to keep him from hitting her during a drunken argument. He was sent to prison for life.

It was sad for my husband to watch this story unfold, feeling that he could have perhaps done more. But George was almost thirty and had been around the block. Not quite twenty-four, Ray liked George, who was an unusual black man in those days, very outspoken, pushing the limits of permissible behavior toward whites. The older man was something of a kindred spirit for Ray, but his life was like a powerful force heading in the wrong direction—Ray tried to change it but was not strong enough—and got no help from a society not yet ready to minister to a black man in the same way as it would to a white.

The Gill Sisters

George wasn't the only interesting person we knew. Next door to the Curry house lived a pair of Presbyterian sisters—Helen and Martha Gill. These two spinsters seemed fond of us from the beginning, including our child David. Their parents, at that point deceased, had been prominent horse owners and breeders. Their house was full of silver loving cups, silver tea sets, and other signs of equestrian pursuits. The two sisters had melted down some of the silver into tableware. So pervasive was the precious metal that the house practically gleamed.

Naturally Ray and I were flattered to be invited over for dinner at this local landmark. On one of the first such occasions, we glimpsed the sweet, romantic nature of these two gentle women. After the meal and a survey of the silver, they showed us a painting done by their Aunt Emma. It was supposed to be a rendering of Little Eva, the character from *Uncle Tom's Cabin* who is the epitome of goodness. Ray took one look and cried out, "Oh that picture, it looks just like Eloise!" He carried a photograph in his billfold taken of me on the bleachers one day at Freed-Hardeman. The photographer yelled at me and snapped the photo when I turned around. So here in this fancy house, three years later, Ray pulled out his wallet and showed the photo to Helen and Martha. They too thought I looked like the girl in Harriet Beecher Stowe's famous novel. Little Eva, who tried to help others both white and black, wasted away in a world coarsened by slavery and the profit motive. She must have been quite a role model for these genteel women. What really touched them, though, was Ray's act of commissioning the picture in the first place. They asked for details of the event because it seemed to them a romantic gesture worthy of the 19th century, and they were incurable romantics. The fact that Ray carried this photograph around made him their romantic hero.

One night years after we left Lancaster, Ray returned (and I with him) to conduct a gospel meeting at the Maple Avenue Church. As he stood at the podium, Helen walked in. She was the scholar of the two, often engaging Ray in discussions of history in general and of the church in particular. She found the connection between the Restoration Movement and her Presbyterian roots fascinating. Anyway, she carried a package wrapped in brown paper and laid it in the back pew while Ray preached. After the lesson she waited until most of the other greeters dispersed to present us with Aunt Emma's original painting. "Emma died last year," she said, "and Martha and I wanted you to have this. You were our favorite couple." Ray was touched by her coming, and we both felt humbled to be the object of such strong feelings.

Admittedly, their interest in us could make me a little nervous. On an earlier occasion, the sisters confessed to us that one evening they had turned out their kitchen lights so they could observe Ray and me having a candle-light dinner in our own little kitchen across the yard. They had watched us the whole time. I can only imagine what Ray and I did or said while under their gaze, but for them it was a scene in our ongoing love story. Perhaps they saw an elegant dining hall and two aristocratic young people feasting on the sight of each other more than on food. From their vantage point our lips murmured words of love, instead of the small talk we were probably making. They created their own fantasy little Eva, who in their version did not die in *Uncle Tom's Cabin* but instead lived to marry the dashing Raymond Lee Muncy of Belle, an idealistic young man who loved her so much he carried a photograph of her beauty in his wallet.

I still have the photograph, and the painting hangs in our living room to this day. And maybe they weren't so far wrong about our marriage. Candlelight dinners need not be fancy to be romantic. If I was Eva, though, I couldn't provide a happy ending for the descendants of the slaves she tried to help. The Gill sisters were the ones who told us what happened to George, Ray's black presser. Drifting away from the Predestinarian Baptist church, involved in petty crime, the jokester and singer languished in prison for second degree murder. Unfortunately, life in 1950 was not all candlelight and romance.

ADRON DORAN

Adron Doran knew how to make an impression. He walked in from the winter day, tall and muscular under a fancy topcoat, hat and leather gloves. He was a stately man with a demeanor befitting someone accustomed to sitting in high places. As Speaker of the State House of Representatives in Frankfort, he mixed with politicians as much as with church members, a dual seasoning reflected in his calm self-assurance. Ray met him when he came to Lancaster to hold one of his many meetings. We also attended his meetings in Danville and Nicholasville. By the time we sat through those sermons and a few private conversations, Doran had helped change Ray Muncy's approach to preaching.

Ray, of course, modeled his style after those preachers he had known in Belle and at Freed-Hardeman. Brother Hardeman himself was a smooth speaker, but he could be bombastic, and most of the preachers we heard as teens veered in that direction. They grew red in the face and seemed to get angrier as they got deeper into the sermon. Their subject matter was often the source of their anger; they preached about the errors of denomination-alism, or the error of instrumental music, or the inroads of modernism into the church. They themselves had matured in an era when contending for the faith was not a mere figure of speech based on a biblical allusion. It was a way of life. They debated Baptists and Methodists; they wrote open letters of disagreement with one another in brotherhood papers; they saw the church as a small body threatened by foes within and without. Thus they were vigorous in presentation, unyielding in attitude, and committed to the Bible as the only source of their preaching. Not all preachers fit this mold, of course, but Ray had seen enough of them that he tended to borrow their shouting occasionally, to inflame his own face with passionate argument against error. And he mostly argued along the lines of logic taught him at Freed: all valid points follow from sound interpretation of scripture. He rarely brought secular references to his sermons. He was like hundreds of young men trained in the tradition of the Restoration. But Adron Doran was dif-ferent enough to cause Ray to sit up and listen.

Doran's wife, Mignon, was the fashion maven of the Bluegrass State. Her striking wardrobe and makeup were controversial in those days. She also wore expensive gloves and always looked delicate, feminine. Her dress-es and the way she wore them remind me, in retrospect, of Loretta Young swirling through her television door in the 1950s. Mignon sort of swirled down the aisle at church, sometimes sporting a fox neck piece. Never immodest, she was always ostentatious, and when we went to these gospel meetings in little towns, as many people came to see what she would wear as showed up to hear what her husband would say.

As flamboyant as both husband and wife could be, Ray went to hear the preaching. Doran took a philosophical approach from the pulpit entirely new to Ray. It was not so much in content as in style that he differed; it was a quieter, more professorial style. No pulpit pounding, no yelling. At this point, Ray lacked the confidence not to yell—at least some. Here was this glamorous man, Doran, however, who began preaching the same year as Ray was born, and who owned not a mere two-year degree but a doctorate in education, softly making his points.

He might be speaking on the importance of education in the church, a favorite subject of his. Ray realized that Doran was applying educational theory to the study of the Bible, advocating children's curriculum to fit the needs of children, not the adults who taught them. He quietly criticized those traditionalists who stood in the way of innovation: "Those who make issues of putting children in classes, using women teachers, employing print-ed instructional materials, and motivating the learning process are forbid-ding many little children the blessings of learning more about Jesus."

He talked to Ray about the good to be done through civic activities. He urged Christians to be involved in their communities so they could be a leavening influence through secular activities. This message was liberating for us. Doran was not alone in proclaiming the need to be "in the world" in this positive sense, but Ray and I had heard little of it in our backgrounds. It opened up new possibilities for ministry. For example, the Home Demonstration clubs that had been part of the American scene since the 1920s could be a site for service on the part of Christian women. Most of all Doran stressed the role of secular schools in the lives of children, urging men and women to become involved in this profession as a ministry.

He combined his educational background with politics and was in the vanguard of those who advocated the need for Christians to be active in gov-ernment. Not only should we pray for rulers, a clear biblical command accepted by all Christians, but we should also take an active role in selecting those leaders, maybe even being those leaders. Good citizenship in a democ-racy demanded, Doran taught, an exercise of the rights and responsibilities in such a form of government. In this way, Christians could better help achieve the peace on earth that was part of God's promise to the world through His Son. Doran took every opportunity to allay fears among Christians who saw politics as a corrupt "kingdom of this world." When our little David was two, Doran took him to Frankfort to make him an honorary page for the Kentucky House of Representatives. It was a thrilling experience for David and typical of the kind of influence Doran was willing to exert.

Like Ray, Doran had graduated from Freed-Hardeman, but he did not consider himself one of the school's favorite sons. In their own ways, both men had been a bit ill suited to the style of the place. Doran once told Ray, "You and I are getting along in spite of our alma mater." Certainly, Doran seemed to have moved far beyond their old junior college, and his influence made Ray realize his need for more education. Doran enabled him to see pos-sibilities of ministry based on his own personality and interests, not based on imitating a traditional style. And I think it planted the seed for Ray's even-tual turn from preaching to teaching. The two men shared a relatively brief time together, but Adron Doran exercised a lasting influence on Ray Muncy.

As charismatic as Doran was, however, his influence on Ray took sec-ond place to another figure closer to home.

POP BROADUS

Our first three nights in Lancaster were spent in the home of one of the Maple Avenue elders. Earl Broadus was the town's tall, graying postmaster, a man whose kind, paternal air led most people to call him simply "Pop." His wife Elizabeth, a tiny woman who wore her hair in a bun, served as a warm hostess until our duplex with the Currys was ready. They endeared themselves to us with their grandparent-like ways and open hospitality. She was involved in the home demonstration movement, as my mother had been and I would be later. We had never met any church members quite as open to the community and to different ideas. To be sure, they were Victorian enough in outlook, but they had a connection to the world outside the church that Ray, especially, never saw in his other mentors. In fact, Earl had an unusual vision of the brotherhood for those times. I think he began to turn Ray around, if any one person did, right there in little Lancaster.

Earl was immensely helpful to Ray in cultivating a tolerant spirit in doctrinal disputes. The big plague on the church back then was premillennialism. The subject came up once during an evening at the Broadus home. Maybe Ray asked the elder for his opinion on how to handle the controversy, which for many in those days centered on the role of former Harding College president, the late J. N. Armstrong. Armstrong was so suspect in my father's mind that he never considered sending me to Harding a few years earlier—even though Armstrong had died in 1944. Ray was aware of how Armstrong was viewed by some in the church, but like many, he did not fully understand the issues behind the furor. So he hoped his new mentor would enlighten him.

"Pop, help me out, if you can. What do you make of Armstrong and the premillennial fuss?" Earl furrowed his brow, as he did when he was thoughtful, and answered briefly and to the point. Even Ray didn't fully appreciate the answer until years later when he read the biography of Armstrong. What happened to this great man was and remains a lesson in how minor disagreements can escalate into major challenges to harmony.

Premillennialism grew out of a mysterious reference in the Book of Revelation to "a thousand years" that would constitute some future triumph of Christ over Satan and serve as a preliminary to God's judgment. This apocalyptic passage, coming near the end of the Bible's most highly figurative book, has stimulated varying interpretations. Those who built on the idea of a thousand-year reign, though differing in particulars, were labeled premillennialists. Most leaders in Churches of Christ saw the belief as mistaken but at the same time saw no reason to make the issue a test of fellowship. Others saw it as a road toward greater errors: distorting the meaning of the Second Coming, dividing the church, and perhaps most dangerously, mixing with denominational groups who embraced some form of premillennial thought.

J. N. Armstrong stepped into the controversy innocently enough. He was president of the fledgling Harding College in 1924 when one of his friends, then later a Harding faculty member, came under attack for believing in the thousand-year reign. Armstrong thought the issue unworthy of time and effort, but in both cases he refused to condemn the men who disagreed with his position. A Little Rock publisher questioned his beliefs; Armstrong replied in an open letter and eventually asked the premillennial faculty member to resign for the sake of the school. Painful as it was, the incident appeared to be over.

It only lay dormant, however, and in 1935 arose again. In his biography of this influential figure, L. C. Sears suggests that premillennialism was a pretext for those who wanted to oust Armstrong, who by this time had stepped down as president and was serving as Dean of Bible. Whatever their reasons, the group again questioned Armstrong's views on premillennialism, often using unfair tactics to try to embarrass him. The constant skirmishing over the issue never threatened the leader's reputation in the brotherhood at large, but it left pockets of critics, most of whom never knew the whole story. The personal sniping stopped only when Brother Armstrong died in 1944, though premillennialism lingered as a brotherhood issue into the next decade.

What Ray saw in the biography, and what reflected back onto Earl Broadus, was Armstrong's amazing tolerance and magnanimity. For over twenty years he absorbed the venom of his attackers without responding in kind. Further, he resolutely refused to censor the premillennialists with whom he associated. His only compromise had been the request for one faculty member's resignation back in 1924, and that was with Harding, not himself, in mind. Ray would have noted these words of Armstrong's as being especially inspiring:

> There is a great need to stress the importance of maintaining freedom of speech in the kingdom of God. Intolerance is dangerous to the future growth of the church.... All progress of truth—all truth— has always depended on free speech and progressive teachers who were not afraid to teach their honest convictions, even though it cost life.... It takes no courage to teach the things one's audience already believes.

Ray had already become interested in Restoration history (Adron Doran had stimulated that as well), so even back in 1950 he recognized the courage of which Armstrong spoke in men like Thomas and Alexander Campbell. Reading this biography of Armstrong, Ray could add another hero to his pantheon, and in retrospect understand why he found old Pop Broadus so inspiring. Broadus, completely unassuming and not a public speaker, had lived his life on the same principles as had J. N. Armstrong—faith in God, loyalty to the church, and tolerance for others.

That's why his answer to Ray's question back in 1950, before Ray was mature enough to fully understand it, stirred him nevertheless. Pop listened to the question about what to make of Armstrong and his supposed millennial views. Maybe his furrowed brow indicated sympathy for all that Armstrong had to suffer, or maybe he knew nothing much of the background himself and was simply formulating his own thoughts. In any case, his answer showed him to be a kindred spirit: "Well, I'm not gonna take issue with Brother Armstrong on this matter. You know we shouldn't make this a test of fellowship. If he wants to believe in the thousand year reign, why that's all right with me."

It may not sound like much of an answer, but it was so harmonious with the old man's life that it meant a lot to Ray—and to me. It was a way of telling us not to get bogged down in controversy when it takes away from a Christ-like commitment to people. Earl Broadus was not some "live and let live" man who would shrug off anything, but he possessed a wisdom about what was most important in life. For him it was serving people—not harping on their disagreements with him.

Pop and Mom Broadus were very good for us because Ray's background, and mine also to some degree, had been anti-civic involvement. Many in the church felt it should be separate from the community because of the dangers of corruption. This separation was emphasized so much in those days that both Ray and I sometimes saw the church as this little group off to itself, not doing this, or not teaching that, and not mixing with worldly groups. Like Adron Doran, the Broaduses showed us that Christians could interact with their communities, including members of other fellowships, and still be Christians; they had ministered long and well in Lancaster. They weren't the only ones; other elders and many members showed the way spiritually, too, but Mom and Pop Broadus were special.

Maybe the best illustration of Earl's personality was his relationship with our son David. Of all the people who lavished attention on him, he loved Pop Broadus the best. At the end of every service at the Maple

Avenue Church of Christ, Pop carried David, who could not yet walk, to the back to turn out the lights. He and Elizabeth were unofficial custodians of the church by virtue of having bought the property on which it was built, a function no one seemed to begrudge them. After the evening services, when the inside lights went off, the wall by the light switch would be illuminated by an outside street lamp, and the shadows of Earl and our baby would be thrown onto the wall. Earl always pointed to the melded silhouettes, first to the big one with long legs, and asked, "Who's that?" David would reply, "Pop!" And then Earl's finger would shift to the small head bobbing next to the big one and ask again, "Who's that?" And David would say, "Dadee." Earl recalled this ritual over and over in the years after David grew up. Even when he was old and his memory impaired, he relived their shadow play. David had become like one of his own grandchildren.

How do you measure the value of his act—taking the time to be a grandfather to our son? And it was something that took both emotional and physical energy, service after service, week after week. Multiply that by hundreds—the children and adults to whom he ministered in ways both small and great— and you can begin to understand why Earl Broadus had no time for premillennial debates.

At some point after we got to know Earl, we learned an important fact about his own childhood. His father was a church treasurer but stole from the congregational funds. The guilt and shame caused him to commit suicide, leaving young Earl and the rest of the family to face the world. Earl's life in some measure was a compensation to the church for what his father took, and his famous empathy for others grew in large part from his own emotional trauma. Earl Broadus simply tried to be for others what his wounded father could not be for him.

MOVING ON

Despite our good experience with the elders and the work at Lancaster, after a year and a half we needed to leave. Financially we struggled in Lancaster despite Ray's two jobs. He still would not hear of my working. Instead I sewed. Mom Broadus taught me how to make my first dress so that more of our budget could go to Ray's preaching clothes and David's needs. In all I made three or four dresses while in Lancaster. With money a problem, Ray sometimes felt guilty for being the focus of our budget. It took money, not to mention lots of washing and ironing (and dry cleaning) to keep Ray in enough shirts.

Despite the hardships and his occasional guilt, Ray was placid about money. Nothing illustrates this better than his job interview in Indianapolis. Realizing the need to improve our situation and motivated to go back to school, Ray had jumped at the chance to relocate when he heard of an opportunity in a larger city. I was excited about better financial prospects, but when he returned from the interview, he didn't mention money at all. Frustrated by his silence on a subject so important to our decision to move in the first place, I interrupted his summary of the trip to ask point blank: "How much was the salary offer?"

Ray said matter-of-factly, "I didn't ask."

I exploded: "RAY! You didn't ask the salary you were going to make?"

"No. I believe the Lord will take care of us, and these are good men...."

Even now I shake my head at his cavalier attitude. Part of it was immaturity. He should have known it was important enough to me for him to address the financial issue. On the other hand, I appreciated his trust in God, for that was a factor as well in his nonchalance. And if he believed in the certainty of God's care, I could not disagree, having seen it time and again so far.

In Lancaster no small part of that care had been provided by the people we met: the dry cleaners, the Currys, the Gill sisters, George Tevis, Adron Doran, and Mom and Pop. They helped us grow in many ways. We had come to Lancaster with a sense of relief at being out from under Ray's parents but knowing so little of the world. We left with a much greater sense of what evil the world can do, of our responsibility to the lost, and of the need for tolerance in this sometimes hurtful existence. As Tennyson says in the poem, we had "become a part" of those we met in Lancaster, and they had helped form an arch to even larger experience. To us, parents not yet thirty years old, Indianapolis "gleamed" as the next stop in "that untraveled world" through which God was guiding us.

FIVE

True Colors

The Indiana Preacher (1951-64)

INDIANAPOLIS: THE "ANTI" CHURCH

"Brother Phelps! What have you gotten me into?" Dear old Brother Phelps had perhaps expected the phone call, but he still acted innocent at first. "What do you mean, Brother Muncy?"

"What I mean is that I've landed right in the middle of an 'anti' congregation here at Washington Street! Why didn't you tell me about it when you recommended I come here?"

The older preacher hemmed and hawed. Ray began to suspect that the man could be an "anti" himself. Phelps finally said—I can't imagine with a straight face—"I figured you could work it out."

"Well, I just don't know. Some of these people have a different attitude than any I've ever seen. They don't want to do anything! I don't know how to work that out."

But Ray Muncy, all of twenty-three years old with exactly three years of experience as a preacher, did work it out. Our time in Indiana is a tale of two cities, two congregations, and one husband showing his true colors under pressure.

The above phone conversation came a few months after Ray first met Aubrey Phelps, a visiting preacher who told Ray of an opening in a church in Indianapolis. By this time, Ray had decided to go back to school, and the

University of Kentucky, located in Lexington, made for too long a commute. Besides, the minuscule salary at Maple Avenue put up another barrier. It seemed like the time to look around, so Ray contacted the elders in Indianapolis, knowing that it was the home of Butler University. Before long, in November 1951, Ray, David, and I were driving in to West Washington Street on Route 40.

The brick church building looked rather new, a good sign, we thought, but bad signs reared their ugly heads too. On the Sunday that Ray tried out, a very pleasant older man who lived in nearby Plainfield drove us in. Ray asked him if the preacher would be expected to do the bulletin. "Oh no," he replied, and Ray had visions of more preparation time, until the old man added, "We don't have a bulletin."

"You don't have a bulletin? Do you mean that no one has been willing to do one?"

"Oh no, Brother Muncy, we feel that any printed material by man is an addition to the Word. We have never had a bulletin. God's word is sufficient."

Ray's heart sank. "Antis." He had been warned at FHC about this branch of Churches of Christ, a group of arch-fundamentalists who suspected any and every doctrine that might pose a threat to their narrow interpretation of what was biblical. While all members of Churches of Christ wanted to avoid unscriptural practices, the "antis" built a reputation of being fanatical about it. Not only were children's homes banned, but Christian colleges were also highly suspect because they threatened to usurp the role of the church in teaching and preaching. The "antis" went so far as to denounce the whole concept of Bible class as unscriptural.

In 1951 the area was influenced by the teaching of Daniel Sommer and Karl Ketcherside. Sommer, who learned at the feet of the great 19th- century preacher Benjamin Franklin, had been a force in the Indiana church for thirty years before his death in 1940. Suspicious of modern, urban influence on the church, Sommer vigorously opposed anything smacking of secularism or elitism, thus his suspicion of the newfangled missionary efforts, of radio ministries, and of Christian colleges. He carried the banner of Franklin, who once expressed his distaste for higher education thus: "We have no patience…with this mere butterfly twaddle, toploftical aircastle, highfalutin and empty thing." This tough independence lived on in the "Sommerites" of the anti-institutional movement, one of whom was Carl Ketcherside of Missouri. He published the *Mission Messenger* for years and was very active during Ray's tenure. These men and their disciples wielded considerable influence in the Churches of Christ.

LEADING THE FLOCK BY HOOK OR CROOK

Needless to say, Ray had not checked things out very well. What should I have expected from the impulsive man who didn't even ask about salary? I went along, of course. I had married him for better or worse. Besides, I couldn't stay mad at him because in those first weeks he reached a low point emotionally. The reality of life at Washington Street was sinking in on him. He had agreed to minister to a group of Christians who thrived on non-cooperation.

After our driver's comment on printed material, we encountered more signs of the attitude we would face, the most jolting of which came some weeks into the work at Washington Street. The elders had provided a house on Jackson Street not far from the building. The house, we assumed, came as part of the salary. Before the first month was up, two elders paid us a visit one morning to demand rent money. As thunderstruck as we were, Ray swallowed hard and agreed to pay. I was ready to pack up for Lancaster—maybe even Belle—but he stayed calm. As it turned out, we paid only two more months before the church took over the rent. When all was said and done, Ray's dictum—that the Lord provides—proved true again.

The Washington Street Church had an interesting history. The deed to the building contained stipulations against Bible classes, college-trained preachers, and extra-biblical literature. The church must have been desperate for a preacher because it violated the second ban—against college-trained preachers—when it hired Ray. Maybe this concession heartened Ray to think he could have influence; maybe he just girded his loins and decided to go down fighting. He began to take on the elders and members in a series of confrontations punctuating our four years in Indianapolis.

The matter of a preacher's study became one of the first issues. The new building lacked a study, and Ray requested one. He needed a private place to prepare his lessons. Even the church in Lancaster provided one. Despite initial opposition, the elders let Ray use a space behind the baptistry originally intended for a classroom. It was small and unattractive, but Ray had won an important victory. As much as anything else, he had proven to himself that he could influence these people. To be sure, not everyone went along with the idea of a new study. A study meant the presence of books in addition to the Bible. After Ray moved his things into the room, former elder and descendant of the owner of the land on which the building rested, Gayle Miller, inspected it. A vocal critic of the decision to allow the study, Gayle took one look at the few commentaries and other reference material on Ray's desk and snapped. He threatened to throw all Ray's books in the baptistry. Miller's passion was convincing, and Ray winced at the possibility of having to restrain the older man physically to preserve his books. Fortunately, Miller never carried out the threat.

The odd combination of a baptistry and office space did result in one mini-fiasco. Located in a large city like Indianapolis, the West Washington congregation got its share of calls from non-Church-of-Christ people asking for help. In his four years as preacher there, Ray performed several wedding ceremonies for strangers who happened to dial the church office or drop in. One Saturday morning he talked by phone with a couple desperate to get married. They were Methodists who had been told by their local church official that they would have to pay what they considered an exorbitant fee to have the ceremony performed. Ray never charged a fee but usually accepted any donations. At any rate, they agreed to meet him at the building that afternoon for a quick ceremony.

Ray greeted the couple and a small party of guests at the door and then escorted the bride and groom to his office to sign the necessary papers before proceeding. Though this was a decidedly informal wedding, both had dressed up. The groom wore a suit and the bride a white wool dress; she also cradled a small bouquet in her hands. Ray too had put on his white shirt, tie, and suit. They were sweet, he decided, all in love and anxious to get this over with.

It was dim enough back near the baptistry that I'm not sure if they even noticed it as they made their way to the desk. For some time we had worried about how open the little pool was, with children sometimes playing in the area. It may have had one rail and was elevated slightly, but it was not protected very well. On their way out, the trio passed by the baptistry again, but this time the bride-to-be caught her heel on something and lost her balance. Ray heard a splash followed by dog-like yelping. The girl was flailing in the waist-deep water, holding her little nose-gay above her head.

"What is this thing?" she screamed.

"It's our baptistry," Ray said, as the groom pulled her out. "I'm very sorry. I should have said something."

"Well, we don't have these in the Methodist church!" she yelled. Her white dress clung to her in wrinkled soppiness. Still apologetic, Ray suggested postponing the ceremony until she could change clothes.

"No! I've been trying to get married all weekend and I'm not going to wait any more!"

So after she used towels from the church linen closet to dry off as best she could, the three went to the front of the auditorium, where Ray conducted the ceremony. As he extolled the sanctity of marriage, the guests in the front pew looked sympathetic, the husband looked distressed, and the wife looked like, well, all Ray could think of was a wet chicken. Water dripped off her throughout the five minutes it took to pronounce them man and wife. After they left, Ray sat in the front pew and stared at the puddle left in her wake, laughing heartily for a good while, then praying that their marriage would be blessed more than their wedding had been.

Happily, other people who entered the baptistry did so by choice, and Ray did reach outsiders with the gospel.

Most of his work centered on the attitude of Washington Street Christians, however. Ray soon grew increasingly restless at all the prohibitions. After getting his study, he decided to challenge the no-literature rule by printing a bulletin. He talked to the elders about the matter, and significantly, they did not veto it. They didn't approve it either. It was almost as if they were letting Ray make the decisions and take the heat, things he was willing to do. He spent several hours writing his short message, detailing his hopes for church growth, our delight to be in Indianapolis (a delight we were struggling to maintain, he might have added), and his desire to become a good servant to the Christians at West Washington.

The following Sunday he kept several dozen copies with him at the podium, and after services positioned himself at the door to hand bulletins to departing members. The first customer took the bulletin from Ray with thanks. However, the next passerby took one look at the folded sheet of paper and threw it back in his face. Ray couldn't believe it. He might as well have been offering the *Communist Manifesto*. Regardless of his dismay, he continued to hand each adult a bulletin. He got a face full of paper several more times for his trouble, but others took one without rancor.

The bulletin was the first big step in moving the congregation off square one. Progress was slow and resistance to any change was certain. Each proposal had to be made carefully. When Ray started a Bible class for teenagers, for example, he listened to older members gripe about imitating denominational ways. He got permission, though, primarily because parents of teens could see the need for something in those changing times to provide fellowship and learning for young people.

By 1955, the last year of Ray's tenure at West Washington, the members reached a tacit understanding with him: "We will never propose to do much of anything, but will let you lead us into new things—up to a point." Ray had learned how far to go to accomplish a good work. No incident better illustrates this fact than his rescue of the destitute Watson family.

A Mr. Watson, it seems, had abandoned his wife and children. In desperation, the deserted family applied for admission to the Potter Children's Home in Bowling Green, Kentucky, but they needed a church to sponsor them. Mrs. Watson convinced someone at the Home that she really wanted a job to keep her family together. A representative of Potters called Ray to see if the West Washington congregation would be interested in providing the needed funds. Of course, Ray knew the congregation's attitude about institutions outside the church, but he had a plan; in fact he had two plans. Meeting with the elders on a Sunday morning before church, Ray began with plan A: "Brethren, we need to help this family. This mother is desperate. If we can give them $200 a month out of the budget, then she can keep her children together. Her health is bad, but when she recovers—and the money will help her do that—she has a job promised by the Home." The elders frowned, stewed and sputtered in a tight circle as they talked among themselves. The three men debated for some time, expressing grave reservations about committing money to such a case. What they didn't express was their distaste for working with a children's home.

When it looked as though a direct appeal might fail, Ray was ready to try plan B: "Brethren, it boils down to this—we can't leave that woman and her children stranded. If we can't give money, we are just going to have to bring them here and take them into our own homes." Ray told me that he had never seen elders scurry so fast to make a decision. Within minutes, details for financial assistance had been worked out and Ray was free to phone the good news to the Watsons. Amazingly, the monthly sum set aside for the family caused no rift, no outward grumbling, among the congregation at large.

Ray visited the family and got to know the children. One of those children, Bob Watson, who was six at the time, never forgot what Ray did. He still remembers Ray sitting in their home, encouraging his mother. Mrs. Watson's stubborn dream of a family came true except, sadly, for one sibling who died before reaching adulthood. The other children survived and prospered. Many years after Ray had come to Harding, someone knocked on his office door one day. A robust man with dark hair entered: "Dr. Muncy, I'm Bob Watson." He wanted to meet the man who had extended help to his desperate family so long ago. He had never forgotten the gesture.

This simple act of charity was the closest we came to a giant step while we were there. Many of the members merely tolerated Ray's efforts to change things. Ray kept his perspective by joining a small group of preachers in the city who rejected the "anti" attitude. For Ray, association with other preachers was one of the best things about being in a larger city, but it meant dealing with strong-willed, opinionated men much older and more established than he. One of those old-timers struck fear in our hearts on every visit. His name was J. C. Roady.

THE ROADY-HOUSE BLUES

J. C. Roady was an old-time preacher, a supreme "anti" with a deep voice and imperious manners. Never without a hat, he traveled to Indianapolis by train to preach, expecting to be chauffeured everywhere. He loved to preach on elders being caught in roadhouses. Standing in the pulpit like a lord of the manor, he would say ominously, "One of the great shames of the present-day church is its failure to repudiate the sin of drink—and of carousing! Why our brethren think nothing of frequenting that den of iniquity itself—the roadhouse. If church members stopped frequenting roadhouses, their business would drop dramatically! And friends—if elders stopped frequenting all roadhouses, these sump holes of sin would close immediately!"

Each time he came into town for a meeting he expected meals and transportation from us. We all wondered what he might mention from the pulpit about some private vice he detected in our lives. One night, during a Roady meeting, just before the evening service, I escaped to the bathroom to get ready. As I polished my nails, Roady's piercing voice penetrated into even this inner sanctum. He called to me from a chair in the living room: "Sister, do you have nail polish?" How could he know? Were all his senses that keen? Why did he want to know? I came in the living room to show him my bottle: "You must have smelled it!" I said as cheerily as possible. Ray drew closer, thinking, as he told me later, that Brother Roady would grab the bottle and fling it away. I expected a reprimand for wearing the devil's paint. Instead, he commanded, "Hand it here!" in the usual rasping, peremptory tone.

Would he smash it, keep it for a visual aid in tonight's sermon, or what? He did none of the above, of course, just unscrewed the applicator and began swabbing a small wart on one of his hands. Ray leaned in closer still, finally asking the question Roady was waiting for: "Why are you doing that, Brother Roady?" The old man continued to apply the red fluid around the edges of the growth: "Oh, this is the best thing for a wart. Seals out the air. This will now be gone in two or three weeks." He handed me back the nail polish without so much as a thank you or a smile. All part of Brother J. C. Roady's perpetual theater.

No matter how much he may have been toying with us, something in his manner made us go to great lengths to avoid his disapproval, and since the list of things of which he disapproved was long and arbitrary, we were always on guard when he was in town. One Saturday during his meeting, we were to take him to dinner with other members of the congregation. A potential problem loomed, though. Ray had been invited to the Indy 500 time trials by our friends the Dickeys. Even before we came to Indianapolis, Ray habitually listened to the Indy 500 on radio. Since our arrival he had become an even bigger fan. Even with Roady in town, Ray was not going to turn down a chance to attend the trials. He returned rather late, just in time to change quickly and pile in the car with David and me. We were to pick up Roady at the hotel. Ray seemed more on edge than usual before a Roady visit, so I waited for him to speak. As he drove, Ray whispered, so our son couldn't hear, "Whatever you do, don't mention that I've gone to the track today." Of course I hadn't planned on it. But Ray was taking precautions: "I just don't want him to know and then to hear about it in tonight's sermon. You know: 'If our preachers stopped going to roadhouses and car tracks....'"

Well, we arrived at the hotel, and I got in the back seat with David (Brother Roady always sat in front, his back as straight as a fence post). After some small talk, Ray hoped to drive in silence to our dinner destination, but Brother Roady kept fixing his keen eyes on Ray's face, a bright red from his day in the bleachers. This attention made Ray nervous, especially since the severe old man said nothing. Eventually Roady broke the silence. Staring straight ahead, he asked: "Well, Brother Muncy, how were the races?" Although I'm not sure why, I was dying with silent laughter in the back seat, as was David, who couldn't appreciate much about the scene except that I was giggly. Ray's face had the stricken look of a trapped infidel, but he managed to say, "Oh fine, I guess. I was invited by some friends." Roady waited a beat and then said as if delivering an oracle: "I don't have any sympathy for the men who drive those cars or for anybody who goes to watch them." Then he turned and stared at Ray, who did not say another word. Mercifully, the Indy 500 did not come up in Roady's sermon that night.

Brother Roady came into our lives like the trains he always took: straight ahead and powerful. As with a locomotive, it was a matter of learning to stay off the tracks when the warning bells and whistles sounded. Ray always reminded me to be courteous to the old preacher, knowing how much I disliked him. The good brother taught us patience if nothing else.

As for the Indy 500 that got Ray in trouble with Roady, it became a part of our lives for the thirteen years we lived in Indiana. If basketball was king in the state, the Indianapolis 500 was the prince-in-waiting. Our son, Marc, who started going to the race after we moved to Bloomington and still attends with his family, remembers the history and allure of the event was woven into the very fabric of the culture. By the time he was old enough to go, he was already captured by the mystique. We all picked out favorite drivers and followed them. As many as 500,000 people would fill the stadium and grounds and would generate an Armageddon-like noise both terrible and exciting.

Attracted by the speed and power, Ray went to the 500 nearly every year we were in Indiana. He even fulfilled a boyhood fantasy when he drove a racing car one lap around a local track in a small town, courtesy of a church member at a gospel meeting. For a few minutes Ray experienced an exhilarating freedom that he could not have explained to J. C. Roady in a million years.

An Awkward Goodbye

Although Ray did not fit with the J. C. Roadys and "anti" groups of the area, he did find some preachers with whom he associated. There were about five or six congregations in the vicinity, with people like Dean and Ruth Clutter and the David Bobo family. Also among these kindred spirits, Earl West preached at Irvington, and Ray's talks with him fueled his growing desire to go back to school. Later the two would get together again in Bloomington. West's expertise in history also solidified what had been a growing interest in that subject At the time they knew each other in Indianapolis, West was finishing his book *The Search for the Ancient Order*, a history of the Restoration Movement. When Ray migrated back to the classroom, he knew it would be in history and philosophy. Unfortunately, he never made it to Butler University. He visited, inquired about classes, and dreamed, but the work of the church kept him too busy. It just wasn't to be. Later, in 1954, when the elders from the Bloomington church came offering Ray a job, he felt it was the Lord's will to get him into school—this time Indiana University.

The congregation at 4th and Lincoln in Bloomington came calling because news of Ray's work had impressed them. Given all the circumstances, we decided quickly. It was time for us to move on. I doubt if Ray could have taken the congregation much further. The membership totaled about 200, but with lots of visitors. In truth, not much evangelism took place. Ray held a few gospel meetings with tepid success. He baptized a few people and restored a respectable number. He left feeling that the church was more progressive, had become stronger in its sense of meeting the needs of its children.

He had low moments to be sure. Although Ray put little stock in outward signs like baptisms, he sometimes felt the pressure to accumulate gaudy statistics, a sense of competition encouraged in part by brotherhood publications. The *Gospel Advocate*, for example, solicited reports from preachers. Undoubtedly this communication had a positive side to it; it could be heartening to see people in other states and other parts of the world coming to Christ. Yet those reports could also serve as self-aggrandizing documents for the preacher. Ray and his like-minded preacher friends used to parody some of the worst offenders in this regard. One of their typical take-offs on the ego-trip report went like this: "Held a gospel meeting, two weeks, three Sundays, fifty baptisms, converted twenty-five from the Masons, and twenty-five from smoking...."

Despite the satire, low-profile preachers needed to feel successful, and my husband wanted a new opportunity to achieve results. Ray told the elders at West Washington about the Bloomington possibilities and requested a chance to visit the congregation there. When he decided to take the new

In 1991 Ray returned to Cloverdale, Indiana, to hold a gospel meeting.

offer, he asked the elders not to announce his departure right away because he felt it would hamper the work at West Washington. Only a few weeks after the agreement to remain silent, an elder began the service with a vague but telling announcement: "We, uh, want to talk to you this morning a little bit about some ideas for someone that could maybe preach for us. Can't tell you the reason right now, but…." When Ray took the pulpit, he was inwardly fuming and decided to announce his departure fully rather than have everyone wonder. The elders thus ended their relationship with us as they had begun it, with an inexplicable lapse of communication. In between, however, they had been more cooperative than Ray would have imagined. Their work together had forged a mutual respect.

Our time in Indianapolis also forged some strong friendships with couples like the Arnolds and the Streitelmiers. We will also remember Indianapolis as the place where David acquired a younger brother. Marc was born in September of 1953. When we left for Bloomington, David was six and Marc nearly two, both the objects of great affection by members at West Washington.

Tragically, the congregation at West Washington no longer exists. For whatever reasons, within a few years the membership declined rapidly. Such was the fate of many "anti" congregations. Like farmers who miscalculate in an effort to control enemies to their crops, the Sommerites, spraying prohibitions like insecticide at every possible danger, poisoned the very vine they wanted so desperately to save. For Ray, the experience helped push him away from legalism and toward the beautiful notion of grace. By that grace of God, Ray's four years in Indianapolis had changed him for the better. It had changed both of us.

THE CONVERSION OF JOHN CLAYTON

Bloomington is the home of Indiana University. Maybe the fact that it was a state college town created a different atmosphere. Maybe our enjoyment of the children, three of whom did a lot of growing up in Bloomington, lent the time there its sheen. At any rate, the nine years at 309 E. 4th, then S. Washington Street, and finally 117 Heritage Road, our three addresses during our stay , seemed carefree despite the rigors of working with a congregation and of Ray's return to school.

We started the first of June in 1955. The congregation was called 4th and Lincoln after its address. The Indiana University campus started at 5th street, making the church building within walking distance for college students, who were to be an important part of our ministry. The church building of Indiana cut limestone seemed an extension of the lovely campus.

Ray and I opened our homes to the youth group. To make a play room, we moved our table and a hutch to the side of our dining room and set a ping-pong table down in that space. We called the remodeled room the Muncy Foundation in parody of the Wesley Foundation up the street. The "Foundation" fulfilled one of Ray's primary directives from the 4th and Lincoln elders: to keep "church kids" from abandoning their faith when they hit campus. We invited students on Sunday and Wednesday nights to play ping-pong and eat and sing—sometimes entertaining far into the night. Many students developed a good camaraderie, including two students named Fred Jewell and Alice Karnes, from down near the Ohio River in New Albany. Fred was working on a degree in political science; Alice was an English major. Both would cross our paths again.

Ray worked hard on his mission to students. In addition to social hours in the ping-pong room, he met with the young people at the church building before Sunday evening services. It was in these sessions that Ray first came to appreciate the give and take with intelligent, educated young adults. The interaction forced him to study all the more diligently and, of course, developed his ability to respond to people. After almost two years of the program, we felt that we had made a difference in the lives of young people who came our way.

Not every student who showed up at the Foundation was easy to deal with. Both Ray's knowledge and patience were tested by our most memorable IU student—a young man named John Clayton, who was dating local Church of Christ girl Phyllis Galyan, a regular at the Muncy Foundation. As early as 1956 Phyllis and I bonded. A member of our student group, she talked to me quite a bit. Though she and John had known each other from high school days and she had strong feelings for him, she struggled to understand his attitude. The son of a department chair at the university who was active in the Unitarian faith, John questioned everything the Church of Christ believed or did. He seemed to be an atheist, really.

Hoping to turn his belligerence around, Phyllis wanted John to come to church with her. He started attending the seminar group that met on Sundays; then he came to our house. He would almost win us over with friendliness, then offend us with obnoxious behavior. He wanted everyone to know that he saw through pretense, that he would not let religion serve as a crutch for the weak of mind. John sometimes sneered openly at comments about things like the resurrection. It was not always easy having him around, and even Phyllis got discouraged at how he seemed to take pleasure in defying her own beliefs. Yet she saw something underneath the skeptical façade. Thanks in large part to her inspirational patience, John began to relate better to those in the group. He changed slowly (and Clayton has since admitted how bad he was: "I don't know how you stood me," he once said), but he did drop much of the cynicism.

While I counseled Phyllis, Ray hoped his lessons would appeal to John. He tried to answer any questions honestly but authoritatively. Would-be rebels occasionally posed hard questions, and while more traditional students rolled their eyes or got mad, Ray tried to go beyond proof texts to engage the questioner.

John Clayton enjoyed the give and take of such discussions, but his fierce independence and rhetorical skills intimidated other students. Most of them had grown up in a Church of Christ background and had no use for rehashing some of the fundamental issues that galvanized John. His intellect was challenged by Christianity; the real question was, would it engage his heart and will?

It was touch and go. Phyllis thought she was making progress, but then he would refuse to come for awhile. I felt sorry for the emotional hardship she underwent because of her desire to save her boyfriend's soul. On the other hand, I admired her tenacity and her faith because anxiety over John did not help her health, either. She was a diabetic who had to be very careful of physical and emotional stress. I could tell the experience wore on her, but she never complained, dealing with her disappointment with the double zeal of an evangelist and a woman in love. One night she came in to report another run-in.

"John and I aren't doing well," she said, near tears. I think I harp too much on what it means to me for him to become a Christian. Mrs. Muncy, he wants to marry me, but I told him that I couldn't marry someone who didn't, you know, share my beliefs."

"How did he react?" I asked.

"He got very angry. I'll never forget what he yelled at me: 'I will not be baptized just to marry Phyllis Galyan!' Then he stormed out. He hasn't been back to a Bible class since. I'm worried that I was too harsh. How can I get him to come back to our study?"

I told her, "Just let him go. Act as if you really don't care. Quit pushing and prodding him. Don't compromise your belief—you keep coming, but I think he derives a benefit from seeing you so upset."

"Do you really think it will work?" she asked.

"Let's try it," I replied. Just don't even tell him—let him make the effort.

This was on Monday. The next Wednesday, February 6, 1957, Phyllis did not attend services at 4th and Lincoln. I wondered if she was just worn down. With her absent, would we see John at all? The answer came soon enough.

As we suspected and Phyllis believed, the crusty exterior of John Clayton hid a terrible personal struggle that brought him to the point of despair. When he first started dating Phyllis, John thought she was "the most bull-headed, the most stubborn, the most cast iron-willed individual" he had ever seen. He delighted in questioning everything, and if he didn't like the answers he got, he said so bluntly. Realizing that Phyllis was a Christian, and having been raised to think Christianity largely bunk, John saw no reason to let his attraction to her change his *modus operandi*. She came in for interrogation too. Do you really believe in miracles? Do you really believe the Genesis account of the age of the earth?

Back of all these scientific questions was Clayton's contempt for the idea that God existed at all. He wore his atheism as a badge of pride. Phyllis couldn't answer many of his questions, but she knew the Bible and was willing to go back to it with an open mind to search for answers. His questions couldn't seem to "break her faith" as they had with other young Christians. Looking back on those days, John says flatly, "She was the first girl I ever met that I felt I could respect."

He admits that her allegiance to the Bible as a source of answers motivated him to read the book carefully for the first time, even if he did so to find scientific errors to "throw back in her face." He wanted to expose this supposedly divinely inspired book as nothing more than superstition. Incredibly, however, the more he read the more he discovered that what he had been taught or assumed was in error, not the biblical record itself. He found that the Bible did not contradict science and that its depiction of God was more complex than he had been led to believe by his parents and Unitarianism. God was not pictured as an old man with a white beard but as a spirit. The possibility of a spiritual realm, something that science could not adequately address, intrigued the young atheist. And his science professors at IU were in their own way reinforcing the lesson.

In one of John's classes, a famous biologist gave a brilliant explanation of how the raw material of DNA synthesized in the "primordial soup" at the very beginnings of time. John was fascinated, so he posed a question. "By what process," he asked, "did the original living cells on earth come into existence?"

"Young man, that's not a question that falls within the realm of science," he was told curtly. Clayton was shocked. He thought science held all the answers, but this professor and others said essentially that when it came to the origin of life, when it came to ethical questions, or those related to the nature of man, humans ought to look elsewhere.

Thus when Phyllis Galyan kept returning to the Bible as her guide, John Clayton took it seriously for the first time as an alternative explanation of the meaning of life. Honest in his quest if nothing else, John began to attend the church at 4th and Lincoln because, like Phyllis, the other members there respected the Book. He did not drop his pose as an atheist and did not make it easy on Christians. His performance in Ray's seminars was often belligerent. In retrospect, John realized that though Ray was a man of "great patience and great knowledge," he wasn't ready to listen to a Christian authority figure just yet. The following exchange is an illustration of the experience Ray had with this difficult student.

After another belligerent question, Ray asked John, "Do you know who Thomas was?" Despite his recent plunge into Bible reading, John needed to be prompted a bit. He looked to Phyllis, beside him as usual, for help, and she said after a long pause, "He was an apostle of Jesus who could not believe in the resurrection until he saw the wounds in Jesus after the resurrection."

"Oh, so I'm the doubting Thomas." John seemed angry with her for providing the answer.

Ray quickly interjected, "Well, you do have something in common with him. He was a kind of scientist, or an empiricist at least."

"I don't apologize for being skeptical; it's the only way to find out the truth."

"I don't think you should apologize. It wasn't wrong for Thomas to want to see the nail marks, either, but listen to what Jesus says after he shows those marks to Thomas:

> Though the doors were locked, Jesus came and stood among them and said, "Peace be with you!" Then he said to Thomas, "Put your finger here; see my hands. Reach out your hand and put it into my side. Stop doubting and believe." Thomas said, "My Lord and my God!" Then Jesus told him, "Because you have seen me you have believed; blessed are those who have not seen and yet have believed." (John 21: 26-29)

John snorted a bit; he looked at Phyllis but said to Ray: "The only way to know if someone has been resurrected is to see him in person. The so-called blessed ones who believed without seeing based their religion on hearsay."

"Isn't it a little more than hearsay?" Ray asked.

"What do you mean?"

"If the man who saw the wounds tells me they were real and tells me Jesus did come back to life, isn't that an eyewitness? And doesn't the recording of his account provide something to be at least considered as serious evidence for the resurrection?"

"As long as you could trust the witness," John said.

Ray smiled. "And since Thomas is the closest thing to a scientist on the premises, do you think he is trustworthy?"

"Thomas may have had a scientific mind, but that doesn't make this whole thing some kind of scientific truth. It's still just a story."

Phyllis sagged a little and Ray changed the subject. John usually wanted to have the last word. Encounters like this were part of his ongoing reevaluation. The more he considered where he was, the less satisfied he was with his place. And though he would not give Ray or even Phyllis the satisfaction of admitting his need for some guidance, his exposure to biblical teaching shook not only his atheism but also his attitude toward morality. For John, atheism was more than an intellectual position; he had been acting on its implications. If there was no God, then there was no absolute moral standard. And without moral absolutes, obedience to anything or anyone, including parents, made no sense to him. From an early age he had stolen, lied, and sought pleasure, but the pursuit had left him jaded, almost exhausted.

He was an unhappy young man on the morning of February 6, 1957, caught between the proverbial immovable object and irresistible force. Atheism and its guilt-free morality had once seemed a formidable structure for his life. Now its walls had been shot full of holes by his own study and threatened by the cannonball of Christianity, the fuse lit by a slim, quiet girl who by his standards should have been no match for him. Privately he was so unhappy he contemplated suicide; publicly he continued to display bravado. For Phyllis it was more than irritating, of course; it was depressing. As an occasional target of John's sarcasm, of his anger, she struggled with her own feelings. For both of them it was a real test of endurance.

The turning point came on that February day when John asked his geology professor one last question at the end of a long final exam. Months earlier at the beginning of the course, John had believed that the atheist professor would help him in his battle to convince Phyllis of the Bible's unreliability. On the contrary, no one answered his questions in a way to strengthen the case for unbelief. Much of the criticism leveled against biblical teaching was directed at straw men. In other words, the professor would misrepresent what the Bible taught in order to more easily tear it down. For example, when the geologist claimed that he would demolish the biblical idea of the earth as only 6,000 years old, John asked him where in the Bible that figure was specified.

"Oh, somewhere in Genesis, about chapter 52—" It didn't take long to learn that Genesis has only fifty chapters. A little more searching revealed that nowhere does the Bible offer an age for the planet. Compared to Phyllis, this famous professor knew nothing about the book. By the end of the course, John was nearing a meltdown from all the pressure to find answers and to lead a better life, so he gave the teacher one more chance. As he handed the final paper in, he said to the man, "Sir, you haven't really shown me any contradiction between what we learned in this course and in what the Bible teaches." Instead of protesting or arguing the point, the professor admitted with some irritation that he agreed: "When you really study it, I guess there is no contradiction."

Such an admission seemed to drain the fight out of John. He was in shock. Just days before he had risked his relationship with the woman he loved by refusing ever to become a Christian merely to please her. John's integrity would not let him compromise his beliefs even for Phyllis. Now, with his last atheist idol crumbling, he saw that integrity pushed him in another direction.

As Ray prepared for Wednesday evening services, he was likely feeling inadequate. At FHC he had learned to type up sermon outlines on five-by-seven cards, headings in red ink, points in black ink, with scripture references at each point. All his sermons fit that format, and each was a model of clear exposition and biblical truth. Yet his growing eloquence reached so few. Apparently it could not reach someone like John Clayton at all. Conversely, in those seminars, dealing with John's hostile comments and questions, Ray had been forced to see the world, or try to, from a totally different point of view. What a slap to the ego to discover how little you know, and Ray now realized he knew little about the world of ideas, of alien world views.

How many sermons of Ray's had John Clayton heard? With his questions about Jesus, did the student listen at all to a lesson like "Looking Unto Jesus," delivered a few weeks before? As Ray compared the neatly typed points in the sermon to Clayton's aggressive questioning, he faced the insufficiency of his own words. It was an important lesson for my young husband. He was not ready to take on a John Clayton yet, to win him over by force of argument, but he was stimulated by the debate. He tasted the challenges and rewards of submitting his faith to secular thinking. Before, his battles had been fought with Baptists or with "antis" or with one-cuppers. Listening to John's doubts renewed his sense of the gospel's importance. Here was a serious seeker after truth who had the courage to test his own skepticism for the highest stakes: eternal life. No matter what happened, this brief encounter with the young atheist (not that much younger than Ray) had borne fruit in the young preacher's mind and heart.

With thoughts such as these, Ray prepared for his invitation on that Wednesday, another routine evening service. Since I had kept him informed of the ups and downs of Phyllis's relationship with John, he knew of the recent blowup and consequently did not expect to see John at the assembly, an unlamented absence considering John's perpetual contempt for the practices of the church at 4th and Lincoln. As far as Ray was concerned, it would be just another night: reassemble after classes, read a biblical passage, have a prayer, extend an invitation, and sing a song to give sinners a chance to walk down the aisle. Frankly, unless it took place during a revival, the Wednesday night service hardly ever generated responses.

When the bell rang at 7:45, signaling an end to Bible class, Ray watched the auditorium gradually fill. He watched the young children scurry alongside parents, stretching their little arms high to show off a drawing done in class. Then teenage girls came giggling up the aisles, followed by slouching teenage boys saying sly things to one another under their breath. Dozens of others poured into the fan-shaped auditorium, very modern in its design, with seating arranged so that not all members were lined up behind each other. The room was supposed to create a more relaxed atmosphere, more open. On this night it seemed a good container for the energy of the crowd, abuzz at the prospect of ending a long day. The fan shape created a wider angle of vision for the preacher as he looked out from the podium. As Ray stepped up, he noticed stragglers rushing in, and one figure entering from his left, finding a seat on the far pew at a sharp angle to Ray's sightline.

When everyone was seated, Ray launched into the routine. Nobody remembers what he said that night, what scripture he read or what song was sung. Ray could have quoted the Koran and the scripture and song could have been in Chinese; it didn't matter. What Ray would never forget is seeing, out of the corner of his left eye, someone get up during that first verse and head toward the back of the auditorium. The person, a male, made his way to the rear and turned right, walking along the very back row. When he got to the main aisle in the center of the auditorium, the figure turned and walked toward the front. He was a young man, about six feet tall, with dark hair. Even before he was close enough to see the fierce brown eyes that had flashed during their conversations, Ray realized who it was.

"It's John Clayton! What's he up to now?" Ray couldn't believe this antagonist was actually obeying the gospel. Maybe he was coming down to denounce the Bible or Ray's comments or to otherwise embarrass the Christians at 4th and Lincoln. Clayton himself remembers a shocked look on Ray's face, but the closer the young man got to the front, the more it sank in on Ray what was happening. By the time the two were face to face, Ray's suspicion had turned to delight. He clutched John in a brief, tight embrace. We all watched expectantly as the two huddled on the front pew. Then Ray faced the congregation.

"Brothers and sisters, we rejoice tonight that John Clayton, an Indiana University student, has come forward to declare his desire to be baptized. We applaud his decision and want to help him do that now. We begin by taking his confession." Ray asked John to stand.

"John, do you believe that Jesus Christ is the Son of God?"

"Yes." His voice was loud and clear, as always, but it seemed unreal to me. I stared at the back of his head as he confessed, this tormentor of the girl I had grown to love, and I couldn't believe it either.

"God bless you for that confession. Now we will have the baptism." Ray himself seemed to be restrained, but, as I've said, in those days it was not as fashionable to wear emotions on your sleeve. As we sang while waiting for John to get ready, I felt as if the whole congregation was subdued, the way events are muted in a dream. But it was real. There was no doubting the reality of John's decision five minutes later when Ray immersed him in the name of the Father, the Son, and the Holy Ghost, for the remission of his sins. Water streaming down his face, as bold as ever beside my husband, a brand new Christian stood before the world. John Clayton was a new creature in Christ, and realizing that, it was as if the water had washed away my doubts about him. What could I do but rejoice?

Later, after services concluded and well-wishers departed, John asked Ray if he could use the office phone to call Phyllis. Ray and I listened as he spoke to her. All we heard, of course, was his side of the conversation.

"Phyllis, this is John. Are you doing okay?"

Here there was a brief silence.

"That's good." He seemed uncomfortable and I wondered if she was a bit short with him, considering the terms on which they had parted.

"Phyllis, I have some news for you. I've been baptized. I've become a Christian."

Pause.

"No, I'm not lying."

Pause.

"Phyllis, please believe me. I was baptized after services—by Mr. Muncy."

Another pause, with John looking more frustrated.

"I'm sorry I upset you and I'm sorry for what I said, but I am telling the truth. I wanted you to know!"

 Pause.

"Yes, she's here."

One last pause.

"All right." John turned to me, partly in frustration and partly in relief: "Mrs. Muncy, she wants to hear it from you. She doesn't believe me!" I had to laugh. He deserves this, I thought. But I got on the phone and gave Phyllis the good news. Once her shock wore off, she was ecstatic. We were all happy. First Ray, then I, and finally Phyllis had trouble believing our eyes and ears, but I don't think anyone was more surprised than John Clayton himself. What he had been trying to deny for months, maybe longer, finally overwhelmed him. For such events as this were the words "Praise the Lord!" created.

From that moment forward John Clayton soared. He became a different person, as on fire for the Lord as anyone we've ever worked with. When John and Phyllis were married about a year later in the little chapel on the Indiana campus, Ray performed the ceremony.

Of course, John has gone on to a wonderful career as a writer and speaker on Christian evidences. His probing intellect has been used for decades to explain and defend the biblical account of creation as well as other doctrines. As importantly, his faith, joined to that of Phyllis, has enabled them to raise a wonderful family of three adopted children, who have been blessed with parents who count the cost and then do the right thing.

IN THE PRESSURE COOKER OF CHURCH POLITICS

I was upstairs wondering when Ray would come home. It was late afternoon on a November day in Bloomington; the sun had already disappeared. I had just taken off my shoes after a day of housework to stretch out on the bed when I heard the kitchen door off the alley bang shut. Not bothering to slip my shoes on, I went to the head of the stairs and called out, "Ray, is that you?"

His voice sounded strange as he yelled back from somewhere in the kitchen. "I can't talk now! I've got to run." By this time he had appeared at the foot of the stairs.

"I've shot Vaughn Clipp!"

"You what?"

Even in the dim light I could see dark stains on his clothing and on his hands. He was covered in blood. His eyes looked glassy and his voice still sounded disconnected to his will: "I've just shot Vaughn Clipp." Then he disappeared into the downstairs bathroom.

By the time I got my shoes on and ran downstairs, he was on his way out, telling me to meet him at the hospital. The bathroom sink was splattered with red drops where he had tried to clean himself up. Several drawers had been opened. I didn't know what to think and was too unsettled to be mad at Ray for not explaining more. "It had to have been an accident, didn't it?" I thought. Ray loved Vaughn, and I counted his wife Faye and daughter Bonnie among my best friends. The two families would never even exchange nasty words, much less shoot at each other!

As I rushed to the hospital, the only comfort I could take was in the certainty of my husband's good nature. "Hunting!" I sneered in exasperation. Ralph Deckard and his hunting expeditions! Looking for someone to blame, I felt myself angry with Ralph. Not knowing if Vaughn was alive or dead, I kept thinking of Ralph's dark wavy hair, ruddy complexion and insistent smile, his desire to be the perfect host, to control the situation.

"Ralph!" I cried. "Why couldn't you just leave Ray alone?"

Once the remark slipped out, I realized that it was not only the shooting I was responding to. It was the years of Ralph's behind-the-scenes pressure on Ray exploding in me like a gunshot.

Looking back on my emotions, I can see how the uncertainty of everything caused me to give in to melodrama. I loved Ralph Deckard, but he became a convenient villain in my turmoil. The first news at the hospital did not do much to calm me either. Vaughn had been shot in the eye, and the doctors were not sure they could save it. Ray was as pale as I've ever seen him. Ralph was there too, of course, trying to reassure us both. It was an accident, they said, though at first no one was in the mood to offer details.

Eventually Ray filled me in. The game was quail, and Ralph brought dogs. Short and a little heavy, Vaughn had grown tired and wandered off, maybe in pursuit of one of the dogs he thought might have a scent. When Ray and Ralph noticed his absence, they called to him. Vaughn, who found himself at the bottom of a little rise, was ready to retire for the day, so he took the shouts as evidence that the other two were finally ready to go. He quickly backtracked up the slope. Unfortunately, the shouts had also flushed a covey of quail. Now a veteran of Ralph's expeditions, Ray reacted to the blur of feathers in the distance. He raised the shotgun to his shoulder and fired into the dusky woods. The buckshot sprayed into the trees just as Vaughn reemerged at the crest of the rise. Ray saw him go down, grabbing at his face.

When he and Ralph got to him, Vaughn lay bleeding from the eye: "It's in there," he cried; "I can't see!" Ray picked him up and carried him almost half a mile toward the truck, having to stop every so often to put his friend down, then hoisting him again in a fireman's carry. With Ralph's help, they got him into the truck and drove to the nearest hospital. Ray had left only to clean up because Vaughn's blood was all over him. He and Ralph had been praying constantly since Ray returned from our house. Joining them in the emergency waiting room, I had plenty of time to dwell on my sudden hostility toward Ralph.

Almost four years before the trauma of Vaughn's accident, Ralph Deckard greeted us with his distinctive gusto after church, our first week in Bloomington. He owned a wonderful smile and a toastmaster's unflappability. He shook Ray's hand as if the two were long-lost brothers, saying how much he looked forward to a new direction for 4th and Lincoln. He spoke highly of Freed-Hardeman. After so much anti-Christian college sentiment in Indianapolis, this overture was disarming. He invited me to attend his class for young married couples: "I know your husband will be teaching a class of his own, but we'd love to have you come, Eloise. You sure qualify as a young—and very pretty—lady who's single for that hour anyway!"

Ralph soon invited us over to his home, a beautiful suburban house on the east side of Bloomington. His wife, Alma, served a great dinner and afterward Ralph entertained us with a tour of the antiques throughout their home, but the most impressive ones were adjacent to the house in a huge garage full of what he called his prize possessions: a dozen or so antique cars. They gleamed in the light of the garage in bright reds, yellows, and greens. As Ralph led the way among the cars, he limped slightly, and I noticed a specially fitted shoe on the afflicted foot. Hobbling among all that shiny metal, he looked like a pedestrian unable to escape from traffic, but his pride in the vehicles forced my attention away from his foot to his face. "They're a present for Norman," Ralph said, referring to his adopted child. "He travels all over the world to get parts for the restoration." During our stay in Bloomington, Ray became a frequent visitor to the garage, sometimes observing the arduous process by which the ancient vehicles became new again.

In addition to this residence, Ralph owned a farm, like the cars bought with profits from his Full-O-Pep auto parts store. We would see his ads all over town and hear the commercials on the radio. It felt good to know a local celebrity who was also International President of the Lion's Clubs of America.

The occasion of our first visit to the farm was Ralph's annual welcome party for Indiana University students. At this wiener roast, we merely enjoyed the fellowship: good food, warm hospitality, and just the right note of religious feeling at the end. Ralph spoke movingly of his hopes for the students. "Don't let your allegiance to Jesus be overcome by the temptations of the world," he said. He introduced Ray as the new preacher at 4th and Lincoln, praising him as if they had worked together for years. He had a way of making himself and Ray intimate partners in this enterprise of shepherding youth through the dangers of the world. I could tell Ray was flattered and inspired by the evening. At some point that night or the next day, as we discussed our first impressions of everything and everyone in our new work, a thought occurred to me. "Ray," I said, "I am so impressed with Ralph. He teaches, he shepherds, he has energy. A faithful child and good home. Why do you suppose he isn't an elder?"

"I don't know," Ray said, "but the congregation can thank God for men like him."

I was thrilled to have friends like the Deckards at 4th and Lincoln, Christians more affluent and sophisticated than those we had grown up with, yet who retained a desire to help others. The congregation as a whole was very conservative, with some of the ever-present "anti" beliefs, but it was leavened with wonderful, forward thinking people who reached out to us.

Kathryn Stogsdill and Alma Deckard, for example, involved me in the Home Demonstration movement than ever before. Under the influence of these mentors, I saw more than ever how it was a way of being a Christian servant within the community, in much the same way Adron Doran had commended community involvement back in Kentucky. The original idea for HDM came in the 1920s, when the government sought to educate people, especially in rural areas, on practical domestic living. Volunteer agents taught farmers how to can fruits and vegetables properly, how to sew, how to preserve other foods—a whole range of skills designed to improve the quality of life for the poor and middle class. By the 1950s, Home Demonstration clubs had become social as well as service organizations. They elected officers and held meetings that both passed along knowledge and helped cement relationships. These clubs were a great way for women to feel useful outside their own homes.

I loved being a part of the group and became very involved with "*Les Bonnes Amies*," as we called our club. Naturally there were other ladies from the church active besides Kathryn. One of these was an elder's wife. Not since Flara had I experienced a personality clash like the one with this person, whom I'll call Joan. She was very intelligent and taught a weekly home Bible class for women. It was by invitation only. I have met very few women with as much knowledge of the Bible. But she was a severe woman, hypercritical I thought, and, since she was an elder's wife, felt free to dispense criticism. Even worse, she would rather die than explain her moods. At least Flara told you why she was upset; Joan used silence as a weapon. It was a long time before I was invited to join her Bible class, and only then did I begin to appreciate her more. Once that happened, we opened up and our problems seemed to go away.

In the meantime, she and I clashed in Home Demonstration because I was elected council president over someone she had supported. As the time of my first official meeting as leader approached, I dreaded having to deal with her. At this point my husband once again exerted his gentle headship. After pouring out my tale of woe—Joan does this and says that—I declared my intention to go to her with my problem.

"I don't think that's a good idea."

"Well, why not?"

"Right now you don't know her well enough and you're too upset. You have to consider the negative impact on her, not just the need to get things out in the open."

"OK, so what can I do?" I probably was pretty shrill.

"Honey," he said, "just rise above it. You are a bigger person than this." I wanted to say to him, "I'm not and that's the problem," but I did not have the courage to confess the depths of my inadequacy. The area meeting of Home Demonstration was out there still, darkening my horizon.

Significantly, at about the same time as his counsel to me, Ray was having problems "rising above" trouble in a relationship.

"It's Ralph," he said one evening. He's pushing me about the elders again." Within months of our arrival, Ray realized that behind Ralph's generosity and intelligence lay resentment and no little ambition. Not being an elder galled him, and he let Ray know his feelings gradually. Ray was working hard with the college students and with the other members of the congregation, trying to visit, to do a radio program, and to keep up with his lessons. He once confided in Ralph that the pace was tiring.

"I understand," Ralph said. "A preacher's job gets hard if on top of study and visiting he has to bear the whole load of counseling too. What we need in the church are elders who see the job as shepherding, not managing the deacons." Ray had to agree that most of the elders at 4th and Lincoln saw their duties along the lines of corporate board members. After all, their success in business had in large part qualified them to serve as elders. They were good men, but tended to see Ray as the pastor as well as the preacher.

At first Ralph did not criticize elders personally, nor did he ask Ray to say or do anything. Eventually he changed from sympathizer to subtle agitator. While he and Ray were in the garage watching Norman paint a Stutz Bearcat—the new color was bright yellow—Ralph said, "You know, Ray, maybe a sermon on the real role of the elders would open a few eyes around here."

"What do you mean?"

"Ray, you and I have discussed this dozens of times. Our elders need to be shepherds and they're not doing it."

"Wait, Ralph. I believe you have talked about this before, but I've been a listener. I'm not sure a sermon criticizing the elders would be a good idea. These men mean well. Even if I wish they were more open to new ideas, I don't see the problem you do. You know they are all good men."

"What about the 'planting,' Ray?" Ralph was referring to a group of families, led by two of our elders, who planned to split off into their own congregation because they held so many "anti" views. This group did not like official support of orphans. They hated the idea of kitchens in the church building. They suspected the scriptural worthiness of the newly published *Great Songs of the Church* because the compiler was a premillennialist. One of the elders leaving with this group believed that communion bread must be baked at home and brought to the church in loaves, because when Christ instituted the Lord's Supper, He broke loaves of bread before others ate it. Therefore, it was crucial not to break the unleavened bread used by the congregation before the leader of the communion did. The women in the church were often in a dither to bake and transport this bread to the church. It was not easy. Once I asked about a lady named Ruby who wasn't at services. Her husband said, "Don't ask. It was her turn to do the bread. She had to bake it three times before I got it here without breaking it. By that time she was sick—went home and went to bed."

Ray knew that this "planting" typified one aspect of his work—not always easy because of the extreme conservatism of some, but he did not want to let it become a bone of contention. He told Ralph that the parting was amiable enough and that 4th and Lincoln would be better off serving the Lord in its role while the new church served the Lord over on Second Street. It would make things easier for men like Ralph to bring about change.

"But more needs to be done. We need new blood." Ray could not disagree, but he didn't want to be put in the position of campaigning for anyone.

"Let's change the subject."

And so the relationship went along for several years. I have to give Ralph credit. Even though Ray did not always suit him, and after a time resisted his private attempts to influence the church through Ray, he never lost his good humor. He would greet us heartily at church, slap Ray on the back, and laugh. "Brother Ray, have you come around yet?" he would ask, able to laugh at his own unfruitful persistence. He never stopped inviting Ray to go hunting.

While Ray deliberated weighty matters with elders and would-be elders, I faced my first meeting of the county-wide council of Home Demonstration clubs. I was taking office after serving for one year as vice-president. I was pretty proud of myself, having been in my club only three years. Presiding over a monthly meeting meant anxiety, however. These meetings were carefully planned and in our case involved dozens of women (two from each club in Monroe County), a meal, and entertainment. We went by strict Roberts Rules of Order, something I was just learning. But what really bothered me was a potential adversary in our midst: Joan. I feared she would in some way show her disapproval of me as a choice for president. Ever since the election, she had been giving me the silent treatment. I dreaded the meeting because of her presence. At the same time I knew it was a chance to "rise above it."

Roll call came first. There in the confines of a banquet room in the IU Commons, tradition had it that we did not merely say "here" or "present." Instead, each member would recite a favorite scripture or mention something in keeping with the month. At this meeting, we were supposed to announce our presence by telling our favorite flower. The social part of Home Demonstration was as important as the service component, and the ladies insisted on a certain level of formality along with the chatter and fun. After conferring with my vice president to confirm the order and wording, I opened the meeting and had the secretary call roll. One after another, the women responded with the name of a flower.

"Ruby Abernathy?"

"Chrysanthemums."

"Belinda Bostick?"

"Violets."

Next we had the treasurer's report. Sure enough, after the report, Joan had a question. But instead of asking me, she addressed our vice president: "Joyce, do we know the status of our fashion show for the fall?" I let Joyce answer. Then, as coolly as I could manage, I went on. We needed to decide future projects, and I felt as if Joan resisted my every suggestion. More infuriatingly, she continued to talk as if I wasn't there. I felt unequipped to fight against her, all the while wondering how many others she may have persuaded to dislike me. For the most part, the meeting went well. In the end, we did settle on some worthy projects, but, for me, Joan's dismissive presence drained the pleasure from our accomplishments.

With business finished, the evening's entertainment came out to a spot near the head table. Flustered on the inside, I was in no mood for the singers we had invited but told myself the show must go on.

"Ladies, it gives me great pleasure to introduce to you the Murphy sisters: Pam, Marsha, Jeri, and Colleen. These beautiful young ladies have been singing together for four years now; most of you know their mother, Christine. We all remember her demonstration of canning peaches last summer. We are very proud of these future Home Demo ladies, who will now sing for us."

The girls, twelve to seventeen in age, took out old beat-up hats and set them at angles on their heads as the applause died down. The oldest then produced a pitch pipe and blew the key of C. She started tapping her foot and patting her right hip. When she opened her mouth, the others came in perfectly with her on this song, sung a cappella to the tune of "Auld Lange Syne":

> We're glad so glad so very glad
> That you are glad we're here!
> We're glad so glad so very glad
> That you are glad we're here!
> And just because you are so glad
> It makes us all glad too—
> And so our host and hostesses
> Our hats are off to you!

They held that last note and doffed their hats very ostentatiously, ending with a bow. Normally I would have enjoyed such silliness. That night it was hard not to dwell on Joan's attitude, which was hardly communicating "hats off" to me. It didn't help when I saw Joan smiling raptly at the performance as if the girls were expressing word for word her philosophy of life. My self-pity ebbed finally as the girls switched to religious songs. The beautiful harmonies soothed my spirit, and I could see Ray when I closed my eyes, whispering, "Rise above it."

I gritted my teeth and got through the entertainment and devotional. Everyone told me the meeting went very well, and that took the edge off my irritation. I arrived home exhausted, ready to get comfort from my husband and kisses from my babies.

When we were alone that night, I said what I should have earlier, when he had counseled me to "rise above it." I reminded him of that conversation, then told him about the meeting and how Joan's presence had spoiled it all for me. "Do you remember telling me that I was 'better than that'?"

"Yes," he said, "and I still believe you are."

"I'm not 'better' than anything. Ray, I cannot love a person like her." I shocked myself by saying those words, but they expressed how I felt.

"I'd be lying to myself and God if I said I could ever feel good about being around her. I know that's wrong but I'm not strong enough to love everybody. It's too hard. " I was deeply ashamed to be admitting this flaw in my being.

Ray was silent for a minute. "What do you mean it's too hard?"

"I mean it's too hard. She doesn't like me and her personality rubs me the wrong way. I feel like a hypocrite being nice to her when tonight I was so mad I wanted to wring her neck!"

"I think I get it now," Ray said. "You don't like her, so you think that means you don't love her? You can't be her best friend, so you feel like a hypocrite for not doing her physical harm?"

"I know 'liking' and 'loving' aren't the same thing, but—"

"I'm not sure you do, honey. I think in spite of yourself you're confusing love with the warmth that comes with friendship. Have I ever told you about the levels of love?"

"The what?"

"In Greek, there are different types, or levels of love, expressed by different words. In English we've got just the one—love, and it means about anything we want it to. But the New Testament takes advantage of the different Greek words. 'Eros' means sexual love. 'Storge' describes familial love, and 'Philia' has to do with friendship. That's what you are feeling guilty about. You lack that kind of love for some people. But we all do, Weezie. Joan may be having the same problem liking you. It's going to happen even in the church."

"Now it's the fourth type of love which takes over when the other three break down or don't apply. I know you've at least heard the term before, but 'agape' is the highest form of love because it imitates God himself."

"Think about God's feelings when He sent Jesus. It was an act, not a feeling. So you're free of having to like everybody. The command is to love all people, as Christ did. If you want the best for Joan, if you can stifle your impulse to throttle her when she makes you mad and pray for her soul, then you are loving her."

"Now that doesn't give you license to be bitter toward her, or to talk about her negatively all the time. But it does mean that you can choose to love her by choosing to seek the best for her."

Ray was asking me to swallow my own sense of justice—and pride. It was his way of phrasing an important biblical principle: "Love one another as God has loved you." Thanks to the impromptu Bible lesson, I learned that love was paradoxically easier and harder than I had imagined. Easier because it freed us from fluctuating emotions. Harder because it called on us to "rise above" those emotions. From that point on, the phrase "rise above it" epitomized my husband's great presence in my life, always calming and edifying me.

We did comfort each other in our little trials, but we were blessed with another couple who acted as surrogate parents. Woody and Kathryn Stogsdill were among the most wonderful Christians we ever worked with. Woody was an elder who gave conservatism a good name. He never separated sound doctrine from good works, and his generosity showed that giving was the most important doctrine of all for him. If someone complimented him on his generosity, he would likely say, "I dish it out in teaspoons and the Lord gives back by the shovelful." When he spoke the words meant something. With his black rimmed glasses, dark hair, tall, lean body, and kind face, Woody might remind someone of Gregory Peck as Atticus Finch in the movie *To Kill a Mockingbird*.

Like Atticus, he dispensed wise advice. Inevitably, Ray came to Woody with his frustration over Ralph. And Woody listened. Ray never said much about Woody's reaction, but I have no doubt that the older man taught patience and understanding. People who knew Ray Muncy never saw him terribly angry or upset. And God did bless him with an even temper. He also blessed him with friends and counselors in times of stress, most of all Woody Stogsdill, whose wise equanimity Ray could absorb and pass on in some measure to men like Ralph Deckard.

I thought of all this—our life and times in Bloomington—while I watched Ray and Ralph in that hospital waiting room. All of us wondering if Vaughn would be all right.

Ralph was almost as shaken as Ray. He began pacing back and forth between the seats and the hallway. I noticed again the slight limp in his walk, and the special shoe he wore on the bad foot. I recalled how oddly vulnerable he had seemed as he walked among his prized cars. I suddenly thought of how Ralph kidded Ray about the length of his sermons—and how I agreed with him. Those years of pressure had also been years of warm fellowship. I felt myself flushed with shame for my angry thoughts. Ralph had given us much more than he had taken.

After a few hours of examination, Vaughn was declared out of danger and on his way to a full recovery. He had been very lucky, the doctor said. The buckshot lodged near the retina but without doing any permanent damage. Vaughn's eyesight would be fine. Ray and Ralph hugged each other in relief. Ralph said, "Preacher, tell this doctor that it was not luck. It was prayer!"

"That too!" the doctor laughed.

There in the hospital, my momentary hostility vanished. I was watching two good men celebrate the answer to prayer.

Not too long after Vaughn's brush with death, Norman Deckard got married, and Ray performed the ceremony in the Deckard home. Ralph seemed very happy on that day as his one son exchanged vows with pretty Mary Lee from Abilene. After the wedding, I didn't hear Ray complain about Ralph as much. It could have been coincidence, or it could have been that Ralph, looking forward to being a grandfather, grew out of his frustration at not being an elder. The story of Ralph Deckard's impact on us, though fraught with tension, ended in our mutual growth. And as that terrible day ended with the two of them praising God for saving Vaughn Clipp, I could relax too, thanking Him for the blessing of Ralph and Vaughn and Joan and all our other Christian brothers and sisters. He led us all safely out of the woods.

LEARNING TO BE PARENTS

Our time in Indiana will always be special in large part because that's where our children grew up. David had been born in 1949 in Charleston, Marc in 1953 (Indianapolis). Kandy and Zac were born in the same hospital in Bloomington. Thus as Ray and I worked through our problems in the church and community, we tried to raise a family.

David and Marc got along pretty well as they grew up, though they did their share of fighting too. Typically on Sunday afternoons while Ray and I tried to nap, we would hear them arguing in the back yard over a baseball game they were playing with imaginary men on each team. "I had an invisible man on second!" one would yell. "No, you didn't!" the other might respond. Once, when the game came to a standstill as they disputed the position of all those imaginary teammates, Ray finally called out the window, "The invisible umpire says 'Play ball!'"

Kandy, our third child, was a very late arrival, causing Ray and me no little trouble in the summer of 1959. July came and still no Kandy. By the middle of the month I was miserable. Even with the boys safely in Alabama with their grandparents, the heat and discomfort wore me down.

My doctor recommended a cocktail of orange juice and castor oil to induce labor, so I swallowed the filthy stuff—with no success. Ray tried to help my evenings by taking me for drives or walks. One night we ended up in a little town called Spencer, where we found a drive-in. I think *Journey to the Center of the Earth* was playing. I remember Pat Boone singing and a goose that kept getting into trouble and big lizards menacing the party as it headed to the center of the earth. By the time Pat and the rest headed underground, I was having contractions. The deeper the movie went, the closer the contractions.

"Ray," I said finally, "I'm sorry but they're getting close—five minutes apart. We'd better go. Looks like this is it." We drove to Bloomington, packed our hospital things, and headed back out. I hated to tell Ray, but by the time we got to the door, I had felt no contractions for fifteen minutes.

"Ray."

"What?"

"I'm afraid they've stopped."

He dropped the suitcase: "That makes me mad! I wanted to get to the center of the earth!"

I had a few other false alarms, but Kandy did arrive. Ray, who had given up on a girl, was ecstatic when he discovered we had a daughter. I thought he couldn't be funnier than at David's and Marc's births, but his elation this time was even zanier. He rushed immediately to the Betty Jean Shop to buy her the frilliest outfit he could find.

Zac came along two years later, in 1961, to complete our brood, so Bloomington will always be a special place of freshness and innocence. In fact, those days exist in my memory like the super 8 movies we took at holidays and birthdays. We transferred them to video tape eventually, but they still have the grainy quality of a silent movie. No music, just very young children and incredibly young parents walking a little too fast and hamming it up for the camera. There are Christmas trees filling our small living rooms and Zac and Kandy tearing open presents. Marc holding a jet airplane as if in flight. David, looking so tall as he tries to appear pleased at a birthday gift—soap on a rope—while the little ones sniff it in curiosity. And the vacations! All of us splashing in lakes, streams, and oceans. Gazing at dams and mountains. Everybody smiling at the camera. Seeing again the houses and

The Muncy family in Bloomington shortly after the arrival of baby Zac.

the parties and the children, more grownup each successive Christmas scene, makes those days in Bloomington poignant almost beyond the telling.

Ray was very busy as usual, but he really tried to make time for the boys, who filled their days in this Big Ten country with sports. Actually, he got a little more involved with each child. Though I had never resented his absence in child rearing before—his combination of ministry and academics made it inevitable—by the time all four children arrived I had to have more help. I can even remember him cutting short his greetings at the door after services to help me in the pew with the kids. Ray never changed one of David's diapers, but he frequently dressed the younger children when they came along. It wasn't necessarily philosophical enlightenment; it was necessity. Yet Ray made the most of the time he did have. When he could play catch in the back yard or take the kids to the circus, he did so with the joy of a father in love with his role.

One of his major attempts to carve out time as a father was to help David prepare for the Soap Box Derby. Back in the 1950s this competition was an important and popular cultural event. Boys aged eight to twelve built their own non-motorized, miniature racing cars according to a set of rules and competed at local, then national levels. The event received lots of media attention because it epitomized mythic American virtues of know-how, integrity, and excellence. In theory, the experience taught a youngster many skills, including self-reliance. In practice, it furnished fathers with lots of work getting their sons through the competition. Let's just say that David was not a natural at constructing and perfecting a race car. Ray got frustrated frequently during the process. I remember one time while they were trying to paint the car, Ray slipped from the garage into the kitchen to tell me how badly it was going. David, missing his dad's support, left his work to find him. As Ray was complaining about David's ineptitude, he looked around to see his son standing in the doorway, paint brush in hand, waiting for him to finish. Blue paint dripped steadily from the extended brush, leaving a small pool on the linoleum. Ray nodded toward the sight and said, "See what I mean?"

Ray did do most of the work that first year, but it was worth it to see David out there at the Derby site, near Bryan Park, with three dozen other racers, lined up Indy style in rows. Since Fran Bennett sponsored David, the dark miniature car had the words, "Bennett Stone Co." emblazoned in white letters across its chassis. We took home movies that day, and I see Ray and an official carrying David's car to the wooden ramp, with slots for the two cars about to go against each other in a heat. I can also see the start of one heat, with David's car rolling off the six-foot ramp onto the long, sloping highway. As the car gains momentum, David does as he had been taught—he leans forward for all he's worth, pushing his car to a greater velocity. Ray, Marc, and I watched proudly as David's car won several heats. After his racing days were over, David's car was converted into a family go-cart. The chassis still languishes somewhere in our back yard.

Because David was our oldest, we tended to be busier with him, driving him to school functions and managing his growing social life. By far the most important event during this period, however, was his baptism, a landmark illustrating his seemingly congenital sensitivity. Once when he was five he exasperated me and I yelled at him, "David, what am I going to do with you?" His response was a meek statement turned into a question: "Throw me away?" Despite his insecurity at that early age, he had grown up experiencing all the church activities, and by the time he was twelve, in 1961, he was thinking seriously about becoming a Christian. His decision came during one of the many gospel meetings sponsored by the 4th and Lincoln congregation.

I was glad David came forward during this meeting if only because such a sweet man was speaking. Eldred Stevens was his name, and he was a big change from some of the more severe preachers who came through. I remember one, a notorious writer of tracts, who became obsessed during his meeting with convincing me that celebrating Christmas was wrong. I told him that I celebrated it as a traditional holiday, not as the birth of Christ, but welcomed the chance for people to think more about Jesus. "I'm not opposed to that, are you?" I asked. "Oh, I've got a tract on it," he said, "and Mrs. Muncy, before I leave this meeting I'm going to convert you—from celebrating Christmas."

Ray, who sometimes got nervous when I talked to visiting preachers, was sitting on the couch during this exchange, and interrupted with forced good humor: "Oh, I doubt that you'll succeed there, brother." It wasn't for want of trying, as the evangelist harped on Christmas from the pulpit, along with Masonry and tobacco and I don't know what else.

Of course, most of the men who came through stuck to preaching the gospel. Hugo McCord was wonderful. And Eldred was too. I don't think he influenced David so much, but it was nice to have such a big event happen while he preached. Ray and I worried that because the age of twelve had become an unofficially mandatory age for baptism, David might succumb to peer pressure rather than real conviction of sin. When he asked me one night if I thought he needed to be baptized, I chose my words carefully: "David, you don't have to be baptized at a certain time. Only if you believe in Jesus and are ready to tell the world. Baptism is an important step. You are turning your back on the devil and turning your life over to the Lord."

He sighed, "Boy, I sure do have a lot of sins to repent of, don't I?" David did not go forward that night, but did before the meeting was over. Ray took his confession in front of more than three hundred people, struggling to keep his emotions in check. Though he knew David was maturing, I think the actual event caught him by surprise. David had grown up during Ray's own last hurrah of youth, and Ray had not been the kind of hands-on dad we now idolize. With his son on the verge of manhood, it was a little like riding in an Indy car to catch up. But he was very proud and talked to David for a long time after the baptism.

We thought he became a better child after his big decision, but he was still an adolescent. He faced all the temptations we worried about, including sock hops. Bedford Junior High held its share of them, but David never asked to attend. One night, however, after David left for a school function, Ray noticed his son's billfold on the counter and decided he better take it to David. Whatever David had told us about the evening, he omitted the part about the sock hop. When Ray arrived at school, David was out on the gym floor, having a good time. He was astounded to see his father pushing through the gyrating crowd. "I thought you might need this," Ray said, handing him the billfold. Then he turned and walked out.

Later, Ray talked to David about dancing. But rightly or wrongly, Ray felt that the stern opposition to dancing so evident in Churches of Christ was driving kids away. He simply stated his preference: "I'd rather you not go." He tried to let God do the rest. He did not want to win a battle only to lose the war. For a preacher in those days, Ray's position was considered liberal, and he certainly didn't advertise it.

This story illustrates the pressures of being in a preacher's family; living in the proverbial fish bowl is not easy. All of us, including David, felt under the scrutiny of not only other Christian parents but also the entire congregation. Thankfully, not every social occasion or institution amounted to a threat.

The boys were active in Cub Scouts, and Ray served as a pack leader with me as den mother. He believed that his influence on people in Bloomington could be more effective if he was doing something for their families. It was simply another area of ministry. And it was fun for our family too.

The boys made good friends in the scouts, and we got to know other parents. One boy, Pilkington, whose father owned a successful business, was one of our favorites; and his dad, who often accompanied him, was fun to be around. We couldn't help but notice that Mrs. Pilkington never came— although she answered the phone to take messages about events. Good old Mr. Pilkington always brought his boy, though, very faithfully. He always took his turn with refreshments too. When later we heard the couple was divorcing, we assumed "poor Mr. Pilkington"—so active with the boys in junior soapbox derby—had been the victim of an uninvolved, restless wife.

At the same time we heard about his divorce, we learned he had been ill—nothing too serious but requiring surgery. On New Year's Day, Ray asked me to visit some church members who were in the hospital. Since Ray had already visited Mr. Pilkington once after the surgery, he knew the room number. So, after calling on our own members, Ray suggested that we see him too: "He's right down here in this corner room," he said, "and I know he would love to see you too."

When I noticed the nearly closed door, I hesitated, but Ray was always full steam ahead. He pushed the door open, ready to wish Mr. Pilkington a

happy New Year, only to see a voluptuous blonde in bed beside the apparently recovered patient. I could see from where I was that the two were
pretty tangled up. Both Ray and I knew she was not a nurse and what they
were doing was not therapy. Everyone was silent for a few awful seconds. I
wondered what Ray would say, or if he would say anything. He looked up at
the television where the Rose Bowl was on. "What's the score?" he asked. I
nearly died—started backing up, in fact, out of embarrassment. Ray finally
emerged with a red face into my embarrassed query: "Do you realize what
you said? You asked what the score was."

"Yes, but did you hear their answer? They said it was a close game. Why,
it was a rout!"

"Well," I responded, "that makes it pretty obvious they haven't been
watching football."

"Maybe they were referring to the game they were playing," Ray mused.

I think the woman in bed was from Pilkington's office—and the divorce
from his wife was pending. At least Mrs. Pilkington's absence from the scene
made a little more sense now.

Although we found out more about the Pilkingtons than we wanted to
know, we did appreciate how the Cub Scouts helped us get involved with
the community. Working with the church isolates you sometimes, and I
shared Ray's desire for outreach. Though I can't be sure of any lasting results,
I do know that one of the scouts from a poor family started bringing his parents to church for a while. And that's what you hope for when you do
good—that it reflects Christ's love and leads someone into His presence.

Ray spent time with the boys beyond scouting activities. For one thing,
his profession of preacher allowed a more flexible schedule than most
fathers could enjoy. In fact, David and Marc wondered what their daddy did
for a living, since he often seemed to be around to take them places in the
middle of the day. When I worked part time in the IU bookstore, he even
babysat with Marc in the undergraduate classes he had begun on campus,
hoping to complete his degree. At any rate, the boys never really pictured
Ray as going to work, until one day when he donned overalls and grabbed
some tools to be part of a church work party. As they watched him get in a
car with other tool-bearing men, they ran to me proclaiming excitedly that
Dad had finally found a job.

Since Marc's early school years coincided with Ray's graduate study, he
had lots of contact with his dad as babysitter. Marc went with Ray to visi-
tations; he even went to a funeral that Ray preached. When he saw the casket, he leaned over to Ray in the pew and asked, "What's in that treasure

chest, Daddy?" Marc often accompanied Ray to the church building, where the five-year old would play church (something that David did as well—both boys started singing before they were two). Once Ray heard him singing "A Wonderful Savior" all by himself out in the auditorium. Charmed, Ray continued listening until Marc finished the chorus, which goes like this:

> He hideth my soul in the cleft of the rock
> That shadows a dry, thirsty land.
> He hideth my life in the depths of His love,
> And covers me there with His hand.
> And covers me there with his hand.

Ray noticed a slight misinterpretation of the last, repeated line, however. Marc closed by singing, "He clobbers me there with His ha-aa-nd; he clobbers me there with His hand!"

For a while when he was about eight, Marc would go to the church building with his dad on Saturday mornings, succeeding David as preacher's assistant. In those days, despite the fact that the Bloomington church was a congregation of four hundred, the preacher had no help: no secretary, no youth minister. Consequently, Ray, as in other places, wrote and published the church bulletin himself. Little Marc came along to fold the finished product. It was one of those temporary routines in the boy's life, something not entirely unpleasant—and unremarkable except for one Saturday.

As usual, about mid-morning, Ray hustled Marc out the door of the Muncy home and drove him to 4th and Lincoln. Since the building was in a business district, there was little parking. On Sundays church members used the Post Office lot, located across the intersection of 4th and Washington, and the Bank lot, adjacent to the narrow strip of church land. This morning Ray pulled into the bank lot where he found his choice of vacant spaces. Soon he and Marc were busy with the bulletin. Another routine day for the boy, it appeared, until the side door to the building opened and in barged an obviously agitated middle-aged man who headed straight for his dad.

"Is that your car parked out there?" the man almost shouted.

Ray said, "Yes."

"Well, who do you think you are?" This time it was a shout; the man was almost in Ray's face. It was a rhetorical question that Ray had no chance to answer before the tirade continued: "I am the president of the Bloomington National Bank back there and that was my spot!"

Marc waited for Ray's reaction, which came quickly: "I am so sorry. Marc, please wait here while I go move the car." He grabbed his keys and headed for the door, accompanied by the bank manager, who still berated Ray on the way out.

It took only a few seconds for the door to open once again, but in that span, the young boy felt the hot shame of humiliation. The sudden attack on his father left his knees weak. He was shocked by the spectacle of it.

Ray came back in and without a word resumed printing the bulletins. The silence forced Marc to realize that he had been waiting for some word from his dad, some sign that Ray Muncy, even if he was a preacher, would not take this. When Ray offered not so much as a "What a jerk," a dark cloud crossed the boy's awareness. "My father was chicken!" he said to himself. The realization seemed to shake the foundations of the building. He knew what he had wanted when both men disappeared outside—to see his dad fight. To have the satisfaction of telling his friends how his dad punched an enemy. He got instead acquiescent silence.

Nevertheless, life went on. The next Saturday the father and son were back at the building—with Ray carefully parked on the street—getting out yet another bulletin. Young boys don't brood too long, and perhaps the worst of Marc's shame had already worn off. Perhaps he felt back to normal with his father. Whatever his feelings, he would not be allowed to forget what had happened the week before. Because once again that side door opened and through it came the same irate executive.

Only this time he was not mad. He was meek. Ray turned to meet him while Marc held his breath, but the man started apologizing to Ray even before he even stopped walking.

Mr. Muncy, I'm sorry for the way I acted last week. I don't know what was wrong or why you let me behave that way. For goodness sake, we're not even open on Saturday. I want to make it up to you."

He extended a piece of cardboard toward Ray. "This pass will allow you to park in our lot any time you want. Please take it as a token of my regret. You did nothing wrong." He glanced at Marc. "I was the one who was wrong."

Of course Ray accepted the apology and took the pass.

"You know," the man said, "one of the reasons I got so angry is that you wouldn't fight back. It infuriated me to be the only one mad. I guess the whole sorry episode made me think about some things, Mr. Muncy."

The two talked briefly before the contrite president departed. While the scene unfolded, Marc was once again gripped by shame, but this time it issued from what he had done. He felt foolish and sinful for his thoughts about Ray. He was ashamed of being ashamed of his father. His immature mind could not articulate fully his complex feelings there in the tiny church

office. Later he would understand that he had just witnessed the power of
turning the other cheek, and at first had been unable to see the
Christlikeness of his father's reaction. To have a rare glimpse of an earthly
reward for such nonviolence brought the lesson home almost too much. If
his father's apparent cowardice the week before hit him like a slap in the
face, the sudden and dim awareness of Ray's righteousness was like a punch
in the stomach because it exposed the boy's own unrighteousness. As I say,
the eight-year-old Marc could not articulate all this, but the older Marc, a
father himself, understood the parable being played out on those two con-
secutive Saturdays in Bloomington.

It was not until after Ray's death that Marc told me this story. He
thought of it when I asked him what he admired most about his father. The
story welled up from deep underground like the tears in his eyes when he told
it. Of course, I cried too, but for joy that Ray's example lives on in my son.

GRADUATE SCHOOL AND THE DECISION TO LEAVE

Our years in Bloomington flew by as Ray tried to be the best preacher
and father and husband that he could be. By 1960, when the conflict with
Ralph had been more or less resolved and three of our four children had been
born, I could see significant changes in Ray. He was more self-assured, more
efficient. His rigorous schedule brought out his best. On Sundays he got to
his office early for a live radio show. Then he preached a sermon and taught
a Bible class. Of course there was the Wednesday night lesson and the bulletin. Since he was committed to visitation, he spent at least two other nights
away from home. A preacher who does not get stronger under that load will
be crushed by it. Ray got stronger.

The changes went beyond confidence and efficiency, though. The spiritual maturity I first noticed in Indianapolis had deepened. He didn't visit
merely because it was in the biblical blueprint; he did it because he was
committed to people who needed the Lord. He was less legalistic in other
ways too. In Indianapolis, he once snapped at me over a remark I made
about a certain preacher's wife, Mrs. Bobo, who stood with her husband at
the rear of the auditorium to greet people after services.

"Isn't that refreshing?" I said.

"I don't like it," he shot back. Case closed! The rear of the auditorium
by the preacher's side was not a woman's place. By the time we left Bloomington, however, he had asked me to join him in that very activity. It is a
small thing, I know, but it was one of a range of discoveries signalling his

growth in the Lord, majoring in majors and not in minors, as we used to hear preachers put it. Ray wanted to do the right thing according to scripture even if it wasn't a brotherhood tradition.

I was very proud to be his wife, and felt that his guidance was helping me to grow as well. His admonition to "rise above it" always rang in my ears when I was tempted to resentment or anger. What made things even better for me was the change in Ray as a husband suggested in some of these anecdotes. He had never treated me any way but well, yet as he matured I felt he respected and trusted me more. He began to consult me on more decisions, even occasionally on tough issues in his ministry. This sharing strengthened our marriage, and as Ray ministered and I helped as his wife, we felt we were serving the Lord. I was happy, and so was he.

If it hadn't been for one thing, we might have lived out our lives in Bloomington as preacher and family. But as happy as Ray may have been with his circumstances, he was also intellectually restless. Back in Indianapolis, he had put his ambition for further schooling on hold. In the meantime his interest in history—both church and secular—was growing. Originally, he thought about a degree as a way to get a high school certificate and therefore provide supplemental income by substitute work. He read a good deal on his own from the beginnings of his ministry, more than needed to prepare sermons. With this reading came a hunger that eventually took his ambition beyond high school teaching. History was not just about events and people; it was about ideas and values. The Bible itself demonstrated that. And his acquaintance with knowledgeable preachers along the way reinforced in him a historical sense. He wanted to pursue and communicate those values and ideas at the highest possible level.

Thus in 1958 Ray began taking courses at Indiana University. He worked his classes around ministerial duties during the day and studied at night. He admired his teachers and loved the stimulating discussions. I developed the role I would continue throughout his graduate work: keeping guard outside his study door so prying children could not disturb him. In fact, to this day I maintain that a good preacher's wife will guard his study door as diligently as she smiles at parishioners after services.

Ray completed an undergraduate degree in 1960 and his master's degree in 1963. He flirted with the idea of going for a doctorate but wasn't sure that he would need it to accomplish his goals. He was wrong about that, as things turned out, though his reasoning was sound. A preacher doesn't need a Ph.D. What Ray couldn't see at the beginning of his graduate work had become clearer by the end of it—he didn't necessarily want to remain a full-time preacher for the rest of his life. That realization came, in part, when at some point during his graduate work, he traveled to Searcy, Arkansas, for the Harding College lectureships. Back on a Christian college campus, Ray began to get the itch, I believe, wondering what life as a professor might be like, sharing insights from history with college students like the ones he loved at Indiana University.

Of course we had known of Harding for years. When we were at Freed-Hardeman, Harding was scorned by some as a haven for premilllennialism (recall that my father had refused to let me consider going there). Since 1946, that stigma had largely disappeared (Ray never put any stock in it anyway), and George Benson was turning Harding into one of the brotherhood's up-and-coming schools. It had attracted national attention with its Freedom Forum and its defense of the American way. The school became more of a reality for us, however, with the arrival of Kenneth Davis in Bloomington.

Kenneth, the choral director at Harding, was in Bloomington for graduate work. He had arrived by 1960, so that he and Ray were on campus at the same time. We grew acquainted because he worshipped with us at 4th and Lincoln. He was pressed into service as song leader and minister, and his influence helped break down the prohibition against Christian college choruses performing in the church building (part of the "anti" heritage).

Impressed with Ray over time, Ken mentioned the possibility of Ray's teaching at Harding. Ray discussed the prospect of such a move with me. Some time later, in the spring of 1964, the offer of an interview came, in the form of a phone call from Dr. Benson himself. Ray flew down in April, warning me not to mention it to anyone. He wanted no premature speculation among church members. Previously, the elders had extracted a promise from him not to move until the new building campaign was finished. They felt that any dissension over the project would be lessened by Ray's presence. Now a potential offer was on the horizon ahead of schedule. Ray decided to interview and see what happened from there.

I knew when Ray called me from Searcy during his interview that he was smitten. He loved Harding immediately and when the school said, "We want you," he said, "I want to come, but I'll have to check with my family." I would have been a mean woman to object to something that filled him with such excitement. "The next thing I have to do," Ray said, "is talk to the elders." His promise to stay through the building program was the biggest potential barrier to accepting the offer. He met with the group immediately upon his return to Bloomington, and they were very gracious.

They said they loved us and the children and would be wrong to stand in our way. We were deeply grateful for their blessing because they would have been well within their rights to use Ray's oral agreement as reason to resist.

Despite the greased path on that front, selling the older children would be more difficult, especially teenager David. Of course, I thought of my unfinished tenure as president of Monroe County Home Demonstration Council, of the new house that we had barely lived in, of the potential trauma for our children. But we knew that children are resilient and that they were going to an even stronger Christian atmosphere. As for our work with 4th and Lincoln, Ray reasoned that with things so upbeat at the moment, the timing could likely not be better. Nine years at one place is a long time. So we campaigned to win the kids over. Ray bought them all Harding College T-shirts. Zac, who could barely talk, would point to the front of his and say, "Hawding Cawedge." David got a letter from Harding Academy football coach Ed Higginbotham about going out for the team. He was impressed by such attention.

By the time of our departure, we were about as ready as possible to leave. That did not mean leaving would be easy.

ANOTHER FAREWELL

In mid-August 1964, the 4th and Lincoln congregation hosted a farewell dinner for the Muncys in the Armory, site of so many youth rallies. Emotions ran high that night. Our family sat at a head table of sorts with all the elders and their wives. The other members were seated at other tables in the drafty room. Things started with a roast of Ray featuring several stories told on us. Ralph Deckard, Mr. "Toastmaster" himself, served as emcee. Most of it was strictly memory lane stuff, funny to those who had been there.

There was the chicken story. Once when Ray conducted a meeting in the southern part of the state, one of the host congregation's members promised a chicken as a bonus. I had not accompanied Ray, but in their usual kind spirit of fellowship, Fran and Hazel Bennett drove the children and me to hear the final lesson and afterwards agreed to follow Ray to the farm where the promised fowl waited. The good brother and owner of the farm was known for dressing and freezing chickens to offer as gifts. After our caravan pulled up to his house to claim payment, Ray was surprised to find the chicken not dressed or frozen, but alive and in a gunny sack. He shambled back to the cars where we all waited. We saw him holding the gunny sack with chicken claws writhing at the opening. The Bennetts, the children, and I laughed until we cried.

"I couldn't turn him down," Ray said, "but we've got to get rid of this thing. We're scheduled to leave for West Virginia tomorrow." It was a problem, but the Bennetts had a plan. Hazel's brother kept chickens, and so we would drive by his house and drop the bird off there. It was late when we got to Bloomington, so Fran and Ray decided to literally drop the chicken off—over the brother's fence—without disturbing him. They sneaked to a spot as far away from the house as possible, to a point where Fran's brother's property bordered his neighbor's, pulled the patient bird from the sack, and tossed him over. The next morning Hazel got a call from her brother, who thought he had foiled a thief: "I'm pretty sure I scared off some chicken thieves last night—from our neighbor's place. They must have panicked and thrown the chicken into our yard, because we had an extra one this morning."

"What did you do?" asked Hazel as she suppressed a giggle.

"Why, I just tossed it back over the fence." Once that little escapade got around, a big plucked chicken showed up on our front porch. At the farewell dinner, someone presented us with a rubber chicken with its legs sticking out of a sack.

Dozens of people stood up with stories like that. Maybe the funniest stunt of all was Vaughn Clipp's. Ralph introduced Vaughn, who gave Ray a jewelry box with directions to open it in front of everyone. Inside, Ray found buckshot where the cufflinks should have been, with a note that read, "Better luck next time." The three of them—Ralph, Vaughn, and Ray—stood together on the dais, able to laugh once again at their near-tragedy.

Then the dinner got serious. We received a cash gift accompanied by a note: "For underpaid services." I received a beautiful clock. Each elder voiced his appreciation for Ray and for us, his tribe. Others offered testimonials too, among them Ralph Deckard, Ray's old mentor and agitator. His tribute may have been the nicest of all, and we knew for sure then that his solicitude had not been self-interest alone, but genuine love. So many dear faces, each with a kindness or service to us etched in its features. The cumulative effect was overwhelming. I know that Ray was moved. The harsh lights of the Armory reflected in his glasses but could not hide his moist eyes as he heard praise heaped upon him.

In the nine years Ray served the congregation, he had grown with its people. The church had shaken off the dust of "anti"-ism: they were no longer as wary of lectureships and choruses and new ideas about how to serve God. Ray was not a dynamo or a maverick. He just preached. During his time in Bloomington he delivered 1,526 lessons in church services, camps, schools, clubs, PTA meetings, on radio and even one on television.

Among his most often delivered sermons was "The Preeminence of Christ," in which Ray took his audience, using Colossians 1:12-18, from Christ's role in creation to His demand for a place in the individual heart. He closed with a simple question: "Seeing that God has given Him preeminence, cannot we do the same?" He preached more on Christ and the Christian life and less on what the church should be against. His last sermon, on Sunday evening, August 23, 1964, was called "Standing in Our Place," in which he said a very personal goodbye.

Ray didn't boast of what he had accomplished, but the record is there. He served the flock in official duties, performing fifty-six weddings and conducting ninety funerals—including on successive days services for a welfare infant and one-hundred-year-old Lydia Duncan. He baptized 150 people into Christ. Those numbers were behind Ray's message to 4th and Lincoln that night: "Our lives have become intertwined with yours. You have taught our children, ministered to their needs, encouraged me and Eloise to greater service. We have baptized your boys and girls, married your young men and women, and buried your elderly soldiers in Christ. We won't live in Bloomington after today, but we'll never leave you."

As he spoke that Sunday evening, I was wishing we had left after morning services. It was just too hard emotionally. Ray was going to fulfill his duties, though. The boys and Kandy especially didn't want to say goodbye to Woody and Kathryn. The night before, having packed our belongings into a moving van, we had stayed with them. When the finality of our departure sank in, all the children cried for Grandpa and Grandma Stogsdill.

Not too long after Ray's last sermon at Bloomington, we were heading south in our maroon station wagon. David was in the front seat with me and Ray. Marc and the two little ones rode in back. None of us said a word for the first twenty-five miles out of Bloomington. From time to time we heard sniffling in the seat beside us. Ray and I knew we were headed for a new and rewarding challenge, but the first part of the journey felt as if some vital part of us had been amputated. It would have to grow back five hundred miles away in hot, humid central Arkansas, in a town called Searcy.

SIX

Passing the Tests

First Years at Harding (1964-71)

FOOTBALL AND NEW FRIENDS

We drove all night. We passed through Indiana, Illinois, and Missouri in the dark. By the time we crossed into Arkansas the sun was up. The drive from Walnut Ridge to Searcy down old U.S. 67 was desolate in the morning light. Faded shacks and peeling billboards were strewn along the roadside, along with rusted car chassis and cheap gas stations. On our house-hunting trip the previous May, Ray kept saying to me, "It'll get better; it'll get better." But with visions of lush, green southern Indiana in my head, the outskirts of Searcy seemed no better to me on this decisive journey.

"It'll get better," he said.

It had to, for the sake of the children, whose anxiety increased mile by mile, and once we saw the city limits of Searcy, block by block. The streets were clean and the yards well kept as we approached our neighborhood, a place called the Sunnyhill Addition. It looked woefully small, though. Our house on 1405 Hillcrest seemed more aptly named "Hillcrammed," squeezed as it was between two other homes on the side of that hill.

It would take us a while to see the potential in this north central Arkansas hamlet. In an earlier chapter, I described Henderson, Tennessee, as "small town America," at the end of the '40s. Well, Searcy, Arkansas, was small town America at the beginning of the '60s. I am echoing Ray in this, for he made the same point in his book on the history of Searcy. But though

Ray emphasized the traditional values he saw in the town, he also knew that the definition of small town America was changing. We arrived in the summer of 1964, when the city was in the middle of its boom. It was still small, only about 7,800 in population, but the Chamber of Commerce had been active and new industry was arriving. As in other parts of the country, people were making more money and spending it on buildings and programs that reflected the great society envisioned by John Kennedy and Lyndon Johnson. It was a synergy of mercantile, educational, and civic forces.

In the years immediately before and after our arrival, these facilities were built: Searcy High School, White County Memorial Hospital, the new Searcy Library, Sidney Deener elementary, the Sunshine School (for special children), and Foothills Vocational Institute. The Chamber's $75,000 "Program for Progress" brought new business: Polar Stainless Products arrived, as did the Speed Queen Plant. Ground was broken on an industrial park. The city had its first parade of homes. The first dial telephones went into use. The Optimist Club, the Civitans, and the Head Start Program originated. Searcy got its first automated car wash. The Rialto Theater downtown was remodeled to look like a glitzy Hollywood showplace.

Social change marked our new home as well. In 1965 Searcy became the first Arkansas school district to desegregate voluntarily, serving as a pattern for other area schools. The very year we moved into a house on Hillcrest, plans were born to build a freeway connecting Little Rock to outlying towns like Beebe and Searcy. It would take a while, but urban sprawl had begun. Searcy would never again be like it was, or like Henderson had been fifteen years earlier. America's post-war boom was inexorably connecting us all, in small towns and large, to a new economy and a new sense of ourselves.

But as day ended in Searcy on August 24, 1964, twenty-four hours after our emotional farewell in Bloomington, most of what we knew about Searcy could be summed up in one word: hot. Only a few weeks earlier, the thermometer had topped out at 111 degrees. Everything seemed baked during the day and desolate at night. When we bought the house earlier that summer, we hired a boy to keep it mowed until we arrived. He told us that we owed him absolutely nothing; no grass had grown. After our first Wednesday night service at College Church, we took the children, who as usual were thirsty and hungry, to look for a store. We also needed coffee for the next morning. We drove up and down Race Street. Beyond the town's drive-in movie theater, we found a drive-in food place called The Pit. It was closed. Nothing that sold groceries was open. After our futile search, the two older boys started rolling around in the back seat. When I asked them what they were doing, one said, "We're rolling up the sidewalks in this town—it's 8 o'clock!" We finally found Bill's Grill, where Ray talked the waitress into selling us three pounds of coffee—after he spent money to feed the family.

We went back to 1405 Hillcrest, to the unpacked boxes in a house smaller than we had hoped, with no friends within easy reach, having celebrated Zac's third birthday without fanfare the day before. We all indulged in a bath of self-pity.

The mood didn't last long. The citizens of Searcy drove it away. We already knew the Davises from Bloomington, of course, and they visited immediately. But new friends came too. Lottie Nichols brought us food. Neighbors like Guinn Pyeatt ministered to us. R. T. and Charlene Clark lived nearby and let us use their car. Alice Ann Kellar volunteered to drive David to football practice, and even before we had moved, she had been instrumental in locating our house for us. When we came down to work on it that summer, the Davises threw a party for us, attended by the Kellars, the Formbys, the Atteberrys and others. When we moved in, we already had a cadre of new friends. Before long the two oldest boys were spending time at other homes and inviting boys over to Hillcrest. As for the younger children, Zac and Kandy soon made friends and began running around the neighborhood.

This warm reception healed the wounds of leaving. In town or on campus, people smiled and greeted us. What a change from the larger Bloomington! The welcoming arms of Searcy enclosed us in a radiant community of God-fearing servants. That's how I can describe the feeling of those first days, as the fatigue wore off and the new relationships began—a reinvigorating bath of light. Not all the strangeness or tension evaporated immediately, but Ray and I, and David and Marc too, felt as all strangers and travelers should feel in the fellowship of believers, like adopted family.

The welcome extended to the community at large as well. The clichés about the friendliness of small towns were true in the case of Searcy. Although we might have had an opportunity to find a house adjacent to campus, we decided early on to live away from the college. The men and women of Searcy civic groups, the parents and coaches of recreational sports, the businessmen downtown all contributed to our sense that their town might just be the last stop on the journey of the Muncy family.

In this new place our lives were to be dominated by three interlocking institutions: the college, of course, the College Church of Christ, and Harding Academy. Private Christian education did not have the national cachet it does now, but the founders of Harding had planned a total environment for their families to attract Church of Christ members. Thus many of the faculty members at the college attended the College Church and many enrolled their children in the Academy. The three facilities were within a mile of each other, and many of the faculty and staff lived inside that same circumference. It was a close-knit community empowered by shared religious values and in many cases long family associations. No one said that the Muncy children had to attend College Church (there were three other Churches of Christ in town), and the Searcy public schools had exemplary reputations. Yet we never really debated seriously either of those choices. If our decision was coerced, it was by the force of wanting to belong to what seemed like such a secure and happy extended family.

Ken Davis and his wife Betty chaperoned us on our first visit to the College Church of Christ. The building itself, set on property almost adjacent to the campus, was, I am sorry to report, extremely unattractive. A large, barn-like auditorium accommodated five hundred people for two Sunday morning worship services (later the auditorium would be expanded to almost double this size). The friendliness of the people and quality of the service were gratifying but typical. When the first song started, however, we realized we lived in a new place. The hymn filled the high ceiling of the auditorium, sounding like a mighty choir, which in fact it really was. At least a third of the voices in that service had been trained in college and most of the remainder had been seasoned by thousands of services of singing parts. The a cappella sound of the College Church of Christ was beautiful—a little bit of heaven in Arkansas. Maybe this is what he meant when Ray told me, "It gets better." Up front at the podium, our friend from Bloomington, Ken Davis, led us with his impeccable voice and phrasing. We placed our membership almost immediately.

Next came our introduction to Harding Academy, and the first activity that loomed large in our collective lives was Academy football.

Growing up in Alabama, I knew the importance of football to the South. Ray's interest in the game went back to his cheerleading days at DuPont High School. He and I had attended many high school and college football games before and were avid fans of the "Hurryin' Hoosiers." Eventually, we became veterans of many scholastic games with our sons and later grandsons on the field. David was thrilled to have a chance to play, but frankly, if he wanted to feel part of the group, he didn't have much choice. In the South generally and at small schools like the Academy in particular, it was understood that able-bodied males played football. For someone uninterested in sports, such expectations might be a burden. In our case, David and Marc and Zac all wanted to play. That first year, the whole family was swept up in the excitement of seeing David go off to his first practice.

I waved goodbye to him early in the morning on our third day in town. As he got into the car with Alice Ann Kellar, her bright smile reassured David, I think, and she bombarded him with information and friendly questions on the short drive. She told me later a special bond developed with David in those few days of taxi service. She was taken with his sky-blue eyes that looked like mine but sparkled like Ray's, and his broad, winning smile. And I think it meant something to him as the stranger in town as well. I soon realized that Alice Ann has never met a stranger. Her friendliness took the edge off his apprehension over entering a whole new world: Harding Academy.

In 1964 Harding Academy was located at the corner of Blakeney and Center, on ground at the northeast corner of the college campus. It consisted of one building with three wings, originally designed for one of George Benson's pet projects, an industrial arts program for the college. The program failed to get off the ground, and by the time we arrived, the building, which featured a box-like middle section flanked by wings with peaked roofs, served to house all 130 or so of its high school, junior high, and elementary students. It doubled as the home of the college art department. The best that can be said for the complex is that it was functional. When President Benson was talking Ray into coming to Harding, he promised a new, modernized academy very soon. His optimism was off by about seventeen years, but eventually the school moved off the college campus and into a new facility (in 1981), after the last Muncy had graduated.

On that first morning Alice Ann drove past the Academy building, with its long sidewalk leading from Blakeney, to take David to practice. She headed south for a few hundred feet and came to a stop where David could take the shortest route to the little concrete building that served as dressing room for the Academy team. It was squeezed between the music building to the north and Rhodes Field House immediately to the south. David would join other boys in the walk past Rhodes, which was actually a transplanted hangar moved to campus during World War II to serve as the college gymnasium.

Behind the field house was the Academy football field. It was bordered by Cross Street to the east and the music building, dressing room and Rhodes on the west. Scrunched up next to the field were wooden bleachers that seated maybe 350 people, home and visitor. On this field early in the August mornings, Coach Ed Higginbotham supervised practice along with assistant Cliff Sharp. It was Ed's first year as head coach, but he had been at the Academy ever since his own graduation from Harding College in 1962. Only twenty-six, the soft-spoken young coach had come to Harding as an indifferent Christian and graduated a committed one. Ray and I were grateful even then for the spirit of Ed and the other coaches. Their dedication shone through even when equipment was scarce and victories were hard to come by.

Among high school players for the first time, David didn't think much about what the team didn't have. He braced instead for the challenge of being one of the new kids—a halfback competing with strangers for a spot on the team. He remembers one of Harding's running backs staring hard at him the first day, but when David was moved to tight end, that budding feud died. He survived other challenges to his manhood and endured with his new teammates the grind of morning and evening practice in the 90-degree weather. The boys sweated in their pads and took salt tablets as the coaches barked encouragement. David came home exhausted and sore, loving every minute of it. The week of the first game, he proudly brought home a scarlet jersey adorned with the big white numeral 84.

Then in September on a warm Friday evening, we took Marc, Kandy, and Zac to the first game. The opponent was Des Arc, a little school about thirty miles south, and the result was pretty much the same as it would be the entire season. The Wildcats, who had gone 10-0 in 1963, got stomped 36-0. David started at tight end. Ray and I sat among the parents: the Atteberrys, the Lawsons, the Harrises. Almost all of the faculty and staff attended too—except Mrs. Ritchie, David's math teacher, who openly declared her conviction that football was a cruel sport. For the rest of us, each game was quite a social occasion, with other parents shouting encouragement to David when he made a play and Ray and me cheering for Rick Harris and David Lawson. We could tell the parents took pride in this group of boys, remaining undaunted despite disappointing on-field results or sometimes bad off-field conditions, including a plague of mosquitoes at Cotton Plant large enough to make us look around for a Moses to lead us out of the swamp.

After that first year, the excitement gradually wore off for all of us. The violence of the game sometimes tormented me. My fears were realized in David's junior year when an illegal block ended his football career prematurely.

Back in 1964, though, before David's injury, Academy football was new and exciting. Despite a seven-game losing streak, loyal fans of the Wildcats cheered the boys on. Finally, in late October, on Homecoming night, Harding eked out a 7-6 victory over Clinton. It was a great feeling, I must admit. From the Academy field bleachers, we could see the shadowy west end of the college stands, and beyond that the almost empty skyline. In those days, the east side of the campus was not surrounded by much but trees and other fields. Beyond to the southeast lay largely undeveloped land. It was like watching a game on the edge of a frontier. But in the crisp night air with Harding's tiny pep band blasting out fight songs, the cheerleaders cavorting below us, the white chalk lines shining on the slightly withered autumn grass, and the clash of home white and visiting red jerseys in the distance, we talked and laughed in the stands as part of the great social drama of high school sports unfolding all over America.

Football remained a part of our lives for the next fourteen years as Marc and Zac took their turns as Wildcats. Both the younger boys earned all-star honors playing for some pretty good teams. Marc especially loved Bill Barden, who took over as coach in 1967. When I asked Marc once if he ever heard us cheering for him in the stands, he said in his laconic style, "Coach keeps us pretty focused when we're on the field." Translated, that meant, "Mom, get serious; this is football. I can't worry about people in the stands." Marc loved the discipline and emphasis on values, not to mention the winning tradition established by Barden. Seven years later, when Zac made the varsity, he wore Marc's number 50 and shared his older brother's respect for Bill. Years later as an alumnus living in Clarksville, Arkansas, Marc paid tribute to the program by providing meals for the team when it played in the area.

It was a good fourteen years. A decade-and-a-half of pep rallies and fund raisers and banquets and load after load of laundry. But we saw in those years increasing emphasis on the sport, increased time demanded by coaches in order for the team to remain competitive. The energy of Harding Academy football was infectious but also tiring. I remember Treva Pryor asking me as Zac's last game wound down in 1978: "Don't you feel sad?" She asked this as smells of popcorn and liniment filled the air, as the sound of cheerleaders and the school band rang in my ears, and as the red and white uniforms rose and fell on the lighted field.

I was nostalgic for a moment as I contemplated the end of an era. Then I got a mental whiff of those dirty uniforms and said, "Oh boy, it's almost over!" I had given my best for the team, and if Ray hadn't been able to be at all of David's and Marc's games, he was there for Zac's. We were ready to move on. Mothers may have an advantage in this matter of giving up sports. You see, fathers and sons find it hard to accept the end of athletic glory; mothers know all along that there is life after football. God made us that way.

Football may have captured the boys' hearts and my time that first year in Searcy, but Ray simply could not get too caught up in it. He fixed his eyes on the goal of becoming a college teacher, and the only major distraction he permitted himself was preaching.

In part, he added preaching to his duties because I wasn't working outside the home at first. Money was not the main reason, however. He repeated to me what he told Ken Davis when the two had gotten serious about Ray coming to Searcy as a history teacher: "Weezie, I don't want to leave the pulpit. I wouldn't feel right not preaching." They say things get in a person's blood and compel him to go on with them even when common sense dictates otherwise. Preaching was that thing for Ray. He had no desire to minister full time, but he wanted to teach God's word.

This desire was not unique at Harding. For years the school had funneled both male faculty and students into small area congregations. These men would preach on Sunday mornings and evenings at places within a radius of about a hundred miles. It was a way for students to gain training, for faculty to reinforce the mission of the college to strengthen churches, and a way for these small, often struggling congregations to sustain worship services without busting their fragile budgets. So important were these Sunday preaching assignments that the college held its classes from Tuesday through Saturday instead of the usual work week. The reason: to make it easier on those who had to travel back to campus late after a day of preaching. The policy was changed in 1965 only after the state board of education ruled that Harding Academy must get its calendar in line with other schools. Saturday classes tended to put a crimp in athletic and other extracurricular scheduling.

In order to join the dozens of faculty and staff who preached on weekends, all Ray had to do was approach someone on the Bible faculty, likely Conard Hays, to secure a preaching appointment. His first was at a place called Oil Trough. It was a farming community about an hour's drive north of Searcy, receiving its unique name from the practice of siphoning bear oil, a most useful commodity in frontier days, into wooden troughs. Speaking of commodities, the good people of the congregation could not pay much, so they loaded Ray's car most weeks with garden produce, fresh milk, butter, beans, and home-slaughtered meat. When he arrived home on Sunday nights, weary from his long day, we would ask, "Did you get your commodities this week?" In reality, Ray took home more than a check and some produce; he shared in a fellowship of common people who loved the Lord and their fellow man in a unique way. As much as he loved the stimulation of college life, he also needed the nourishment of Oil Trough's sincere hospitality. He took me and the children about once a month, and we would spend the day with the Sineles or some other host, watching our kids play among new friends and enjoying the view. In a few years Ray moved on to Pine View, another wonderful place with the added benefit of requiring only one lesson on Sunday. Nothing spectacular happened during his pulpit days in these little communities, but Ray renewed himself as he helped them do the Lord's will.

By the end of our first month in Searcy, the family routine had been established: church in Searcy and Oil Trough, college for Ray, the Academy for the children, and home for me. With these various focal points, the Muncy family settled into life in Searcy and Ray geared up for life as a college teacher. Before moving to his challenges at Harding, I must mention the man whose presence was inevitably part of all three of our domains: church, college, and school. Adjusting to Harding meant adjusting to the powerful George Benson.

GEORGE BENSON

When we arrived in Searcy, George Benson was the dominant figure at Harding. In one sense he was Harding. When he had assumed the presidency of this small college in 1936, it was embroiled in the premillennial controversy and was losing support from local congregations. In a bold move, Benson went outside the brotherhood for funding, tying the future of Harding in part to corporations and conservative politics. The plan worked and Harding began to grow. The political leanings of the college made it friends and a few enemies, but once the ball started rolling, the church support regained momentum as well.

As he restored the flagging finances of Harding, Benson also fired its missionary fervor, leading the way in establishing efforts in Japan, China, and elsewhere, most famously perhaps, much later in his career, in Zambia. A man of inexhaustible energy, Benson was often caricatured as willing to use any pretense to raise money for Zambia. Even in his later years when his powers had declined, he never missed an opportunity. Reportedly, Benson sometimes took catnaps in elders' meetings at the College Church. During one such snooze, a budget manager for some ministry admitted that he had a surplus of $200. Immediately the silver-haired Benson opened his eyes and said he'd be glad to take the surplus for the good work in Zambia. Perhaps he did less sleeping than some supposed.

It took a strong man with vision to accomplish what George Benson did. He was gifted in many ways, and the ability to control his employees ranked among his best talents. Anyone who went to work for Harding during his administration had to pass whatever test he might have in mind. I'm not talking about the standard matters of being a member of the Church of Christ or being at least reasonably conservative in outlook. Benson prized a loyalty to Christian education that would rise to the top during tough times. He wanted people who didn't covet high salaries or material possessions. Above all, he wanted people who shared his dedication to the idea of Christian service.

Maybe that's why Ray and I heard others tell stories about Benson's "tests." Harry Risinger, Benson's pilot on the college plane, recounted a time he was flying his boss to Chicago for an important conference. Dr. Benson told Harry to wear a blue serge suit. Harry had no blue serge suit, so he bought one, supposing the financial sacrifice worth it if the school president needed him in the meeting. When they deplaned in Chicago, Risinger started to accompany the president to the meeting site. Benson stopped him: "I don't think I'll need you today, Harry; why don't you stay here and wash the plane?" So the loyal employee washed the plane wearing a suit that he did not need and could not afford.

Another employee, Guy Petway, a retired Air Force man who came to Harding to run the new American Heritage Inn, also learned the mysterious ways George Benson used to impart life lessons. At some point Petway was given the title of Assistant to the President, but had no idea what that meant. Combining a pleasant personality with a military bearing, Petway was prepared for anything, he thought. On the first day of his new job, he reported to work in his usual suit and tie. Benson greeted him, then said, "Let's go to the farm." At that time, Harding raised crops and livestock on college property located some distance from campus. Once they got to the farm, Benson ambled up to a pile of manure next to a wagon. He grabbed a pitchfork and started shoveling the manure into the wagon. Petway watched, nonplussed. After a minute, Benson paused.

"There's another pitchfork," he said.

At noon, Loudine Petway had lunch ready for her husband. "So what did the president's assistant do on his first day on the job?" Petway laughed, "You wouldn't believe it if I told you."

One other story, about Camp Tahkodah in Independence County, Arkansas, illustrates this dimension of the Benson style. Camp Tahkodah had been a special project of Benson's. According to John Stevens, he bought the land for it in 1942 with money from an insurance policy he cashed in. Over the years, it served not only as a boy's leadership camp but also as a retreat for Benson and his friends and colleagues. He kept horses on the grounds and liked to surprise campers gathered for assemblies by riding up on a majestic equine and dismounting to deliver an impromptu speech on self-reliance.

With so much financial and emotional investment in the place, he naturally guarded it against intruders. He maintained a strict policy that no one be allowed in the cabins unless he or the caretaker knew the visitors personally. Once when he returned to his own cabin, Benson was greeted by a newly hired caretaker: "You know, Dr. Benson, some fellas came up here wanting to use the cabins, but I did like you said and told them no. They were pretty upset, but everything turned out all right. Afterwards, I got to thinking how the problem came up so soon after you warned me about it. It occurred to me that those fellas coming as they did might have been a test."

Dr. Benson's eyes twinkled: "You passed the test, didn't you?"

If Ray was subjected to a test, it took the form of a late night call soon after his first semester of teaching began. That first semester was very hard on Ray. He was not ready for the amount of needed preparation, and he worked late every evening, sometimes returning to the office after supper. On this occasion he had just gone to bed when the phone rang. It was President Benson. He needed to verify a date for something he was writing. Ray said, "I don't know offhand, but I can have it for you in the morning."

"I'm over in my office now," Benson said; "I need it before 11:30 tonight."

"What did he want?" I asked, when Ray hung up. Looking rather pathetic in his pajamas, he said, "I've got to go the office." So he did, finding the information and taking it to Benson. Since the President never asked anything like that of Ray again, we wondered if he had designed the task as a way to test his new employee's readiness to serve. In any case, Benson produced that effect on all who worked for him. You might not like his tactics on occasion, but you stayed on your toes. He commanded respect and not a little fear.

This demanding nature formed one side of President Benson as we knew him in those first years, but we saw other sides as well. He and his wife, Sally, were wonderful and gracious hosts who invited us to their home several times along with others for dinner, teas, and receptions. His graciousness was combined with an old-style formality. For example, at one luncheon to which we had been invited, Dr. Benson rose immediately after the meal to announce that other obligations forced him to leave: "But my wife is an excellent hostess and will entertain you." And Sally did just that, with artifacts and stories of their travels in China together. At the receptions, we had a chance to mingle with Harding's guest speakers. Herbert Philbrick, at the time famous for his book *I Led Three Lives*, the story of his years as a double agent for America in the Cold War, spoke at Harding several times and even enrolled his daughter as a student. The book had spawned a 1950s television series of the same name. The "three lives" consisted of his cover as a Boston advertising executive, his evening charade as a member of the Communist Party, and his after-hours role as an American counterspy. As usual the topic of discussion at Benson's gatherings was politics, and like the other wives gathered in the living room, I listened while the men talked. Ray did find Philbrick interesting and not as rabidly anti-communist as some of the speakers.

Benson's alliance with the aggressive anti-communist segment of the right wing was part of his American Studies Program, with its offshoot, the National Education Program. The NEP, from which Harding had severed official ties in the '50s, had been a lightning rod for both praise and criticism because of its association with anti-communist propaganda. By the time we arrived in 1964, Harding had been the victim of national press attacks for its perceived association with far right movements. As baby boomers began to come of age and the Cold War dragged on, the first stirrings of reaction to it were setting in, and our campus felt those tremors as the '60s progressed. Benson and his conservative promotion of Americanism never received much public criticism on campus, or from Churches of Christ in general, but the media outcry had drawn negative attention that occasionally discomfited the Harding population, or even embarrassed it.

Ray never got embroiled in the controversies. Privately he voiced concern about the danger of identifying too much with a political position. Hardly a critic of the free enterprise system, he never saw the need to go public with his concern. He and his fellow history faculty members felt occasional pressure to conform and resisted it, standing for academic freedom above party lines. In a 1966 yearbook picture caption that Ray did not exactly appreciate, he is described (standing in his checked jacket looking at a blackboard) as "compar[ing] the values of our American society with those of non-competing economic systems." Ray did discuss that topic perhaps, but he thought the caption distorted the purpose of the department by depicting it as part of the fight against other "economic systems."

There was pressure at Harding, as there is on any campus, to conform to the dominant ideology. Benson had built the school's financial base on the cornerstones of faith in God, constitutional government, and free enterprise economy. The intertwined nature of the spiritual and political was captured in a painting included in the 1965 *Petit Jean*, Harding's yearbook. Across the bottom of the canvas the tops of trees are visible, and the rest of the background is a huge, slate sky with billowing clouds. A few faint rays of sun light are breaking through those clouds. In the middle of the painting, suspended between heaven and earth, is an open Bible, and above it, almost as if growing out of the book, is an unfurling American flag. The caption reads: "America can find her 'place in the sun' if she remains loyal to God's word and the principles of freedom." Ray was not comfortable with such imagery. The sentiment is inarguable in theory, but in the messier practice of partisan politics, it can create problems.

Though officially no Harding administrator completely identified Christian values with Americanism, some school personnel and its supporters at times acted as if the two were completely synonymous. One teacher was so obsessed by the Cold War that students used to ask, "What is he calling his course on communism this semester?" Ray experienced the pressure one year not long after he became chairman of the history department. The NEP influenced some students from politically conservative families to attend Harding, and one of Ray's colleagues in the department ran afoul of the father of one such student.

Joe Segraves was an Arkansas boy and Harding alumnus who returned home from Ohio to teach history at his alma mater. Ray hit if off immediately with fellow novice Joe, a quiet, dignified young man with smooth good looks and a soft voice. When Ray was named chairman in 1965, Joe, a bit surprised because Ray was as inexperienced as he, never resented having his friend as supervisor. In fact, the two young teachers feasted on the Harding experience. They had the energy to embrace the "do-it-yourself" attitude encouraged by Benson and made necessary at a small college without much academic budget. Ray and Joe often bought their own office supplies, and they shared one typewriter, which was old and worse for wear. It had a chink in its roller, for example, creating an uneven surface that spoiled sections of the print. One day Joe found Ray bent over the machine wedging freshly chewed gum into the chink. Amazingly, the gum seemed to work as a kind of peppermint caulk.

The two colleagues, who in Ray's first year *were* the history department, along with a few adjuncts, also managed to endure the crowded office space in the American Studies Building where the history department was housed. The massive red brick structure was also home to the education department, the fledgling foreign language department, and eventually the English department. Given such crowded conditions, student conferences became an exercise in musical chairs. When Joe needed to see someone, Ray excused himself, and vice versa.

If Joe ever entertained any doubts about Ray as department chair, they were quickly dispelled by Ray's leadership style. The new chair was hands-on, willing to do the routine tasks like class-change sessions at the beginning of semesters. Some chairmen delegate others for the hectic activity. At first Ray did it out of necessity, but even after the department grew, he retained the duty. He also maintained a heavy counseling load. Joe never felt as if Ray were his boss; the two always operated as colleagues—and friends, of course.

The friendship was cemented at some point early on when Joe said something in class that a student reported to his father. The father happened to be a staunch conservative who saw Harding as a bastion of anti-communism, and Joe's comments seemed sympathetic to communism. Who knows what it could have been? More likely Joe had failed to denounce Russia sufficiently in the father's mind, and of course he got his information through his child, so it was second hand at best.

Even though the red scare of the '50s had passed from the national scene, Benson's Freedom Forums and other NEP propaganda had kept alive in some an unhealthy paranoia. A few citizens of Searcy, for example, were convinced that Russia had George Benson on an atomic hit list and that in the event of war Harding would be a primary target. Such fringe thinking was in the small minority, but it persisted into the '70s, made worse by the left wing's anti-American agitation so visible in the media. For many, the issue had become so visceral that the slightest remark could be interpreted as deadly right- or left-wing poison. Whatever may have been his mindset, the father paid a visit to Ray and actually said something to this effect:

"I suspect that Joe Segraves may be a Communist."

"Really. What makes you say that?"

"Well, in his lectures he blah blah blah blah." Whatever the man's imagined evidence, Ray listened politely and then assured him that he was quite wrong. Later he dropped by Joe's office, which by this time was separate from Ray's, and closed the door.

"You have so-and-so in your American History class, is that right?"

"Yes."

"Well, you know his father came by this week to register a complaint about you." Joe wasn't sure at first what this could be, so he waited.

"Yes," Ray said very gravely, "it seems that, according to Mr. So-and-So, you are part of the Red Menace."

"What?"

"I have one question for you, Joe T. Segraves." Ray was already smiling by this time: "Are you now or have you ever been a member of the Communist Party?" Then Ray broke out into his deep, rich laugh. They never heard from the concerned father again.

There may be other isolated instances of harassment, but for the most part Benson's conservative political machinery brought relatively little in the way of outside grief to faculty members. Internally, feelings were mixed, but civility usually prevailed even in matters of political debate. One of the reasons we came to Harding—its religious emphasis—kept political division from running too deep. At most the arguments ruffled feathers, as when Evan Ulrey complained during a faculty meeting about getting political material in his mail box. At Harding such mail meant pleas on behalf of Republican candidates from zealous advocates. The more liberal faculty members, always in the minority, saw themselves as put upon but not censored.

As great as George Benson was in the history of Harding, he had only one year left at the helm when we came. In 1965 Cliff Ganus assumed the presidency. Benson, who had exceeded the school's mandatory retirement age of 65 by two years, still could not resist voicing displeasure at the inevitable exit. Marvin Robertson, then a student at Harding, recalls the grand old man's farewell speech in chapel in which he groused about being led out to pasture like "old Ned."

The retiree had long served as chancellor of Oklahoma Christian College, another Church of Christ school, and agreed to oversee the development of their American Studies program. Benson never stopped working. His efforts on behalf of a Christian school in Zambia, under way even before his retirement, escalated afterward. Though his American Studies program inevitably grew beyond his control, it remains a legacy. He died in 1991, a giant in the brotherhood.

Ray had relatively little contact with Benson after those first few months, and as his retirement began in 1965 the two saw each other even less. He did appreciate Ray's scholarship, however, and the 1974 yearbook has a picture of the chancellor honoring Ray for the publication of his book *Sex and Marriage in Utopian Communities*. The only other memorable Benson moment came later and was part of an eyebrow-raising second marriage for the ex-president.

Sally Benson died in 1979, a loyal wife who sacrificed much to support her husband's career. Two years later, George Benson approached his fellow elders seeking permission to date his long-time secretary, Marguerite

O'Banion. He felt enough time had passed and did not want to be alone. The elders, perhaps surprised that Benson sought their approval, saw nothing amiss in the timing or person, and readily agreed.

Dating quickly turned into marriage plans. Benson's choice of place, the College Church, seemed fitting, but his choice of preachers may have surprised some. He wanted Ray Muncy to perform the ceremony. Ray at first had no inkling as to why he was chosen over other men who were more associated with pulpit work than he. My son Zac remembers Ray telling him one answer Benson gave to the natural question of "Why me?"

"You have the most resonant voice, and are the most easily understood preacher at the College Church," Benson declared to Ray. Ray was hoping for a more ringing endorsement—maybe something about the content of lessons or his towering spirituality. Whatever reason lay behind Benson's decision, it reaffirmed for us the affection we had felt some fifteen years earlier in our first semester at Harding. Wondering in spite of himself if this was a final test, Ray agreed to do the wedding for his fellow elder.

Of course the wedding was the talk of the campus. While no one raised any moral questions, some clucked their tongues, maybe feeling queasy about the age of the couple or the decorum of marrying a secretary. Most of the reaction was more amused than critical. Our daughter Kandy joined in the fun when Ray told us that the wedding would be videotaped. At the time use of camcorders was still a novelty, so I joked that the ceremony must be scheduled for television. "But which program?" I wondered. "*That's Incredible,*" Kandy said without hesitation. No doubt many people either joked or complained about Benson's last hurrah. Nevertheless, the man who had faced down Senators and raised millions of dollars from the most powerful men in America didn't let any such ripples affect his plans.

As for his age, Benson would have snorted in derision at suggestions that he was too old to marry again. In fact, in a story that I cannot swear is factual because I didn't hear it from my husband, the groom asked Ray to accompany him to World Travel to help with plans for a trip to Hawaii after the wedding. The young travel agent, intent on selling the complete package, tried to interest Benson in one excursion after another: "Sir, you and your wife would love this bus ride to the Mauna Loa Volcano."

"No, thank you," Benson replied.

"Well, there is a beautiful flower tour each afternoon in the Kauai Island region, and at a very reasonable price too."

"No, thank you," Benson replied.

"OK, but may I suggest a one-day excursion in the—"

"Young man, I don't need to do any of that. I'm on my honeymoon!"

As for the ceremony itself, Ray received only three instructions from Benson: First, that Ray omit the phrase "with thee I endow all my worldly goods." He and Marguerite each had their own money and there was no need to mix it up now, he explained. Second, Ray was also to omit the words, "you may kiss the bride." Benson offered no explanation for this taboo or for the third and last request: he wanted to strike the clause, "If anyone objects...let him now speak or forever hold his peace." The august ex-president also requested a lapel microphone, an unusual request by a groom, but who was going to say no?

The wedding, directed by the estimable Bessie Mae Pryor, wife of Academic Dean Joe Pryor, was beautiful. Benson looked as magisterial as ever, and Marguerite, for whom this was a first marriage, drew comments (not all of them admiring) with her white tulle outfit. Music was provided by a college choral group. The most striking thing about the arrangement was the number of candles positioned behind the bride and groom. Dozens of them cast a gauzy halo around the couple and Ray as the ceremony began. The audience could not help but notice, however, that the light was considerably brighter by being reflected off the bald heads of those who lit them, both of whom were well over forty. The intensity of the glare also made the white-clad bride positively radiant. Meanwhile, Kandy saw Benson's lapel mike at the beginning of the ceremony and said, "Oh no, he's going to ask for donations to Zambia!"

Ray's remarks were short and to the point. Then he presented the bride and groom to the audience with none of the forbidden language about kissing. Nevertheless, Benson gallantly took Marguerite's hand and kissed it, the lapel mike amplifying the smack of his lips on her flesh as the audience tittered. Now it was time for Benson to assume his favorite role as speaker. To Kandy's relief, he did not solicit funds for Zambia. He only thanked the guests for coming, for supporting him and his bride in their new life together. It was quite touching, really, but the remarks were almost cut short by a comic disaster. As he stepped forward to speak, the long mike cord had become wrapped around one of the sizable candelabra, which started to teeter as Benson unknowingly tightened the pressure of the cord. He took another step and the candelabrum inched toward a sure fall, impelled by gravity to crash right behind the appreciative groom. Ray, behind Benson and facing the audience with him, saw the situation and reached out just in time, deftly catching the candelabrum before any of the candles could dislodge and spoil the effect.

During the reception, Marguerite sidled up to Ray, asking him to make sure that Dr. Benson had the airline tickets. Safely married, the couple flew to Hawaii, where I'm sure the honeymoon went exactly as planned.

INITIATION INTO ACADEMIA

When Ray came to Harding as a teacher of history, he was a successful, veteran preacher. He had been in front of people on a regular basis for fifteen years. For at least ten of those years he had been preparing in some way to become a history teacher. Not only had he earned an M.A. from Indiana University but he had also taught in high schools as a substitute. Each year his love of learning about the past, about great ideas, had grown, so that by 1964, teaching in a college classroom seemed the inevitable goal of his whole adult life. Ray was prepared academically, experientially, and emotionally for this sea change in his life—this brave new profession.

And it nearly killed him before the end of his first semester.

Oh, he loved the academic life, and his time in front of students was rewarding from the first. He even adapted to the small offices and scarce resources of the college. What nearly did him in was the preparation. At first glance, this might seem an unlikely stumbling block for someone who wrote several sermons a week every month of the year from the time he turned twenty. But that kind of preparation was different, focused primarily on the Bible and a small range of commentaries and histories.

In his new role, however, the fields of learning had multiplied. In addition to survey courses for freshmen and sophomores, he taught courses for majors; these demanded all his master's notes and much more. Courses like Ancient and Medieval History and International Relations took him from antiquity to modernity. Ray first had to absorb the material himself and then organize it for presentation. In some classes the text book helped do that. In others he was on his own to find a structure.

Thus beginning in August, Ray's life became a cycle of reading, notetaking, and writing lectures. Often he would return to the office after supper to finish up, especially to prepare tests. Oh, those tests. They might have been the biggest challenge for the new teacher. Ray began learning the art of test making as most teachers do—by trial and error and stealing ideas he remembered from his own teachers.

Weekdays were hectic, with Ray out the door and to his office early. He taught five classes that first semester, with a total of more than one hundred students. In addition, he had to learn the routine and jargon of academic life, which was changing rapidly in the 1960s. The 1,400 students at Harding did not realize how the educational establishment, spurred on by the prospect of a staggering number of increasingly affluent students approaching college age, was scrambling to satisfy the expectations of the post-war generation for higher learning.

In his first year Ray may have been the chief scrambler. Perhaps I can make the point of Ray's distress then by describing something of what he became much later on. A former student from the 1980s once remarked on the amazing polish of Ray's lectures. He would begin by writing a list of important terms on the board, often filling the forty square feet with a glossary for the day. At the sound of the bell he called roll, then took the students on a journey through those terms, creating a set of amusing and interesting anecdotes around them that had the effect of erecting the larger, coherent story of the day's segment of world or American history. The explanation of the last vocabulary word would still be echoing in the students' minds when the dismissal bell rang. Once in a Western Civilization class, Ray was able to use the day's newspaper headlines for his last lecture because he had brought the students to that exact point in the present. To the admiring student, it was a magical performance. To an experienced teacher, it is, if not routine, at least a matter of knowledge and structure.

In 1964 Ray could perform no such magic. He could lead the students through history, but could not yet make it seem his own back yard. To put it another way, he depended on constant study of a map to get the students through; he had not yet become his own cartographer.

As a result, our home life suffered some. Inevitably the children did not see their father as much, and I was left to do more errands on my own. David's greatest regret about Ray is that his father was not there often enough for his football and basketball games. I don't know if Ray struggled greatly with decisions about his time with the children. Both of us occasionally felt as if we were "turning our kids over" to the care of the Harding community. Our busy schedules seemed to dictate a version of the *in loco parentis* philosophy. Devotional and recreational activities abounded for all four of our offspring. Maybe it was a way of rationalizing his absence from games. At the time our full life seemed to leave us little choice. David, Marc, Kandy and Zac often went in four different directions themselves for supervised activities.

We adapted to this new mobile lifestyle and, though we realized the drawback of lost time together at home, believed that our family benefited from the larger community of faith in which we lived. In light of subsequent events involving some of our children, we questioned our decisions in these first years at Harding, but I'm convinced we chose as best we could, and whatever mistakes we made occurred with the best of intentions. Despite all Ray's duties and the kids' activities, we did have a normal home life and sought "teachable moments" long before the term became fashionable.

Ray devoted weekends to preparing his sermons for Oil Trough. I continued my role as guardian of his office, which by 1967 was a small room upstairs at 1002 Hayes where Ray's dual ribbon typewriter allowed him to highlight scriptural references in red. Zac and Kandy heard the clackety clack of the machine on Saturday nights and would often want to see what was going on. "Sorry," said the gatekeeper. Then on Sunday Ray would do last-minute preparations in his easy chair. He would come downstairs wearing only his dress shoes, long dark socks, and sometimes a robe. He didn't want to wrinkle his shirt or suit by studying in them. He would sit in that chair, sipping coffee and going over the lesson, while I tried to ready the four children for College Church. Ray stayed at Oil Trough all day on Sundays, visiting and studying after eating lunch with a church family. He left for home around eight and arrived at nine or so. It made for a long day and meant that he took advantage of Harding's odd schedule to rest on Mondays. After 1965, when classes reverted to the typical Monday-Friday routine, he made sure his Monday classes were ready before Sunday.

The rigors left Ray tired and distracted sometimes, and the routine extended to June, when he taught in the first session of summer school. By the end of the spring semester in 1965, more precisely on June 3, I realized how distracted he had become. Ray was in the middle of final exams, grading long essay tests for more than fifty students. That morning before he left for class, and before I realized his state of mind, I said provocatively, "Ah, seventeen years ago today it all started." From the look on his face I knew immediately that he had forgotten completely about our anniversary. He just laughed and tried to cover his surprise.

In a few minutes he excused himself, saying something about the need to get to the office. I couldn't resist eavesdropping on his call to Parker Florist. Later, when he returned from class, I hugged him: "The dozen roses were beautiful," I said. "You are so sweet to remember."

He kissed me, but looked uncomfortable. "Oh Weezie, I didn't remember. I absolutely forgot. This year has me spinning, I'm afraid. I'm so glad we've got a break coming. Forgive me?" Of course I already had, when the roses came. That year—1965—was the first and only time Ray ever forgot our anniversary.

Despite testing the limits of his energy and resilience, the first semester went well. Like the good teacher he was fast becoming, Ray learned more than the students even as he taught them. He loved the ideas at play in history, and occasionally a student caught the enthusiasm. In History 408, European History, he taught a young man, a senior Bible major, who showed promise. His name was Richard Hughes. When Hughes came to Ray's tiny office on the first floor of the American Studies Building, he wanted guidance on choosing a topic for the class project. Hughes recalls , "For some reason, he encouraged me to do a paper on the debate between Luther and Erasmus concerning 'The Freedom of the Will.' He may have encouraged me in this direction since he knew I was a Bible major with a strong interest in religious history." The two met often on the project, and Hughes says that the paper captured his imagination and that Ray "nurtured and encouraged" him to pursue the research.

I do not doubt Ray's enthusiasm for the famous debate. It had the highest stakes for thoughtful Christians—the exact nature and role of God's will and His grace in human freedom. To indifferent students, such abstract ideas tasted bitterly unlike real life. To Ray such topics were the elixir of life, and his emerging gift was the ability to rescue them from abstraction to live for students who were ready. Hughes doesn't recall what was said in those meetings, but he came out of them considering for the first time a career as history teacher or church historian. Looking back on those days, he says it was not so much Ray's knowledge (Ray probably would say his knowledge was skimpy enough at that point) but his friendship that launched Hughes on the productive career he eventually embraced.

But the comfort of such reflections were not yet possible to Ray in the summer of 1965. He had another semester to get ready for and a new duty to assume. In the spring Harding had "put old Ned out to pasture," and Dr. Cliff Ganus was named the new president. Since Cliff had been chairman of the history department, his inauguration created a vacancy in that position. As I mentioned earlier, Ray was chosen to succeed Cliff. I've already recounted his willingness to be a hands-on leader, but when he took over he was anxious about his ability to do the job. One of the first things he did was to seek the advice of other department chairs. Harding's small size and common faith made that an easy task; Ray was fast getting to know and to trust men like Evan Ulrey, head of the speech department. At the time Evan's department, with its drama and forensics branches, was as respected as any on campus. Evan still remembers Ray's humble manner in asking, "How do you make a department succeed and grow?" Evan's answer out-humbled him: "You just do the best you can and hang in there."

Ray's search for advice went beyond Evan to include other chairmen at Harding like Ed Sewell of education, and the answers or non-answers he got taught him that the role of a chair can mean very different things to different people. The duties seem straightforward; he is to manage the budget of his department and the teachers within it. He assigns classes and offers new courses for approval by the larger college community. He approves travel for his departmental members. He handles student questions about courses. He meets with the administrative counsel on decisions about curricular and other academic needs. He does all this in return for one fewer class each semester and no extra salary.

Ray did it because he had grown to value history and its cousin in the social sciences—political science—as vital to the education of Christians. And in one year he had become loyal to men like Benson and Ganus, who perhaps most represented what Harding stood for. He wanted to please them. His loyalty went beyond the obvious leaders, however. Men like Joe and Evan and Ken Davis—not to mention those supporters of Harding within the Searcy community—Tom and Mary Formby, Wayne and Alice Ann Kellar—had all won him over. In some ways, Ray was like the West Virginia kid he had once been, awake in an academic soda fountain, better than the one at Kresge's in Charleston. God had set him down in a place of sweet intellectual and biblical delights. He could hardly believe his good fortune.

He pressed on excitedly, if a bit fearfully, to find a formula for success as department chair. The anxiety arose because, when he added up all the advice he was able to get from his well-meaning but busy colleagues, it came down to "We had to find our own way and we're sure you can too. Good luck!"

In the end, Ray became the only kind of chairman possible, given his personality and teaching philosophy. On the one hand, he wanted to make the history department known for high academic standards. On the other, he sought a truly collegial atmosphere among his faculty members. Even if an administrator had decreed that he rule with an iron hand, he couldn't have done it. He led by example and encouragement. That early group of teachers included Joe Segraves and Dallas Roberts, a veteran political science teacher who was congenial from the first. Over the twenty-nine years of his tenure as chair, the cast would grow and change, but the spirit of collegiality remained pretty much the same. As we will see, the job was not without its drawbacks and Ray was not without faults, but his final record more than justified the appointment of this second-year teacher as department chair.

DIRTY DOG

While Ray was trying to adjust to leading his new department, he was also trying to improve as a teacher. From the time he agreed to come to Harding, it was understood that he would pursue a doctor's degree, and in 1966 he began the process. The doctorate would ignite Ray's ambitions as historian more than ever. In the meantime he had already developed a vision of pedagogy in the history classroom. Students, he felt, should expect to absorb details about history and to think about it. One without the other would be like the canoe without the paddle—no one could get up river.

Before the first year was over, even casual observers like Dennis Organ, a junior from Louisiana, got the impression that the new guy Muncy was a good teacher. Students standing in line at the old Pattie Cobb dormitory and dining hall might mention him. On a spring day in 1965 the line for supper might stretch out the double doors that led to the basement cafeteria all the way out to the Lily Pond, and students would get bored enough to mention classes and teachers. By the end of the first day on campus, an inquisitive newcomer could acquire a complete list of those to avoid and those to take. In their better moments, students appreciate good teachers of all stripes, but when push comes to shove, they will sacrifice the beauties of intellectual challenge in a heartbeat to see that A on a paper or test. The trouble with new teachers is the unknown factor. It takes a semester to rank them properly. By the spring of '65, the lines at Pattie Cobb and the dorm bull sessions undoubtedly included Ray's name on the list of hard teachers. Those who had taken him unawares would be the most vociferous in their admonitions to freshmen. By the time he went away to graduate school in 1967, his reputation as a demanding teacher was cemented and on its way to legend. The following story helped a great deal to that end, if not in the eyes of the students, in the eyes of those who heard Ray repeat it, which he often did.

It's hard to recall the exact date of this episode, but I'm quite sure it occurred sometime in the '60s, likely before Ray's graduate work. I know he was still in the tiny office on the first floor of the American Studies building. A room of sufficient size had been divided by partitions into two offices of insufficient size, the second space occupied by Billy Ray Cox and his secretary. Ray happened to be in his office one day at the end of semester when many finals had been given and many grades already known. As was the custom, Ray posted final grades for his classes on his office door.

As he read at his desk, he heard the sound of students coming down the hall. He could tell by the murmuring of their voices that they were female.

Their progress stopped outside his door. He sensed the apprehension in the voice of the one who apparently was looking for her grade on the list. In the brief silence, Ray could imagine her finger going down the Social Security numbers until she found hers, and then following the horizontal column to her final exam and final course grades. The explosion of her voice told him that she had found what she was looking for.

"Why, that dirty dog!"

The frustration in her voice struck him like an angry child's blow might impact an adult's body—both violent and amusingly irrelevant. Reflexively, in the spirit of West Virginia and Freed-Hardeman humor, Ray responded with his own explosion. He barked.

Immediately after emitting his "bow wow" from behind the closed door, Ray heard the scurry of feet recede down the hallway.

Whenever he told this story, he ended it with laughter. The self-deprecatory nature of the laugh marked Ray in people's minds as unconcerned with his reputation. And most of the time he didn't mind it.

Very soon after the dirty dog story, Ray met with a young lady at an advising session. While he finished with the student before her, he noticed that she carried a paper with two clearly labeled columns: Teachers to Get and Teachers Not to Get. Since the list dangled from her hand, he had to read it upside down, but the first name on the second list was printed clearly enough even at that angle: Ray Muncy. Obviously she did not know who he was, having approached his station in the advising session. When Ray turned his attention to her schedule, he noticed that, ironically, his was the only open section of a needed Western Civilization course. He related the bad news: "I'm afraid the only teacher available for that course is Mr. Muncy.

"Oh, but I don't want Mr. Muncy!" she said.

"Why not?"

"Because he's too hard."

"Well, why don't we see if you can get into another required course, so you don't have to take him?"

"That'd be great." So Ray found another course, double-checked all the information, and then signed his name on the advisor's line. He handed the trial schedule back to her, adding instructions on where to go next in the process. She said, "Thank you very much, uh—" then she looked on the sheet for his name, immediately turning a deep shade of crimson when she found it. Ray dismissed her stammered attempts at apology good humouredly, and wished her a successful semester.

Paul Haynie remembers deciding to take a course from Ray because he was interested in ancient history and because the books appeared useful. He bought *From Tiber to the Tigris* and attended one class. After hearing the requirements, he dropped the course, deciding that, as a senior biology major, he did not need the extra hard work. He did keep the book. Twenty years later, championed by Ray, Paul came back to Harding as a history teacher. At some point in their relationship as colleagues, Paul remembers Ray coming to him with a worried look on his face. It seems that a young lady who was taking both Ray and Paul for history classes had complained to Ray that while she was failing his class, she was getting an A in Paul's. The implication was clear: You, Dr. Muncy, are unreasonably hard. Ray wanted Paul to confirm her comparison. Paul discovered that she had overestimated her grade in his class—it was actually a C. Ray was relieved. "I can live with that," he said, "but an A to an F would have made me wonder."

Though Ray was not oblivious to the potential negative side of his reputation, he never backed off his standards. Among history majors, he was less feared, but like general education students, they had to adjust to his expectations. Kevin Klein's experience was perhaps typical. He thought he was prepared for the first test in Ray's Early National America class. It was his first experience with essay questions on a test, and he did not manage his time well. After giving what he thought were solid answers on the first two of the three questions, he saw that only a few minutes remained in the period. He scribbled an outline of an answer and appended a note: "Time got away." When he got the test back, sure enough, he had an A on the first two questions and an F on the last one, with a return note: "Sorry your time got away; make sure the next time it doesn't."

Kevin says it was a useful lesson, and I think it shows the way Ray operated. With little background in educational theory, he knew only one method: recreate his own fascination with the past by telling it as fully and vividly as possible. He wanted his students to do the same, on papers or on tests. History was the perfect discipline for the man who loved stories. And Ray's amazing memory enabled him to produce hundreds of stories, seeming sidelights of history that made it come alive. Rachel Robertson, who served as departmental secretary from 1974-92, remembers early on in her tenure sitting at her desk in a straight-back chair, typing some test as the sound of Ray's voice drifted down the hall from American Studies 211. Its mellow enthusiasm mingled with the clack of her old typewriter and made her want to wander down the hall to catch more of what he was so happy to be talking about. As Kevin puts it, the problem for students was that they got absorbed in the stories to the point of not taking notes on what the stories were supposed to illustrate. And, Kevin says ruefully, they would not be tested on the stories.

Undoubtedly teachers were not as solicitous in those days. They felt free, for example, to test without any real review or suggestion as to what students should study. Students, the thinking went, ought to measure up to whatever rigor was imposed by the professor. In practice some teachers tested on whims, and even the brightest students could not prepare for the occasional question coming out of a private left field. Joe Pryor, the academic dean at Harding for most of Ray's tenure, made periodic pleas to faculty to "be sure to test on only what you actually teach." At times Ray leaned in the despotic direction. Tom Howard, another former student who eventually became a colleague (and who succeeded Ray as department chair), remembers a brutal question on one upper level English History exam. The class had been assigned W. E. Lunt's massive *History of England* as out-of-class reading. On the final exam, Ray asked only one question from its 970 pages: "Henry VIII is well-known for his divorce, but there was another king who had a divorce. Name the king and discuss the details of the divorce and its impact on English history." According to Tom, Ray probably did mention the case in class, but he never hinted at its importance on the final. Pretty rough for an undergraduate to measure up to the kind of responsibility, not to mention memory, demanded by such questioning.

I think Ray learned to be a better tester. Despite his best efforts to be fair, Ray's tests remained the cause of the most severe criticism he received. Mike Cope joked that Ray learned testing under the Nazis. One of David's friends, a baseball player, took a required history course under Tom Statom precisely because he had been warned that to stay eligible, he must avoid Muncy. Fate intervened in the form of a broken hip, which Tom suffered in a fall on icy sidewalks. During his six-week convalescence, Tom's classes were taken over by several different faculty members. The baseball player got Ray. His distress gave way to delight after the first few periods, however, and he reported to David that his dad was a great lecturer. He was loving the class. Then after a couple of weeks, Ray gave the first test—his own, not Tom's. Reportedly, Tom received a get-well card the next day with heartfelt wishes for his speedy return to class.

Ray's reputation for being tough affected the manner in which some students handled meeting his deadlines for papers. Fearing the consequences for their grade of a late assignment, they sometimes went to extraordinary lengths to get it in on time. For example, a young man once rushed a paper to Ray's office only to find the secretary gone and apparently no one else there either. By the time of this episode, Ray's office was on the second floor of the American Studies Building, and once again a large space had been partitioned to provide several offices. In this case, the partitions did not reach all the way to floor or ceiling—a cost-cutting measure no doubt but one that gave the student hope. With the deadline of 4 P.M. approaching and the office empty, how could he verify that he had met the deadline? He saw the solution to his problem in the narrow space between floor and bottom edge of the partition.

Meanwhile, behind that partition, Ray was quietly and contentedly reading. He designated a reading time every day during which he was not to be disturbed by routine matters. I can picture him leaning back in his chair, feet up on his desk, enjoying a tome by Schlesinger. Imagine his surprise when he heard a scuffling sound beneath him and looked to find the right arm and leg of a human being squeezing under the partition. The hand of that arm held a manuscript. A few seconds later the other limbs followed along with the face of the intruder, whose surprise at seeing Ray, I imagine, equaled or surpassed Ray's at seeing him. Scrambling to his feet, the young man apologized profusely, explained why he took his unusual route, and apologized again.

"That's quite all right," Ray said, "but you ought to try knocking first. That's a lesson I've learned the hard way myself." The student took the point and bent down, apparently ready to crawl back under the partition.

"Uh, Kirk, why don't you just use the door this time?" Kirk thought it was a good idea.

One student didn't fare as well at squeezing in under a deadline. Harding security found this young man stuck in a window on the first floor of the American Studies Building. He had missed the official deadline and hoped that by slipping the paper under Ray's door before office hours the next day, he would "finesse" the points. The officers helped him out of the window, but the paper was late anyway. The fact that both these students have since become solid and very successful citizens testifies to the power of reputation. Under normal circumstances they were both logical human beings. Faced with the Muncy aura and prospects of losing points for a late assignment, they acted impulsively, leaving themselves with, so to speak, little room to maneuver.

General education students avoided Ray's classes his entire career, scared off by the stigma of tough tests, yet, as Rachel observes, Ray's tests seemed no tougher than Tom Statom's or Fred Jewell's. She adds that Ray's grades matched up pretty well with those of the other department members. Perception is reality, I suppose. Part of the perception of him as difficult may have stemmed from reality, however, for during much of our first seven years in Searcy, Ray was involved with his own study at the graduate level. He was thinking through some of the difficult questions about the science and art of writing history, of what history really is. He was forging maxims like the one that became so familiar to history majors: "Historians reflect the temper of their times." What he brought more and more to the classroom, especially in upper level courses but maybe to a slight degree in the survey courses as well, was historiography, the study of how history gets written. Living as a graduate student in the upper reaches of his discipline, he may have, more than others in the department, tried to lift students higher than they were ready or willing to go. He was not afraid to put someone on the spot in the classroom, to ask the difficult question.

Ray ended the '60s at Harding loved or feared by students, depending on their readiness to absorb all that he asked them to absorb. He ended the decade as a student himself, and that part of his story leads me back not to academics but to the personal and spiritual.

SEVEN

Distinguished Teacher

Graduate School of Life (1966-71)

THE LOST OXFORD SERMON

As I try to recall things for this account, time and memory threaten to defeat my best intentions. Not only do daily matters get lost in time, but also crucial events grow dim. I suddenly recall a time during Ray's doctoral work that he did something he believed was very important, something in which he felt very much an instrument of God's will. Yet I had forgotten it until my search for the past glimpsed it as a furtive form caught in a beam of light. Because I was not there and because so few survive who were, I may never illuminate it fully, but with the help of the Doug Shields family, I will try.

It involves only one summer night in 1968, and that night is not recorded anywhere in the newspapers or even in official church records. It certainly wasn't recorded on the official University of Mississippi transcript listing the courses Ray took and certifying that he completed all requirements for his doctorate in the summer of 1971. It's not something he talked about much afterward. We can't know how much of an impact it really had on the people involved, except for one—Ray Muncy. Before it happened he agonized over his role and afterward felt blessed for what he had done.

I admit that to posterity it may not be significant. The story of his time in Mississippi is mostly about doctoral course work and missing his family. Let me tell that story first and save what I know about the special night until the end, which is its proper place anyway.

In the summer of 1966, determined to earn his Ph.D., Ray packed up for Oxford, where he had been granted provisional acceptance by the University of Mississippi until he satisfied a French language requirement. He got a leave of absence for both fall and spring semesters in the academic year of 1966-67 and also spent the summers of 1967 and 1968 on campus finishing course work. He completed his dissertation, a word the children came to despise, by writing part time until 1971. For the first two semesters, Ray actually lived in a dorm—not the ideal place for a forty-year-old preacher. Despite the oasis of Christian friends in Oxford, Ray missed his family.

Back in Searcy, the children missed their Daddy and heaven knows I did too. When he could not come to us, we went to him as many weekends as we could afford. It was hectic making the then four-hour trip. In the first place, Ray betrayed his chauvinist side by worrying about me driving the station wagon in Memphis traffic, so I traveled with his judgment hanging over me. Second, it was sometimes like handling a twisting snake to get everything together for the trip. We planned to visit one Saturday that happened to be Kandy's birthday. She wanted to be with her dad on this occasion. A day or two before, though, Marc, who was mowing lawns to earn money, had broken the rear window in the wagon trying to get the mower in the back. I was lucky after three or four phone calls to get the window fixed in time to leave Saturday morning. We made the trip safely, but not before I took a wrong turn coming through Memphis and got the small children upset: "Mom, it's hot—when are we going to get there?"

"Listen, children," I said, "we are coming out of the big city now and will see Dad in less than an hour. But remember, we don't need to tell him about Mommy getting lost. He has a lot on his mind and we want him to concentrate on Kandy's birthday." An hour later Zac and Kandy began chanting "Popeye! Popeye!" when they saw the familiar campus looming in the distance. Specifically, what they saw was the top of the Athletic Center, which to the children was shaped like Popeye the sailor's nautical hat. Shortly afterward we pulled into the drive leading to Ray's dorm, and Kandy burst out with a loud , "MOM! LOOK!" when she saw a big sign in Ray's window that read: "HAPPY BIRTHDAY, KANDY." She hugged Ray tightly when he came out, but before he could release her and say hello to Zac, the little show-off blurted out my secrets: "Dad, did you know that Marc broke out the rear glass and Mom got lost in Memphis?"

Our visits were always fun, filled with news from Searcy for Ray and his tales of campus life for us. Despite being a middle-aged married man among younger, mostly single males, he got along fine in the dorm. And he loved being on a university campus to read and exchange ideas, even if he did have some bizarre teachers. His German professor was blunt to the point of cruelty. He once corrected a student who had translated a phrase as "steam machine," by saying, "That's 'steam engine,' stupid." At one point in the class, the professor began telling each student whether he would pass or not. Right out of the blue! And with still several tests to take. When the professor predicts your failure in front of the entire class, it's embarrassing to say the least. When he got to Ray he hesitated, then said, "Pass." Another of Ray's history professors actually lectured with his back to the students! After the July 4th holiday he surprised them by facing the class as the beginning bell rang. He silently counted the students, pointing at each one, and said, "Oh hell! I was hoping some of you would be 4th of July fatalities." Then he turned his back and started lecturing.

Ray didn't let that sort of attitude intimidate him. He had more practical problems than sourpuss profs. As I suggested, his schooling had created a financial strain for his family. Harding did not pay full salary during a leave of absence, so our income fell from $7,500 a year to $5,000. Marc remembers how frustrated he got as a young teenager who wanted desperately to attend the Tahkodah summer sports camp. He was showing promise as an athlete in both football and track and knew that campers would get one-on-one instruction in fundamentals. Watching his Academy friends take off for Tahkodah was hard on him. When he asked for the $50 it cost to attend, I fell back on what he says was my stock reply during Ray's graduate years: "Marc, you can't have some of the things you're used to having because our income is $2,500 a year less than it was." To soften their sense of deprivation, Ray sat down with the kids to explain the coming hardship, but it was difficult for them to understand.

With our reduced income, we faced the reality of double college expense—Ray at Ole Miss and David, who would soon enroll at Harding in 1967. In the fall of 1966, Ray agreed to preach for two congregations near Oxford: Enterprise and New Albany. He drove to Enterprise for an early service and then made it to New Albany, which was between preachers. It made for a grueling Sunday, but despite a grant and my new job, we needed the money. Besides, once a preacher, always a preacher. Enterprise paid a whopping $40 a sermon and New Albany chipped in with $45. Ray could get by with only two sermons each week, since the Enterprise lesson could be repeated at New Albany in the morning. Still, it was a challenge for him to digest the material in courses like Historical Criticism and Historiography and spend weekends in Bible study and preaching.

Everyone old enough took jobs to help out. David and Marc both worked summers and part time while going to school. I had to go back to work in 1967, my first job since Bloomington. I sold women's clothes at The Ideal Shop. With David busy in college, Marc became my right-hand man in domestic matters. He was wonderful. I'll never forget how so often, at fourteen, he patiently babysat with Kandy and Zac in the afternoons until I got home—and on Saturday. It was not easy on the children being without their father. Kandy seemed to suffer the most. She was often grouchy and irritable and ran to Ray in delight when we visited or he came home. He would call her his princess and, if possible, take her and Zac to the country, where they could enjoy his presence in a peaceful, safe environment.

During this period we also moved from Hillcrest to 1002 Hayes Street, a distance of about half a mile. Despite our financial burdens, the larger house in a newly developed area came at too good a price to turn down. Besides, the sale of our Indiana home allowed us to break even in the move. Zac and Kandy loved the surrounding trees and Gin Creek that flowed a hundred yards from the back of the house, and for me entertaining became easier overnight.

We got through it all, Ray included. At the end he endured a rigorous five-day oral examination, with questioning about a different area of history each day. To make matters worse, a late addition to the committee examining him seemed to be bent on raking him over the coals. For those who have never experienced doctoral comprehensive exams, it's hard to know what it must be like, but someone told me once to remember the worst final I ever took in high school or undergraduate college work, and then imagine that the teacher had a chance to critique each answer on the spot. And imagine further that he didn't much like me and kept bringing up stuff I'd never heard of.

Well, Ray had several days of this. By noon Saturday, after the last session, he was numb. As he headed home he realized that he had not gone to the bathroom all day, so he pulled into a Stuckey's on Interstate 55. Reliving all those answers in his head, and berating himself for things he had forgotten to add, he stumbled into the restroom and practically collapsed into the nearest stall. As he sat there in the cool silence, the door opened and footsteps sounded on the tile floor. The clatter stopped as the visitor apparently stood outside the stalls. Then Ray heard a female voice say, "I thought this was a ladies bathroom!" Only then did Ray look down and see the high heel shoes belonging to the speaker. He retracted his own feet as far as possible and waited for her to leave. He waited a long time to make sure no one else was in the room. Finally he scurried back to his car and set out for Searcy, thinking that the unknown woman's challenge had been an appropriate ending to a bad week. One more hostile questioner with him on the hot seat and stuck for an answer.

The last year of Ray's doctoral study was bearable. He stayed in Oxford only during summer sessions, so our family life returned to a semblance of normalcy. The final summer session he attended came in 1968. This time, Ray was hired as pulpit minister for the Oxford Church of Christ. Although he had preached only once or twice for them during his main stay on campus, he had endeared himself through his knowledge and occasional work with the college students at the Christian student center. The temporary arrangement meant that Ray would give two lessons on Sunday and continue ministering to college students as much as possible. He was working with the elders, primarily Doug Shields, a professor at Ole Miss and one of the most hospitable men we had ever known. When our family visited Ray, we knew where we would eat. Though other families made us feel welcome, the Shields house was our most frequent home away from home on weekends in Oxford.

Although I wasn't there to see it first hand, I know from what Ray and others have said that Doug and the rest of the eldership did wonderful work during this period. But it wasn't always easy. The summer of 1968 was a volatile time across our nation—especially in matters of race. By the time Ray resumed his graduate classes, Martin Luther King had been assassinated in April, Bobby Kennedy in early June, and racial tension was at an all-time high almost everywhere. Only five years before, in 1963, federal troops had been called to Oxford to protect James Meredith, the first black student to enroll at the University of Mississippi. Though things had settled down on the campus, Oxford was a town with unresolved problems, and the church was not immune to the sin of bigotry or the pain of rapid change.

One night that summer I got a phone call from Ray. He was in as much turmoil as I'd heard in a long time—maybe since the hunting accident over ten years ago in Bloomington.

"The elders want me to speak this Wednesday night," he began. Ray had been hired strictly for Sunday mornings and evenings, but something had come up—an emergency in the eyes of those who requested the lesson. Unfortunately, the passage of time has made the details unclear, but I distinctly recall that the issue had to do with racial tension. Based on what Ray told me and what Doug Shields remembers, I can piece together a probable context for the elders' request.

Doug was a leader on the eldership in pushing for integration, and many supported him. Inevitably, some did not. Doug does not remember it as any kind of open fight, just a struggle over separate incidents. For example, some members were known to stand by the door on Sunday mornings to make sure that any potential black visitors could be directed to the nearest black congregation—the opposite of a welcoming committee.

When Doug invited black children from a nearby Church of Christ to attend a youth program, some members saw it as the last straw. It is worth mentioning that one of the elders was also a member of Oxford's White Citizen's Council. In other words, any whiff of sympathy for integration would have upset him and his fellow segregationists. Suddenly Doug received word of a hastily called church meeting. He showed up to find a sizable portion of the congregation and all the other elders there. The man who had called the meeting delivered a diatribe against Doug's "self-willed" leadership. Then he called for Doug's resignation from the eldership. Shaken, Doug left the meeting promising to consider the demand. Although the official complaint was his so-called "domineering" manner, he remains convinced that it was a pretext to thwart his pro-integrationist efforts.

Doug considered resigning. The shock of this little rebellion forced him to reexamine his own motives and behavior. If self-doubt ever pushed him toward giving up, though, his allies helped pull him back. Doug recalls standing in his back yard with Ray, listening to the young preacher talk him out of resigning. Buoyed by Ray and no doubt others, he made his decision.

But Ray's role in the resolution of this crisis went beyond personal counseling. In an attempt to preserve unity, the elders asked him to speak to a Wednesday night service. The principal issue would be the relationship of elders to the flock. Thus his worried phone call to me: "Eloise, I haven't been able to study or sleep much since I found out about this. I don't really have time for it. I am praying that I can say the right thing, but I just don't know what to say. I'm essentially a stranger to most of these people—an outsider. I just don't know. Better pray for me, too, honey."

I tried to reassure him, of course. When we hung up, though, he wasn't convinced that it would go well. His call came on Monday, two days before the service. I wish I could verify exactly what he said on that Wednesday, but Ray's own meticulous records bear out that he did make the talk. In his ledger, there are eleven Sunday morning and eleven Sunday evening sermons (at $25 a sermon) for the Oxford church recorded between June and the middle of August. Sandwiched in between is a meeting in Enterprise. According to the ledger, Ray delivered only one Wednesday night lesson that whole summer, at Oxford, for no pay. It is titled "Responsibilities of Elders and Members," and there is no exact match for it anywhere in his outlines. I conclude that this must be the lesson he was agonizing over, and it must have had something to do with the lack of harmony at the church over race.

Ray would have used the Bible for every point he made. He has an outline of a sermon called "Elders and the Flock," which might be a clue to some of the things he said. It's a very simple outline. He begins by asking the question "Why have elders?" and answers it with Paul's directions in Titus 1:5: "The reason I left you in Crete was that you might straighten out what was unfinished and appoint elders in every town, as I directed you." This verse implies that every congregation needs elders to be complete. In his outline, Ray has the word "wanting," which is the King James translation of what the NIV renders "unfinished." I wonder why that word interested him. Maybe he saw in it a sense of our mutual dependence on each other. Isn't that the basis of life in the body anyway?

The outline consists of two major sections: Duties of Elders and Duties of the Flock. As I look at both lists, I am reminded of how simple the relationship between the two groups is supposed to be. Elders care for the congregation, and its members obey and respect them for the sake of the work they do. Yet the Oxford congregation, like so many others, had found it hard to keep that delicate balance between leaders and followers. In the cauldron of racial strife and personality conflicts, the members needed to have reaffirmed how important harmony is to the work of the Lord. If Ray's sermon that night was anywhere close to the outline I found, then he simply took them back to basics, back to the Word.

But Ray called back late Wednesday feeling that something remarkable had occurred. Maybe hearing those scriptures from an outsider was the catalyst, or maybe, as Ray told me, it was something more dynamic.

"Weezie, the Holy Spirit was with me tonight. I felt guided by a hand not my own." His message had struck a chord, and Ray was giving the credit to God. I've never known him to be so exultant about a lesson. If only I had asked him to keep a copy of it, or to tell me more details. Perhaps he was right, that it wasn't so much what he said as it was the presence of Christ in his heart—and in the room.

The following Sunday morning, Doug Shields walked down the aisle. He faced the congregation and asked its forgiveness for any "self-willed" actions he had taken. To Ray, Doug's words were amazing—this elder was humbling himself before the congregation in an attempt to heal its wounds. But he followed this gesture with a statement that made Ray equally glad. "I will not resign," Doug said.

A better man because of the controversy, Doug stayed on and fought for what he believed to be a scriptural attitude toward all people, regardless of their skin color. It sounds like a rather trite principle now, but it could be a costly sentiment in those days. Doug did leave the eldership many years later after a long career of service. Ironically, the congregation tried to dissuade him. Looking back on his career as elder, Doug says that the two best decisions he ever made were, first, not to resign when people seemed to want him to, and second, to resign when people wanted him not to.

On the matter of elderships, I'll offer one more detail from Ray's old outline and speculate a bit on it. Ray's last point was that elders have a "fearful responsibility," and thus the congregation needs to "know" them. His reference for that word is I Thessalonians 5:12, again the King James version. It has all sorts of connotations for the special relationship between elders and members. Later translations use words like "respect" or "honor" to render the meaning of verse 12. Perhaps those are more accurate. But perhaps Ray saw in the King James language a sense of the intimacy we as Christians ought to have with each other. He saw, on the one hand, the need for empathy—the ability to walk in the leaders' shoes, to understand the "fearful responsibility" given them by God. And, on the other, the need for transparent spiritual leaders who let themselves be known, who don't "lord it over" their flock.

With God's help, maybe Ray had been able to show those Christians that every divisive issue, even race, can be solved in the intimacy of our shared knowledge of Christ and of each other as members of His body. How can someone not be convicted of the need to treat all people with honor when God's word makes it the focal point of life in the church?

As I said, we may never know exactly how much impact this night had on the church at Oxford. Nothing dramatic happened right away. But we do know that the eldership survived the challenge to it and the congregation did do better in its treatment of African Americans. The segregationist elder left and started his own congregation. Change occurred as it usually does—slowly.

No, whatever happened on June 26, 1968, my husband was not a hero riding in to save the Oxford congregation. He was a preacher doing his job. Let's just say that whatever the impact of his talk, it was part of God's plan for the congregation and for Ray. Who knows? Maybe Ray's intense feelings about his lesson came in part from his own growing understanding of the eldership. He had now worked with various elders for eighteen years. Within three years, he would be asked to assume the role of elder himself, and would get a chance to live his vision of what that special servant should be. He would be ready because God had been preparing him for such a role all his life.

THE END OF THE '60S

Clifton Ganus, Jr., is an imposing physical specimen who, as president of Harding from 1965 until 1987, spoke softly and carried a big stick of optimism into every problem. Actually, his sunny disposition was more like a carrot than a stick, for he continually challenged his faculty to be positive, to work hard, to make Harding the haven for Christian ideals that it should be. The only big stick he carried was on the softball field, where he crushed the high arcing pitches of hapless students, who watched the softball fly across the road serving as right field fence and bounce all the way to the door of the old Rhodes Fieldhouse.

Like Ray, Ganus had come to Harding as a history teacher after a brief career as preacher. Unlike Ray, he came from an affluent family who had bred him to leadership. Ray and I loved his graciousness. As formidable as he was on the softball field or handball court, he was humble and deferential behind his desk or at the podium. Blessed with patrician good looks and a soothing voice, he brought a warmth to the presidency that may have been lacking in Benson's later years, and a dignity that both faculty and students respected. Stepping in as he did in the middle of the most prosperous decade in American history, with the reputation of Harding on the rise, and with his own less political persona, he seemed the perfect choice to lead the school.

No one could foresee the series of crises that would plague his first four years and that, while they may not have threatened the foundation of Harding, certainly threatened to damage the unusual harmony of the students and staff. Even the genial Clifton Ganus himself admits as much about the racial strife that briefly flared on campus, and the internal rancor that led to the resignation of one of Harding's best and most respected teachers. I don't want to be misunderstood as equating what happened at Harding in the last years of the decade to the more volatile events on secular campuses and society at large. What happened here was mild by comparison. Still, the events of those years tested the unity of Harding's loyal staff and probably forced everyone to reexamine a host of assumptions and values.

Harding had finally integrated in 1963, with very few ripples in daily life. One student at the time remembers a Mississippi girl being called home immediately by her parents, and no doubt others objected, vocally or otherwise. Nevertheless, when the administration called a special chapel to introduce the three local African-Americans to the rest of the student body, the newcomers were given an ovation. For some who had been advocating integration for years, it was a great day and seemed to reflect the relative tolerance exhibited by the Searcy community. By 1968, however, with twenty-six blacks on campus, many of them athletes, the mix was less harmonious. Some of the black students felt that they were treated unfairly. Offended by some of the rhetoric of the American Studies program, young black men toyed with militancy. Virgil Lawyer, dean of students at the time, got word at the end of the 1969 spring semester that a few black students had threatened to burn down a building. With volunteers watching from the roof of the library, the last few days of the term passed without violence of any kind.

Still, the tension wore on a community unused to these things. President Ganus himself became the focus of complaints. His supposed insensitivity to the needs of blacks led some to walk out of chapel one day. He had to suffer the further indignity of the *Arkansas Gazette's* attempt at muckraking. Smelling a scandal at a college with which it had little sympathy, the paper sent a reporter or two to cover the protests, such as they were.

Fed by television reports of racial violence all over the country, the relatively mild unrest at Harding divided students and faculty to some degree. A few younger faculty members, especially, wanted the school to move faster in its attempts at integration. They pleaded for greater understanding of the disaffected blacks; some even advocated relaxing the rules for them as they adjusted to Harding. Other staff disagreed with such suggestions and wanted to proceed more slowly in breaking down all the old racial barriers. All in all, while the school was not in the vanguard of social change, Ray was glad to see some well-intentioned efforts to support it. Race is still a sensitive issue, of course, and like America itself, Harding has never completely solved the problem of how to incorporate minorities into its mainstream. But thank God we've had men of good will who have tried in true Christian fashion to extend Harding's mission to all people.

More worrisome than those few years of racial strife was the controversy that overlapped it and, though it focused on one English teacher, brought to light the tension between religious conservatives and progressives.

James Atteberry met us the summer before our first semester at Harding back in 1964, at the party given for us by the Davises. He was charming and friendly, but it didn't take long to see that he was also brilliant. He could speak of Shakespeare and Jesus with equal eloquence. We immediately liked him for his wit and stimulating conversation. He and his wife, Ruth, joined our new circle of friends.

As Ray got to know the academic terrain better, he saw that Jim was an outstanding teacher, a model of the intellectual polish Ray himself desired. In fact, he rivaled Ray in the minds of students as a difficult teacher who did not put up with half-hearted effort. In faculty meetings and other college gatherings, Jim spoke out on behalf of his discipline and the liberal arts in general. It was he who championed the adoption of a foreign language department and pushed for high standards in grading. The small number of English majors on campus respected, if not loved, him. Additionally, he was able to attract other English teachers with impressive credentials to the department.

He also made some people nervous.

He had the same receding hairline as Ray, and the same dark-rimmed glasses. He looked and acted the part of a college professor, gazing at the world with a decorous but slightly imperious air from above the bow ties he usually wore. I'm not sure when the trouble between him and some in the Bible faculty began, but we could sense it at times from things Jim said. Frankly, he thought some members of that department retrograde in their thinking, and some of them mistrusted his overt intellectualism. From 1964 until 1969, the level of tension between the two parties rose, some siding with Jim in a subtle war of words and ideas. As one friend of Jim's told me, "Jim decided to pick a fight with these people. To him it was partly about truth, partly a game of wit. He didn't realize how seriously the other side took his game."

While this observation may or may not be at the core of the problems that disrupted the spring semester of 1969, the enmity between what amounted to two factions was unmistakable. It permeated faculty meetings, leading some teachers to be careful about where they sat, so as not to leave the impression of being "with" a certain group. Ray was like the majority of his colleagues: he did not have a dog in the fight and was uncomfortable with the tension. Fortunately for him, he was away at Oxford a good deal working on his doctorate while the clash escalated. One person who was around at the time, an acquaintance of Jim's, told me that one day while watching a track meet on campus, he was approached by one of Atteberry's known antagonists. Leaning against the chain link fence on a cool spring day, he greeted his visitor, who made very little small talk before telling him: "Your friend [Atteberry] and I don't get along very well. Everyone has forced me to be quiet, but I think the time has come to fight."

It was a chilling moment. The speaker had the weight of the conservative majority behind him. Jim had a relatively small group who, like him, had alienated some in the Harding community with their supposedly liberal views on key issues. Though opinion is divided (or not forthcoming) on what all those issues were, most agree that the catalyst for a final confrontation came in the form of a speech given by Jim to faculty members at Camp Tahkodah. In it, he used language suggesting that truth is something we pursue, not something that we possess completely.

I'm not sure how those outside Churches of Christ will understand the serious implications of such a suggestion. The brotherhood to which Ray and I had belonged our entire adult lives made absolute truth the bedrock of its faith, and that truth was found in the Bible, the unerring word of God, His once-and-for-all revelation to humans about His nature and plan. The church was founded on that bedrock. To question the nature of truth was to question the legitimacy of the brotherhood itself. In the atmosphere of the late '60s, when society seemed bent on challenging so many heretofore absolute Christian values, such a statement by a brother in Christ shook some to their very souls. It was bad enough to be threatened by outside forces like the sexual revolution, black power, anti-war demonstrators, and relativists of all stripes. To be threatened from within was intolerable.

By no means did all readers of the speech regard it as heretical. In fact, in an irony worthy of Greek tragedy, Harding's academic dean, Joe Pryor, urged Jim to give the speech after hearing him deliver it at an Alpha Chi convention. And Dr. Ganus himself read it beforehand. With the blessing of the two most powerful academic lights on campus, the speech was delivered in September of 1968. Its stated purpose was to reaffirm the concept of absolute truth in an age when it has been questioned, and to create in faculty members a needed humility in the face of such a grand notion of truth. Although later Jim would say he was approaching the subject philosophically and not theologically, his mixture of scripture and abstract philosophical concepts of truth seems in retrospect a risky strategy before a Harding audience. This audience included some uncompromising opponents of anything even appearing to question biblical truth. To his face no one said anything derogatory about the talk. Behind his back the speech was being analyzed with a hermeneutical fine comb.

His enemies now had enough to go to the college's Board of Trustees, themselves a conservative group. Eventually a special meeting of the board was called. It took place on April 7, 1969, in the American Heritage Center on campus. According to his friends, Jim went to that meeting without any idea what its purpose was. When he walked into the room to face the Board, he was told he could make an opening statement. "An opening statement about what?" he asked. So began a session that would later elicit cries of protest from many, and lead to a North Central Association accreditation team's use of the word "reprehensible" to describe the conduct of the board. Although some faculty members had been alerted to be outside the meeting room on the chance they might be called as witnesses, they waited in vain. Before an hour had elapsed, Jim Atteberry walked past those colleagues, speaking to no one. According to one description, he looked "thunderstruck." A few seconds later, President Ganus emerged from the same room to say that the faculty would not be needed after all.

Before the week was out, news of Jim Atteberry's dismissal spread. A week later, in a faculty meeting, Dr. Ganus explained in general terms what had happened at the meeting, the result of which was the Board's directive that the administration either "request [Dr. Atteberry's] resignation or take action to terminate his services." Dr. Ganus, who told me many years later that releasing Jim was the hardest thing he ever had to do, ended his report by urging the faculty to "be Christian" in their reaction.

After a long and no doubt heated discussion, the faculty prepared a statement to be delivered to the Board of Trustees. The motion by Dr. Joseph Pryor reflects the fear of most faculty members that the lack of due process in Jim's case threatened them all. If the Board had been frightened of Jim's theology, Harding faculty now feared the Board's seemingly absolute power over their lives. After some tinkering with wording, the motion was sent in this form:

I move that the faculty of Harding College through President Ganus express its deep concern to the Board of Trustees, in full recognition of the ultimate responsibility that the Board has for the College, regarding procedures that are used in investigating faculty members. I also move that the faculty urgently request that the procedures outlined for years in the Faculty-Staff Handbook be followed; namely, that a faculty member on tenure is to be notified in writing of the charges against him in advance of such a meeting, and that he is to appear before a joint meeting of the Executive Committee of the Board and Executive Committee of the Faculty for a review of the charges. I further move that according to the well-established policy for many years at Harding College that the president of the college serve as the liaison between the faculty and

the Board in order that there may be stability within the institution, that justice may be equally extended to everyone, and that
times of crisis be avoided.

It passed by an 82-19 vote. A committee consisting of Ray, Erle Moore, Evan
Ulrey, and Ed Sewell was elected by the faculty to study the goals of Harding.
Its purpose, according to faculty minutes, was "to work with the Board and
the Administration in reviewing and clarifying the aims, ideals, and objec-
tives of Harding College as a Christian liberal arts college." I have been
unable to discover what, if anything, it reported or what may have happened
as a result of the committee. Ray never talked about it specifically, and time
has dulled the memories of those still around with whom I've talked.

In the aftermath of the firing, several other faculty members resigned.
Though no longer teaching, Jim mounted a campaign to clear his name while
he pondered whether to resign or force a dismissal. Other disagreements and
suspicions were fueled by this incident. I have not talked to anyone from the
era who does not feel it was the worst time in Harding's history. Almost everyone involved was tarnished some. Feelings were running high. Tape recorders
were smuggled into faculty meetings and classrooms to ferret out unsound
doctrine or damning statements. As in the case of the racial unrest concur-
rent with this ideological dispute, or series of disputes, Harding's turmoil was
mild compared to what went on across America's campuses, where property
was destroyed and lives were lost. Yet for Christians it was an unpleasant
reminder that we are susceptible to Satan's snares, that divisive attitudes can
overcome our bond in Christ, and that fear can lead to abuse of power.

Don England, one of Ray's best friends and a wise man, once told me that
he despised the terms "conservative Christian" and "liberal Christian." With
those soulful blue eyes and fine white hair, Don looked for all the world like
one of the Bible's hoary-headed elders as he said, "I don't think there ought
to be liberal and conservative Christians. Just Christians." Sadly, in 1969,
that plea was largely unheard. Perhaps the most telling story to come out of
the Atteberry mess, one that sounds apocryphal but has been related to me
by several people who swear it really happened, occurred in that fateful April
7 meeting. When Jim tried to defend his Tahkodah speech by appealing to
Harding as a liberal arts college, a board member interrupted him to declare,
"We are not a liberal arts college! We are conservative arts school!" The
speaker was probably not typical of the group's level of sophistication, but I
wonder if the two factions represented in that room really spoke the same
language.

I tried to keep as much of the unfolding scandal as I could from Ray. I wanted him to be able to concentrate fully on his comprehensive exams, which had begun on April 6, one day before Jim's dismissal. Of course he had to know sooner or later, and when he did it distressed him greatly. He spent time talking with friends. He spent time with his Bible, contemplating the issues. Joe Segraves, away at the time doing his own doctoral program in Lexington, Kentucky, showed me a letter Ray wrote to him a little more than two weeks after the Atteberry incident. It suggests the results of Ray's meditations. It hints at his awareness of the dangers to faculty posed by the Board's action, but it shows his essential moderation on such matters. I offer it not as the definitive wisdom about the crisis, but simply as a record of my husband's priorities as chairman and Christian:

Dear Joe,

I guess by now you would have heard of the recent rumblings here at Harding. I feel that some of our colleagues have acted quite hastily in this matter and have resigned. I do not believe Harding will collapse, for throughout the years she has been able to absorb some pretty severe shocks. Now is the time for those of us who hope to build an even greater Harding to unite our efforts and begin picking up the shattered pieces.

I trust your decision to return to Harding has not been altered by recent events, for we need you now more than ever before. Your balanced judgment, academic efficiency, and dedication have brought you great admiration on the part of the faculty and students alike. I believe that we can build a strong department at Harding, but it will take a determined faculty and one that is willing to cooperate to that end. I have tried to steer clear of the polarization which has come about within the faculty, for I sincerely believe that there is room for moderation. I am confident that you will join me in seeking the middle way. I do not feel that the history department has ever been limited in the exercise of free exploration and explanation of knowledge. There is no single dogma imposed upon members of our faculty in the history department.

I think you will find that the current upheaval has to do with liberalized teaching along theological lines and it is presently devoid of either conservative or liberal political overtones. If it were a matter of political points of view, I would be all the more disturbed and seriously consider my resignation. But since it involves the future direction of the church and whether or not we should adhere to the principles enunciated by the leaders of the restoration movement, I feel compelled to remain and do what I can to maintain the ideals for which Harding was initially established.

Please let me know as soon as you can how you feel about these matters. We have been counting the days until you return. We need you now, Joe, more than ever before.

Please give my regards to Shirley and the children.

Joe did return in the fall to rejoin Ray in "doing what they could" for the department and for Harding. Jim Atteberry eventually gave up his struggle for justification and resigned, taking a position at Pepperdine University, where he taught until his retirement. It took time and some other departures for the tensions to ease, but eventually they did. Some people never completely got over it. Others refuse to talk about it even today because of its unpleasant reminders of the fallibility of Christian servants and intellectuals. What strikes me as I revisit the incident after thirty years is that the damage was not more severe.

No one should misunderstand. Jim's fall was tragic, no matter who bears the greatest blame. Other lives were affected for years to come. The legacy of the scandal for me, however, is not that a few men let their differences get out of control, but rather that the majority of men and women never for a moment let the passion of disagreement, as serious as it might be, alter their loyalty to the school or to each other. I admire my husband's letter for its moderation, its appeal to the greater cause, and its devotion to Restoration ideals, but Ray and Joe were not unique. That's the lesson of the end of the '60s, with headlines screaming revolution and panic in the streets.

To be sure, Harding changed in the decade in many ways, including the loss of its innocence perhaps, but Ray was right—the stability of the institution was never really threatened because the faculty and staff cared less about the "issues" than they did about restoring the Christian atmosphere at their school. No doubt some were motivated by conformity or fear, but most, under the leadership of Cliff Ganus, who emerged from these trials as a better president, chose a path of perseverance out of love and duty. And as Ray knew very well, those traits are as much a part of sound doctrine as any of the issues that made the end of the '60s such a sad time for the Harding community.

GRADUATION DAY

As bleak as August can be in Searcy, April and May can transform the town into a momentary garden. The same is true of Harding's campus. By early April in 1971, the pear trees around town blossomed all white, joining the redbuds and dogwoods on God's palette. Later in the month the flowers around campus were blooming, and the quadrangle, bordered by the stately red brick buildings that formed the main facilities of the campus, had turned green. The grass was pale, but the oak trees towering over the Lily Pool were a dark forest green. At the other end of the quad, near the gate that spelled out "Harding" in its crowning arch, bloomed purple irises.

Perhaps nowhere in America does spring quicken the step as much as it does on a college campus. The greenery reassures students that rebirth is real and that summer vacation beckons like a beautiful love. Love was indeed in the air, much to the dismay of Virgil Lawyer, the dean charged with enforcing college rules. If in spring a young man's fancy turns to love, better to have him attend a public ceremony than engage in private pursuit of romance. So it came to pass for as long as people could remember, that Harding women wound the May Pole.

Held on the Saturday nearest the first of May, the winding ushered in spring for Harding. It was a yearly project of the Ju Go Ju women's social club. Students voted for a May Queen, and all the other girls' clubs selected representatives to help in the ceremonial winding. Then on Saturday morning, after ballots had been counted and practices had made perfect, the festivity began. The event was sure to be well attended by students because of the competition for queen, but the spectacle of the ceremony brought faculty and staff out too.

May Day 1971 was typical. A crowd of five hundred or so, including a sprinkling of small children, gathered in a semi-circle around the white May Pole, which stood twenty feet high and was festooned at the top with blue, yellow, and white streamers. A procession of Harding coeds (as female students were known then) marched through the crowd to the pole. Each wore a long gown of white or powder blue or pink—and white shoes. At the signal, each girl picked up a streamer where it lay on the ground. She then began to walk slowly, the loose folds of the streamer coiled in her left hand while her right hand held the remaining length taut to its fastened point on the pole. Two dozen of them would then circle the skinny tower, crisscrossing in patterns designed to wrap the pole from top to bottom in pastel. The crowd murmured appreciatively at their precision marching. The girls wore solemn looks as they concentrated, their bouffant hairdos of black and blonde shining in the sun.

Later, with the pole completely adorned, President Ganus took charge for the crowning of the queen. The candidates were seated on a white wooden platform under the trees. As the crowd shifted position to have an unobstructed view, preliminary thanks to all the people who had made the day possible and kind remarks about the young ladies-in-waiting delayed the culminating moment. When the winner was announced, the president, in the spirit of the day wearing a white sports coat, placed a laurel of white on the happy girl's head, while she cradled a bouquet of roses. Students stomped and cheered and the older adults applauded. And so the ceremony ended. May had been ushered in and the race to graduation had begun.

Ray and I were among the ones politely applauding. He was amused that this ceremony, which the college community took so seriously, had derived indirectly from a pagan practice, one that migrated to the colonies in the 17th century only to be outlawed by the renowned Puritan preacher John Endicott. Ray joked that if Endicott were alive and happened upon our young Harding girls bowing before the May Pole, he would descend on them in fury and rip the streamers to shreds—and likely clap President Ganus in stocks for countenancing such frivolity.

Ray was in too good a mood not to joke at least a little. We were finishing our sixth year at Harding. In a week he would officially become Dr. Muncy when he walked across the stage at Ole Miss. It had been an arduous six years, especially the last three, spent teaching full time while writing a dissertation. On this beautiful Saturday, Ray looked relaxed in his open-collar shirt and slacks. He was wearing his sideburns fashionably long and sporting a mustache. The hair on his head was a bit further back than when he came to Harding in 1964 (although he had learned to comb it to cover some of the baldness). The smile and laugh, however, were the same, and so he was going to enjoy the winding of the May Pole to the fullest, which meant teasing about its "paganism."

I enjoyed the ceremony. It was something we seldom missed, another part of the Harding tradition of which we now felt a part. I had become a sponsor for the women's club Zeta Rho and wanted to see my girls perform. More than that, I was excited for all that was about to happen. In a matter of a week or so, no less than four of our family would go through some kind of commencement. In addition to Ray, Kandy was moving on from sixth grade, Marc was finishing high school, and David was graduating from Harding College. Only little Zac had not reached some watershed year in education.

And me, of course. But as mother and wife, I needed no diploma; I owned instead a family pride that glittered like the May Pole upon which I still gazed as we left the quadrangle. Besides, I told Ray, "I earned a share of every one of those diplomas, if for nothing else than the driving time getting all of you to and from school."

As proud and as excited as I was, the next few weeks were hectic. Kandy's little commencement came first and involved an hour on a Friday morning, but then the family, minus David, drove to Oxford on Sunday, May 30, for Ray's afternoon graduation. Marc, Kandy, Zac and I sat in the Athletic Rotunda trying to spot Ray among all the milling mass of undergraduates and grad students. I tried to direct the children's attention to where I thought their father might be, but Zac, who was ten and into sports, had discovered something that made it hard to get his attention. Listed in the program was none other than Archie Manning, the All-American quarterback from Ole Miss. To think that the legend from Drew, Mississippi, who had captured the imaginations of fans across the South, was down there somewhere, excited

The Muncy family graduates pass under the Harding sign in 1971.

Zac far beyond any feeling for his dad's accomplishment.

"Oh, look, I think I see your father!" I said.

"Mom, I'm looking for Archie!"

To Zac's disappointment, the newly married Mr. Manning did not attend the ceremony, and we had to be content watching from a distance as bespectacled Dr. Raymond Lee Muncy walked across the stage, looking in his robe like a caped insect of some kind. But we all applauded in spite of not being able to see him very well.

Three hours after we met Ray on the field for a brief celebration, we pulled into the parking lot behind the Harding Administration Building in Searcy. Inside, David's baccalaureate was half over, but we slipped in for the final moments.

Marc's big day had been the day before, when the whole family was able to see him graduate as an honor student. Then on the following Thursday morning, the family once more took seats in the auditorium for David's commencement. I sat in the balcony with the rest of the family, which was now larger by one. In March, to inaugurate this hectic spring, David had married Candy Cleveland, daughter of Harding English professor Jo Cleveland. Candy sat between me and her mother looking beautiful and no doubt eager to get this day over so that she and David could leave for their new home in Virginia. I tried not to think about their imminent departure while Ray took his place with the faculty down front. Decked out in academic regalia, the faculty looked strange and wonderful.

It was Ray's first Harding commencement as a doctor, and he enjoyed the little perk of being able to wear the doctoral hood and to put the tassel of his mortarboard on the left side, signifying his new status. No matter on which side it hung, it managed to cling to the rim of his glasses as he marched. He would flick the strands from his eyes and before he went ten steps the tassel would sway back up into the angle where rim met lens. I watched this little struggle while hordes of parents and friends strained to spot their own special one out of the group of two hundred graduates.

Our graduate, David, had hardly been around us that week, between exams and work. He and Candy needed every dollar they could get for their new life. We watched David laugh as the line of graduates paraded in to recorded hymns by Harding's chorus. It would be more than a decade before the a cappella religious songs gave way to the mellifluous organ notes of "Pomp and Circumstance." Back in those days, students had not grown quite so nonchalant about formal occasions as they are now, and I remember David catching himself short in the laugh as if someone might think him rude to snicker in the face of "Onward Christian Soldiers."

Finally, President Ganus rose to the podium on the stage and the ceremony began. First, he welcomed parents and visitors; then he introduced the person leading prayer. As the amen sounded, I started looking at the commencement program and calculating how long it would be before David actually walked across the stage. As I browsed through the names and cast an occasional eye on the children, I realized that President Ganus was mentioning Ray's name. I looked up to see my husband walking onto the stage. It took a moment before I realized, with the help of the program, that Ray was being presented with one of the Distinguished Teacher Awards. President Ganus shook Ray's right hand and placed into his left a check. Along the way I heard the figure $1, 000. The audience applauded.

I couldn't believe it, and, it turned out, neither could Ray. The DTA had been established a few years after we came to Harding as a way to honor and stimulate good teaching. Ray even sat in on some of the debates over what criteria should be used to determine the award. It turned out that the heaviest weight was given to student evaluations, and I knew as I watched him return to his seat, that realizing his students had rated him highly more than made up for all the hard work, for the fear some had of his classes, and for the demands of his position as chairman.

"Ray, my dearest," I thought as I watched the back of his head from a distance, "you have arrived! You are among the best this college has to offer. The Lord has blessed your decision to come to this place."

Soon my pride in David pushed such thoughts to the side, and I saw through tears our oldest son, who had overcome adversity to have a fine college career, receive his degree in art. Candy also beamed. The sight of her young, fresh face saddened me, for the anticipation on her features reminded me that in less than twelve hours, she and David would leave Searcy for a new home and job in Virginia. The goodbye gripped my thoughts. It was unfair to have our firstborn get married, graduate and take a new job all in the same spring. Then I remembered that today, June 3, was the anniversary of my wedding. My life had come full circle. I was saying goodbye to my son with the same mixed emotions with which my mother bid farewell to her newly married daughter in 1948.

The year 1971 was our *annus mirabilis.* Four graduates. Four lives with accomplishments behind and the promise of more to come. Later that day, after the celebration had subsided and Ray and I were alone, working in our new garden, he asked, "Does it seem like twenty-three years, Weezie?" He was digging the grass from around our most recently planted row of Kentucky

Wonders. "And come August it's six years here." Then he went back through the week, commenting on things Marc, or David, or the other children had done or said. "That Zac," he laughed, "the rascal looking for Archie Manning instead of me!" Then he stopped weeding and straightened up. It was almost dark. "I've been thinking of a passage that comes pretty close to describing how I feel today. Do you want to hear it?"

"Do I have a choice, Dr. Muncy?"

"No," he smiled. "It's from your favorite epistle, though." Then he quoted the passage from Philippians verbatim, something he could do on occasion but most of the time shied away from, as if it were almost too preacherly. The words came out not as in a sermon, but softer, hushed to fit the quiet evening and the mixture we felt of emptiness at David's departure and happy exhaustion at the day's celebrations:

> Rejoice in the Lord always, again I say rejoice. Let your gentleness be evident to all. The Lord is near. Do not be anxious about anything, but in everything, by prayer and petition, with thanksgiving, present your requests to God. And the peace of God, which passeth all understanding, will guard your hearts and your minds in Christ Jesus.

"You know, Paul wrote that from prison. I'd be ashamed if, well, if I couldn't amen what he says on such a great day. It does feel grand, doesn't it?"

"A little sad too, but, yes, it feels grand. I just hope David and Candy will call as soon as they get there tomorrow. I'll feel better when I know they have arrived safely." Ray stopped weeding and stretched. "You are a mother to the end; that's one of the things I love about you." He reached over to brush some dirt off my pants. Knowing that we had postponed the dinner marking our own wedding day until tomorrow, Ray said, "It's getting too dark to see. I don't know about you, but I've had all the celebrating I can stand. By the way, happy anniversary!"

We got up, a little stiff, and went inside. Weeding the garden could wait for a while. Tonight we felt like enjoying our harvest.

EIGHT

The Scholar Gypsy

Ray Speaks to the World (1971-85)

WHAT ARE YOU READING?

Tom Howard, Tom Statom, Virgil Lawyer, Rod Brewer, Larry Long, Rachel Roberson. He asked them all that question and more than once. It would come out of the air while students hurried past on the way to chapel, heading toward the Administration Building in the '60s and '70s, then toward the Benson in the '80s and '90s. It created pressure because the people being questioned knew that the questioner was no doubt reading something. Indeed, they suspected what only the children and I knew, that he was reading three "somethings" simultaneously. As Zac puts it: one for the office, one for the easy chair, and one for the bed stand. Thus whatever answer came out, it would not measure up, or so his companion thought.

But no one seemed to mind. After all, the questioner was Ray Muncy. Reading books was what he did. Rod Brewer once lent Ray a book that offered a feminist interpretation of Queen Elizabeth's life. An English teacher who felt the pressure I spoke of above, Rod felt good about being able to add to Ray's reading. "One day," Rod thought, "after Ray has a chance to read it, I'd like to hear what the historian has to say about the book recommended by the literary man." He was surprised the next day as he walked toward chapel when Ray fell in beside him. In his extended hand was the book: "I enjoyed it," Ray told him, "but I probably can't use it in a course."

Ray shared a love of American frontier history with Virgil Lawyer, who had come to the history department in 1971 after serving as dean of students during the late '60s. In fact, around 1974, when the department decided to add Frontier History to the curriculum, Virgil wanted very much to teach it despite not having seniority, his love of the period dating back to graduate school. Surprisingly, Ray let him have the course without discussion. As Lawyer recalls it, Ray simply announced to the group, "Virgil's going to take the Frontier and the Civil War." Virgil silently rejoiced: "I would have been happy with just one!"

Ray's own research in frontier history led him to many different kinds of books. Among those he enjoyed most were accounts of frontier dialect and storytelling, in part because in his youth and as a preacher he encountered his share of colorful speakers. Old Brother Nunn, for example, in Bloomington, exhibited the combination of ignorance and invention that exemplified frontier speech. Once when Ray asked him how he was doing, Brother Nunn replied, "I ain't no good. I just went to a chiroplasterer and he says I got three vertebells out of place."

Ray loved to share these examples of speech with colleagues. He might leave his office with his copy of Thomas Clark's *The Rampaging Frontier*, a collection of humor and manners from the early 19th century. He would nod to Rachel and stroll out into the second floor hall, then make his way to Virgil's office, where he would offer to read a particularly good passage. Virgil remembers one chapter of which Ray was fond. It featured stories about frontier preachers and ended with the sermon of an unnamed but colorful backwoods proclaimer.

This brief sermon consists of a purported exposition of each phrase in this parody of scripture: "And they shall gnaw a file, and flee unto the mountains of Hepsidam, whar the lion roareth and the wang-doodle mourneth for his firstborn." Claiming the verse can be found somewhere in "Second Chronicills and the last chapter of Timothytitus," the old preacher clarifies nothing in his "commentary," which is mostly an adventure in rhetorical improvisation. When he finally gets to the curious phrase, "Whar the lion roareth and the wang-doodle mourneth for his firstborn," he claims that it does not symbolize the "howling wilderness," but instead is a figure for New Orleans, a city full of sin. Ray loved to read aloud the phonetic reproduction of dialogue, as in this excerpt excoriating the Queen City:

> Whar honest men are scarcer than hen's teeth; and whar a strange woman once took in your beluved teacher, and bamboozled

him out of two hundred and twenty-seven dollars in the twinkling
of a sheep's tail; but she can't do it again! Hallelujah—ah! "For they
shall gnaw a file, and flee unto the mountains of Hepsidam, whar the
lion roareth and the wang-doodle mourneth for his firstborn"—ah!

Ray guffawed as he read (supporting Betty Davis's contention that his
humor was pure corn pone). The two men laughed together, not only at the
ridiculous bogus sermon, but also at the picture of robust life in a bygone era.
Like Don England, Virgil shared with Ray humble beginnings and a conse-
quent appreciation for the poor, the uneducated. These stories of the frontier reminded both Virgil and Ray of their own past, with parents and grandparents not that far removed from the conditions described in those pages,
and though the two did not miss the hard work of the frontier, they gladly
exercised a little historical imagination to revisit it in their beloved books.

SEX, MARRIAGE, AND SCHOLARSHIP

I think my husband enjoyed this reputation of his in the '70s and '80s
as a great reader, yet in the decade and a half that ended in 1985, it was the
writing of books, not the reading of them, that occupied him. In those years
he published two major books and, with research help from its members,
wrote a history of the Cloverdale, Indiana, congregation. He contributed to
several other books and wrote dozens of articles. He became something of a
specialist in 19th century utopias, traveling the country and Europe to learn
and present history—all while maintaining his courses, serving as chairman,
and helping found the Arkansas Association of College History Teachers.

Ray's first and most successful book grew out of his dissertation, which
he finished in 1971. Within two years a revised version was published by
Indiana University Press as *Sex and Marriage in Utopian Communities: 19th
Century America*. The book's title was suggested by Ray's advisor on the dissertation, Joseph Kiger, who found what Ray planned to call it—*Views
Toward Marriage*—too tame. Dr. Kiger was adamant: "Muncy, you've got to
change it. Anything on sin, sex, or the South will sell like hotcakes."
Although Ray took the suggestion because the term "sex" did convey an
important part of the book's subject matter, he worried that his fellow
Christians might consider it salacious. The book was far from "dirty," as we
used to say, but did contain frank discussion of sexual mores and behavior
among the utopian communities in question. Later, when Ray lectured on
part of the book for a Harding Elderhostel presentation, he was amused to

learn that one lady chose to sit in the lobby of the American Heritage and read the then new biography of George Benson rather than hear some of his stories about the communes. Apparently she was nervous about their content. To his relief, he never received any official complaints.

The specific thesis of the book answers a question posed by a communitarian leader: "Did any successful communal experiment ever accept marriage as traditionally constituted?" The answer for Ray is "no," because monogamy posed a threat to the aims of most communes. Whether they were religious or secular, these social experiments, like Robert Owen's New Harmony group or Charles Fourier's "phalanxes," wanted to challenge social institutions such as marriage. To many of the various communitarian leaders, marriage was part of the system of private property and individualism that had corrupted Christianity or society, depending on their agenda.

Ray took pains to write in a neutral voice, keeping his conclusions modest and his own views unobtrusive. But he wrote the book in part as a response to the various attempts in the late 1960s to revamp traditional ideas of social order. In the wake of the sexual revolution and the explosion of new communal living, the book's findings are an indirect reminder that God's plan for the family is the natural and best foundation for society. Ray does not attempt any daring new argument, but he does pull together several valuable primary sources for future study by social historians. The presentation of the material contains his own implicit question to would-be reformers of the 1970s: "What do you do with the idea of family when history proves that even the most determined efforts cannot replace it in the hearts of humans?"

The book was reviewed fairly widely, suggesting its importance as a historical work. Even *The New York Times* featured *Sex and Marriage* in its book review section, a moment in the limelight both pleasurable and painful for Ray, because the reviewer lambasted what he claimed were serious flaws in the study and what he perceived as conservative bias. He especially rebuked Ray for the book's dismissal of Margaret Fuller as a "pathetic creature" who wanted marriage in spite of her campaign for women's liberation. In using such a phrase, Ray guaranteed that anyone sympathetic to Fuller or women's liberation would come down hard on him. In the study, Ray acknowledges that communes often sought the equal treatment of women, but he does not necessarily endorse any of those attempts. This neutrality on what was very much a *cause célèbre* at the time, coupled with his less than glowing summation of Fuller's character, made Ray sound retrograde to feminists.

Ray took his lumps like a man (pardon the pun in this context), and admitted that the reviewer had some valid points. Yet he was encouraged to see other reviewers treat his work more kindly. As things turned out, the book generated dozens of other opportunities for Ray. He delivered lectures on the subject of sex and marriage in communes, he wrote chapters for other books, and he even participated in an international conference—all because other scholars had seen and approved of his study. In 1993, before his heart attack, he was looking forward to retirement as a time when he could develop a sequel to his original work. Ray's long hours of research had paid off by opening up a new world of scholarly interaction.

One later opportunity to capitalize on his status as an expert was amusing. Largely on the strength of *Sex and Marriage*, Ray was asked to write a brief history of the Kinsey Institute for an encyclopedia of foundations and institutes. I say amusing because it made Ray a little nervous to be considered an expert in matters of sexuality, and when the 1981 *Petit Jean* announced his commission to write the history, he cringed to see his name and the infamous Alfred Kinsey's together—in a Christian college yearbook no less. Coincidentally, Alfred Kinsey lived around the corner from Elm Heights Elementary School in Bloomington, where David attended for six years.

Based on what I observed of Ray in the years it took to write *Sex and Marriage*, he was fulfilling both his function as a scholar and asserting his world view as a Christian. The former purpose was primary in this case, but I do not think he separated the two functions. In order to sacrifice the family time it took to finish the project, Ray had to be motivated by concerns beyond his role as social historian. The book shows that social history cannot be divorced from the moral and spiritual history of a people. As a Christian scholar, he was reacting to a drift away from values integral to his life. I know I am speculating some here, but I will offer one more piece of evidence that this book was a subtle tribute to marriage. Between the copyright page and the table of contents page are two words in flowing script on an otherwise blank sheet: "To Eloise."

I was Ray's wife and the mother of his children, and we all had lives during the writing of his big book. I was working at the Ideal Shop selling ladies clothing. David and Candy were in Virginia, Marc was a sophomore at Harding, Kandy was a proud Beta Club member as an eighth grader, and Zac was living the carefree life of a sixth grader. Zac, a lovable little guy who occasionally dropped by Ray's office, also developed the habit of watching the evening news with Ray. Kandy, who had been taught how to play football by David and Marc, did not fit the mold of dainty femininity of many girls in her age group. Marc was doing well in school and in track at the college level. He was soon to meet Tina Kinman, however, who would take his mind off running and a lot more.

On May 11, 1974, Marc and Tina were married in Clarksville, Arkansas, where Marc would eventually set up his dentistry practice. It was a beautiful wedding, of course, but the most memorable episode for me was the preacher's emotional breakdown during the ceremony. The preacher was Ray. Thinking that his previous experience at David's wedding would make him impervious to attacks of sentiment, he had prepared personal remarks for both Tina and Marc. He made it through his speech to her with flying colors, only to choke up almost from the instant he faced his son. Afterward he apologized to Marc, but in the meantime I was hearing rave reviews of Ray's performance from the sweet old ladies of the Clarksville congregation, who considered his display of emotion very endearing.

His feelings revealed that for him marriage was more than a research topic; as father and preacher he celebrated the sanctity of the institution about which he wrote as a scholar.

MANAGING THE DEPARTMENT

Despite some change, the History Department remained stable during Ray's tenure in the '70s. Joe Segraves stayed on, but Dallas Roberts, an avuncular presence for Ray's first seven years at Harding, retired. In the meantime, as the school grew, new departmental members were added. Ray hired several ex-students, including Tom Statom, who came on board in 1967. In 1968 another new history teacher from Ray's past came to Harding, but this one was not a former Harding student. Fred Jewell, fresh from his graduate work at Indiana University, agreed to come to Harding after more than a year of persuasion by Ray. Frankly, Fred was not impressed with the campus on his first visit, and only when the school could offer his wife, Alice, a job in the English Department did he agree to come. Fred and Alice had been part of our student fellowship in Bloomington, and Ray sensed their rightness for Harding. As things have turned out, my husband proved a prophet. Both spouses have served long and well at the school and as members of the College Church.

Before the decade was out, Virgil Lawyer moved to the history department and became a fixture there until 1989. Adjuncts and others turned out to be short term, but the core of the department changed little in the early '70s.

In 1972 another former student at Harding and a political science major, Tom Howard, returned as teacher. Not long after he joined the department, he incurred Ray's wrath, such as it was. The story illustrates Tom's respect for Ray as well as Ray's propensity to turn the tables on himself even when he was the prosecutor. The problem developed because Tom preached for a small congregation in Poughkeepsie, Arkansas. The members there begged him to go hunting with them come the start of deer season. Tom agreed after relentless friendly pressure. Before making the trip, he would have to reschedule one of his classes in order to save the lecture time. The whole affair might have gone off smoothly except for one student who had missed the new arrangements and came to Ray complaining about an empty classroom on Friday.

When Tom returned, Ray jumped him pretty hard about the situation, and Tom felt terrible. Ray seemed upset at Tom's failure to notify him as well as the rescheduling of a class meeting time. It didn't seem to make any difference that Tom had not actually missed the class. Tom accepted the reprimand as evidence of Ray's high standards. But when Ray even brought it up in the next departmental faculty meeting, Tom's colleagues provided another view of the standards.

After hearing Ray's warning about the dangers of canceling class for trips, Virgil Lawyer thought for a second and said, "Why, I've done that before."

"Well, actually, so have I," someone else volunteered.

Ray looked lost for a moment at this rebellion, then, with a slightly crestfallen shrug, said, "Come to think of it, so have I." The matter was left somewhere between Ray's original indignation and his realization that flexibility matters when the faculty can be trusted.

Rachel Roberson, who became departmental secretary in 1974, remembers all the veteran teachers carrying themselves with Christian forbearance and kindness. Ray's leadership consisted in large part of never abusing their good faith. For one thing, even when he got mad, he couldn't stay that way, as the story about Tom's unauthorized trip shows. Further, Ray permitted friendship to win out over most other concerns. Members of the history department enjoyed each other's company. In the '70s Ray and I maintained our custom of having a departmental dinner each fall semester. It was typical of the fellowship among most faculty at the school, but I doubt if any group was more convivial than these men.

Ray also established a tradition of informal Christmas parties for the department, one of which produced a classic story. These parties came to be strictly for teachers. The men gathered at the departmental office for food, pleasant conversation, and inexpensive gifts. One year Ray had noticed that the newest fashion in stationery consisted of pads with the phrase "from the desk of so-and-so" embossed at the top. Those pads, and the plastic trays that served as receptacles for them, provided a nice desk display. They would, he concluded, be the perfect gift for his teachers. He placed an order for five kits (each with stationery and tray) in time for the names to be printed before the party. When the package of kits arrived from the local office supply, Ray eagerly opened it for inspection.

He was dismayed to discover a problem. The pads were too big to fit into the trays supposed to hold them. Even when he shoved hard, one edge of the pad stuck out over the rim. He couldn't believe the supplier had gotten it so wrong; he had placed the order personally with explicit instructions. Fearing that he could not get new kits before the party, he grabbed the contents of the package and drove to the business. He rushed through the front door carrying the box and headed for the first person he saw. A pleasant clerk, a young woman, watched as Ray plunked down the box with its defective trays and over-sized pads. "Look," he said, "wedging a pad of stationery as best he could into a tray, "these are too small." Before Ray could say more, the clerk picked up the pad in one hand, the tray in the other, turned the tray over, placed it on the counter, and slid the pad into its slot. With the right side of the tray now facing up, the pad fit perfectly.

Ray stared at the stationery. He looked up at the clerk.

"Oh," he said. "Never mind. Thank you." He reclaimed his package and headed for the car. His colleagues treasure the story more than the note pads.

If any dissatisfaction developed among the department members, it was that Ray did not fight as strongly for their budget as necessary. According to them, his fault was almost a virtue when they considered the attitude behind it. It might be characterized as a meekness, a timidity in front of his superiors. In other words, Ray did not have the heart to ask for extra money on behalf of the department. History had one of the school's lowest budgets, in part because it was a low-tech kind of discipline: not much beyond maps and maybe videos beginning in the early '80s.

Equipment was not the only legitimate expense of a discipline, however. The history faculty noticed, for example, how other departments used graduate assistants in the office for a variety of tasks. The blessing of graduate students came with the change of Harding's status from college to university in 1979. Not only does their presence relieve teachers of some grading, testing, and even substitute teaching, but also the students themselves get valuable experience. As the decade of the 1980s neared its end, the history department still used only an undergraduate helper—for a mere five hours each week.

Ray's colleagues knew that within the history department this need for graduate help had been discussed and that Ray had promised to ask for it. As years passed, however, none was forthcoming. Tom Howard, Fred Jewell, and others did not view the matter as cause for much criticism, having grown accustomed to the way things were. Nevertheless, they wondered why Ray, an old union man, was ineffective in getting the grad student help. Later, after he had assumed the chairmanship, Tom asked Dean Priest, head of the College of Arts and Sciences, about the lack of a graduate assistant for history. "Oh," Dean said, "you never asked." Tom protested that Ray claimed to have asked several times. "Well, he asked. But he never *asked*," Dean replied. His verbal italics on the word conveyed in a flash the unspoken rules by which a chairman must play the game. Tom got the message. He *asked* and history had its graduate assistant the next budget year.

In the 1970s, Ray's meek pursuit of money was tolerated, even regarded with some amusement, in part because the other teachers understood it as an extension of his own sacrificial spirit. Tom Howard refers to Ray as a member of the "old school," the Dr. Benson way of thinking about money. At a Christian college, it was a duty to get by on as little as possible. Benson used to return from fund raising trips with donated tape recorders in the back seat of his car, dispensing them to a grateful Evan Ulrey. As for Ray, he learned to scrimp as a child. After all, he grew up pulling greens from a mountain pasture so that he and Flara and John D could eat supper.

Though the history department rolled along with few changes in personnel and almost no dissension, it was during this period that Ray had his first experience dealing with ineffective teachers. He hated it, and probably did not act quickly or decisively enough to protect both the students and the teachers in question from undue stress. In two cases Ray's involvement with the families of these professors made his ultimate decision almost torture. Kandy baby-sat for the little boy of one such teacher, but a tragic illness took the child's life. Ray preached the funeral. It is hard to fire someone with whom you share such emotion. Afterward, when our daughter died, this teacher came to our home, remembering happier days for both families, and said, "Now my son has a baby-sitter in heaven."

It hurt Ray so much to reprimand, much less dismiss, anyone, because beneath the incompetence or the struggle with detail that plagued an occasional colleague, Ray could always see the human situation—the family in need of money or stability or comfort. As he discovered in the latter stages of his work on *Sex and Marriage*, sometimes the family in need turns out to be yours.

MOVING JOHN D

On Labor Day in 1972, Ray and I took a quick trip to West Virginia to see John D. Muncy. It had been three years since Flara died, and Ray was worried about his foster father. We knew that all his friends and family were dying off, and Ray felt uneasy about letting him live alone. His church ties were about all he had. Weakened by age and a variety of ailments, John D was getting closer and closer to being dependent on others.

Eventually we sat down with him in his new Oak Hill home. He was haggard, often rubbing his white head with his hand as he stared down at the floor. "Dad," Ray said, " I've been thinking this over real carefully and have prayed about it too. Eloise and I want you to come live with us in Searcy."

"I ain't a-comin'!" he almost yelled, sounding very much like Grandpa Joad in *The Grapes of Wrath*. And even though Ray pled his case at length, the conversation was essentially over. He had things to do, John D said. "What things?" Ray asked him.

"Well, I have to go down and tell Flara about things. She needs to hear about our story." The two had become fans of the television soap opera *Days of Our Lives*, and for a while after her death, John D visited her grave every day to share the latest plot developments, but he had not been there in months because of his disabled condition. He insisted on his responsibility, though. "You see, Mickey has this heart condition, so Laura ain't gonna leave him after all. And it's tearin' her boyfriend up—Bill, yes, that's his name. It's a mess. I don't know how it's gonna get straightened out!" Ray and I looked at each other as he recited the plot details with such passion. We returned to Searcy without him.

Before leaving, we hired someone to look after him every day and keep us informed. For a while this arrangement made us rest easier. Then in October we received a phone call from Ernest Lowery, John D's cousin. It seems that the nanny had taken several days off without telling anyone. When Ernest and his wife Chloe dropped by for a visit, they found John D lying in his own waste, a box of Ex-Lax beside him, its contents drained to fight his troublesome bowels. They found no food in the house and the old man seemed near death.

Ray did not know how, but he was going to get John D away from there. Remembering his foster father's previous refusal to go, he called again, expecting a battle. I heard Ray's end of the conversation as we stood in the space between family room and kitchen. I could see the nervousness reflected in his body language as he told John D that we wanted to come get him. A moment of silence was followed by Ray's relieved "Well, good." He hung up shortly and told me, "Dad says he's a-comin'."

Exactly how we would transport him to Searcy was another matter. He would not fly and Ray feared that his condition made traveling by car dangerous. He secured permission to borrow one of the college's nine-passenger station wagons, into which we crammed a twin mattress. Sure enough, when we put the old man in there, he was as comfortable as he could be outside an ambulance. Still, Ray worried throughout the first stages of the trip, wondering what we would do if John D worsened or even died. We left about five in the afternoon and drove at night. By the time we were almost out of Kentucky, we stopped for gas. Ray decided to get some food from a greasy spoon next to the gas station. Since we didn't want to jostle or wake John D once he got to sleep, we pulled into the station slowly and talked in hushed tones on the pavement beside the open passenger door. Inside the car the old man breathed loudly but regularly.

"Can you eat a hamburger?"

"Yes," I said, "and get me some coffee too, if you don't mind."

Before Ray could leave for the diner, John D rose up from his mattress and said, "Get me a burger and coffee too." Ray and I looked at each other in consternation. We thought he was half-dead. The old codger ate every bite of his hamburger before going back to sleep.

Back in Searcy, we fixed up the downstairs bedroom for him. He was sweet most of the time, but this new life was a big adjustment for him, never having lived anywhere else but West Virginia. The man who had once battled American troops in the hills around Logan could now only sit in a strange house in a town far away from the land he thought he was fighting for back in 1921. The man who had soothed Ray's fears as a little boy now needed someone to soothe his. The peacemaker between Flara and me all those years ago could have peace only between bouts of incontinence and diarrhea.

There were frictions for us too, of course. Ray had to give up his easy chair—the Archie Bunker chair we called it, the one that faced the television. He didn't mind that, but he did mind the odor it took on from John D's urine and defecation. We finally bought a chair for our guest and resorted to recovering it when it had absorbed enough punishment.

And the kids were embarrassed to bring friends over while Grandpa was sitting there with his coffee can spittoon in his lap, chewing the Red Man that Ray bought for him. Those trips to get tobacco embarrassed Ray (an elder in the church!), but he didn't have the heart to deny his father this pleasure. Thus eventually I was delegated to make the purchase. As if a spit can in the family room wasn't bad enough, Kandy once discovered John D urinating in it. From then on she stayed out of the family room if he was there, in spite of missing *American Bandstand*, a show he ridiculed as she watched anyway.

We tried to police John D's diet, but sometimes his bowels were out of control, and in the aftermath of an attack he was apparently oblivious to the damage he'd done. One morning I looked in on him in his bedroom to see if he was ready for a bath. Not only had he managed to soil himself and the bedding, he had also smeared the walls above the bed with fecal matter. I was almost overcome with nausea. Alone in the house except for John D, I wanted to walk out and lie down somewhere with breathable air.

"I've just got to clean it up right now!" I finally said to myself, while John D lay there very quietly. I started by maneuvering him onto some clean sheets. As I struggled with him, he remained very passive, but fully awake. Looking up at the ceiling he said, "You know old Frank Aliff's in a bad way."

"Is that right?" I began to wipe him off.

"Yes, I hear he can't do a thing for himself."

"Well, isn't that a shame," I said.

Ray had to be away for school trips in those days, especially that first summer for a commitment to the International Studies program. When he was home, he did his share of cleaning and had his own confrontations with John D. I mentioned that John D sometimes urinated in the chair or in his spittoon. Ray talked to him about that and finally the old man started making an effort to get up when he felt the urge. When he went to the bathroom, however, he urinated in the sink instead of the commode. Ray was dumbfounded and issued a severe warning never to do it again. Later, during one of Ray's trips, a morning stench from the downstairs bathroom betrayed John D's disobedience. I walked over to his easy chair, put a hand on each arm, blocking his view of the television, and stuck my face right into his: "Dad, you've pee-peed in the sink again."

"I never done it."

"You remember what Ray said, don't you?"

The old man snorted, "Just cause Ray says it don't make it no stronger."

John D often complained about living in Searcy. He would compare it to West Virginia. "I need to see some mountains!" he would say. Then he would go on and on about how ugly Searcy was. After several months of his bad habits and growing cantankerousness, caring for him became too much. In August of 1973, John D took up residence across town at Leisure Lodge. Before long, however, we got a call from Mrs. Angel, the proprietor of this rest home for about eighty elderly people. John D would have to leave the lodge, she said, because the women there were all afraid of him. It seems that Grandpa Muncy liked to run his hand up and down the legs of any female within reach. Although Ray said, "I don't think they need to be afraid; that's about all he's going to do," he understood the reasoning of the nursing home. Fortunately, about this time we learned of a Mrs. Holden, a lady who lived in Clay, near Pine View, who had an opening for an elderly lodger. Her home was clean and the care he would get seemed good. What's more, the area featured some hills, not exactly West Virginia-size scenery but a better view for the old mountaineer. John D lived out the rest of his life in that setting, dying two years later, on September 16, 1975.

It had been a long three years since we first moved him to Arkansas, and in many ways a difficult three years. We drove to Oak Hill, West Virginia for the funeral, with Zac and Kandy. Ray didn't say much during the service, but at the graveside he wept. Age had robbed John D of the gentleness that sustained Ray as a child, making it easy to forget how the ex-miner and Flara had plucked the boy from sure destitution and misery to give him a chance at life. The next day we visited the grave site a final time. I could tell it hurt him to let go of John D, the last real link to his childhood. Maybe that's why he lingered a while, welcoming memories in a mixture of grief and gratitude on a windy hillside in his home state.

Seven years later, in 1982, death would take Ray's biological father, John Jack. Over the years Ray had grown to appreciate the man, though he could never feel for him as he did for Dad Muncy. To his credit, John Jack persisted in keeping contact with Ray. He became a Christian and remarried. About a year before his death, in the presence of the two surviving sisters, Thelma and Charlotte, John Jack presented Ray with his old railroad pocket watch. He made a speech choked with tears. It seemed to give him pleasure to call Ray "son": "Son, I want you to have this…" And Ray accepted the shining gold orb and chain with gratitude, thanking God for John Jack, the prodigal father who returned, and for John D. Muncy, the father who gave him a name.

Before his death, John D played a small yet pivotal role in one of our family's most traumatic experiences up to that time. Years later it seems relatively trivial, but at the time it momentarily challenged the faith of practically every family member, especially Ray.

CHRISTMAS FIRE: LOOKING FOR LESSONS

The reflection of flashing red lights in our rear view mirror scattered the images of Christmas dancing in my head. The fire truck interrupted my thoughts of how hectic the season is, but how rewarding. Today, Saturday, Christmas Eve of 1974, had been the perfect example. I had run myself ragged but was anticipating with great satisfaction our arrival back home.

The day had begun leisurely enough with a late breakfast. The house would not be crowded with family this Christmas. Until Marc came over in the evening, Zac and Kandy had the run of the place, walking amidst presents and decorations with adolescent restlessness.

As Zac came through looking for the *Gazette*, I told him, "Don't forget we go to have Christmas with Grandpa Muncy this afternoon."

"Joy to the world!" he said, then broke into that famous melody to improvised lyrics of his own: "John D we come, to bring you cheer, and make the bathroom clean!" Mercifully, his invention failed, so he started humming the tune. It had been over a year since we decided to move John D out of our home, but Zac still remembered the occasional hassles and couldn't resist an attempt at satire. I couldn't blame him for having mixed feelings about his grandpa. He and Kandy could once again enjoy their home, a fact which helped Ray and me find peace with our decision to move Dad Muncy. Since we planned to be at Mrs. Holden's by 3 o'clock for our visit, I would need to hurry to get everything done. By 2:30 that afternoon I was still hurrying, trying to collect all the presents to take on the trip.

The gift exchange at Clay relaxed us all. Grandpa enjoyed the gifts and the company. Mrs. Holden loved her gift, too. I could tell that Ray felt good about doing this little duty and having all of us take part. On the way back home, I was marveling at the prevailing Christmas spirit and, I confess, admiring the image of our house, with all its holiday decorations. Though I was thanking God for this home, now ours for nine years and one that fit us so well, I suppose I was congratulating myself too, on our beautiful tree, decorated with everything from tinsel to glass-blown ornaments, and on the wreaths hanging from door and window, and most of all on the beautiful candles placed around the house. Then flashing red lights spoiled my reverie.

"Dad, it's a fire truck!" Zac shouted.

"That's the slowest fire truck I've ever seen!" Ray said, watching the vehicle turn from Main onto Moore behind us in the near darkness of late afternoon, a light rain turning silver in its headlights. It did seem odd that the truck was going so slow if there was a fire. Never offering to pass us, the driver almost appeared to be looking for a place to turn.

"Oh, isn't it a shame to have a fire on Christmas Eve!" I cried. I pictured a little shanty with a brood of hungry children running around. The 10 o'clock news would probably blame an overturned space heater for the blaze. It made me sad.

The truck stayed behind us all the way to Hayes, but continued east on Moore as we turned left. "That's strange," I said, as if the tiniest pebble had been tossed into the calm waters of my mind. When we started down the long hill leading to our house, the ripples got larger.

"I see smoke coming from the bottom of the hill," Ray said. I still couldn't believe it: "Isn't that fog?"

"Hey, there's a bunch of people in our yard!" Kandy and Zac yelled.

Now within sight of 1002 Hayes, we could see that the smoke was coming out of our house. As we pulled up, Ben Berry greeted us almost in relief:

"Boy, am I glad no one was at home! I was ready to break out a window to make sure someone wasn't inside. We called the fire department, but they haven't shown up yet."

"They missed the turn," Ray said.

"Where's the fire?" Zac asked. It was strange to watch the house because no flames were visible, just billows of smoke. Within seconds flashing lights illuminated our yard as the fire truck pulled up. Several men dispersed, unreeling hoses and circling the house. Quickly Ray asked the firemen if we could try to retrieve some presents, but they said it was still too hot. It now dawned on us that if we couldn't salvage any presents, Christmas was spoiled for the children. "Tell me what stores are still open, then, so I can go buy more presents!" I frantically asked anyone who might be listening.

By this time the firemen—who were volunteers on duty for the holiday—had already checked the house. One of them emerged from the garage.

"I can see the presents," he yelled. "I think they're okay, and I think we can get them out now just in case." He escorted us inside. The air was still smoky and the walls were stained, but except for the kitchen, not much of anything had been ruined. The top of our tree was singed. On the floor near the presents glittered a tiny Christmas tree pin, a present from Marc long ago that had hung from the tree. I snatched it up immediately. Meanwhile, someone grabbed a present and handed it to Stan Green, who handed it to Betty, who handed it to Bob, who handed it to Ben. Ray and I realized that a host of neighbors had shown up and were forming a gift brigade. The line extended from inside our family room all the way to

Dottie and Carl Lindsey's front porch, while Dottie fed Zac and Kandy inside the house.

Inside our house Ray and I assessed damage and took inventory. We arrived back at the Lindsey porch when almost all the presents had been placed there. Ray stopped, seemingly lost in thought for an instant. Then he bent down and started plowing furiously through the boxes: "One of my gifts is lost!" His moment of panic ended when he secured a tiny box from the pile. I found out later that it contained an opal ring for me. The children came out and danced around the recovered presents.

By the time the fire cooled enough for a more complete survey of the damage, it was too dark to see much (no electricity). After fearing the worst when smoke filled the sky, we were actually relieved to see how relatively little damage had been done. The kitchen and utility room appliances were ruined. I lost a painting or two, all of my recipes, some of which had been in my grandmother's original hand. Yet almost all of our possessions remained intact. The major problem was smoke damage. Only an adjustor could tell us what insurance would replace, but in any case a major renovation of the house seemed mandatory. It would be a while before we lived there again.

The inspection revealed the cause of the fire too. Some of my precious candles. My favorite arrangement featured a bowl of bayberry oil with floating wick candles. I lit them in the morning, never thinking of them again in the rush to get out to Clay. My mistake was to let Christmas paper fall in the bowl. The fire must have started minutes after we left home. Needless to say, I was crushed. Ray heard the cause from the firemen without a word. He was very quiet the rest of the evening.

Before we left for the motel, a flood of sympathetic friends came carrying food or offers of help. It was a little overwhelming. Only six hours earlier I had been sympathizing rather smugly with the poor victims of the fire. Now we were the victims receiving invitations from friends to spend the night with them. In the general melee, Kandy heard these offers and made a U-turn away from us.

When Ray and I could be alone with her, she was crying. Standing amid all those offers of charity, she had suddenly been hit with her own status as victim. What hurt the worst was the loss of her recently redecorated room, which she and I had worked on together. "We just did that room and now it's ruined!" she bawled. Ray winced at the force of her lamentation.

Trying to console her, I said, "Kandy, don't cry. We have insurance and can replace those things."

She stopped abruptly: "We have insurance?"

"Yes," we have insurance."

"I didn't know we had insurance." Then in a firmer voice she added, "But I don't want to spend the night with anyone else."

Ray asked, "Why not, princess?"

"Because I don't want to be a charity case! I mean, if I have to go because of the money, I guess—" Her voice trailed off.

Ray said, "If it makes you feel any better, the insurance will pay for time in a motel, too. So you don't have to go. I'll tell everyone we're staying at the Holiday Inn." Looking even more relieved, she went in search of Zac. As Ray prepared to go back to our visitors, he said, "We need a family council."

It was Ray and I who had the council, later, at the Holiday Inn, where we moved into adjoining rooms. With Zac and Kandy asleep in the other room, Ray and I lay in bed to assess the day's events. I had noticed his subdued nature during our pep talk with Kandy. Alone with me, he let his full feelings show. He was depressed, worried that the insurance would not cover all the costs. He was especially worried about the carpet. "What if they pay only to have it cleaned? Weezie, it needs replaced entirely. If we have to pay for that, I don't know where the money is going to come from." He seemed fatalistic about our chances of coming through the ordeal solvent. Even I, unversed in finances as I was, knew that we would be okay. I can only surmise that Ray was feeling the burden of his role as provider. As a rule he preferred not to think about money at all; now he was obsessed with a fear of losing ours. I decided to play the role he typically took—Barnabas to a worried companion.

I started by reminding him of the many gestures of good will we had received that day. Several different families volunteered to transport portions of our frozen food to the freezers of J&J Beef. Its owners, Jackie and Jody Taylor, offered their equipment free until we could reclaim our provisions, a value worth at least $200. Good old Ben Berry, among the first on the scene at the fire, had provided lots of those sturdy egg cartons made by International Paper to help pack up our things. My final argument against his depression came from an incident earlier in the day, when Marc and I surveyed the damage together. After staring at blackened walls and smoky curtains, we found our way to the back yard. Like Ray, Marc was low.

I said, "Marc, God uses the strangest ways to slow us down, doesn't He?"

Our college senior, an honor student and a good kid, thought for a moment before saying, "Mom, we haven't had much in the way of trouble." He was right, of course.

"You know," I said, "I don't think I've ever been more prepared for Christmas morning than I was this year. I have been so preoccupied with small details. I think I needed to be reminded of who is in control." He smiled and nodded. We gazed at the house until Marc broke the silence.

"That reminds me. What are we doing for Christmas dinner tomorrow?" I shuddered at the thought of my cinnamon rolls, yule log, and glazed ham all stained with smoke. "We'll give our meal a try!" I laughed. Marc had begun his recovery, I could tell. He was not going to brood about the situation.

As I finished the story, I said, "Honey, don't you brood either; we'll be all right." Ray had tears in his eyes. "Let's pray," he said. And we did, far into the night. When we went to bed, however, he had not shaken his anxiety.

Christmas Day came and went. My ham and side dishes were inedible, incidentally, "double smoked" as someone said, so at the insistence of Bill and Lil Harris, we enjoyed a great Christmas dinner in their home. We went to church where still more sympathy was showered on us. We joked at our predicament, but although Ray put on a good front, I could tell he was still gloomy.

The next day Mae Anne Tucker, wife of Harding's chief business officer, opened the front door of their house on Harding Drive to a forlorn Ray Muncy, come to ask about temporary lodgings on campus. When she first saw him, she thought he had come to report a death in the family. Her husband Lott quickly arranged for us to live in the married student apartments until the remodeling was finished. For three months a tiny apartment there was our home. On March 12, 1975, we moved back to 1002 Hayes.

No one moment snapped Ray out of his depression. His spirit was refreshed in stages, and he always put on a better face to others than he did to me. The closest thing to a dramatic turnaround came when the insurance adjustor told us the company would pay for new carpets. This news was not exactly a dove descending from heaven, but we felt it was an answer to our prayers that night at the motel. Maybe the work of restoration itself brought him out little by little. The busier we got, the less Ray played the part of destitute sojourner. Life became a matter of resuming our routine as spring semester classes began and of accepting, day by day, our daily bread.

It was curious how much harder Ray took the fire than the rest of us. We all struggled to some degree, but he lingered over it longer. In a way, we saw it with more unclouded vision. Ray seemed bogged down in money concerns for maybe the first time in his life. I worried too, of course, but used most of my energy to encourage him. Zac and Kandy displayed the most unfettered view of the Christmas fire. Their relative innocence helped them accept the obvious lesson. It was Zac, echoed by Kandy, who later named the Christmas of '74 as his best: "The fire taught me that there were more important things than presents."

So what did God intend Ray to learn from the fire? Was it patience? Was it dependence? Was it a fuller measure of the traits God had already blessed him with? The grand lesson, if there was one, might be the simple principle of how God works on any of His servants—one decision at a time. As one old preacher put it, "It's called growth, son."

March 12 was cause for celebration. Zac and Kandy had grown sick of the apartment, christened "the prison" by Kandy for its concrete and metal spareness. On the morning of our move, we awoke to a snow-covered Searcy. Going back and forth became more difficult, but we loved it. At dusk, with all the essentials restored, we used the one new feature in the remodeled home—a fireplace. Ray could not let the irony pass unnoticed: "We need a place to keep our fire," he said, "and this is much preferable to what we tried before." Soon we gathered around a roaring blaze, drinking coffee and hot chocolate. With snow on the ground and a warm fire in the hearth, we celebrated the Christmas we foolishly thought had been missed.

CITIZEN OF THE YEAR

The fire was a major interruption in our lives, but despite his brief emotional struggle in its aftermath, Ray did not let it affect his work. He stayed extremely busy for the rest of 1975 as he did throughout the decade. Though family events like Marc's graduation from Harding sweetened his life, he threw himself energetically into work.

Ray would continue to write and lecture on communal living for the rest of the '70s and into the '80s, but he acquired another book project soon after the publication of *Sex and Marriage*. During his first decade in Searcy, Ray had not been in an ivory tower. He made friends in the community as a member of the Kiwanis Club, as a speaker at banquets and 4th of July celebrations, and as a concerned citizen. Therefore it came as no surprise when he was asked to write a bicentennial history of Searcy.

The idea for a history dated from the spring of 1975 in a Searcy Library Board meeting. The Bicentennial Committee soon got behind the notion, and Mayor Leslie Carmichael and the city council agreed to fund half the project. The other money came from government grants and private donations. Lee Biggs, chairman of the Bicentennial Committee, wanted a competent writer for the history, which had to be completed in one year to be ready for bicentennial celebrations.

Biggs no doubt knew of Ray's work in history, but it was Mayor Carmichael who really knew him personally. The two were in Kiwanis together, and the

Ray delivers a 4th of July address on the Searcy courthouse square.

mayor had called upon Ray to deliver talks to various civic groups. In short, Ray knew the right people. His price was also right. Ray wrote the history *gratis*. He spent a year of his life doing the research—while remaining a full-time teacher—but felt he was fulfilling a civic responsibility as well as a Christian one.

Ray set up headquarters in the Arkansas Room of the Searcy library, where he taped note cards to one of the walls to create a chronological chart of the city's history. As a non-native, he depended heavily on newspaper clippings , donated photographs, and personal stories. In this sense the project was truly a community effort. Almost two dozen volunteers helped research and file material. If Ray ever felt pressure, I saw no evidence of it. He did work nights frequently, and the time constraints forced him to write hurriedly. He knew going in that it would be difficult to polish his prose, and the book reads more like a compilation of events and people than a synthesis and interpretation of them. Still, he managed to evoke a distinctive spirit of the "frontier town that grew up with America," as his subtitle put it.

When the book became available on July 4, 1976, Searcians celebrated with a ceremony in Spring Park, followed by a book signing for hundreds of people. Some civics teachers used the book in their classes. Perrin Jones, editor of the *Daily Citizen* and one of Ray's helpers on the project who became a friend, wrote a glowing review of it. Others offered praise too, and a year later, the National Association of State and Local Histories presented the book with a National Award of Merit. The most meaningful award came from the Searcy Optimist Club, which in 1976 named Ray the town's Citizen of the Year. It was quite an honor for a West Virginian who had lived in Arkansas for only twelve years.

I suppose Ray became something of a celebrity at the time, as much as anyone can be in a small town without winning a state championship or killing somebody. School officials at the nearby town of Bald Knob may have coveted the presence of author and Citizen-of-the-Year Ray Muncy when they asked him to judge a beauty contest sometime in the late 1970s. Unable to refuse but uncomfortable with the obligation, Ray talked me and Gary Elliott (Harding English department) and Gary's wife, Cheryl, into joining him as judges. We drove together to the school and sat in front of a stage where junior high and high school girls paraded by in formals. As we eliminated candidates during the pageant, the crowd started showing some disapproval of our choices. In the backs of our minds was the reputation of the town, which at the time, fairly or not, was known as a rough place. A few years earlier, shortly after we had moved to the area, Kandy said a prayer in which she included a petition for "our boys fighting in Bald Knob." What she had meant to say was "our boys fighting in Vietnam," but in her child's mind the propaganda about Bald Knob got mixed in with what she knew about the war.

Ray and Gary were not quite that credulous, but the catcalls and occasional booing made them nervous. After declaring winners, we retreated to our car and headed for Searcy, not wanting to wait for a chance to test our impression of the crowd's dissatisfaction. On the way back the two men, sitting in the front seat, became convinced that a car was following us. "Why did you vote for that one girl?" Gary asked. "She was the ugliest one on stage!" Ray answered, "She looked like she could make good cornbread." Cheryl and I laughed ourselves silly as the guys imagined scenarios of violence at the hands of Bald Knob ruffians. The car followed us into Searcy, down Race, onto Moore and all the way to Hayes—our street—causing true anxiety to mingle with the joking. But the car did not turn behind us at Hayes, and soon we were safe within our homes in Sunnyhill, appreciating the confines of Searcy and wondering how we ever let Ray talk us into judging a beauty contest in the first place.

The year 1976 was a good one for Ray. In addition to finishing the book and earning Citizen of the Year recognition, he was named a Distinguished Teacher for the second time. In many ways Ray was at the pinnacle of his career, and his happiness showed. Between the writing of his two books he had squeezed in two trips to Europe, along with art professor Elizabeth Mason and others forming the vanguard of what would eventually become Harding's Inter-national Programs. Unfortunately, this incarnation of the future existed for only two years before running into funding problems. While it lasted, Ray and Elizabeth had so much fun teaching in European settings that they irritated some of the students. Steve Davis, son of our long-time friends, Kenneth and Betty, amazed at how much energy Ray could muster to talk about ancient religious architecture, promised half jokingly that if someone would divert Ray, he would run ahead to the next town and burn down the churches to forestall any planned lecture.

These journeys only whetted Ray's appetite for more cross-cultural experience, and in 1981 we would be among the second group to go to HUF, the Harding University in Florence program. Such travel became a regular part of Ray's life in the decade of the 1970s and into the 1980s. His favorite trip came later and marked an unofficial end to this era of scholarship.

IN THE HOLY LAND

In May of 1985 Ray flew to Tel Aviv for the International Conference on Kibbutz and Communes, at Tel Aviv University. He delivered a paper based on his book *Sex and Marriage in Utopian Communities* and did research for a comparative study of the modern kibbutz and American communes, intended as a sequel to the book. The conference invited only two Americans. Since it was by invitation only, spouses could not attend.

The trip was more than a chance to engage in additional research. Under the auspices of the conference, Ray would be able to visit the Holy Land for the first and what turned out to be the only time. Although he enjoyed the company of fellow conference attendees, Ray made the sightseeing into a personal spiritual journey. He witnessed the sad evidence of Arab-Israeli conflict and saw the commercialization of biblical historical sites. But political and social eyesores could not spoil his sense of wonder at being in the cradle of Christianity.

He delivered his talk on "Sex and Marriage in Utopian Communities" on Monday, May 20, as part of a workshop session on family. The talk went well, but his real interest was in interviewing members of the kibbutz, or the Jewish version of communal living, for his new study. He left recordings of those sessions.

The interviews, conducted in individual apartments at several communes, are informal, with young children interrupting in Hebrew. Ray's voice is softer on these personal encounters than in sermons or chapel talks, but it is still rich. And as the interviewees responded, he had a soothing way of saying, "I see" or "Yes."

For selfish, not scholarly reasons, I include one excerpt from the four interviews he brought home. It is with a very frank and charming couple. The wife, Rosaria, speaks in one of those small, pinched voices that you can envision as modulating into a wail of anger or grief. She answers forthrightly. Having written in his book that many American communes tried to enforce a kind of unisex dress code to diminish sexual desire among members, Ray notes that Rosaria dresses "more effeminately" than most women in the commune. He asks her about this decision. Rosaria says that she values choice, that everyone was not meant to be exactly alike. At times her husband has to translate the questions and her answers. Children can be heard in the background. When Ray asks if she ever gets jealous, Rosaria is passionately playful with her answer:

"Many times! Every day!"

After a brief silence she adds, "I don't like him looking at young women, especially the volunteers." She waits again as if building emotion.

Finally she says, "I can't stand it." Ray has begun chuckling by this time and the volume of his laughter increases with her repeated expressions of dissatisfaction.

"Even one little look! I want him to see only me!"

At this point the husband interrupts to say that he has dark glasses so he can look without getting caught. Ray is close to an all-out belly laugh as he observes the interplay between the couple, each flirting a bit with the other during the answer.

"Ha ha ha ha ha ha," Ray laughs, "I see!"

As the interview progresses, I hear the reporter, the scholar, and the fundamentalist in Ray's probing. In this and other interviews he sought to understand the degree of commitment on the part of kibbutz members, both in and out of marriage, sometimes getting answers offensive to his beliefs. Yet he obviously enjoyed being with these people. Listening to the tapes, I realize, sadly, that this is my only record of Ray interacting with others. I am hearing again the warmth he exuded, the love of people.

Even more than his research, the land of Israel itself energized Ray on this trip. His spare moments were spent in absorbing and recording the sights and sounds of the country, first at Yad Tabenkin during the Shavout festival, or festival of first fruits, then on his journey through the famous landmarks of a world rich in history.

He brought back dozens of photographs and recordings of music from two different Shavout festivals. Those photographs and recordings remain as shadows and echoes of the joyful story he told when he returned to Searcy. What follows is my rendering of those sights and sounds as I pore over his memorabilia from the trip. Poor substitutes for Ray's telling, they remind me of his face and voice as he shared his journey with me.

Ray took pictures of the austere Golan Heights. He photographed a kibbutz at Daphne on the Lebanon border: beautiful trees just beginning to bloom bowered a sidewalk and young girls danced in white swirling dresses. One song was very recognizable, fast-paced, joyous but with that Hebrew sadness or drivenness or intensity in it too. He heard Shavout music at the Godot kibbutz, featuring a haunting solo in Hebrew by a woman accompanied by guitar. Then at Godot he heard the same tune as at Daphne—lively, sung by a group this time. It's a melody suggesting pride. Israeli soldiers sat on the ground around the outdoor stage watching the dancers and listening to the songs. An Egyptian tank was displayed in the kibbutz.

He floated in the Dead Sea, obeying the posted rules: "Don't attempt any breast stroke. Your head might sink and it's dangerous." He shot the desert around Jericho. He traveled through Hazor, to Masada; he saw the Ebenezer and a first-century olive press ringed by a small stone wall. He walked the streets of old Jerusalem with traditional markets featuring garments and vendors, old hooded women driving donkeys through one-way stone streets, and a Kodak shop. He watched wrinkled, bearded men with yarmulkes standing and sitting at the wailing wall with their pocket-size scriptures resting on crevices in the massive stone blocks. He saw a bar mitzvah.

He shot the narrow Jordan River in its winding path south of the Sea of Galilee. He stood by its water in his two-toned green and maroon golf shirt and white sailor hat. He visited the reputed site of the Sermon on the Mount, the Mount of Olives, the Kidron Valley (Jehosaphat's tomb), and Damascus with its stone gates and narrow streets. He photographed an olive tree in Gethsemane. And, yes, he retraced the steps of Jesus along the *Via*

Dolorosa to Golgotha, which really does look like the place of the skull if viewed from below, with dark holes carved by time in its ravaged stone side, staring like hollow eyes of death.

God blessed my husband with this trip. It was a respite from family and professional concerns. It promised future work in his area of expertise. It allowed him to luxuriate in the Holy Land, to reflect on the geography of his faith, as it were. He came back renewed for whatever challenges lay ahead.

THE DEMOCRACY OF LEARNING

I have attempted only a brief and partial account of how Ray talked to the world through his writing and speaking. For some, such subjects may seem dull enough to wish for even less extensive treatment. For anyone who values history, however, my husband played a small role in an ongoing vital job—the preservation of the past. Speaking as objectively as I can, I admire his work. It will not place him in the highest rung of the profession, but his labor has benefited and will benefit students in places beyond Harding.

Take for example, Ray's contribution to Frank McGill's *Great Lives from History: A Biographical Survey.* Thanks to the book on communes and other writing connected to it, Ray was asked to do profiles of four historical figures: Thorsten Veblen, John Peter Zenger, James Conan Bryant, and Louis Agassiz. During the academic year of 1985-86, he wrote a 2,000-word entry for each man. In 1987 the book was published. I wonder how many people in the years since its publication have been introduced to one or more of those influential men by reading Ray's entries? How many book reports used this basic source? How many students got their first desire to study natural history because of Ray's summary of the life of Agassiz? Or how many learned something of Veblen's theory of "conspicuous consumption" because Ray's entry was in their library? Or did some budding Bob Woodward find inspiration in reading about the Zenger trial, the "morning star" of American liberty and free press?

In these essays Ray relied on previous scholarship. His task was to condense reams of material into 2,000 words and supply a suitable bibliography for those who might want to study further. In the great scheme of institutionalized knowledge, such a contribution is modest. It is the ground-breaking specialist who earns his own place in history books. Unfortunately, most readers never make it to the landmark book or essay, and if they do, they likely can't get through the technical language. Much of Ray's work was like his politics and religion; he served the ordinary person. He provided the general reader with knowledge or the student with a foundation on which to build more specialized expertise. I am proud of my husband for his role in the democracy of learning.

It takes thousands of men and women like Ray to codify what we know into a form accessible to the public. All those encyclopedias and dictionaries and bibliographies and biographies require an army of faceless academics to make them available. Only my academic was not faceless. He was a small, balding man with a beautiful smile who took on this assignment as extra duty. During that academic year he read dozens of books on these four men while teaching his full load of classes and serving as an elder and trying to parent one of his children through a heartbreaking divorce. And he was home every day by 5 to see his wife. He was paid $400 for his trouble.

I think he loved every minute of it.

One of Ray's friends, an English teacher, said that Ray reminded him of a character in Chaucer, a clerk (scholar) who is described in the general prologue of *The Canterbury Tales* as poor, spending all his money on books, too unworldly to have any power, and always in prayer for the souls of others. The final and, for my purpose here, greatest compliment paid to the clerk consists of a very simple statement of his creed: "Gladly would he learn and gladly teach." The drive behind Ray's accomplishments during his "renaissance" of the 1970s and early 1980s comes down to that twin desire.

But I take my chapter heading from another poem. Mathew Arnold's "The Scholar Gypsy" is about a scholar who ran away with the gypsies and thus preserved himself against the "disease of modern life." The allusion has both ironic and straightforward relevance. Ray did not run away from the world during the 1970s; on the contrary, he conversed with it and partook of it. Like the hero of the poem, though, he retained a delight in what he did that made him seem forever young in those days. After all, he traveled with gypsies in his boyhood too, and in his scholarly journeys, literal or intellectual, he explored life with a boy's pure passion for discovery:

> But none has hope like thine!
>   Thou through fields and through woods doth stray,
> Roaming the country-side, a truant boy,
>   Nursing thy project in unclouded joy,
> And every doubt long blown by time away.

NINE

Second Honeymoon (1981)

GETTING THERE IS HALF THE FUN

It started in our own cozy home on 1002 Hayes Street, surrounded by all the things dear to us and by memories of the many going-away parties. Best of all was the family dinner with Zac and Kandy—Chinese pepper steak and Moo Goo Gai Pan. The two children were almost deliriously silly at dinner, maybe because they were anticipating living at home without Dad and Mom for a few months (although we had a neighbor all set to check on them regularly). Marc and Tina called to say goodbye, as did David and his kids. After the pressure of getting ready, those last few minutes of my last night in America seemed dreamily pleasant.

The next morning we had everything loaded by 7:30 A.M. of what would be a long and exhausting day. We met up with Carl and Frankie Mitchell, our faculty partners in the adventure of chaperoning two dozen Harding students during a semester in Florence, Italy. After delays in Little Rock and the flight to Chicago to catch a 747 KLM plane, we finally headed nonstop for Amsterdam. Ray and I folded the arm rests on the seat to make a bed. We were drowsy over Lake Michigan, falling asleep over Canada, and oblivious to the charms of Iceland. Warm under KLM blankets, we even ignored the oohs and ahhs of students and slept through the Northern Lights.

We touched down in Amsterdam on a cold February morning with light snow on the ground. After one day in the city of Rembrandt and Anne

Frank, we took a night train along the Rhine River, heading for Florence (Firenze), Italy. Luzerne was unearthly in its frozen beauty: deep, fluffy snow sprinkled with evergreens at the foot of rugged mountains.

Eventually the countryside grew hilly and green, and there it was—Firenze. Our first look was hardly romantic: aside from the train yards, we saw only the backs of decrepit apartment buildings, five or six stories high, each floor with balconies from which hung laundry—enough to furnish (dirty) underwear for an army, it seemed. Finally, about three blocks from the station, we glimpsed the famous Florence Duomo (cathedral), or the dome that crowns it. This dome, designed and built onto the cathedral in the early 15th century by architect Filippo Brunelleschi, looked like a brilliant red egg shell hugged by vertical arms of limestone ribbing, with a white cupola at the pinnacle. By the time the covered platforms of the train station blocked our view of the duomo, the cold fire of its red brick had burned away images of dirty laundry and made us feel we had truly arrived in Italy.

All twenty-eight of us managed to get away from the station with baggage intact and soon arrived at number 24 Via di Spadini at the Scuola Biblica at Scandicci, the home of Harding University in Florence, the HUF program Ray had helped start. After dinner Carl directed someone to drive Ray and me to our apartment on Claudio Monteverdi Street.

Number 69 Claudio Monteverdi was a two-story Italian stucco, right on the street. Its entry way had a beautiful Italian marble surface, and the rooms were small but comfortable. We awoke to a chilly Sunday morning and soon found that the tiny, steam-heated kitchen was warmer next to the burner, beside which we huddled to eat Melba toast and fresh sliced apples. Before long, Bibles in hand, we were on the way to our first church service in Italy.

DO YOU KNOW THE WAY TO MONTEVERDI?

When Ray and I left Claudio Monteverdi for Porta di Prato and on to the Scuola, our confidence soared because we took a bus—number 27—with no problem. Maybe being without a car would not be so bad after all. Making the right bus connection had not been that hard.

The morning service was a mixture of comedy and inspiration. The comedy was provided by Ray and Carl Mitchell, who showed up wearing the same outfits, both bought at a sale in Cothern's department store in Searcy. The inspiration came courtesy of our worship in the "summer" sanctuary when we stood under its domed ceiling singing "O Lord, Our Lord," as a skylight let in the harsh winter sun.

After evening worship and fellowship at the Scuola, we left for our bus stop that evening, planning to retrace our morning path. Nobody told us, however, that bus 27 did not run from the Scuola to Firenze on Sunday night. So there we stood on a Scandicci street corner, waiting and waiting and waiting.

Suspecting nothing out of the ordinary at first, Ray saw a photo booth nearby and suggested that we have our pictures made. We needed them for bus passes anyway. He approached the machine and, thinking he saw a sign that said "change," inserted a 500 lira bill. Instead of the sound of change being made, what he heard was the sound of pictures being snapped by a camera hidden in the machine. The first snapped his face looming right into the lens as he inserted the money. The second picture caught his glasses falling across his nose as he bent forward trying to figure out what was happening. As the third photo was taken he finally understood his mistake and managed to strike what he thought was a serious pose for the fourth and last photo. It turned out to be the silliest looking one of all.

When the photos emerged from the booth, Ray and I burst out laughing. I think it must have been a release of all the fatigue and tension of the trip, or maybe it was the excitement of being alone together in a strange place. But we lost it. We could not stop laughing. We waltzed around in hysterics on the street, tears streaming down our faces and guffawing like a couple of teenagers at the thrill of doing mischief. Fortunately not many people were on the streets at that hour. Later, we sent the pictures to Kandy, who put one on the fridge with a caption: "Would you buy a used car from this man?"

After our mirth subsided, an Italian passerby made us understand that we would have to go to another bus stop to get to Claudio Monteverdi Street. Once on the alternate bus, however, we ran into another problem—we recognized no landmarks in the darkness and did not know where to tell the driver to let us off. Consequently, we rode all the way to the end of the line, watching the other passengers get off in twos and threes until we were alone with the driver. After he parked the bus in a deserted lot, Ray tried to make him understand that we needed to get to Monteverdi, but he just stared impassively. Then he said something in Italian which neither of us could catch. Only when he put his hands together and leaned his head against them did we realize that he was telling us he wanted to sleep. When Ray and I looked at each other, we each saw a bit of helplessness in the other's eyes. Well, we got to watch our bus driver nap for thirty minutes! And had to be quiet so as not to wake him. He snapped to attention eventually, started the bus, and off we went on the return trip.

I must say that the famous bridge, the Ponte Vecchi, is beautiful at night, all lit up, but although we recognized it and the Duomo, we could not make out a place to get off anywhere on the journey back in. Obviously frustrated but trying to stay calm, Ray said, "We'd better try it once more." On the second round trip we still could recognize nothing! Ray decided to get off at Porta di Prato rather than face the prospect of another round trip. From there we walked about twenty blocks until someone who understood our pronunciation of "Monteverdi" gave us directions. It was 12:20 A.M. when we got to our little apartment. Poor Ray still had to prepare for the first day of classes—not the way he wanted his semester to begin!

LIFE IN FIRENZE AND BEYOND

Those first few days were a whirl of getting lost, shopping for groceries, figuring out the crazy washing machine in our apartment, and learning to avoid the equally crazy Italian drivers.

On the first day of classes, I stepped off our bus and was almost hit by the cars that whizzed by in spite of a clearly marked pedestrian right-of-way. A policeman standing nearby, who should have been enforcing traffic laws, simply turned his head. Ray muttered, "I guess he can't stand the sight of blood." We realized then that pedestrians were on their own in traffic.

We arrived safely at the Scuola where I attended Archeology and Ray's Humanities and Ancient and Medieval History classes. He and I both took Italian (Ray later had to drop because of his workload). We were quite the students, reviewing together at night; at least once Ray read the vocabulary words to me while I needlepointed and tried to translate. I learned a lot in all the classes, but the most lasting lesson turned out to be that my husband was a great teacher.

I recall the first days of his Humanities class and the talk about art. The students seemed excited at the way Ray could depict a painting or sculpture. Even when they seemed less than excited, he would pull them in. One day after a trip to the Galleria degli Uffizi, Ray wanted to talk about Botticelli's famous *The Birth of Venus*, which the students had seen. Since this 15th century work shows Venus coming out of the ocean nude, it elicited a few giggles from the guys, I'm sure, and in class there was a bit of that along with one student's mock groan at having to study this artsy stuff. Ray seized on this slight resistance. "You sound like the old boy who first said 'you can lead a horse to water but you can't make him drink.' Well, I suppose that's true, but I would hate to think that we led you all the way across the Atlantic to

Florence, Italy, the wellspring of some of the most interesting, vital Renaissance history and art—and we can't get you to drink." Of course, Ray was smiling as he boomed out this remark, and the student who had groaned was ready to backtrack.

"You know," Ray added, "someone once said that 'there is many a horse who does not know how thirsty he is until someone leads him to water,' and before we leave Italy, I wager that you are going to realize how thirst-quenching this course is!"

"Take this Botticelli painting, for instance. By the way, did you know that Sandro Botticelli took his name from a nickname for his little brother, 'Il Botticelli' or little barrel? But back to his painting. We look at it and see a naked woman on the sea shore, but for the Renaissance it represented an attempt to unify the pagan and the Christian. To a man like Lorenzo di Pier Francesco de' Medici, who commissioned the painting for his country villa, the ancients had a superior wisdom. Therefore, a pagan legend like this one must have a symbolic meaning—a Christian one. Venus, the epitome of beauty, is a type of the Virgin Mary. This vision of beauty emerging from the sea became for the Medicis a way of depicting the grandeur associated with the spiritual beauty of Christ."

"So it's not just a dirty picture," the student said, smiling.

"You're learning!" Ray laughed. "And if the connection between Renaissance and Christian world views doesn't interest you, maybe you'd like to talk about the painting as part of the early stirrings of capitalism?

"What? Do you mean that Botticelli sold this painting?"

"Not exactly. It was commissioned, as I mentioned, but the wealthy people like the Medicis needed these paintings to decorate the walls of the huge palazzos they were building, so they became patrons of the arts as a kind of what you might call conspicuous consumption.'"

"What does that mean?"

"It means that art became a way to show off their wealth and their culture to others. As they did that, they also gave art a commercial value—a dollar and cents value. And *voila!* Capitalism! *The Birth of Venus* is not just about a naked lady; it's about beauty, capitalism, and Christianity! So even though this painting looks like it belongs to a very different world, that world has helped produce ours."

I watched during this little exchange. His facts were precise and detailed, but his delivery seemed completely natural. He lectured from the bottom of his feet, with his whole being.

Teaching was only part of the new, arduous routine in Florence, and the rigors of the hectic pace took a toll on Ray. Sinus problems plagued him throughout the winter. Sometimes he would forget to take his blood pressure medicine; sometimes he would stay up late preparing. Once our European washing machine blew a circuit while I was doing a late-night load of clothes, and I had to wake Ray to fix it. He was up until the early morning hours. Nevertheless, the next day we hauled ourselves out of bed to be at the Scuola Bibilica by 7:30. Later that morning in Italian class, I was having trouble keeping my eyes open. I leaned over to whisper to Ray that I could not stay awake, but he couldn't hear me—he was sleeping soundly.

Though my interest in classes waned, I managed to take a book's worth of notes. Once in the middle of a hectic day, it dawned on me that I was studying abroad, like some wealthy heiress. I took the Humanities final without studying, just to see how I would do. Ray handed the test back and said, "Congratulations, Weezie, you did well." I felt as proud as a school girl. If I read the satisfaction in his voice correctly, he was more than proud of me; he was flattered that I had taken his class. Funny, the pleasant little turns a marriage can take.

Life with the students went well. We had no major problems during our months in Europe. One student left because of illness in the family, and there were the usual ups and downs of relationships. We could always tell when the students had traveled the weekend before because they came in mopey on the following Monday. But the bonds forged by HUF more than compensated for the occasional fatigue or emotional immaturity of the students. When we left America, we had two non-Christians among our group. By March 4 we had none. Two baptisms occurred within our first month, and they resulted from Bible study and the concern of sincere, loving students.

In Florence, Italian history was inescapable and amazing, but the city became only the first site among many in our ever-widening explorations. After seeing dozens of the country's other cities, we toured Germany, France, Switzerland, and Greece as well. I absorbed a great deal in those three months. To be surrounded by ancient art treasures and to see the site of such momentous world events meant nonstop revelation.

In February we visited the hillside suburb of Fiesole, where, for 300 lira we toured the Etruscan ruins there. During our visit Ray thrust his hand into the earth and discovered an ostrika (piece of pottery). In the chill of that winter day, he gestured to the crumbling brick walls, inside which Roman nobility once luxuriated in hot baths, his hand pointing me back in time to see the whole pottery in the hand of a housewife, or servant, carrying steaming water to replenish the bath of her master.

On we went, to Pompei and San Gimignano and Athens, each spot moving us further back in time, it seemed.

It was the biblical sites, however, that meant the most to our group. I can still see Ray reading Acts 17 on Mars Hill in Athens, where Paul had delivered the original version of the passage. Later, we attended a Greek Orthodox service. The high point of our trip to Greece occurred in old Corinth. Because the city was destroyed in 146 by the Romans, the ruins of the Temple of Apollo are all that remain of the original Greek civilization. But extensive Roman ruins exist, including the location of the apostle Paul's appearance before the Tribune, as recorded in Acts 18. Our students gathered among the ruins. The Mitchells produced grape juice and crackers. After communion, Carl spoke briefly and someone read scripture. Ray led one of the prayers. Then we sang. Below us on the hill, I could hear the songs of an Assembly of God tour group from Michigan. In the stillness of the moment, it seemed right for all of us to be there, connecting to the roots of our faith.

APRIL IN PARIS

By the end of the first full day on campus, our little home had become a refuge. That evening, Ray and I prepared the first of many meals together.

Ray and Eloise enjoy the ruins of old Corinth after a worship service there.

Being in a small house in a strange place made us feel newly married. Even more than that, here we were both students again. It was a second honeymoon and beyond. The sense of adventure made all the little things more vivid and intense. After years of work or kids or other routine getting in the way, I was alone with the man I loved.

Of course, even overseas, romance is not without obstacles. I got sick in spite of taking precautions, and so did Ray. Mine was a cold and came and went within days. His was a sinus infection that came on slowly and lasted for weeks. Poor Ray. While I was sick, he did the laundry, cooked, cleaned—then prepared for class. In the evenings I sat wrapped in blankets, one for my feet and one for my shoulders, watching him study. He was growing a beard, and by mid-February it looked good—salt and pepper. "He's a cutie," I thought to myself from under the blanket, "a real doll." My mind flew back to Freed-Hardeman days when I would watch him from afar. When he went to bed, it was all I could do to finish my journal because I wanted to join him there, to get warm beside him under the heavy blankets.

On Valentine's Day he bought red tulips for me, recalling our engagement in 1948. Later the same day, on a trip with the students, we put our hands in the water of the Arno River where it emptied into the Mediterranean. Close by, an Italian girl played as we looked for shells on the shore. She was dark and beautiful like so many of the children we saw in Florence and around the country. I picked up an exotic shell that, if it had been large enough, might have held Botticelli's Venus in the painting I loved in Florence and that Ray had discussed in class. In the painting, she seems to have just floated in from the sea, modestly covering her nakedness, the center of attention from humans and gods alike. The goddess of love rising up out of the sea. As the little girl walked in the cold waves, she too could have been a creature from the ocean, quite unlike the figure in the painting but just as beautiful. To have seen the painting, then to have stood on the shore of the Mediterranean with Ray at the mouth of this ancient river, left me overwhelmed. All I could do at the end of the day was thank God for allowing me to see this beauty.

The three days we spent in Rome were like a dream. Although our youth hostel's limited accommodations forced me to share a bathroom with eleven students, Ray and I had a tiny but comfortable bedroom to ourselves. When we arrived there after an exhausting day of sightseeing, Ray pushed the twin beds together. "No way we sleep apart in Rome," he said. The next day I threw three coins in the Trevi fountain, and Ray and I drank from its water. The ruins and surviving buildings alike were dazzling: the Appian

Way, the catacombs of St. Sebastian, the Colosseum. We walked in the cold sunshine, eating ice cream (gelati), drinking caffi and routinely gasping in wonder.

Even the little misunderstandings did not spoil the trip. On one occasion our tour bus was stopped by a policeman outside one of the ruins. Ray and I looked anxiously out a window, along with dozens of students, as Carl talked to the officer. We saw the man listen as Carl spoke. Then he gazed right up at Ray and me and said something to Carl, who smiled and replied. After a moment, the policeman seemed satisfied and left. "What did he say to you?" Ray asked as Carl reboarded. "Why did he look up here?"

"Well," Carl said, "it seems that some unauthorized guides are bilking tourists out of money, and the police are double-checking all buses. When I assured him that our driver was legitimate and that this was a registered group of college students, he looked up at you two and asked, 'Then what are those old people doing on the bus?'" We laughed along with the others, but the thing was neither of us felt old. We got tired but rarely ran out of energy on the many trips we took.

In Austria we took the "Sound of Music Tour," a series of sites involved in the real-life story of the Von Trapps upon which the famous movie was based. Even before this trip, my family teased me about how much I loved *The Sound of Music*. On the grounds of the Von Trapp's ornate palace, we entered the little glass house, where a Japanese boy took a picture of Ray and me. Like so many other tourists, I suppose, we did the obligatory kissing scene from the movie. Another scene, though, fit my mood better. It featured the older lovers. Maria and Von Trapp declare their love for one another at night, silhouetted against the glass walls of the gazebo, as they sing these words:

> Here you are standing there loving me,
> whether or not you should.
> So somewhere in my youth or childhood,
> I must have done something good.

Ray and I didn't sing, but we did embrace in the same doorway, and the words, which I confess did not come to mind at that exact moment, nevertheless could have expressed perfectly how I felt as he kissed me for the stranger photographing us.

Not every excursion was so perfect. Our trip to Naples, though fun in its way, included irritations typical of traveling abroad. By the time we returned to Florence, I had picked up some kind of bug in that filthy town, and the new shoes bought before the trip had worn a blister on my foot. When yet another bus strike hit Florence the next week, and when we learned that our photographs of the trip had not turned out, I was definitely out of sorts. The strike forced me to walk a good deal of the way to school one day—on the blister. I limped into chapel feeling a mess.

Ray was speaking. His talk was on the "Happiness of Psalm 23." "Ever since Aristotle," Ray began, "man's ultimate goal has been happiness" (women too, I thought), "but the question has always been where to find it" (*not in Naples and not in these shoes*). It was hard not to let my mind wander. Each time he said something, it seemed to go right to the heart of my discontent. When Ray mentioned the false happiness of wealth, I said to myself, *the fortune I'm spending on cold medicine and bus passes that I can't even use half the time.*

"The 23rd Psalm tells us where happiness is," he said. *It's here with you,* I thought, suddenly, looking at his now fully grown salt and pepper beard. *Oh woe is me! This blister is making you delirious!*

"Man is unhappy in the wrong places, and how often, when he tries to direct his own steps, does he end up in a wrong place. The good shepherd leads us to the right places. . ." *You are my good shepherd; you have led me here, and no bus strike or blister should make me forget that. I am so very tired. Forgive me Lord; I know you are the good shepherd, but my dear husband is mine too, at this moment.*

"This psalm tells us that we have happiness in life, in death, and in eternity—if we are led by the Lord—He who has the words of life." *Thank you God for letting me be here and giving my husband the calling to preach, and for directing him on this day, even when he didn't know how I felt, to be the prophet through whom you restored my soul in its little moment of darkness.*

As Ray stepped down from the podium to make way for the song leader, I realized that in six weeks I would leave Florence, fly to Chicago from Amsterdam, and then, eventually, return to 1002 Hayes Street. I would not cross the Arno River every day with the Ponte Vecchio in the distance. I would have to leave Ray. He was staying on for a month to do mission work in Zurich, and I began to dread the day of parting.

When I think back on this second honeymoon, I realize how much of it was physically demanding or unpleasant. Only it didn't seem that way while we lived it because of the glamour of the new and the shared discomfort of the hardship. It really was like being young again when every cost is not counted, when the intensity of the experience is worth the pain. And Ray went through many physical ailments. He battled fatigue, a chronic sinus infection, toothaches and never once complained or declined to take me somewhere. He was determined to be my full-time guide and protector no matter what.

He led me through a near-riot in Madrid and over the exhausting hills in Greece, where we slept on a park bench—first me with my head in his lap, then with his in mine. To and from Greece we shared a small ship's cabin with Frankie and Carl Mitchell and had to go through all kinds of contortions to get dressed and undressed while still preserving everyone's sense of modesty—sometimes Ray and I huddled together in the miniscule bathroom just to change. Sitting in our family room in Searcy I might have called all this an inconvenience. Looking back on it now, the only word I can think of is "romantic."

So was our last major trip of the semester—to Paris. But to the casual observer we were just more tourists, a couple whose means were too modest to do much besides sightsee, walking most of the way. The observer could note that this couple had to take a small room in a cheaper hotel. The two had to walk in rain much of the time, and it was cold enough that both had winter coats on. The couple saw the usual things in a criminally short time: the Louvre, the palace at Versailles, the Eiffel Tower, hurrying from one to another without time to absorb fully the art. They stood with mouths open on the first floor of the giant Paris department store, Printemps, to gaze as far as their eyes could see at counter after counter of perfume and cologne, unable to comprehend an entire floor devoted to these products. They sipped coffee outside a shop in Montmartre, trying to ease the chill as they watched the street artists and musicians perform.

Our observer might have noted that early in the tour the woman turned her ankle while stepping off a curb and began to limp noticeably. Had he followed, he would have noted that in spite of the injury, she accompanied her husband on the long walk down the Champs Elysee to the Arch d'Triomphe, a journey made with a light rain in their faces. Had the observer been close enough, he would have seen in her face the pain of each step down coming out of the Louvre.

What the observer might not have seen was the color in the woman's face, and it wasn't from the cold or pain. It came from this momentary residence in the city of her dreams. Each landmark a new thrill. Seeing the Eiffel tower from a distance in those first moments was almost better than standing at its foot in the rain. In her first glance it shimmered like the Paris of all the novels and movies of her youth. For thirty-six hours she could stand the pain for the sake of the dream.

And besides, the observer could not have gone into that cheaper hotel at night with the woman and her husband. He could not have seen her gingerly remove her shoes and stare at the swollen, purple flesh of the injured ankle. What's more, he wouldn't have seen—as she did not at first—the husband sit quietly on the bed, watching her. When she did look up to meet his eyes, he asked if he could help. He ran hot water in the tub. He helped her take off her outer clothes and stockings. He helped her get as comfortable as possible on the edge of the tub. He tested the water with his hand, then gently lifted her leg by its calf, raised it over the edge and guided the tender ankle into the steaming bath. When she gasped in a combination of pain and relief, he laughed a little, telling her to soak it for a while before her full bath. He then brought her a towel.

After that he left her alone to her bath while he lay on the bed, waiting for her. As he waited he jotted down some thoughts running through his mind. His wife did not know until later that on the bed he began his own memory of their two days in the city of her dreams. Much later he gave the finished product to her as a memento, each word of which still acts as a code for the richness of the time. Even the casual observer could read the meaning of their marriage in the poem's lines:

> *Le Printemps en France*
> Do you remember, my love?
> The train moved through a field
>   yellow with Dijon's yield
> Past farms and villages
>   do you remember, my love?
> The South Station in Paris
>   awaited us that day
> A franc exchange and we were on our way
>   do you remember, my love?
> The Bastille, the Ile de France
>   you stumbled on the quay
> Pont Neuf, the Eiffel tower, our first glimpse I say
>   do you remember, my love?
> Down the Champs Elysees, the arch of Triumph
>   the Invalides
> Napoleon resting, the Seine cresting, birds nesting
>   do you remember, my love?
> The cloud, the rain, the sun again

I gave you a flower in front of Le Printemps
  do you remember, my love?
The observation car, quaint Versailles
The majesty of the Sun King
A mighty empire has fallen
  before liberty, equality and fraternity.
The Metro, St. Denis and Montmartre,
The Bohemian, Sacre Coeur
There she lay: the city of our dreams
  do you remember, my love?
Ah, *le Printemps en France*.
  I remember, my love!

LAST DAYS IN THE OLD WORLD

May the First in Florence! Ray and I walked to Cascine park and found ourselves in an eruption of people. The closer we got to the park, the more

Ray Muncy reading his poem, "I Remember, My Love," to Eloise at the 1988 Sig Tau Spring Banquet.

people materialized, as if a great national holiday had been declared. A profusion of old and young no longer able to stay pent up in those small apartments with almost no lawns. As we neared the park, the roar of an even larger crowd occasionally overpowered the hum of leisurely families walking, sitting, playing along the way. Ray and I picked our way through them toward a racetrack with stands full of cheering people. Entranced by the sight of the horses running against the backdrop of the Duomo and May sky, we almost got run over by a small armada of baby carriages. Did all the young mothers of the city decide at once to take their infants outdoors? The sleek horses on the track and the bright strollers outside raced as if to impart a pleasant energy to our step.

Amid all the spring-like freshness was an inevitable sense of winding down. Everything sounded a note of finality. On May 1 Ray gave his final exams. On May 2 I spent my last hours at the Scuola. I did my last shopping in Florence, attended the last church service, took the last walk in Florence with Ray, where I saw from the highest hill in Fiesole the dark red tile of the city's rooftops.

On our last night together in the apartment I made supper while Ray took my bags to the station. I wanted the meal to be Italian and special. I invited him into the dining room and had him sit down; then I served the meal course by course: our pasta was rigatoni in spicy tomato sauce. "Oh, excellent, my dear chef," Ray said. "Excellent!" I stood over him like a maitre'd. "But I'm not finished," I said, producing a bowl of freshly grated Parmesan cheese and sprinkling it over the pasta. Then I brought out a chicken fried steak with mashed potatoes, fresh asparagus, Bibb lettuce, sliced tomato and purple onion salad. Ray played the satisfied customer to perfection and we ate the food slowly. Unfortunately, Ray reminded me, his chef had some studying to do. "Oh yes, the Italian test. Do I have to?" He shrugged and began cleaning up the dishes. I helped and sighed about the test. I wrote until I couldn't stand it. "I'm going to pack," I declared. "I'll finish this thing back in Searcy."

"I'll permit such slackardly behavior on one condition," Ray said. "Make some peanut butter fudge."

I'm glad we were alone that night in our little "fortress." I will always remember living within those walls, as dirty as they were. I would miss the upstairs neighbor's dog traipsing up and down the stairs right over our heads. I would even miss the cranky washing machine and the clothesline. Now, for a moment I could savor our Italian home. The patio doors were open to the little garden where our Italian helper toiled over the flowers. Green vines clung to the lattice that he had built a month ago. The sun was shining and the birds singing. I had an urge to rush out and see all the historic ruins one more time. Most of all I thought about leaving Ray.

There he sat, as he had for so many nights, across from me, reading. As I watched him on this last night we would spend together in Florence, I prayed silently, "Lord, take care of him for me. I can't think of my life without him." We would have the night and then travel together for a few days before having to say goodbye at the airport. Of course, I would see him again within a few weeks of my departure from Amsterdam, but I couldn't shake the sorrow clinging to me more closely than the blanket around my shoulders.

Summer Arrives in Searcy

Since Ray and I were both taking planes to our different destinations, he would be able to accompany me by train to Amsterdam, where we had a single day to enjoy the city once more. All the while the thought of leaving Ray became more unbearable. I suddenly realized that at no time in our marriage had we spent more time together or been so intimate. I prayed repeatedly, "Lord, keep me strong for him."

It was raining on the morning of our departure from Amsterdam, but Ray insisted on heading in the opposite direction from the train station. He steered me back down the street of flowers I had so loved on our first visit and paid seven and a half guilders for twenty baby yellow rosebuds. He had planned it all along. Thrilled, I put them on top of the things in my carry-on bag before we headed to the station to retrieve our luggage.

Once we arrived at the airport time went too fast. The Harding students were gathering and I did not want to make a scene in front of them, so I fought back the tears. Ray and I embraced. "Lord, please take control," I prayed silently. I got on the long conveyor to Gate 53D and watched Ray stand there alone, getting smaller as I moved farther away.

The long trip was unreal. Flying over Scotland, then Iceland, was like looking down on green and white planets in a different solar system. I thought of my children, whom I had not seen for so long. While we were separated, David and Candy had celebrated their tenth anniversary and Kandy had been accepted into the nursing program at Harding. Zac had successfully managed the house, an outside job, and his school work. The longer we were in flight, the more they became real to me again.

At 10 P.M., some forty-eight hours after I left Ray, I pulled up at 1002 Hayes. Jet lag weighed down my steps but seeing Kandy and Zac energized me. The house was full of clutter and dead plants but it never looked better to me. By midnight I had been awake for twenty-four hours, and I drifted off to sleep thinking, "My children look beautiful and I have been blessed."

I arrived home on May 6. Ray was to work in Zurich until June. I would not see him for five more weeks. The next morning I was still suffering from jet lag and was grateful for the quiet house. I was greeted at the kitchen window by cardinals, chirping as if to welcome me back. Then I went outside to size up the yard work ahead. I planted cuttings from the Amsterdam rosebuds Ray had given me, crying a little at the thought of how he had presented them to me so proudly less than seventy-two hours before, and how I had to argue long and loud with customs officials in order to keep them.

Those minutes alone were important, but activity helped me get through the coming weeks without Ray. Visitors came and went in the house at a rapid rate. Welcome-home calls kept the phone ringing. There were gifts to buy for graduation. I rediscovered the joy of driving and of using my own oven. I made jam, went to graduation, and worked in the yard and garden. I prepared for a job with Lab of Pathology to begin on June 1. At night I wrote letters to Ray and missed him terribly.

In late May a torrential rain made everything grow like a jungle. The yard and garden were green, really green. But my Amsterdam roses were dying. Nothing I did seemed to be able to salvage them, so I took the sickly surviving buds and pressed them in an album. Alive they had been an extension of my time in Europe. Between the pages of the book they reminded me that my romantic second honeymoon was in the past.

Mother's Day came and went with phone calls, flowers, and joy. So did the Indy 500. Signs of summer abounded: Kandy's softball season began, wedding showers beckoned, and the days were sunny and beautiful.

On Tuesday, June 9, Zac and I drove to Little Rock to pick up Ray. He still had his beard. He hugged Zac but gave me the big squeeze, lasting long enough to embarrass our son, had he not been so happy for us.

"How are those Amsterdam roses doing?" Ray asked.

"I'm afraid they didn't like the Searcy weather very much."

"So they didn't last?"

"No, I'm sorry."

"Oh, don't be," Ray said. Then he reached into his carry-on bag and carefully removed a long shallow box from it. Before he opened the box I knew what was in it. He balanced it on the bag, unwrapped some wax paper protecting the contents and produced half-a-dozen long stemmed pink roses.

"From Amsterdam," he said.

TEN

The Death of Kandy (1983)

I think of Kandy often, of course—especially the good times, but since her death, my memories of her childhood can't help but take on a different feeling. Back in Bloomington one summer, before any clouds had appeared on our family's horizon, when she was all of four years old, Ray had taken us on some kind of outing, and on the way back we passed a carnival. It was one of those cheap traveling carnivals set up on the parking lot of a shopping center on Third Street. Kandy was intrigued by the bright lights and sounds of music and started begging to go. Ray said what parents usually say, "Not now, princess; maybe we can go later." Since she didn't put up a big fuss, we thought no more about it.

The following Saturday afternoon was a beautiful summer day, and the men of Bloomington were out doing yard work. Ray was mowing our lawn with the old push mower. Thankfully for him it was a pretty small yard. Over ten blocks away, with a major highway separating the two neighborhoods, our good friend and elder Woody Stogsdill sat atop his riding power mower as it circled his expansive lawn. It sloped gently down to the road where a small bluff partially hid a ditch that separated his property from the street. He had already cut the grass closest to the ditch, but as he swung the mower in a path parallel to it he thought he saw something move. A closer look revealed nothing, so he continued mowing. The next time around, the movement again caught his eye, and he could tell it was a human head peeping up from out of the ditch. It quickly disappeared, but Woody thought he knew who it was. On the third revolution the blonde head bobbed up again, only to disappear once more. Woody stopped the mower and ambled over to the ditch. Sure enough, there on her back lay a little girl with a blonde ponytail.

"Is that you, Kandy?"

"Yes."

"Why don't you come up here to see me?" She got out of the dirt and he helped her onto the grass. He hugged her and asked gently, "Did you cross the highway by yourself?"

"Yes." Safely in his embrace, she answered in a trembling voice suggesting a belated sense of danger.

"Where in the world were you going, sweetie?"

"To the carnival."

Later, when Woody told me how she had dared to cross all that traffic to get back to the carnival, I did not know whether to laugh or cry. What went on in her four-year-old mind to make a brief glimpse of neon lights so compelling? It shook us even at the time to know so much desire could be secretly operating in her—what determination could beat in her little heart. After almost an hour of panic at her disappearance, all we could say was "Oh Kandy," and thank dear Woody for being there to gather her up into his arms and bring her home. That was the first time she ran away. Now, twenty years after our daughter set out so irrevocably on her last journey away from us, we can only pray she arrives safely at the house of the One who has the power to return all lost children.

DISAPPEARANCE

On the night before that terrible day, she seemed happy. She stood before me—suddenly a young woman with short, dark shining hair, that athlete's body not quite at home off the field, and those blue eyes so like Marc's. "Mom," she said, "I am having a good week, counting the days till graduation."

I did a lot of reading on suicide afterward, of course, and remember the experts saying how calm the suicidal person is after the hopelessness has taken hold, what a relief the decision seems to be. I wondered if her serenity that evening and the days preceding stemmed from such a black well of despair.

On March 4, 1983, I awoke to the scraping of shoes, the flutter of paper, and the slight thumps of a moving body coming down the stairs. It was Kandy in the hallway on her way out. We talked through the closed bedroom door right off the passageway to the front door—the kids had exiled us downstairs because they said we were too noisy upstairs with our late-night rambles. I don't remember exactly what Kandy and I talked about because it all seemed so routine. I do remember that she wanted to take her own car to Little Rock. It was to be her last day of hospital rotation. One more day at the Children's Hospital in Little Rock before performing the very last hospital duty in Harding's nursing program. Her desire to drive instead of joining the usual car pool grew, I assumed, from her eagerness to get on with things, so we probably just rehearsed the routine: "Yes, Mom, I'll be in Little Rock until noon; then I've got my afternoon classes. Yes, I'll be careful. Yes, the car has gas. Love you too. Bye."

She seemed cheerful enough. And why not? After so much soul-searching about her educational future three years before, graduation was a few weeks away. After that a job awaited. As I lay in bed and heard the door shut, I couldn't help but be happy too. Kandy had come so far. All my children had made it just fine and I felt blessed. Zac was getting married in June. David seemed to have weathered a business downturn in Virginia, and Marc was already enjoying a successful dental practice. It sounds like a cliché, but I had no reason to suspect any trouble that morning.

I got up soon and dressed for work. For two years I had worked for the Lab of Pathology, one of a series of jobs I took to help get the kids through school. Even with Harding's 75 percent tuition discount for children of faculty members, financing four college students was taking its toll. I didn't mind the work, though. It made me feel good to contribute in that way, and it challenged me to learn new things. On this job I had to master a filing routine for insurance claims. Friday was always an important day because we had to meet deadlines. I was in the middle of entering data when I got a call from Kandy's nursing supervisor, Nancy Clark, who asked if I knew where Kandy was, because she had failed to show up for an afternoon test. I was at a loss: "I can't imagine where she is," I said, "and I can't imagine why she would not come in. She seemed fine this morning when she left home."

"Oh, then Kandy hasn't told you what happened today?" Nancy's voice was flat with the burden of having to break the news. "You see, Eloise, I had to reprimand Kandy today—pretty severely. She accidentally doubled a dose of medicine for one of our patients, a little girl." I tried to say something at that point; the news gave me such a shock. Nancy reassured me: "Don't worry, we caught it in time, and even if we hadn't, in this case the overdose would have done no real harm. But as I told Kandy, that kind of carelessness just can't be tolerated. I'm afraid she got pretty upset when I made the point.

That's why I called today when I realized she wasn't going to make the test."
I didn't know how to react to this news: in trouble at work and now missing.
"Where are you, Kandy?" I thought. In light of what happened later, the possible impact of Nancy's reprimand would echo in our minds, but every time
I was tempted to blame her for being too harsh, I thought of Ray's tough-
minded attitude toward lapses in efficiency or competence. It was a teacher's
task to do what she did. I thanked her for the call, then tried to reach Ray
at Harding, but he was in a committee meeting, a fact which would have
irritated me more had I not been so worried. Within minutes I was on my
way home.

I was hoping to find Kandy, of course, but found instead one of her
nursing classmates. Janet Kirby just wanted to help me look for Kandy, she
said. Her quick arrival should have warned me that the people at Harding
knew more than they were telling, but I was too anxious to find evidence
that she had been home to worry about the significance of the girl's unexpected presence. Just to know that Kandy was back in Searcy and not lost
or hurt somewhere between home and Little Rock would be a little solace.
In the kitchen I found a glass with melting ice. In her room was an unopened
backpack that she would have taken had she been on her way to class or to
study. Her blue student uniform lay across her bed and the white shoes rested nearby. Beyond this scant evidence there was nothing. Obviously she had
been home and left again, but not to go to school.

The afternoon turned into evening, and as it grew dark, our phone calls
multiplied. We tried Kandy's friends in Little Rock—maybe she wanted to
check on the little girl to whom she had given the wrong dosage. We tried
friends in Memphis and, naturally, in Searcy. Meanwhile a steady procession
of visitors rang the doorbell to offer comfort. Cathleen Smith, head of the
Nursing School, came by with her fiancé, Sam Shultz, to sit with us. As in
the case with Janet that afternoon, something in Cathleen's demeanor bothered me; or maybe my memory is affected by hindsight. Cathleen seemed a
hair's breadth more solicitous than the situation warranted, friend though she
was. I speculated on this and a hundred other minute things. Waiting in the
darkened front room was like staring at a huge painting, so big you can't
make out details, so you try to find the smallest swatch of color or form to
make sense of the picture. Was Cathleen hiding something? Whatever she
might be withholding, she was with us and that helped. Operating on the
information we had, Ray and I felt that Kandy had retreated from the hurt of
her mistake to be with someone. We didn't phone the police. We believed
she would call when she felt safe, or had exhausted her turbulent emotions.

As she had almost four years ago when she took off for the north Arkansas town of Harrison without a word.

FLIGHT TO HARRISON

Of course, Ray and I couldn't help but think of the Harrison episode as we waited helplessly that Friday night in 1983. The trouble then—in 1979—was rooted in Kandy's indecision about a major. She began college in journalism, but despite promising high school experience as yearbook editor at the Academy, she disliked the technical aspects of journalism. She soon switched to English.

Kandy always had a gift for wry, imaginative expression. Maybe she thought an English major would give free rein to some of her humorous flights of fancy. One of her assignments from high school illustrates why straight reporting and technical detail were not for her:

> Probably
> What shall I do after school today? I'll probably come home and get a bite to eat and then receive a phone call from President Ford, Then I'll probably meet him uptown to talk about important business...Then I will [go back home] to watch Bozo for a few hours....Billy Jean King will probably come over about 4:30 for a few sets of tennis. I will probably beat her, like I always do.... [Then] the lady next door will probably have a heart attack, and I will have to give first aid...thus receiving $10,500 in reward money. Then I will probably look at the mail and find a letter from Tony Orlando, asking me to be on his show next week. I will probably take out a few sheets of paper and write back that I can't because I probably have to clean my teeth Wednesday night. But right now I had probably better finish this report before class is over.

To me this brings out something of her playfulness. She could always make me laugh, as much as or more than any of my children. In retrospect, though, I see her restlessness in that fantasy; it conveys an energy of possibility but also of dissatisfaction. Is it much different than what any fifteen-year-old would express? I don't think so. But after all these years it's hard not to look for clues. All in all, Kandy's imagination as we experienced it was fun- loving and healthy. And we were proud of her writing ability.

But for whatever reason, the English major did not work out either. I wish I could say more about her confusion, wish I understood it better, but that was an area occupied largely by Ray. He was always there for her; they spent long hours poring over class schedules and catalogs. He thought English was a good second choice that she never gave a chance because at this point she was growing disenchanted with Harding itself.

I'm afraid it's a familiar story, especially for children whose parents work at a Christian college. Kandy felt closed in, restricted, by the rules. Ray and I could sympathize, having been at Freed-Hardeman as students. But when it came right down to it, we hadn't minded the regulations. We had been away from home and relatively free, or so we thought. Kandy was part of a very different generation. She had been raised in a culture that assumed an almost absolute freedom for the young; now Harding seemed to stifle her. Even back at the Academy, where she was generally happy, there had been occasional friction. Nothing so bad that I can't look back on it and smile now, but at the time it could be exasperating. She didn't always respond well to dress codes and other restrictions.

If anything, her dissatisfaction with Harding stemmed not from restrictive rules but from the overpowering atmosphere that seemed to value sameness and therefore deny her space of her own. No doubt conformity ruled in those days. Shortly before Kandy left home for Harrison, she told Ray she was dropping out of her English major. When he asked why, she said with a disgust toward older generations only a twenty-year-old can muster: "I'm just sick of seeing everybody shake their legs in those wingtip shoes!"

Wingtip shoes were not the source of her problem, even if every male teacher and all the Bible majors seemed to wear them. As the daughter of a prominent faculty member, she had been exposed to all things Harding for most of her life. All her brothers went to Harding, her dad taught there, her mother worked for the Associated Women for Harding. Perhaps the school threatened to swallow up her sense of family. Or her sense of identity. She was tired of being David's sister and Eloise's daughter and Ray's daughter, she once said, then added, "I want to be myself!"

By the time she entered college, Ray and I believed that "self" to be a beautiful young woman with great potential. Her features linked her inescapably to the rest of us. Kandy had rich, dark Muncy hair. She had a broad smile like Marc's and a hint of younger brother Zac's mischief in her eyes, even though they were blue, not brown like his and Ray's. Her gestures sometimes imitated my body movement. But Kandy was her own person, whether she felt like it or not. She wanted to think for herself. She wanted to be an athlete, not to have to wear makeup when she didn't want to. At the Academy she had longed to play basketball and hated the double standard that would not allow girls to play unless they wore long pants. Yet she would have gladly worn them just to have a chance to participate. It never happened in high school, so, unlike her brothers, she had no scholastic outlet for her athletic prowess. Only in recreational tennis did she have a chance to shine, beating most opponents including her brothers. In school she wrote for the newspaper and yearbook, made the honor roll, sang in the chorus, and served as class officer. She made *Who's Who*. Despite these accomplishments, our daughter felt the "self" behind them was elusive, not yet distinctive.

One episode from Kandy's first year in college illustrates her mixture of independence and sensitivity. She had the courage to do what none of her brothers would attempt: she took one of her father's history courses. It was Western Civilization. Of course she didn't tell us, not even Ray. So when he called roll the first day of class he had no idea she would be there. In those days Afros were in style, and over my objections Kandy had tried one out of a perpetual dissatisfaction with her hair. On that first day before the bell rang, Ray kept noticing a frizzy-haired person on the back row, but whoever it was kept ducking behind the student in front of her/him, preventing a good look. Strolling down the aisle, he finally realized the furtive student was Kandy.

She whispered urgently to him when he bent to greet her, "Daddy, please don't tell everyone that I'm your daughter. Please don't embarrass me." Ray was amused and proud. In truth he was a little hurt over his boys' reluctance to sit in on his classes, though he understood the pressure they felt. Seeing Kandy in the classroom inflated his ego despite her fear of being singled out as a Muncy. He would get to teach one of his own children after all! I always suspected she was in the class because it was the only section she could get, but why not let Ray have his moment? And he took as much advantage of the moment as he could. Although he honored her request not to call her by name, he couldn't resist teasing her slyly in front of the others. It wasn't long until Kandy came home complaining to me: "Mom, do you know what Dad did today?" She then told of how Ray, who of course made a practice of drawing students into discussion and who would by this time know the class roster, had called on her like this: "Oh, the girl on the back row with the brown hair, what do you think?" Kandy's complaint was mixed with the pleasure of a little girl glad for Daddy's attention. But the discomfort was real. As she told us later, she had to get away from Harding and the family so closely associated with it in order to appreciate what school and family really meant. That's where the flight to Harrison came in.

Her departure was sudden and frightening. One Sunday night not long after the beginning of her third year—fall semester 1979— we got a call from a man asking for Kandy; he told us she had inquired about buying a little motorcycle from his dealership. Since this was news to us, we called her downstairs to the family room. When Ray asked her if she was planning on taking a trip on her new vehicle, she began to cry immediately, confessing without any further prodding that she had considered leaving. He escorted her over to the couch beside me, asking what was wrong. "I'm so mixed up!" she said. "I'm tired of school; I just can't go—and I don't know what to do!"

Her breakdown filled us both with pity. It was one of those moments in which parents see in a flash what they couldn't see coming—the months of doubt, frustration, and failure our Kandy must have felt to be so low. I put my arms around her, "Kandy! You don't ever have to go to school again if you don't want to. We won't love you any less." In response to this she sobbed more convulsively, sitting between Ray and me. Ray echoed my words. He began to explain that college is not the be-all and end-all for everyone, that time off never hurt anybody.

Sensing her guilt over letting him down, in particular, Ray talked softly about the "body language" of parents who gave so much time to Christian education. "Kandy, we tried never to pressure you into going to Harding— or to school period—but maybe we unconsciously pressured you just by the way we talked and acted about college. Maybe we sent you the wrong messages by our looks. If we did, we're sorry. I believe in education with all my heart, but going to college is only one way to learn where you fit in life. You know, believe it or not, the Lord won't be standing at the Pearly Gates to check diplomas." Even Kandy couldn't help but smile through her tears at the twinkle in Ray's eye.

As we continued to talk, she regained her composure. In fact, she was happy almost to the point of giddiness, as if the proverbial monkey had been taken from her back. We considered what immediate plans to make. Ray and I offered to take her to Little Rock or even Memphis to set her up in an apartment and help her find work. The night was full of possibilities for the future. Kandy thanked us for being so understanding. We hugged and went to bed.

The next day she disappeared. She withdrew all her savings, bought the motorcycle from the dealer (it was bright red), and took off on Route 65 toward Harrison. On a small motorcycle not designed for highway travel, she could manage no more than thirty-five miles an hour on the straightaways. Once she got into the mountains, she barely chugged up the winding road, sometimes stopping to let the engine cool or to let impatient traffic pass.

Somehow she made it to Harrison without incident. Once there, she made a beeline for the local Church of Christ to inform the preacher of her desire to find an apartment and a job. Eventually she got a job, then another one, and stayed for seven months.

The first twenty-four hours of that stay, however, left Ray and me in anguish. In her determination to do it "her way," she never thought of how we might feel. We had no idea where she might be. Her disappearance was announced in chapel, and we alerted the police. When she did call a day or so later, she issued a tearful apology: "I feel awful! I didn't handle this right." Ray listened to her explanation without saying one unkind or angry word, but when he hung up he told me, "She says she went about this wrong! Boy, is that the understatement of the year!" The last thing she said to Ray was, "I think I'll like going to church here. The preacher and his family have been real good to me."

We went to Harrison the next weekend, taking requested items, among them her stereo, a basketball, and cookies. We helped her settle into an upstairs apartment in the home of a nice couple. On Sunday we discovered that the church was already becoming like a second family to her. The preacher welcomed her, as did many members. Though their names have faded from my memory after all these years, I can still see their spirit of caring, etched like beautiful faces in my mind. Comforted by the kindness of the Lord's body at Harrison, we decided to honor her desire to be on her own. Back home I cried a lot and we both prayed continually. Ray quietly missed his princess.

If we gave her space, the world was giving her lessons in life outside the haven of campus. Her first job was as a seamstress for a Levi jeans factory there in Harrison. We couldn't help but laugh—she certainly never sewed pockets on her own jeans! Her first letter—twenty handwritten pages—conveys several emotions, not the least of which is pride in her work: "Today they moved me from my nice little training-room position to the main floor area at the factory. Yeah boy, I can cover anything from Levi's 'David Hunter' jeans to the thick heavy-duty stuff."

She babbles on in the letter about the tricks and perils of shopping. With a tune-up on her moped due, she visited car lots and dealt with aggressive salesmen. She brags about finding a "consumer's" grocery store with good specials. Using crude drawings, she describes the excruciating task of trying to balance a sack of groceries on the tiny rack of her motorcycle.

About half way through her narrative of daily life, Kandy turns philosophical. It's a passage that saddens me—yet I cherish it:

I'm just enjoying being by myself awhile. It's funny, I feel like I
don't hardly know myself very good. I know it's not good to always be
by yourself and I try to get involved with others if I feel it's good. But
it's not as if I go absolutely crazy if I have to spend time by myself. In
fact, I kinda like it—time to think and enjoy the simple things...
Sometimes I do get lonely. But down deep inside I'm content. I'm not
all mixed up and unsettled.... I'm able to realize who I am....
Therefore I'm not so bitter, critical and cynical toward others.... The
Lord has opened my eyes to the truth, to what life is really meant to
be like.... With Him in my heart I feel as safe and strong as a soldier in armor, yet I don't feel burdened down by its weight because
I want to do good (Hooray for the cowboy in white!). I've also come
to see how wonderful Harding is, what it stands for, its purpose....
Hav[ing] grown up under Harding's shelter [I] am now anxious to
practice the principles which I have been taught.... I wanted to
"get a little exercise".... Is that being rebellious? If it is, I sure don't
know what I'm rebelling against.

Reading that lovely letter now, I frankly am not sure what to think. Did
she really find contentment and then slowly lose it after her return home?
Or did she write to reassure us and convince herself? I choose to believe the
former. She was more at peace and more sure of herself after time away. Also
in the letter are descriptions of sojourns into nature, out to the Buffalo
River, exploring caves, taking in the grandeur and exclaiming, "I just love
what God has made!" Ray and I agreed that it would be a denial of our own
faith not to believe God was with her, teaching Kandy about Himself.

When Kandy returned to Searcy in May of 1980, she brought a renewed
energy and a new major, this time a firm choice. As Ray had predicted after
our visit, the Levi factory didn't last, and Kandy was hired as a nurse's aid at
the local hospital. From the first she loved it. Later, in the summer, she
enrolled at Harding as a nursing major, and for three years it seemed as if she
had put her troubles behind. Her grades, always good, became even better.
Even under the pressure of a tough nursing program, she never expressed anything but satisfaction in her major. Beyond that, her bitterness toward
Harding disappeared in a rush of good times and new friends. The only shadow on this sunny time came early on when Kandy refused our entreaties to
seek counseling. She did not get hysterical about it, but kept us at bay. By this
time she was almost twenty-one and we could not force her to get help. Her
behavior and academic success allowed the issue to fade until, three years

later, on the verge of graduation, with everything to live for, Kandy had vanished again, and there in our darkened family room we relived the nightmare.

THE ORDEAL

At about 9:30 P.M., with Kandy missing more than fourteen hours, I heard her car. Cathleen and her fiancé, Sam, were still there on the couch. Zac and his fiancé Connie huddled together on the other side of the room. Ray sat in his easy chair. I was in the corner chair by the window. Rain fluttered steadily against the house, keeping time for us, lulling our tense bodies into peace. Suddenly a faint, dry hard cough sounded in the spaces left by the falling water. When I realized the new sputter was the putt putt of Kandy's Volkswagen, I snapped up in the chair: "Ray, that's her car."

"Oh, Weezie, it can't be."

"I tell you it is; I've heard it too many times!" We all headed for the window, but before we got there the engine stopped, then started again. Through the window I caught a glimpse of a VW, a ghostly white under the street light. It was backing up. Quickly it stopped and zoomed back down Fox street. For a moment I doubted if I had really seen anything.

"What do you think?" I looked at Ray. The others had not gotten there in time to tell. Ray nodded. He said, "She may have seen Cathleen's car. I wonder where she has been?" We clasped hands and each offered a silent prayer of thanks: she was all right. Nothing to do but wait. At that moment I thought she would come back.

Cathleen and Sam left right away, hoping an empty driveway might encourage Kandy to return. Just before midnight Connie left for her apartment in Beebe. Ray and I talked for a while, then decided to do our situps. You know, keeping the routine going. Ray was serious about losing his tummy. He put his feet under the couch, hands behind his head, making little grunts each time his back left the carpet. There I was, my head a few feet from his trying to breathe properly with each situp. Two middle-aged parents having a last go at keeping in shape, when the phone rang.

It was a young policeman named Sean, who had gone to Harding. He was calling from the White County Hospital. The only words I recall—and they still sound strange to my ear, like a foreign language—were these: "Mrs. Muncy, you need to come to the hospital right now. I'm afraid your daughter has shot herself."

Ray and I fell against each other in shock, tears welling up in both of us. An instant of panic paralyzed us in each other's arms. I remember the rustle of my running suit as Ray embraced me tightly. I think neither of us wanted to be the first to break away because of where we must go from there, what we had to face. I could hear Zac running down the stairs to find out what had happened. He joined us there by the phone in our embrace.

The next twenty-four hours still blur before the eye of my memory in a welter of hospitals, weeping friends, and the gnawing inner tooth of doubt, guilt, and fear.

The first hospital was White County, a few minutes away right there in Searcy. Dr. White met us and after a few amenities said the only thing approaching comfort he could summon: "I've seen worse than Kandy who lived. We need a CAT scan at Central; then we have to get her to Little Rock as soon as we can." We piled in the cars for the ten-minute ride to Searcy's other hospital, where Dr. Elliott met us. As we waited for the test to finish, the questions pounded on all of us.

"Why didn't she come to us?" I asked. Zac sat in a chair, beating its arms and repeating angrily, "Why did she do this? Why did she do this?" He and Kandy had grown up together, a second generation of children to us. Even as college students they remained close. During her sojourn in Harrison, Zac drove to see her and the two had a cathartic reunion. Zac told us he felt very good after that meeting. Now, like Ray and me, he was bewildered, chastising his absent sister: "All the stuff we've done! Why didn't you look me up?"

Our entourage arrived in Little Rock about 2 A.M., joined by a few nursing majors from Harding early on. Kandy was in a coma. By the time they got her hooked up to the needed machines, more Harding students had arrived, as had Marc and Tina. When the neurosurgeon called the family aside, he told us that with surgery she had at best a fifty-fifty chance. The operation would begin at 5 A.M. Until then, the doctors agreed to let people see her—family first, then students. Before the family went in, the neurosurgeon took us aside: "Look, you're going to notice some flinching, and it may scare you. It's the machines—they cause involuntary spasms. Don't worry about it; it's just mechanical." He paused before removing his hand from my elbow, finishing in a softer voice: "But if you get tears, that's a human response."

We paused awkwardly inside the intensive care room. Her bed was almost lost in a forest of tubes with metallic trunks. Screens with green letters and numbers scrolled by like signs on Times Square. Underneath it all lay Kandy, her skin yellowish in the hospital light. Her head was swathed in bandages. She stayed very still for a time; then her arms or legs would convulse, or her eyelids flutter. Marc was the first to approach the bed. He leaned down, one hand on the metal rail, and began to speak to his sister's inert form: "Kandy, you hang in there! You're going to make it! You are going to make it. You're a fighter! You've always been a fighter!" As he spoke his voice rose in volume and intensity. By the time he finished he was nearly yelling. The body in the bed twitched once—twice. The eyelids blinked rapidly as the words flew out of Marc. I wanted to believe that the movement meant she heard him, but the doctor had been clear: electrical response. Her flesh getting random and garbled messages from a damaged brain.

When Marc finished, his emotion momentarily spent, I saw something run from underneath Kandy's fluttering lashes. Out of each closed eye a tear trickled. Ray saw them; the others too. "If you get tears, it's a human response." We were all crying too, of course. I heard a sharp intake of breath from Ray, bless his heart, as he reacted to the sight, not wanting to sob openly, loudly. He drew the emotion back inside as if he needed the control.

Soon he took his turn at Kandy's bedside, with me. We murmured our love with our faces as close to hers as possible. We talked to her in short whispered bursts followed by broken prayers. We told her that God was listening and that she should be strong. That He wanted her to live and be strong and serve Him. And again the salt water dripped slowly down her face to her lips. With one finger I wiped the tears from her cheeks. I'm not sure about Ray, but whatever I said came instinctively, without thought. All I knew was that we had to say something and that Ray was there beside me, his thirty years of preaching echoing in his low, soothing voice. At that moment his faith may have been sustaining us both. I seemed disconnected from my own feelings, my own conviction. I was in the worst dream of my life.

Eventually, students and faculty came, sometimes in twos or threes, to offer encouragement to Kandy. They paraded slowly past her comatose body for an hour. Zac could not do it. He was too heartbroken. Later Ray gathered the family in the first-floor chapel for a devotional, one of many we had there in those forty-eight hours. It would be a long night, too much time to think, to come back to the same questions. "Why did she not come to us?" I would ask again and again. "Why did she take things so hard? What could we have done to help her?"

I prayed for David's safe arrival from Virginia. No one was safe, I realized, not even our children. I thought of my own mother and father and Ray's long dead Flara and John D. I saw Connie, Zac's fiancé, talking, and thanked God for giving her to Zac. Then the stolid face of Lona Jack stared at me as I remembered her mysterious death and a question Ray asked during our courtship—about whether committing suicide is proof of insanity. And he added fervently, "I don't want my mother to be insane!"

These and other unbidden thoughts alternately plagued and comforted me during the long minutes of waiting. Most horribly, I kept thinking of Kandy with a gun; it was inconceivable. And the place the police had found her, not two miles from our house on Hayes. At least we had been spared the agony of it happening in our home. At least we had that.

The Assembly of God church building on the intersection of Benton and Cloverdale is a contemporary gray and white brick building with a spacious parking lot that in 1983 looked nearly deserted even during services. At the time a narrow drive looped around the building alongside a makeshift softball field bordered by a cornfield and rickety wooden bleachers. Next to the field under some trees were three concrete picnic tables and a barbecue pit. Close by stood a sagging volleyball net. From the grove you could see beyond the firehouse and Oakley's Garage on either side of Market out to Race, narrow, pothole-riddled, busy Race. Still the main drag in Searcy. In those days you could see the golden arches of McDonalds too, before the store moved out closer to the freeway, and it was there that Kandy and her fellow nursing students, after a day in Little Rock, would grab some food—cheeseburger, fries, coke—and drive over to the church. They drove around back. In good weather, they would park on the grass and eat on the picnic tables. Surrounded by the traffic of Benton and Market and Race, these college kids felt that they had found a haven. It was one of those places where you could watch the world go by—even if it was just the little world of Searcy, Arkansas—while resting from its pace. It was a vantage point to make the world manageable. The cars sounded faint and looked smaller. The traffic did not threaten but opened up its pattern to your omniscient gaze. So you laughed and talked and ate and let the day uncoil loosely at your feet in the shade of the trees, as your elbows rested against the cool concrete of the tables.

Sometime shortly after midnight on the morning of March 5, 1983, a few hours after she pulled out of our driveway, Kandy made one more trip to the Assembly of God. She stopped the car on the pavement close to the picnic tables and turned off the ignition. In the dark she reached for her perhaps already loaded gun. A yellow receipt for the weapon lay beside it.

I cannot imagine what went through her mind in the moments—seconds?—before she put the barrel to her head and pulled the trigger. I can think only of what her friend finally told us about her last conversation with Kandy. When Kandy turned up missing, Stacy had rushed to join the other nursing students who were with us, fearing the worst, but she could not bring herself to tell me then of Kandy's ominous mood the day before—the day of the overdose and reprimand. It was not until a week after we buried Kandy that Stacy rang our doorbell to give us the complete story of March 4.

As they drove back from Little Rock, Kandy had asked her, "Can't you tell I'm depressed? What about my music?" She was referring to some gloomy choices on the cassette. Stacy did not know how to react at first, but she grew uneasy as Kandy continued to talk. Finally Kandy said, "When I get depressed like this, I think of taking my life." In near panic, Stacy began to sermonize on the wrongness of such thinking, talking fast, ticking off reasons to live. Whatever she did or might do, Kandy said, had nothing to do with her parents. "It's me," she said; "I am the one who sets these goals for myself." Then she recited a list of her past mistakes, her "sins." Still Stacy preached hope, change. Finally, Kandy seemed to relent: "No, I wouldn't do that—I couldn't do it to my family."

Cathleen Smith also told me of a curious question Kandy had asked her not long before March 4. It concerned a recent suicide, someone known to the Harding students, but instead of asking why or raising philosophical questions, Kandy had asked Cathleen which method would be the most painful—poison or gunshot.

I don't blame either Stacy or Cathleen for not telling me right away about these conversations. Cathleen had no alarming context in which to place those questions, and Stacy was a young woman who had less than twenty-four hours to sort out her friend's seemingly speculative remarks before they were acted on. Sitting in her car on a rainy night in the Searcy Assembly of God parking lot, Kandy could see only the lights of Race and the field before her in shadows. Of course I've wondered what she thought of as she sat there. Did she stare into the darkness and see the future? Did it seem threatened because of her mistake? Or did she see only the sins of her past floating over the dark field, never to leave her? Maybe when you reach the point at which she had arrived, there is nothing distinct in your mind. Just the darkness—without form and void. Ray and I wondered many times, but maybe it's a blessing not to know.

Sean, the young policeman, had actually seen the Volkswagen pull into the church lot. He recognized it as Kandy's because he knew her. Approaching the car, he saw her with a gun and yelled, "No!" Maybe because of his shout, her first shot missed. Then she fired again.

FINDING OUR WAY BACK

By midnight Saturday the needles on all the monitoring machines had steadied some and Kandy could breathe a little on her own. Slightly encouraged, Ray and I finally fell asleep. We had decided not to call David until after the surgery, since he lived in Virginia and, realistically, could not arrive before it was over anyway. He walked into Baptist Hospital sometime Saturday afternoon. It was a comfort to be able to wait with all our family present. David looked tired from his flight to Memphis and two-hour drive into Little Rock, but his embrace seemed to give Ray renewed energy. Otherwise he was quiet, looking as small and isolated to me as I felt, trying to keep some sanity while the doctors did their work. I saw his head bowed often. After David spent a few minutes with Kandy in ICU, we rehashed with him what we knew. All of us finally drifted into fitful sleep. At 8 A.M. Sunday, stiff from spending the night slumped in chairs or curled up on short sofas, we were in line to see Kandy in ICU when a "code blue" sounded. "That's Kandy," I said, as the dispassionate voice on the intercom repeated the words. The others did not like the calm in my voice and asked how I could know the alert was about her. "I don't know," I replied. I just did.

An hour later the surgeon came out to the waiting room. Without small talk he told us that Kandy was not going to make it. I don't remember my first reaction with clarity. The next scene I can visualize in any detail occurred in the little chapel, where Ray had once again gathered us: me, David, Marc and Tina, Zac and Connie. He spoke gently but firmly, making three points about which he had thought a good deal during the night. "First, we are not going to question the eternal destination of Kandy's soul over a few hours of recklessness. She had an illness that left her unable to cope. We're going to trust in God to take care of her. Second, we are not going to blame anyone else for this. Not the teachers, not the students, not anyone. We don't want to go down that road—it leads to bitterness, which is maybe the worst sin we could be afflicted with outside loss of faith. Third, and last, we are not going to blame ourselves. We did what we could, given our human limitations. We loved her and she knew it. Her needs—whatever they were—were beyond us." It was very quiet when he stopped speaking. We sat on the small padded pews, most of us sobbing, but even so silence reigned for a moment. Then we prayed.

Many people came that afternoon—more than three hundred. The hospital provided a private room for us, to allow escape from the crowds occasionally. Maybe the greatest value in the large numbers of visitors was in the distraction they provided. With hundreds of students to talk to, I thought less of my despair. Together we kept the death watch. Finally, at around 8 A.M. Monday morning, Kandy was pronounced dead. We stayed a while making arrangements. There were papers to sign, phone calls to make, plans to discuss. Her organs were to be harvested for donation. It was late morning before we headed to Searcy, exhausted emotionally and physically.

In the car on Route 67, I silently dreaded the next twenty-four hours. First, I dreaded the funeral, which was set for the following day at the College Church. I had a long-standing distaste for funerals. In my capacity as a preacher's wife, I attended too many of them. The music would start, the family would fall apart, and I would think, "This is absolute torture! To bring people into an auditorium like this, with the casket up front, then sing songs designed to bring on the tears. It's barbaric!" I don't know why I harbored such feelings; maybe it was because death had not yet invaded the deepest recesses of my being. At that point in my life, I saw death as this painful experience to be endured somehow privately. I couldn't get past the starkness of it. Even the custom of sending flowers seemed distasteful to me. They were an expensive cosmetic, like the makeup applied to corpses, an unnatural attempt to cover up ugly reality.

I was not articulating such thoughts in the car—even to myself. In retrospect, though, they were behind the acute dread I felt about the funeral. My second anxiety was more immediate: I did not want to go home. The idea of walking through our front door into a house forever bereft of our only daughter overwhelmed me. "God," I prayed, "give me strength. Do not let me give in to despair!" I said nothing to Ray, and he spoke only occasionally, just perfunctory remarks. Somehow, by the time we pulled onto Hayes, I had steeled myself. With God's help I could get through the door and through the funeral the next day. Absorbed in my own thoughts, I had lost track of what Ray or the others were saying or doing. All I remember is being at the door, fighting off this sense of emptiness, of being more tired than I had ever been in my life. I was even feeling thankful to God for what little resolve I had to press on. In my ignorance, I was crediting Him with granting me minimal emotional survival when, in fact, on the other side of the door lay a small miracle of emotional healing.

It still seems like a dream to me. In our absence, friends and neighbors had cleaned the house, but frankly I didn't notice that until later. I didn't even notice all of them: the Greens, Betty Davis, Jo Cleveland, and many others. And David's wife, Candy, had arrived with my grandchildren. The house was full of people, and they all reached out to me in slow motion, it seemed. I got passed around like a broken doll, each hug a small repair to my spirit.

And surrounding these warm, living human beings—filling my vision— was a profusion of flowers. In my memory they seem to festoon the walls and furniture like a fabulous garden. My living room, kitchen, and family room had become Searcy's version of Eden. Mixed spring bouquets of pinks, white daisies, red carnations, and yellow jonquils dotted the rooms. A large basket of pink azaleas decorated the kitchen table. I saw white spider mums, pink carnations. Brilliant orange spider mums too, with tiger lilies! The colors swam before my eyes until the whole world was a hanging garden of soft rainbow petals. And in each of the arrangements a card with names of friends near and far. Now for the first time I knew, knew, the value of flow-ers, of all the ritual surrounding death. The flowers softened and absorbed the harsh reality—did not cover it up—but made it bearable because each arrangement, each brilliant color, each delicate petal, symbolized the love of those who sent them. But beyond that, the flowers betokened the return of life after death. We decorate our caskets with flowers because we believe that death is not the end. Even in the tragedy of loss, we can enact the cen-tral truth of our faith. I was overwhelmed.

Again, I did not—could not—think all of this at the time. But I felt it. I have never had a surer sense of Blessing. The friends who escorted me around my home might as well have been angels, for they were acting as ministering spirits, reacquainting me with familiar territory: "This is your house, Eloise, but you may have forgotten what it is made of. It is a house not made with hands. It is held together with love: the Builder's, your own, Ray's, your neighbors, brothers in Christ, yes, even Kandy's. Hers lives on here too. Life goes on."

"Life goes on!" How different that cliché becomes in the context of God's blessings. It's not that all my negative emotions were suddenly replaced by happiness or total acceptance. Indeed, Ray and I would suffer much more in subsequent months. Even so, God gave me a miracle on that day. I call it the miracle of the flowers! It refreshed me like an oasis in the desert revives a worn traveler not yet at the end of the journey.

At some point, I completely lost track of Ray. As everyone, mostly women, tried to comfort us, see to our needs, Ray had slipped out the back door. When I finally noticed his absence, I thought I knew where he must have gone. Ever since our move to the house on Hayes, all of us had loved the big back yard that extended more than two hundred yards down to the creek. Ray especially cherished time spent on the bank of the stream. I think it reminded him of his boyhood, those dangerous but exhilarating times on the Kanawha River. As a historian, he always had a strong sense of place, too, not the color on a map alone, but the rocks, soil, and life particular to a real place where real people lived. This little creek put him in touch with all that. It had been a favorite place of Kandy's too. Father and daughter spent much time here. As I thought of all this, I went to the back window and saw a distant figure disappearing into the foliage hiding the creek.

I excused myself and went out the back door. I hurried past our unplowed garden, through the pine trees transplanted from Daddy's place in Alabama, down the soft green slope to the concrete picnic table where we liked to cook out. The rusty horseshoes were probably piled on the old slab from the days when the water treatment plant owned the land. I followed the path Ray had cleared through the undergrowth until I joined him. He stared into the creek, which gurgled against the rocks in mottled currents. Pin oak trees grew up on both sides of the water; the smaller saplings jutted out overhead, seemingly growing out of the creek itself. The cloudy March day was cool. Ray didn't say anything, so I asked him if he was all right. He said yes. We said nothing else.

He may have been recalling the times he instructed Kandy on the flora and fauna of this bit of nature. Maybe the time he saw a beaver gnaw a tree to the thinness of a toothpick and then lunge against it to send it crashing into the creek. He had not called the children for fear of scaring the animal, but how he loved to tell them the story! The creek was a place for children. I stayed with him until he was ready to go back.

The funeral the next day served as a bridge back to our lives. But it wasn't easy. Twelve hundred people crowded into the College Church, and though their presence comforted me, I could not focus on others for very long. Ray seemed better able to talk to the many sympathetic Christians who filled the aisles. The boys did not talk much at all. Both the Chorus and the Chorale, Harding's two singing groups, gathered in the balcony, led by our old friend Kenneth Davis. Despite my best efforts to concentrate, I heard only snatches of the lyrics, but the sound was full and deep from the opening verse of the first song: "When peace like a river attendeth my way, when sorrows like sea-billows roll..." All 150 of them sang slowly—the sopranos holding the notes and the men answering—filling the auditorium with echoes of "it is well with my soul."

The family sat in several front pews: David and Candy and our two granddaughters, Ericka and Ami; Marc and Tina; Zac and his fiancé, Connie; my parents; my brothers, Frank and Bill; my sister, Nancy; my nephew, Kenny; and others. We listened as Cliff Ganus recited the official statistics of Kandy's life. How cold they sounded to me in a way: "Kandy is survived by..." Cliff closed with a mention of the memorial we had set up at the Children's Hospital; always the good promoter of worthy causes, he urged the audience in his soothing voice to consider a gift to the memorial: "And I know this would be pleasing to the family," he said.

And then the young voices sang "Be Still, My Soul," a song that I cannot hear today without a moistening of the eyes:

> When disappointment, grief, and fear are gone,
> Sorrow forgot, love's purest joys restored;
> Be still my soul, when change and tears are past,
> All safe and blessed we shall meet at last.

Like our lives and our hope, the music seemed to be suspended between joy and sorrow. Someone read Psalm 55, someone else led a prayer, and then came "O Lord, Our Lord," its majestic melody asking me to lose my grief for a moment in the adoration of God. And for a moment I could. Ray did too, I think, if his steady bass voice meant anything.

Neale Pryor walked to the podium. It seemed natural to ask him to preach Kandy's funeral, the way he brings together the Bible and homespun wisdom. He spoke of our need for good memories of Kandy, of our need for not only the tight circle of family to close the hole left by her departure, but also for our larger family circle, the church, which was even in this room, he said, gathering around us in love. He quoted several scriptures, but the one that stirred my heart most, I think, was a mention of Ishmael. The child of Hagar, he had been banished, and in his wandering began to cry out for help. Neale said, "In Genesis...there is one little statement that caught my eye: 'And God heard the voice of the child when he wept.'"

Bless Neale's heart. He intended that news to comfort us, but like everything else it came with mixed results in my psyche. I tried to picture Kandy being heard by God, tried to envision one of His angels swooping down to lift her from the desert and take her to a place where she would suffer no more. What kept intruding on that picture was the question, "Why didn't you hear Kandy when she was alive?" I felt an immediate stab of guilt, both for questioning God and for the responsibility I might have to bear for not hearing her either. My thoughts climbed up, plunged down, and rattled around with each new thing said or seen.

Yet I can still say that the funeral was wonderful. True, I vacillated during the ceremony, but the songs, the Bible verses, and most of all the people kept me afloat. I saw Kandy, too, as she lived. The good things came back as I heard the prayer, the sermon, and the songs. Even without those positive memories, Neale's last story would have eased my grieving heart—and Ray's. He read from a note Kandy had left for her secret sister in Zeta Rho. It was the best way to end the service and the best way to remember our daughter on such a sad March day. It began with this biblical passage from the story of Moses: "And the Lord said to him, 'What is that in your hand?' And Moses said, 'A staff'" (Exodus 4:2). Here is Kandy's message for her friend drawn from the verse:

> Only a staff… and yet with it (and through God), Moses part-ed the Red Sea, amazed Pharaoh [sic] with it, brought plagues, and called water from a rock. And God says to you, "What is that in your hand?" And do you say, "only my life, a few talents?" After see-ing what he can make of a staff, imagine what He can make of your life! Love, Your Secret Sis.

Somewhere in her heart, beneath the pain, Kandy believed this great truth about God. It is the message I still take to groups of teens when I am asked to speak of Kandy's tragic death. I believe she lives through those words and am happy to bring the news to those who may need it. Hearing Neale

Kandy's senior picture for the Nursing Department (1983).

read them renewed my pride in her great value as a person even as I cried for how she failed to see her own worth clearly enough to go on. I left the church building a little stronger, knowing there would be lingering heartache to face in the coming days.

There seemed to be so many places to go, so many things to do, before we could put the death behind us. In what amounted to therapy, we wrote hundreds of thank-you cards. We donated Kandy's clothes to some families in need. Kandy would have liked that. We planted a tree on Harding's campus as a memorial.

One day Ray asked me to go to Little Rock. We drove down 67, onto I-40 and into the city, where we took the exit at Rodney Parham and I-430, to a little shopping center called Trellis Square. Within two minutes we came to the front door of a sporting goods store. It advertised a variety of gear including firearms. We looked at the display window for an instant; then Ray led the way inside. I was nervous just to be in a room with all those guns—everything so brightly polished, rows of rifle barrels and cases gleaming with small arms. There were a few customers in the store, and an older man behind the counter.

Ray introduced himself and me to the man, the proprietor, who, it turns out, was a retired Air Force man. He wore a mustache. Ray showed him the gun and bill of sale retrieved from the front seat of Kandy's car and said in a soft voice, "I'd like to know who sold my daughter that gun." The old man dropped his head and immediately started to cry.

"I did," he said.

Ray asked him if he knew what had happened.

"I read it in the newspaper; I remembered her."

"Tell us about it," Ray said. "Did you not pick up on anything? How long were you with her?" Before he could answer, I broke in, "But she didn't even know how to fire a gun!"

The old man, his eyes still wet, said, "I showed her how!"

We must have been staring at him in disbelief, because he said, "Look, I have three sons myself. I am heartsick over this. She came in and said she needed a gun for protection, that she and a friend were moving into an apartment in the city. She—she was convincing. I took her out back to our target range and showed her how to hold and fire the pistol. I'm so sorry," he said.

Finally Ray asked, "Could we see the form she filled out?" Zac had told us to take a look at the form, thinking it might provide a clue to her state of mind. Statistics show that even when deflected from their purpose, suicidal people tend to come back to death as a solution, but we agonized over the possibility that a few days might have made a difference. Her fatigue, her guilt concerning the overdose, her sense of failure, might have dissipated with a new day. At this point we still wanted those elusive answers. So we honored Zac's request to look at the form for clues. When the store manager handed the application to us, I noticed the almost perfectly printed information. It was as if she wrote with the poise and calm of a new contentment. Like the bill of sale and all the other evidence, the receipt was as mute or as eloquent as our tortured spirits wanted it to be.

There wasn't much more to say. Ray thanked the old man, whose tears seemed genuine. Other customers had momentarily turned their gazes from golf clubs and fishing gear to the trio of parents weeping for lost children.

RAY'S DREAM

The death of our child clung to us both in the weeks following the funeral. It was like a veil through which we viewed everything else. For Ray, it was also a palpable burden, an almost physical trauma. Thankfully, spring break came a few days after the funeral; Ray needed the time. Even after the break, he told me that going to class was worse than taking a beating, this admission coming from the man whose love of the classroom was the one thing in our marriage approaching infidelity.

One of the hardest things on Ray was the disposal of Kandy's things. Noting the mass of items in her room, Marc urged us to begin cleaning it out. "If you don't," he said, "you might end up making it a shrine." Of course, we decided to keep certain mementos: letters, books, trophies, school work. Nevertheless, most of the things in her room—clothes, stereo—must be moved out or given away, and in doing so Ray could not escape a feeling of betrayal. I watched him drag Xerox boxes of paper to the curb as if he were dragging Kandy's body itself. Most of the paper was in the form of study notes, in perfect order, for the State Board nursing examination in July. It was as if the removal of these bits and pieces of her life and work was a kind of rejection of her. Ray didn't say much about guilt, but he felt its burden. He found it harder to live up to his hospital chapel speech than the rest of us did. "We mustn't blame ourselves," he had said. But it was impossible not to. Guilt slipped into the quiet spots of the day.

It was hard on Ray to give away Kandy's two most prized and valuable possessions: her bicycle and car. I do not recall who got the bike, but we gave David the Volkswagen. That little white car was special to Ray because he and Kandy had spent days shopping for it upon her return from Harrison.

After looking in vain on car lots in Searcy, the two went to Little Rock. When they returned, Kandy beamed with pride because not only had they found a car—the white Volkswagen—but she had watched her dad haggle successfully over price. "Mom," she boasted, "the guy said we'll take $650 for it. Then Dad said 'Give you $550'—and the man agreed!"

Now the VW was gone. The garage seemed vacant with both car and bike given away. Shorn of its surplus of paper and clutter, Kandy's empty room reminded Ray of life without Kandy and reproached his role as chief disposer of her possessions. Following hard upon his powerlessness to keep his daughter alive came this sense of giving her memory away. It may have been irrational, or it may have been a saving deflection of deeper questions, but his guilt focused on what we let go after her death.

He went on in this almost zombie-like state for weeks. I too felt that life had stopped. I had no desire to cook, to go out. Ray and I, in fact, forced ourselves to go places. We prayed daily, we drew strength from the friends who constantly called or came by. Still, we felt stuck in a routine of deadened senses. We were surviving. I feel no shame in admitting this. If the writers of the Psalms could be honest enough to confess their doubt and pain to God, Ray and I could claim no false optimism or comfort. In fact, the book of Psalms was about the only biblical book I wanted to read at that point. My only other interest lay in books on suicide. I read seven or eight in the months following Kandy's death. Ray continued to preach, study the Word, and teach. We knew God was there, but we also knew we were walking deep in the valley of the shadow.

Then came one of those rays of sunshine that promised a way out. Early in the morning about two months after the funeral, I was in the kitchen when Ray came in, and his face looked different. Before I could ask if something was wrong, he said, "I had a dream last night, Weezie. I know that it's all right, what we've done." I wasn't sure what he meant, but I could see he wanted to tell me the dream, so I sat down with him at the kitchen table. He told it as vividly as it must have unfolded in his mind—Ray always said he dreamed in Technicolor—and I'll never forget the dream or his sense of wonder as he spoke.

He is asleep in his chair in the family room, a typical night, when Kandy comes through the room from the hall. She brushes his head as she passes and Ray jumps up, eager to talk to her. Kandy, wearing her new red sweater, happy for his attention, nevertheless tells him that she has to see me in the kitchen first, and that she'll be right back. Ray experiences a sweet anticipation while she is gone, one of those dream spans of time seemingly long and instantaneous all at once. When she returns, they are sitting in the family room. Earnestly but matter-of-factly she says, "Daddy, I've decided to come back to Harding, but I don't know what I'm going to major in!" Ray loves the way she says it, as if she is enjoying the joke with him—good old Kandy, still can't settle on what to do with her life. Then suddenly the conversation is over and Ray is looking at Kandy asleep on the couch, the television on with some movie she had been watching. As he has done dozens of times, he tiptoes over to cover her with the blanket draped on the back of the couch.

Like a jump cut in a movie, it is morning. Ray and Kandy are ready to leave. She is excited at the prospect of driving her car to school. With a stab of regret, Ray tells her, "Kandy, I'm afraid we had to give your car away." Without missing a beat, Kandy smiles from her warm red sweater and says, "That's OK; I'll just ride my bike." Ray shrinks even more. "Honey, we had to give that away too." As Kandy moves, Ray realizes that they are standing in the garage. He watches her open the passenger door to his car: "No problem, Dad, I'll just ride with you!" Her absolute joy, her confidence, her contentment, sweeps over Ray in his dream and carries him from sleep, out of bed, down to the kitchen, to tell me that it is all right. What we've done.

We sat for some minutes at the table holding each other, crying thick, bittersweet tears and feeling that we were not alone in our house.

ZAC'S WEDDING

Not long after that dream we headed off to Michigan for Zac's wedding to Connie Mansell. Connie was an auburn-haired elementary education major whose quiet, purposeful manner had won Zac during the spring of 1981, while we were away at Florence. She was two years older than Zac, the same age as Kandy, and had been teaching already, most recently in Beebe. Ray and I had liked her from the first. Something in her unassuming manner communicated genuineness. She seemed more than ready for marriage, asking me for homemaking tips and proving to be creative around the house and in the classroom herself. As time took us further from the day of Kandy's death, Ray seemed to depend a little more on his relationship with Connie. Part of it was convenience; she and Zac were around.

It was more than convenience, however. Although Connie did not know Kandy well, she had asked our daughter to be a bridesmaid. Connie's mother made the muslin pattern for Kandy's dress. The death left Connie with a void in the wedding to fill, so we suggested Tina, Marc's wife. Hesitant at first because she did not know Tina, Connie seemed grateful for the offer and accepted. About three weeks after the funeral, she came to Ray and me in the kitchen, where we sat one evening doing crosswords. Her presence in the house was no longer unusual, so we greeted her as we would have one of our own children. No doubt Connie had been observing our struggles since the funeral. She cleared her throat and told us she had something to say."

"I know I'm not Kandy. No one can replace her in your lives. But I'm here if you need me." Those few words meant so much. We both jumped up and hugged her. Not much more was said; not much more was necessary.

On June 25, 1983, in Midland, Michigan, Ray performed the marriage ceremony for Zac and Connie. Despite the shadow of Kandy's death, the wedding was joyous, filled with much of the usual silliness and pratfalls, the weeping of parents, the giggling of nieces and nephews. At the rehearsal Ray forgot Zac's name. The joke was that Ray should call him "Dave—er, Marc—er, Zac," just to be safe, and Zac threatened to wear a sign with that composite name stitched to the outside of his wedding jacket.

Rehearsal dinners are almost always a combination of tension and silliness, but I knew that Ray's laughter was forced the slightest bit. Later in the evening at the Holiday Inn, he confided to me his dread: "I hope I can get through it tomorrow." I shared his fear and the feelings out of which it grew. No matter where our thoughts led, they returned to the one inescapable fact: someone was missing. Ray said, " Zac and Connie are our living children and this is their day. We're not going to let it be spoiled."

The next day the weather was unseasonably warm but beautiful as cars turned into the parking lot of the Midland Church of Christ. David and Marc, looking handsome in gray tuxedos, escorted me to the front. I know they joined in the ushering because they were worried about my state of mind, and it did feel reassuring to have them at my side as we walked down the darkened aisle, with candles lighting the way. Ray and Zac appeared up front in their gray tuxes, both sporting mustaches and pink boutonnieres. They looked very much like father and son.

As the wedding party waited for the bride, the words and music of "God Give Us Christian Homes" serenaded the audience. Finally, to a hummed rendition of the Wedding March, Connie and her father walked slowly down the aisle. She looked lovely in her lace-trimmed white dress, with its graceful train. She wore an open-crowned white hat and carried a white and pink arrangement of flowers.

Ray watched this procession as he had done for hundreds of weddings, for David and Marc, and now for the last of his children. I could see the emotion welling up in him even before it was time to speak. He did not forget Zac's name this time as he began:

> Zac and Connie, your parents have looked forward to this moment with prayerful concern for many years, for we realize that outside of the gospel call, this will be the greatest decision of your life…. Zac, you've been a dependable and model son in every way. Your mother and I have been justly proud of your many accomplishments. We've watched you grow from an impulsive towhead that your brothers and sister loved to tease, as the youngest in the family, to a mature person with excellent values and great promise for the future. We wanted you, like your brothers before you, to choose a Christian woman for a lifetime companion. We were thrilled when you told us it was Connie.

Then Ray turned to Connie, and it was in this speech that the pain, mingled with gratitude, resurfaced.

> Connie, we love you as our very own. You've been very close to us in recent months. We know that Zac has made the right choice and wish to express our gratitude to you for having accepted his proposal of marriage. You and Zac had similar backgrounds and position in the family and similar moral upbringing. The values that Mr. and Mrs. Mansell have instilled in you are nonpareil. They will serve you well in establishing your home as God would have it.

At this point Ray's voice betrayed him some, beginning to waver: "You have the capacity to enjoy life like a little girl, yet you have the judgment of a mature woman with both feet on the ground." He gathered himself and continued, "Connie, you have stood by us—" Ray had to stop. After a few seconds of silence he went on—"in very troublesome times." His voice shook more on that line and again he stopped before regaining his composure: "And you have given very freely of your strength."

I couldn't see the look on Zac's or Connie's faces. Ray's eyes were moist. As he said those last nine words to Connie, his voice shuddered with the effort to keep from breaking. But he regained command. The deep, rich voice reasserted itself as he talked about commitment in a throwaway society. He talked about trials, about sadness. He painted a picture of the bride and groom as an aged couple, looking back over their lives:

As you relax your grip on life, you mutually share a garden of memories that you have planted and cultivated together through the years. And this is the sweetest time of all—as you relive at will the steps you've taken along the way, some in joy and some in pain, but all precious, nonetheless.

His comments seemed very somber. His description of married life sounded almost elegiac. He then turned to the Bible and read from Matthew and from Ephesians, ending with the passage that identifies marriage as part of the "profound mystery" of the church. The word "mystery" struck me amid a jumble of images: Kandy's cold body, Ray's face as he told me his dream, my hands secure in the arms of David and Marc, and Christ on the cross.

"Will you please join hands?" Ray repeated the vows. In meek voices they both said, "I do."

"Are there rings?" Ray asked. With a minimum of fumbling, the rings were produced.

"These beautiful golden bands are not mere pieces of metal, but they are symbolic of promises made. As you gaze upon these bands in the coming years, you will think of this day because of the promises you made and received…. Connie, are you willing to accept this ring as a token of the vows that Zac has made to you?"

Connie affirmed she was and repeated after Ray the vow:

"With this ring, "

"I thee do wed. "

"With all my heart's faithful affection,"

"I thee endow."

After Zac repeated his vows, Ray pronounced them husband and wife. His prayer following was beautiful but laced with a sense of life's trouble. He ended it with this petition for Zac and Connie: "We pray, Father, that as they walk down the pathway of life and their backs bend back toward the dirt out of which they originally came, they may clasp their hands and walk together as they face the sunset of life. We pray Father, above all, for the salvation of their souls. In Jesus name, amen!" Then to continue the prayer the group sang, "May the Lord be gracious unto you, and give you peace." Its echoing refrains filled the auditorium with the sounds of benediction.

Ray closed the ceremony by inviting everyone to the reception, which would begin in an hour at the Midland Community Center. As the wedding party first and then the guests filed out slowly, the group sang "God is Love."

The song has one of those subdued melodies with almost an alto-dominated harmony. It is not a traditional recessional.

> Come let us all unite to sing,
> God is love.
> Let heaven and earth their praises bring,
> God is love.
> His blood has washed our sins away;
> His spirit turned our night to day.
> And now we can rejoice to say
> That God is love.
> He is our sun and shield by day,
> Our help our hope our strength our stay.
> He will be with us all the way;
> Our God is love!

As more of the audience stood and exited, the more the song became mingled with sounds of their talk. By the time the last chorus ended, the talk and laughter had almost, but not quite, overwhelmed the lyrics and melody. It was as if the song itself had reanimated the people in the auditorium. In the crowded foyer immediately after the wedding, Ray embraced Connie in one of his patented bear hugs. He was becoming famous in the family for reserving those especially for daughters-in-law and grandchildren.

At the reception Ray seemed to be his old jolly self. As he and Connie stood together for a moment, amid the laughing wedding guests, framed by a huge white heart drawn on the brick wall with the names Zac and Connie written inside the heart, I noticed again her dark hair and the trace of freckles across her nose. And her open, friendly face that joined others in the endless smiling of a wedding day. "Welcome to the family," I whispered.

What do all these fragments of memory add up to? The annals of 1983 will forever record that the Muncy family experienced a death and a wedding. Only God can say—and maybe He will tell us some day—whether those two events, so common to humans, balanced out in Ray's heart or in mine. In the aftermath of our tragedy, finding answers consumed both Ray and me. Standing there in Michigan in June, I believed, and do so to this day, that I had just witnessed one answer. Now I don't bother too much about the whys and wherefores of the first, terrible element in the equation. I simply cherish the memory of Kandy, and know that all of life's promises don't come true. But I also know who is in control of life and death and time and space. And I know that He works everything for the good of those who love Him. I cherish the family He has added over the years. I hold on to my children—and grandchildren—a little more tightly, more aware than ever of the number of hairs on their heads.

Ray and I learned all this together.

ELEVEN

Where There is Vision

Life as an Elder (1971-93)

WHAT DOES IT MEAN TO BE AN ELDER?

The College Church building faces Race Street in Searcy, just east of the old Piggly Wiggly. It has a standard sign board in the front lawn, framed in brick and usually featuring a scripture or maxim along with worship service times. Since we started worshiping there in 1964, the building has acquired a fancy new facade and new driveways, more spacious parking lots, an expanded auditorium, and two educational additions. Located a block and a half from Harding's campus, the College Church has always loomed large in the minds of faculty and students, even when it was just a main auditorium with a few classrooms. It serves as a place of worship and study for more than a thousand Christians every week and the seat of vast mission enterprises, the extent of which would surprise the skeptic who sees religion only in its Sunday morning guise. It hums with activity on Sundays and Wednesday evenings.

I say "hums," in the present tense, but the truth is that now fewer people come to the building for midweek classes, what with the advent of home Bible study groups and teen "Huddle" groups, resisted at first but finally accepted by the College Church somewhere in the '80s. Back in 1985, though, you could count on a nearly full parking lot on Wednesday night at 7. Neale Pryor or some other luminary conducted his auditorium class for adults. Other classrooms were filled with younger adults, teens, and children.

The Wednesday night Bible study, such a distinctive part of the church and college sense of themselves, shows a secular world of recreational sports and television and working late where our priorities lie. By eight o'clock, as the parking lot clears out and friends say their good-byes, the midweek has come to an official close for members of the College Church. They leave feeling tired but good about themselves and the tradition in which they live. But for those entrusted with maintaining the integrity of that tradition, the night is just beginning.

By 8:15 the lights in the auditorium go out and the building is largely dark, except for the conference room next to the main office, across from the ladies bathroom. Its light stays on behind closed doors until nine o'clock. Ten o'clock. Eleven o'clock. Then the door opens and about twenty men begin to file out. Middle-aged and older, they wear suits mostly, with some sport shirts and a few pullovers and jeans. Some make small talk and laugh, but all look bone tired. Their day is now pushing eighteen hours. In groups of two or three they drift out to the remaining cars. It is fall and that means the air is clear and chilly.

Two of the men walk toward a white 1984 Cadillac. One, his glasses gleaming in the street light, chuckles, "I see you drove the Caddy tonight." He is small and his dark hair is receding. He is afflicted with a slight middle-age paunch.

"Yes, I didn't want to see you walk home in the cold." The owner of the Caddy is Tom Formby, and occasionally he likes to drive his Mazda, just to test the other's resolve never to ride in a foreign car. He laughs and unlocks the doors. Tom, a medical doctor who has practiced locally since 1953, is even smaller than his rider, and has white hair. His face retains a youthful playfulness despite the wrinkles. If ever someone's eyes could be said to twinkle, Tom Formby's do.

"I could live ten miles from church and walk home before these meetings end," his passenger says. "Oh, well."

Tom shakes his head: "I wish they'd consider my idea."

"You mean Saturday meetings?"

"That's the logical way to solve this problem of fatigue. We'd all be fresh on Saturday morning."

"Oh yes, but you know why that can't work?" The two have discussed this issue before.

"Football," sighs Tom. "I know. They don't want to give up those games."

"Well, in fairness, it's more than football. It's family time on the weekend—a valuable commodity."

"I know," Tom says, "but I still think that when we're tired, we're prone not to be as kind to one another as we should."

His passenger looks at him with affection: "I was kind to you tonight, wasn't I? I rode in your car."

While they talk, Tom pulls onto Grand Avenue and then onto Moore. He turns left on Hayes, remembering the time that his friend had indeed walked home from church rather than ride in the Mazda. The gesture was part playfulness, part a blue-collar heritage that would not die even in the relative affluence of the 1980s.

Ray Muncy may have left West Virginia long ago, he may have become a Reagan Democrat, he may even aspire to drive his own Cadillac, but he is never going to forget the workers of America, the kindred spirits of his own miner forbears. A small gesture, maybe, but he has stuck to it for years— even when his son Marc, with all the insolence of the young, reminds him that American cars contain many foreign-made parts.

Tom admires this stubbornness in his friend Ray. Nevertheless, the memory of Ray negotiating the narrow shoulder of Moore to get home makes his eyes twinkle. It also makes him think of the time he served up a hot pepper fresh from his garden onto Ray's plate. It was a special pepper just for Ray, who understood the challenge and began eating. Everyone watched as Ray took bite after bite of the long red hot pepper. He ate every blazing inch of it, tears streaming down his face. He would have finished though it killed him, Tom thinks. No one considers his friend a competitive person, but in his own way Ray has a will to fight.

Tom pulls into Ray's driveway at the bottom of Hayes Street's long hill. He turns off the ignition. The two men slump in the car seats and begin to talk about the meeting. Earlier tonight, for almost three hours, facing each other in a circle of folding chairs in the small conference room, twenty men wrestled with decisions involving millions of dollars, with the most intimate details of the lives of church members, most of whom are either friends or relatives of one or more of them, and with the question of how to interpret vague or disputed passages in the Bible. Though the meetings were never about a Bible passage, they often came down to one. The men argued and prayed. They did not like each other very much some of the time and at other times felt the deepest kinship.

Tom and Ray are worn out but cannot let go of the emotions, cannot get out from under the weight of the responsibility. They rehash the issues. They reiterate their positions—and say to each other what they would not say to the group. They repeat their fears, especially for the people who will be affected by what they decide. Will that young couple really survive financially if we follow through with our plan to help them escape debt? Is the accusation of abuse legitimate, or is she striking back at him in the worst way possible, by asking them to take the children from him? Most agonizingly, does the traditional interpretation of these scriptures really stand up, or are we risking irreparable damage to someone because of our rigidity?

At this hour they are humble men who have fewer answers than they want. Comfort comes in the presence of that friend against the other window. It is as if God has said in their hearts, "I won't give you all the answers now, but I will give you each other." And after twenty or thirty minutes, the conversation ends as it always does, with one of them saying, "Oh well, there's a better day a-comin'."

Inside our house I wait, unable to sleep. When the door opens, I notice that it is midnight. I hear Ray come up the stairs. He says, "Hello, dear. Can you tell that we didn't stick to the agenda?" I offer to fix him something to eat, and we go downstairs. Ray says nothing else about the meeting and I don't ask. Instead we catch up on family news and other routine matters. After he snacks a bit I hand him the *Democrat Gazette* and follow him back upstairs carrying my copy of the *Searcy Daily Citizen*. We get into bed and turn to the crossword puzzles in our respective copies. Ray always does the Little Rock paper because it is the more challenging of the two. Silently we work our crosswords until far past midnight. Even when we turn out the lights and sink our heads into our pillows, Ray will toss and turn some more before he can get to sleep. I offer a silent prayer on his behalf and, even though I don't know all their names, for all the people whose lives he helps to shepherd. In four hours he will wake up and go to school, living his other life while this one haunts him with its awesome responsibility.

What does it mean to be an elder in the College Church of Christ? I have just described it. At least I have described part of what it means. The long Wednesday night meeting is one of the truths about eldering. That's why I chose to tell it in present tense; I remember those meetings, and Tom's reminiscence about them, as if they are eternally present. But such a description is, of course, a view from the outside, suggesting the emotional and physical toll of eldering—and the bond between fellow elders that sustains them. There is so much more to say, but how to tell it—from the outside as I must—is a problem I'm not sure I can overcome. I know only that Ray dedicated himself to it as much as to any academic ambition, and his closest friends tell me that it may have been his greatest accomplishment.

Ray became an elder in 1971, the same year he earned his doctorate in history at Ole Miss and just three years after his sermon on elders and members at the Oxford Church. The call came when Cliff Ganus, Ray's boss at Harding and a long-time elder at the College Church, pulled into our driveway one summer evening. Kandy and I were coming around from the back of the house, dressed in shorts for a walk. Instinctively we stopped, fearing that President Ganus might disapprove of our attire. When Ray invited him in, we headed for the street. By the time we returned, Ray greeted us as a candidate for elder at the College Church.

He did not accept the candidacy immediately. The challenge was sobering even for a preacher of more than twenty years. He never said so directly, but during those few days before he accepted, I perceived a sense of inadequacy in Ray. He must have prayed privately about it. His experience as preacher told him that if the congregation approved his nomination, he would be taking a new journey out of the comfort zone he had built as preacher, teacher, and now doctor of philosophy. He knew that he would be giving up part of the family life he had reclaimed after years of preparation for his Ph.D. He knew that he, and to some extent the rest of us, would be subjected to a new scrutiny on the part of fellow Christians. Most of all, he realized that if he joined the eldership, he was promising God to "feed the sheep." Such a promise to such a one required some prayerful delay. Yet in the end he accepted, and the congregation accepted him as one of their newest elders.

The story of his life as an elder goes back further, however. It begins with the elders at Belle, West Virginia, who made him see his need to serve God. His grooming for the eldership began under the unofficial tutelage of men like Hubert Peck, Earl Broadus, and Woody Stogsdill. He learned about being an elder from working with four different elderships as a preacher. He saw some men of very limited vision who taught him mistakes to avoid, and he was influenced by some wonderfully wise men who acted as fathers in the faith.

By the time Ray was established in Bloomington, he had on file at least four sermons concerning elders. Fred Jewell, a student at Indiana University at the time, remembers that in those days Ray seemed to admire not just individual elders but the very concept of the eldership. Don England, the chemistry professor who first met and befriended Ray in Oxford and who served with him as an elder, condenses the concept into three key biblical words that mean "elder." They translate as first, "old man," with the implication of wisdom; second, as "overseer," with the connotation of supervisor; and third, as "shepherd," with its metaphorical association of one who tenderly cares.

All those words are important in defining what an elder can or should be, but of the three, the one that in Don's opinion described Ray the best was "shepherd."

He cultivated his talent for shepherding while a preacher. Zac remembers banging through the front door, returning from a ball game, to find Ray huddled with someone in the family room, deep in conversation. While Zac hovered in the kitchen, gathering snack food, he tried to hear what was being said. It was no use; the family room might as well have been a confessional. His glimpses into it revealed a father different from the one who watched *All in the Family*, even the one who preached and taught. In the dim light of the family room during these mysterious sessions, the father he saw leaning forward in the Archie Bunker chair had a quiet, benign authority. The posture suggested concern; the face said to his visitor, "You are important to me and in this room your needs can be expressed and protected from prying eyes. Only God and I will hear." The father in that pose was an elder.

As I have spoken over the years with Ray's fellow elders, they too have provided glimpses, images of the eldership that linger after the specific business of a given situation has faded from memory. More often than not, these scenes involve the friendship between Ray and someone, as in the case of Don England, with whom Ray had long talks after chapel. High up in the balcony of the cavernous Benson Auditorium, the subject inevitably turned from small talk to their tasks as elders, proving in the process that "two are better than one" in withstanding the pressure of the calling. Whether in meetings with Tom or after-chapel talks with Don, Ray's life as an elder often unfolded as a soul-sustaining partnership.

WINFRED AND RAY

Ray sat in the car with Winfred Wright. They were parked in front of a suburban home, clean red brick, manicured lawn. Nice neighborhood. They both knew the couple who lived there, and knew their parents, who also lived in Searcy. Neither man wanted to get out of the car. The early evening air was cool, no rain. But if it had been possible to put the key back in the ignition and go home to their wives, they would have done so in a moment. And it could have been another neighborhood and a different season. It didn't matter where, and most of the time it didn't matter who. What they had to do was rarely easy or desirable.

I don't know what Winfred may have been thinking, but Ray often said, "We lose more of these than we win." It was not a pessimistic sentiment, just experience talking. On this occasion, as others, Ray hoped that he and Winfred would succeed. In fact, before they got out of the car they prayed to that end. Then Ray said, "Well, are you ready?" Winfred said he was. The car doors slammed one after another. The two men walked up the clean sidewalk to the door, where, when the husband or wife, who would be expecting them, answered the door, Winfred and Ray would say something pleasant and the man or woman would invite them in. The greeting would of course be awkward, even subtly hostile, because the real reason for the visit flashed like a neon sign in the minds of all involved: We are the elders who have come to try and save your marriage.

What does it mean to be an elder in the Church? It means two men accepting the hard task of applying biblical teaching in the messy lives of real people. Ray and Winfred made their share of these kinds of visits. They learned things about each other in the process. Each observed the other respond to pressure and each gauged the spiritual commitment of the other. Each came out of the cauldron respecting and liking the other.

Maybe it was because they had faced tense times together, but Ray and Winfred could relax with each other too, each possessing a contagious sense of humor. In fact, Winfred and his wife Dottie were a couple with whom we could laugh and talk about everything and about nothing. Being silly was one of God's gifts for coping with the heavy business sometimes faced by elders—or any Christians, for that matter. Our two families grew close in the old car-pooling days when our children were young and then ministered to each other in the sorrow of death when we each lost a daughter. Some weeks after Winfred's and Dottie's middle daughter, Susan, was killed in a car wreck, we took them and another daughter, Sandi, out to eat, as they had done for us when Kandy died. Our night out fell on what would have been Susan's birthday.

We chose The Terrace, a Little Rock Greek restaurant that on this night, to our surprise, featured a belly dancer. She jangled and shimmered among tables, eyelids lowered seductively and her midsection undulating. Men occasionally stuffed money into her waist band (which was a little lower than her waist). When Ray made the mistake of casting a sheepish glance her way, she writhed in our direction. "Oh, no," he said, and bent forward. She danced beside him, arms above head, stomach thrusting toward him. All the while Ray stared into the skirt of the table cloth. With each pass of her arms in front of his bowed head, he seemed to shrink smaller into his chair. His complete lack of defense, his pathetic suffering in her presence, reduced the three of us to helpless laughter. Little Sandi, however, did not know what to think, so to save both her and Ray from corrupting worldly pleasures, we left the restaurant as discretely as possible. Ray endured much teasing about his animal magnetism, as well as his sophisticated response to women. But for a little while at least the grief was drowned in laughter.

For Ray, teasing was a measure of intimate friendship, and one of the best chances he ever had to tease fellow elder Winfred unfolded on a more typical night of entertainment for our circle.

At a gathering of friends at the Wrights' home, two conversations developed at either end of the rectangular living room. Ray and Winfred sat in a "no-man's land" where they could hear snatches of both conversations. On one end of the room, someone mentioned a woman known to most of us who lived in French Lick, Indiana. Some basketball fan called out, "Hey, that's the home of Larry Bird," at the time a big NBA star. The odd name of the town amused all who heard it, but the buzz in the room was loud and two-directional, and the speaker had run the words of the phrase together.

Winfred, trying to listen to this and the other conversation, heard repeated references to what sounded like some creature, so he finally got the attention of the group to say, "I don't believe I've ever heard of a homolary bird. Could someone please enlighten me on that species?" Home of Larry Bird. Ray stared for a moment, then burst out laughing, as we soon all did, once the inadvertent pun was explained. Winfred too, of course, his good humor prevailing over embarrassment.

Part of the code of faculty friendship, a code that in Ray's case was indebted in no small part to the Bull-Bat Club, I'm afraid, was that you never let a friend live down any gaffe. For months Ray teased Winfred about the new creature he had given life. He might stick his head inside Winfred's office, point to the window, and say urgently: "Quick! Get your binoculars; I think I see a homolary bird in the bushes!"

I'm not sure Winfred was always amused, but he was always a good sport, even after Ray ran the joke into the ground. After what we had been through together, what was a little teasing between friends? That too is the meaning of being an elder.

THE PREACHER'S ELDER

Mike Cope remembers one thing about Ray Muncy from his time as a Harding College undergraduate. His roommate, Buzz Ball, took a history class under this Dr. Muncy, who on the first day of class called roll. "Buzz Ball," he read. "Hmmm. Sounds like some new game." Buzz loved that.

In July of 1984, six years after graduating from Harding, Mike was back in Searcy trying out for the pulpit job at the College Church of Christ, wearing his only suit, one just bought for him by his dad. He must have worn it well on his slight frame, and his neatly combed dark hair and pleasant voice must have put everyone at ease during the interview process. Only the piercing eyes behind his glasses hinted at the dynamo beneath the surface. He got the job and in September of that year settled in with his wife Diane and two very young children, Matt and Megan. He would be working with twenty-four elders in our huge congregation, and I'm sure the process of getting to know them was a little daunting.

We had his family in our home not long after their move in September, also inviting Zac and Connie to help welcome them. After food and small talk, Ray and Mike got around to the subject of Plato's *The Republic*. Ray was delighted to hear that the College Church preacher had read this long philosophical presentation of the ideal state, written before the founding of Christianity. As Mike said later, he too was impressed with Ray's range of interests, his depth. He once told Mike that every preacher should be familiar with Studs Terkel's *Working*, and when Mike read it, he knew why. The book formed a connection with American culture, the blue-collar people from whom Ray came and to whom the gospel still needed to be preached. Plato and Studs Terkel: now that was a pair of opposites who together spanned the socio-economic scale and set even an ambitious preacher a formidable task of knowing his potential audience.

That night began a seven-year relationship between these two men, one a mild professor, the other a fiery student of the Bible and of the world in which Christians must apply that book. Mike was hungry for knowledge—he audited three of Ray's history classes during his stay in Searcy, learning along with Ray's majors the mantra: "Historians reflect the tenor of their times." Historiography helped Mike see more clearly the forces at work in theology, in the traditions of the church. Here is how he put the lesson: "There is such a thing as true, objective, unbiased history. And it is in the possession of God. The rest of us see darkly, as in a mirror. For Ray that didn't lead to pure relativism or futility. It was an admission of humility."

This humility did not mean that the two men shied away from intellectual challenge. Mike and Ray were invited to be among the founding members of the Searcy chapter of a men's club patterned after one in Little Rock. It was called simply "XV," for the maximum number of members allowed in the group. Membership was highly selective, and the club's by-laws required dinner meetings in formal dress followed by programs of specialized learning.

Meeting once a month in the homes of members, the tuxedoed men tackled knotty issues such as the assassination of John Kennedy, a discussion that led Mike and Ray to read part of the massive *Warren Report*. The group helped the two bond even more.

Mike saw in Ray, then, a man of knowledge who could nourish him, but he was hungry for action too. He wanted the church to move, to break out of some of its old ways of doing things. He admits he was a maverick, and his tendency to push for change made Ray a perfect confidante. First, Ray could be sympathetic to many of Mike's more radical ideas. Second, he could talk him out of actually trying them! Ray's sympathetic ear and judicious eye for restraint in sessions with Mike led a fellow-presbyter to dub Ray "the preacher's elder." Ray was not the only elder who encouraged Mike or in whom the preacher trusted, but my husband did earn a special place in his heart. Mike arrived in Searcy at a volatile time in his own life and in the brotherhood.

In 1984, the very year Mike began his ministry at the College Church, Rubel Shelly shook the Churches of Christ by publishing a book called *I Just Want to be a Christian*. Until that book, Shelly had made his reputation as an arch-conservative, aggressive prosecutor of any error in the church. He was respected by some, feared by others. Over a period of time, he came to see his approach as part of a sectarian spirit that had invaded Churches of Christ and damaged the work of the Lord. He appealed to church members to be "Christians only" instead of thinking of themselves as the "only Christians."

Shelly was one of several voices within and outside the church urging a reconsideration of what they felt was an unchristian combativeness on matters of fellowship and dialogue among people of faith. To some this new attitude of Rubel's sounded liberating, or more precisely, like a return to the full spirit of the Restoration Movement which had given rise to Churches of Christ. Many others saw his new approach as forsaking biblical truth. Christianity was by its nature exclusive, his opponents said, and to forget that was to invite "another gospel," thereby betraying Christ.

Needless to say, during Mike's tenure with the College Church, this issue generated its share of debate. Much of the leadership came down against Shelly's revised message. In fact, one of the hardest things Ray ever had to do as an elder was to "uninvite" Rubel to a meeting in Searcy. Ray had been chair of a committee assigned the responsibility of finding a speaker for one of the major gospel meetings of the year. Rubel Shelly's name was as well known as any in the brotherhood, and initially the committee's choice met with approval. After all, Rubel had spoken on campus before. However, as the date of the meeting approached, complaints surfaced; some feared the negative effects of having the newly controversial speaker in town and on campus at Harding. When the elders voted on the matter, Rubel lost. The majority of elders preferred being safe to being sorry.

Outwardly Ray strove to preserve unity; inwardly he was saddened that external pressure had forced the elders into repudiating a man he thought to be an excellent teacher. Ray liked Shelly's call to rethink brotherhood attitudes. He agreed with Shelly's contention that *I Just Want to be a Christian* called for no renunciation of doctrine—only of any divisive spirit that may have grown up around the desire for doctrinal purity. Bound by the vote to find another speaker, Ray's committee pressed on. Ray, however, simply had no heart to break the news to Rubel. It was a matter of conscience with him and most fellow elders understood. Someone else made the call.

Attuned to such brotherhood tension, Ray became a "safe" place for Mike to go. Mike saw the call to a new, less exclusive attitude as faith-invigorating, as biblical. When he grew frustrated with the prevailing climate, he found solace in talking to Ray. Ray agreed with him on the general rightness of his feelings, but at the same time counseled patience, tolerance, and love. It was like letting off steam with a trusty safety valve in the room, one that kept the pressure from mounting too high but also insured that it would not all dissipate in wasted anger or action.

What Mike and Ray had was not one-sided. Ray loved Mike as a son, and he respected him as an intelligent, sincere servant of God. Arriving only a year after Kandy's death and during trying times with David, Mike ministered to Ray. The preacher's famous sensitivity allowed him to see when Ray was hurting. I was not privy to their conversations; I know only that Mike understood the burdens Ray carried and that he did his share to lighten them. Mike often visited Ray in his faculty office. He loved the broad smile he almost always got from Ray, but one day he walked in to see "a plastered smile under heavy eyes."

He understood in a flash. It was near the anniversary of Kandy's death. Mike could recognize those times that, as he put it, "her death washed over Ray again." Not long after he arrived in Searcy in 1984, he noticed on Ray's desk a calendar, one of those with a leaf for each day. The date showing was March 7, 1983. In answer to Mike's question, Ray explained that his daughter Kandy had died on March 7, 1983. After this revelation, Mike could never see Ray's calm exterior in quite the same way, realizing that his friend and mentor ministered to others with part of his joy frozen in the ice of one terrible day. But he also remembered seeing the line from Tennyson that

Ray and I kept framed in our home: "Better to have loved and lost than never to have loved at all." I think he learned something of how to deal with death from watching Ray. Again, I cannot say to what extent the two men talked about Ray's grief. Mike, however, did tell me in regard to their intimacy: "Little did I know that in some ways Ray was preparing me for the death of my own daughter years later [of aspiration pneumonia]."

Mike Cope became an extremely popular preacher, not just in Searcy but around the country. College students, others too but especially that age group, loved his passion and dynamic presentation. Everyone admired his devotion to the call of preaching. When he left it was a sad day for many in the congregation. Ray felt he was saying goodbye to a surrogate son who was also his valued brother in Christ. Both men believed they were moving on from a relationship fostered by the providence of God.

SUICIDE CALL

Innocence is good, but naiveté is bad. A trusting nature is refreshing but can be taken advantage of by the unscrupulous. When it came to innocence and trust, Ray Muncy sometimes walked a fine line between the good and the bad.

His naiveté sometimes showed in humorous ways. Many of his friends remember the story of our trip to the West Coast in 1975 for the Pepperdine Scholars Conference. Ray was on the program and decided that he could combine the speaking engagement with a family vacation. Zac and Kandy still lived at home and were excited about the prospect of seeing Disneyland—they called it the trip of trips. Ray planned the drive as a leisurely tour through the West, wanting to stop at historical sites along the way. He mapped out the itinerary so that we would arrive in San Francisco first to visit his sister Charlotte and then drive down the coast to Los Angeles in time for the conference.

The plan had one flaw: Ray's terrible sense of geography. For years we had traveled from Arkansas to Indiana or West Virginia, and he got into the habit of measuring distance by the number of states crossed. Since it took us a certain number of hours to cross two or three states to reach Bloomington or Charleston, West Virginia, he thought that the same number of states out West would mean approximately the same time. Further, he planned on the assumption that the Mississippi River flowed through the center of the country. Thus he projected making it as far as Denver by the end of the first day's drive with no problem. Then the second day we would drive on to California.

So off we went on our magical vacation. As usual Ray pointed out historical markers along the way, and as usual Zac and Kandy made fun of his mania for them. "Hey, Dad, I think you missed a marker back there." The weather was good and the teasing benign, but at some point Ray began to have doubts about his schedule. It was late afternoon and we still had half of Kansas to go. Eventually we neared the Colorado state line and saw the Rocky Mountains shimmering in the distance. Zac's and Kandy's flagging energy was revived. Ray and I told them, "We should be in Denver soon, now!" We drove for three more hours, well into Colorado, and the mountains seemed no closer. Zac would periodically exclaim: "Oh, look, it's the Rocky Mountains! We should be there soon!"

By the time we did reach Denver, very late that night after a twenty-hour drive, Ray realized his mistake. Our leisurely trip turned into a forced march, although we did make the conference on time. The vacation was a success anyway, but as a navigator Ray failed miserably, all because he had never once considered how much larger the western states are. Here was a man who had already traveled abroad and who taught the history of the United States, but who could not calculate the distance between Searcy and Denver. When he returned to campus he told the story to Virgil Lawyer, Gary Elliott and others. It became one of their favorites and, although he never lived down his attempt to move the Mississippi River four hundred miles west, the story remained one of Ray's favorites too.

I suppose the faulty navigation illustrates his problem with trusting naive instincts, but Ray could display the same dangerous innocence when it came to trusting other people. Once in the early days of our life in Searcy, Ray worked with the family of a young man (I'll call him Jim) who wanted to go to college. Realizing that the child likely had a troubled past, Ray helped him get into Harding, counting on good influences to turn his life around. Before long, however, Ray received bad news about Jim.

At first Ray knew only that he had been stopped by the police in another state and discovered to be driving a car not his own—a Cadillac, no less. Ray tried to communicate with him, but the distance between them prevented that. By the time the boy returned to campus, the Dean's Office had become involved because of the police report. It did not take the Dean of Students long to find out what Ray had completely missed. Jim was a homosexual and the out-of-town trouble was related to his lifestyle. Ray missed the obvious signs. He had taken at face value the family's word about the boy's background, and in the intervening time failed to notice any problem. As the Dean told me after Ray's death, Ray's trusting nature had allowed the boy to take advantage of him. I believe Ray would have helped Jim anyway, but at least he would have been forearmed to deal with the trouble.

And it wasn't as if Jim and his family had lied to Ray maliciously. They did so out of fear and shame. The boy had genuinely wanted to do better by going to Harding; he simply failed to resist temptation. He was dismissed from college and disappeared for a time from our lives. When we did hear from him, it was a frightening experience that gave me a taste of what it is like to be a shepherd.

One night I got a call from Jim. He wanted to talk to Ray, who was out of town. It was very late. He said he was calling from Memphis and was contemplating suicide.

"I've got a gun right here," he said. I was in near shock, having had no training formal or otherwise to handle such a statement. My own terrible first-hand experience with suicide still lay in the future. I had known Jim to an extent but was not ready for this. Of course I told him that he should not even think about it. I urged him to remain calm, to think things through and not act hastily.

"I'm going to end it all," he said. I pleaded again. My mind was a jumble of confused thoughts. At one point I feared he might get in the Cadillac and drive to Searcy to see me. I asked if anyone was with him. I tried everything to get his mind off what he claimed to be contemplating.

No matter what I said he repeated his threat. I was on the phone for more than an hour going round and round with him. Finally my fear turned to weariness, and I lashed out: "If you take your own life, you're just admitting to the world that you are a coward. If that's true and you can't face life, you are admitting failure!"

His voice sounded charged with the energy of my rebuke: "I'll do it! I'll do it!" Although I could barely believe what I was saying, I told him, "It takes courage to live!" We spent another few minutes on this merry-go-round before he finally seemed to tire. He said, "I'm glad you talked to me, Mrs. Muncy."

As soon as he hung up, I called Ray. He listened to my story and did not reprimand me, but I wanted him to say something, so I asked, "What would you have said?" I honestly don't remember exactly how he replied, but it was something to the effect of "maybe Jim needed to hear someone call his bluff. Maybe he needed straight talk." I am not sure if Ray believed that as much as he wanted to calm me down. I could not sleep much of what was left of the night, and the next morning I scanned the paper to see if there had been any suicides reported. There hadn't been, but of course that didn't mean much—it was a Little Rock paper.

Later Ray managed to contact Jim. He told Ray that talking to me had saved his life. I pulled no punches, he said, and gave it to him straight. Who knows? Ray worked with him in the months following his dismissal from Harding trying to help him live a better life. We don't know if those efforts bore any fruit. But Ray tried, and so did I, on that scary night when I substituted for him. The boy I am calling Jim was an outcast at Harding because of his homosexuality. For all we know, he disappeared into the gay community, and a part of me—of us—finds relief in such invisibility and silence. The world does not often grant such peace, though. No matter how badly you may want a certain issue to go away, the phone will some day ring, or maybe the door will open, and it will walk right into your congregation.

LOVING THE OUTCAST

The scriptural qualifications for elders do not specifically mention trust, nor do they spell out that elders need to love the apparently unlovable, the underdog. Obviously these are Christ-like qualities to be imitated by all His followers. In Ray those two qualities went (imperfectly of course) hand in hand.

They enabled him to serve for sixteen years on one of the most difficult committees at Harding—Student Affairs. Its chief function was to hear appeals from students whose violations of campus rules have resulted in expulsion. Those appeal sessions were often long and gut wrenching, and Ray would come home late and limp from them. For students and committee members alike, a meeting was often the fiery furnace of testing where, unseen by the rest of us, not only was the integrity of students on trial, but also the wisdom of their judges. When this court of last resort turned down an appeal, it was to uphold the integrity of what Harding stood for; nevertheless, Ray and his colleagues felt the burden of someone's now uncertain future. Over the years his shoulders grew weary from the weight, but he wanted to be one who helped bear the load, for the sake of his university and for those students in distress. Sometimes, the appeals were granted and the burden of judgment was eased by hope of a second chance.

His friends on the eldership talk about his passionate speeches on behalf of the person in trouble. Since the speeches dealt with confidential matters, most cannot be shared. Perhaps I can convey the importance of those qualities for Ray by telling a story that has been made public, and one that involved him only peripherally. In fact, the story praises the courageous and measured spirit of the entire eldership at College Church, the tolerance of their congregation, and the inspirational life of one repentant sinner.

One day during the Christmas holidays, Ray received a call from Tom Formby, who at the time was "chairman" of the elders, a title putting him in charge of any business that arose during his six-month term. He asked Ray if he could come to the counseling center to talk to someone. The center was actually an old white house on church property used for counseling. When Ray walked into the thinly carpeted front room, doubling as a reception area, he saw Tom, Don England, Evan Ulrey, and a slender young man he did not recognize, but who looked like a smaller version of Tom Selleck, with his thick hair, prominent nose, and mustache. His name was Jody Wood. He had a pleasant manner and face and was dressed "right out of a fashion book," Tom recalls. When the meeting began, the young man spoke very politely:

"I want you to help me go to heaven."

"What's wrong?" one of the elders asked.

"I'm homosexual. It's a shameful way to live; I know that now."

"Do you believe what the Bible teaches about homosexuality?"

"I do believe."

"Jody, are you willing to make changes in your lifestyle?"

"I am willing. But there's something else. I'm HIV positive."

In the late 1980s, no scarier words could be spoken, especially to church-going middle-class Americans who still knew little about AIDS. This was the era of Ryan White, of tremendous fear about how the disease was transmitted, and of intense homophobia. While AIDS activists sometimes overstated the paranoia among middle America, anyone who admitted to having the disease risked being ostracized or worse. Tom, himself a physician, realized the implications more than most. This revelation of Jody's made his confession all the more poignant and made the need for a godly response all the more important.

The men talked with Jody for almost two hours, making sure that he understood what his decision would mean. He had been suspended from Harding because of his sexual orientation, so his life was at a turning point. As they finished, Tom told Jody that the elders would do all they could to help him make changes and to deal with his disease. The meeting ended with a prayer. Ray, Don, Evan, and Tom felt good about the session and hoped to see Jody follow through on his pledge to change his lifestyle and become a part of the church. They did not foresee how literally he aimed to do just that.

A few days later, Jody was back on church grounds, walking into the main building to apply for a job. Travis Blue, serving as business manager then, called Tom. Jody claimed that he had computer skills, Travis said. In those days the church was not fully computerized and needed help getting on line. Travis wanted to hire him but asked Tom if it would be all right. Under normal circumstances the answer would have been easy, but Jody's confession complicated everything. Tom confided to Ray his fear that many members at College Church could not handle the news that an HIV-positive gay man was working in the church building. With so many elders gone, Tom sought the advice of those whom he could reach, including Ray. It came down to four other elders, who told him the same thing: "Do what you think best."

Tom asked himself a question that had become fashionable among young Christians but that was the implicit and continual question of Christians of any age, elders most of all: "What would Jesus do?" Would he turn his back on Jody? The answer to that was certainly no. But would he give him a job at this point? Tom considered the alternatives. The worst case scenario was that without a job, Jody would be forced, or choose, to live out on the streets. He might go back to his gay friends for help and solace. His parents loved him dearly, but for several reasons the family might not be able to care for him fully. A better prospect had Jody finding a job elsewhere; some Christian might hire him. In that scenario, Jody could live on his own until the virus made it impossible to work. What then? He would have no health benefits. Who would take care of him at that point? The church could arrange help, Tom realized, but much would remain contingent on exactly what Jody's situation was when the illness took over. Tom considered these and other permutations of the outcome if the church did not hire the young man.

If Jody worked for the College Church, the congregation could monitor his illness, provide a support group for his battle to leave the gay lifestyle, and minister to the full range of his spiritual needs. And if Travis Blue was right about Jody's ability with computers, the church could benefit as well. As Tom argued the options in his mind, he kept coming back to the principle of compassion. He and Ray talked a lot about the compassion of Jesus, and the need for it among Christians. Ray often made the distinction between supporting programs and supporting people. As he got older, my husband seemed more convinced than ever of the danger of the church emphasizing its institutional identity at the expense of its spiritual core.

That core was the person of Jesus Christ.

We all pay lip service to this truth, of course, but elders like Ray and Tom must wrestle with what it means in the tough issues of life. I remember hearing those two talk admiringly of how Jesus did not back down from the contemporary issues of his time. When followers or skeptics asked about marriage, or allegiance to government, or bigotry, Jesus took a stand. He didn't always say what his listeners wanted to hear. Or centuries later He doesn't always say what we as readers of the Bible want to read. He didn't always offer enough detail to satisfy us. Thus Tom did not know exactly what Jesus would have done had he been an elder in the College Church of Christ, but he knew it would have been compassionate and courageous. Mike Cope fully supported his thinking. Remarking on the case later, Mike said, "The church had the chance to drive Jody back into the gay community or it had the chance to love him into spiritual health. With the leadership of Tom—along with Ray and others—the latter is what happened."

This healing love did not burst into view all at once. Few if any churches had a ministry to gays. Doing what Tom did, showing compassion for a person in trouble, would have been unremarkable except for the fact that the object of the compassion belonged to a group officially outside the borders of ministry. When other elders and members returned from vacations and word of Jody's job circulated, many worried and some were outraged, partly because Tom would make such a major decision without consulting more of the eldership and partly because of the ramifications of the hiring. All the questions about AIDS and homosexuality that Tom and his advisors had mulled over thundered in the din arising from many concerned people. Tom felt battered for a while, but he explained his reasoning to his critics as calmly as he could. And he stood by it.

No matter what some may have thought, Jody Wood was on the staff at the College Church, and by all accounts he performed his duties well. His main task was to work with computers, both creating programs and using them to enter checks and maintain other financial records. Cecelia McLeod, church secretary at the time, says that Jody was a "people person" whose presence in the office lifted the spirit of others. As for worries about his steadily worsening AIDs, a briefing by Dr. Mike Justus on how to handle the danger from blood (should Jody be injured and need attention) relieved her fears. The other office personnel, Travis and Mike Cope, had no problems either.

Jody, the computer whiz, seemed to love working there. It had been his choice not to go home to Missouri, and when the church found him a small rental house on its property, he felt he had made a new home. If the occasional murmuring against his presence bothered him, he didn't show it. Cecelia describes his typical reaction as a laugh and head shake, saying, in effect, "I can't control what others may think." Besides, as he said once,

"Nobody has burned a cross on my lawn." In the meantime, he ingratiated himself to almost everyone who took the time to know him. Cecelia points out a psychology at work for some in this whole ordeal: the people who knew Jody before he confessed were able to relate to him as a person, not as a member of an outcast group. In other words, God, knowing that we are not as loving as He calls us to be, provided extra help in this case. If it was impossible to love gays, it was easy to love Jody.

Jody had his own burdens to bear in the last three years of his life. Even though he ministered by speaking to youth groups about homosexuality, it was not easy to keep his commitment to avoid the gay lifestyle. He wanted to help in the fight against AIDS, for example, but joining the cause meant involvement with other gays. As long as he lived he would face temptation. He may have stumbled in his walk with God, but Tom and Rowan McLeod, Cecelia's husband, picked him up again. Others helped too. In fact, some of the people who had expressed disagreement with the original decision to hire Jody relented and joined in efforts to minister to him.

After nearly two years on the church staff, Jody grew too sick to work. Even before he left, we could see the lesions on his face. He started losing weight. In and out of the hospital, he was now officially a PWA—person with AIDS. The first full blast of the disease tested his resolve to stay hopeful. In a videotaped interview, Jody recalls a night in the hospital when his IV popped out and he awoke in terrible pain. "Is this the way it will end?" he asked himself. He had never felt so alone; all the strength he had demonstrated over the previous months temporarily deserted him. He reached for the phone and called Rowan and Cecelia. It was eleven o'clock, but they came right away. While they held his hands, he broke down and cried. Slightly embarrassed at his own display, he said, "I guess that was stupid." Rowan and Cecelia corrected him gently: "You did absolutely the right thing."

Eventually his parents, both retired, moved into his rental house at Jody's request and cared for him until the end, which came almost two years later. By that time Jody was bedridden in White County Hospital, where his family was joined in the slow, painful deathwatch by some of his faithful brothers and sisters in Christ. The disease ravaged him. He weighed only 90 pounds and couldn't walk. Finally, on March 1, 1993, he died in the hospital room where two dozen supporters had gathered. Ray and I joined the Formbys, the McLeods, and others in prayers and singing on Jody's behalf. We were keeping vigil with Jody, our brother in Christ.

I mentioned the video interview given by Jody. Significantly, he closes it with a song. He had come to Harding on a music scholarship and wanted to dedicate the number to fellow AIDS patients as well as the health care professionals who served them. I had never heard of the song, called "The Blind Plower," but Jody's talent came through in his singing of it. I couldn't help but notice the very last line of this 19th century air, which praises God for the beauty of nature but even more for redemption from sin. The speaker, the blind plowman, concludes by exclaiming this final praise in the face of his handicap: "God took away my sight that my soul might see." Even years after Jody's death, the words seem a poignant commentary on his attitude toward affliction. I picture him singing them amid rejoicing angels of God.

THE THERMOSTAT LEGACY

The help extended to Jody Wood blessed the church and glorified God. By leading the way in securing that help, Tom Formby deserves a great deal of credit. He demonstrated a quality that Ray had written about almost a decade earlier in the *Gospel Advocate*. In 1981 congregations across the land were implementing the latest educational and organizational techniques for involving their members. Partly in reaction to some autocratic elderships of the past, younger elders wanted to assure more congregational input on important issues. Anyone active in church bureaucracy in the 1980s remembers the advent of focus groups, giant writing pads on easels for brainstorming, small-group leaders, congregational surveys. These imports from business helped create a new style in many congregations; younger professional men brought statistics and pie charts to the work of the church. Much of it signaled a new openness. Ray was all for that. One downside, as he saw it, was a herd mentality that valued consensus over leadership.

Thus he wrote a little piece called "Thermostats or Thermometers" (September 3,1981). The title and central metaphor of the article announce the same simple idea: elders must set the mood of a congregation, not merely reflect it. The deeper issue is what he calls "visionary leadership," by which he meant a focus on the "panorama" of God's will, which, in turn, came down to the gospel, that "mystery," that "hope of Israel" and once-for-all revelation of Christ as Lord. If elders can make that grand vision the emotional setting for their congregation, all the so-called programs—education, benevolence, etc.—will flourish. Leadership in this large sense demands shepherds who "know the chief shepherd and know where the heavenly sheepfold is located." By their commitment to the majesty and rightness of God's universal will as revealed in the gospel, they "provide the pleasant atmosphere in which the congregation can march towards accomplishing God's will in all things."

To me, this article explains a good deal about Ray as a person and elder. As a person, he was moved by ideas. The gospel was quite simply the greatest idea he had ever encountered. History documented its power and the church confirmed its ability to foster unifying love. As an elder, Ray combined conservatism on most of the big doctrinal issues with passionate advocacy of love as the "mark" of all Christians. By holding firm on doctrine, the church kept its identity distinct in a world of religious eclecticism, and by never compromising on the doctrine of love, the church kept its essential relationship with God intact.

My husband was never on the cutting edge of change in the brotherhood. He often remained silent on the big brotherhood debates because he hated their divisiveness. He rarely failed to speak up for an individual in need of support or help, however, because in those cases he saw the chance to preserve the spirit of the One whom the writer of Hebrews, quoted in Ray's article, calls "Lord Jesus, the great shepherd of the sheep." Ray closes his article with the rest of Hebrews 13:21, which encapsulates the vision of God's expansive will for the church. The writer's prayer is that God, who sent Jesus, "make you perfect in every good work to do his will, working in you that which is well-pleasing in his sight, through Jesus Christ; to whom be glory for ever and ever. Amen."

After the death of Jody Wood in 1993, Ray could feel good about Jody, who was going to heaven, about his friend and fellow elder Tom Formby, who had served as a human thermostat for others, and about his congregation, whose decision to do the right thing for a single outcast had, Ray believed fervently, pleased God and confirmed that His people in Searcy were being made "perfect in every good work to do His will."

I have not conveyed my husband's life as an elder to my own satisfaction. As I said, some have suggested that in his role as elder he found his niche. I tend to agree, but I can offer only glimpses into that part of his life. Certain words keep leaping out at me in this account: leadership, trust, compassion, discretion, counsel, courage. In fact, when Ray made his own list of leadership traits for a sermon on the topic, it bears resemblance to those gleaned from the images I have collected from his fellow elders. According to Ray, God's leaders need to be

> *consecrated*
> *capable*
> *courageous*
> *compassionate*
> *cooperative*

Using preacherly alliteration—all those hard "c's" to help us remember the points—this list not only shows what Ray valued, but it also introduces the word that may best describe his legacy as an elder. To one degree or another, I think, Ray was capable, courageous, compassionate, and cooperative. He was also consecrated. He was consecrated in the sense of setting himself apart for important tasks. He took on supervision of the educational director for several years, meeting with the man weekly to insure that Bible classes went smoothly. When Life Groups made a comeback in the early 1990s, Ray conducted meetings in our home that had true devotional content and at the same time ministered to those in the group, especially the needy. When those groups mutated into zone care groups, Ray tried diligently to make them work.

Ray's involvement in the Searcy community was also a form of consecration based on an often overlooked criterion for being an elder: his reputation among non-Church of Christ people was excellent. The many duties he took on, the speaking engagements, the civic organizations he supported, all showed Christ to those who may have been outside Him.

Ray consecrated himself in an even more fundamental way too. After Kandy's death, I noticed his demeanor changing. In part this was grief. Subsequent events in David's and Zac's lives took a toll on him as well. Some of his friends have mentioned to me that he grew quieter. I agree. It would be a mistake, however, to think that he was somehow in decline. Instead, he was, I think, drawing closer to God. If he at times seemed more distant, it was because his eyes looked beyond the present. He began to live more as a sojourner in this world than as a permanent resident. I think Ray's life as an elder enabled him to desire more strongly and to claim even more consistently his citizenship in heaven.

TWELVE

In This World You Will Have Trouble

(1982-93)

OF BLACKBOARDS AND THE ADVANCEMENT OF LEARNING

> We call those studies liberal which are worthy of a free man: those studies by which we attain and practice virtue and wisdom; that education which calls forth, trains and develops those highest gifts of the body and the mind which ennoble men, and which are rightly judged to rank next in dignity to virtue only.
>
> —Pietro Vergerio, *Concerning Character*

The 1980s were touted nationwide as an era of booming economy and materialism. In higher education things changed too, but not necessarily in the direction of financial good times. The Harding faculty minutes record several warnings from President Ganus about the diminishing student pool and the hard times that might follow. The Baby Boomer rush to college had peaked, and for the first time colleges were faced with selling demanding customers on their institution rather than gathering in flower children who wanted to pursue the finer things. The new demographics and increased competition for students created a new mind set at many colleges. The traditional disciplines associated with the liberal arts could no longer sustain enrollment alone; they were supplemented or even pushed aside by newer courses of study designed to meet the needs of a technological and business age.

Harding, now a university, had changed over the years to address these new trends. In the mid-'70s a nursing program had been added, which by the mid-'80s had been upgraded to a School of Nursing. Obviously computer courses entered the curriculum. The School of Business became high profile, attracting significant numbers of new majors. Harding was still a liberal arts school, but the liberal arts were no longer undisputed king.

Ray did not entirely like the winds of change blowing through his school of nearly twenty years. People began calling him a champion of the liberal arts. He had been one ever since he came to Harding, but with increasing challenges to the traditional curriculum, Ray came to be known more and more as the defender of the old guard. These challenges came in the form of new programs like nursing and in changes to old disciplines such as music or education, which had national accrediting bodies making demands for more rigorous requirements in their areas. To add a course in a specialized area, however, usually meant subtracting one of the general education courses.

Ray was foremost among those who disapproved or dissented when these changes came up. He and his allies usually lost such arguments. It was in 1982, for example, that the music department proposed a waiver of eight general education hours because of its accrediting body's requirements. Ray went on record as opposing the change, calling the proposal detrimental to Harding's purpose. He urged his fellow faculty members to hold the line. The proposal passed anyway, 64-13.

When he was asked to deliver the closing speech at the 1982 Tahkodah Faculty Conference, Ray seized the opportunity to present his case to fellow teachers and administrators. The speech, titled "Achieving Our Goals in 1982-83" and delivered on August 20, has occasioned more comment than almost anything else he ever said in public. I want to quote parts of it to make clear the well spring of Ray's thinking. It was a summary of his own ideals as a teacher and a rallying cry for the future on behalf of liberal studies.

He began with quotations suggesting that modern aims of education are often confused or unfocused. Mindful of his audience, Ray said, "Most of us are groping in a forest, tapping the familiar trees of our own discipline." He noted the threat of "professional jealousies" even at Harding, and pled for the more comprehensive view: "It is at a time like this, here at Tahkodah, that we have occasion to scale the heights and to take a panoramic view of Harding, and not only Harding but hopefully to catch a vision of hills and valleys beyond and see that we are part of something much larger than ourselves."

After detailing the need for student-centered education, Ray got to the heart of his speech:

Harding University, in addition to her biblical emphases, is a liberal arts institution. The fundamental aim of a liberal education is to open up minds, with a crowbar if necessary. To challenge students to think, to love and search for wisdom, to pursue an argument where it leads, to delight in understanding for its own sake, to engage in a passionate quest for dispassionate reasonableness, to will to see things steadily and to see them whole.

Why is it that our degrees have not served to open a common preserve of the universal interest? I believe it is largely because the liberal arts theory of education is being superseded by another theory: the vocationalist. The pressure upon students from their home, from their own impatience, and from a society built upon materialistic values, is all but irresistible, and they insist on appraising a subject in terms of how it will help them find a job, make money, and be "successful." With a wave of the hand, music and art appreciation, literature, the sciences, mathematics, history, government, foreign languages, and speech are brushed aside as not contributing to their avowed purpose of getting out in a hurry and doing something important, like making a living.

Against the "vocationalist" view of things Ray offered Aristotle's definition of happiness, which is identified with contemplation or mental activity. He cited Thomas Jefferson as an Aristotelian. As proof of Jefferson's anti-vocationalism, Ray recalled the statesman's change of the original formula in the Declaration of Independence ("life, liberty, and property") to the famous list that ends with "the pursuit of happiness." With Aristotle and Jefferson on his side, Ray argued that the liberal arts become the best means to the end of happiness—a state and activity of mind putting us in touch with the most important questions of existence and thus connecting us most nearly to God. In other words, the liberal arts, by supplying broad knowledge and the power of thought, lead to a "fuller understanding of the meaning of life," something that the true teacher is compelled to share with others.

Ray closed by exhorting teachers to be enthusiastic sharers of knowledge but never to forget the source of all knowledge. The discovery of the new will lead the open heart back to God and supply the humility to admit that knowledge cannot save a single soul. Thus, the Harding motto (at the time) becomes the culminating lesson of the liberal arts: we are "educating for eternity."

It was a stirring speech, but whether it changed anybody's mind or not is debatable. Certainly most students were not going to buy the argument that education's prime goal was higher thinking. Some faculty members no doubt judged Ray's picture of the present as too gloomy. After all, with its emphasis on Bible, Harding held on to the liberal arts ideal of holistic learning more than many colleges. And others probably saw Ray as a bit of a dinosaur on this issue. They would argue that if we did not provide vocational opportunities at Harding, then we could not compete in the contemporary market. Moderates might reconcile the two approaches. For Ray, the issue remained central as the decade of the 1980s wore on.

This concern surfaced in many of Ray's activities, but his reputation was made in faculty meetings, where his ironic laments for history's skimpy funding punctuated many discussions of budgets and programs.

Faculty meetings and the budget process were two things for which Ray had little use. I should explain that, unlike many colleges its size, Harding has retained the practice of having not only departmental meetings but also school-wide faculty meetings. Though Ray was not alone in professing disdain for the minutia of such gatherings, their existence in those days did allow a forum for discussion. During Ray's first years the meetings were held in the old Emerald Room on the second floor of the Ganus Student Center. Later, the Heritage Auditorium became the favorite site. The meetings were designed to satisfy both social and academic needs, but many non-academic issues got on the agenda, from health insurance to salaries, to less important items.

Ray sometimes complained about the relatively trivial issues that occupied faculty time. The low point for him came in the early 1970s. Ray would come home and say, "I wish that someday we could talk about something else besides short skirts and parking!" The latter issue came down to a question of whether or not to penalize faculty for parking violations. The topic of skirts challenged Harding's dress code in a then unprecedented way, and debate raged over hemline length. Finally, after a long discussion, President Ganus actually called for a secret ballot, asking each teacher to suggest an acceptable length. When the results were announced, the winning length was "two inches above the knee," followed by "four inches above the knee" and "knee-length." Ray laughingly reported that four people had actually voted for "six inches above the knee": "That's what happens on a secret ballot," he said.

When hot-button issues such as these (the college finally started issuing parking tickets to faculty in 1976) did not consume time in meetings, budget matters sometimes did. As time went on and Ray's concern for the status

Ray relaxes in his office recliner with one of his precious books.

of liberal arts grew, he loved to play up the history department's poverty at every opportunity. Intended as humor, his laments also seemed designed to remind the faculty that Ray was on the side of the angels when it came to money. His department had none, illustrating the inequity of a system that tended to neglect the liberal arts. A chairman of one department might argue for major new technology in his area, only to have Ray comment, "Yes, and the history department would love to have some colored chalk."

The most famous of Ray's catch-phrases involved "the blackboard." Although it took on legendary proportions, the blackboard was real, located on the second floor of the American Studies Building, in Room 211, where many history classes were taught. As Tom Statom remembers it, the writing surface on the board had deteriorated so much that a teacher could not produce legible script: "You might as well have a piece of soap." When Ray complained about it, someone came over to repaint the surface, but the new surface retained the old problem. The chalk still slid right over it, leaving the barest of traces. Such a condition was bad for anyone, but for Ray, the king of blackboard fillers, it was potential disaster.

Who knows how many times he seriously requested a new board? At some point that ceased to matter. The blackboard became a symbol of the lower status of the history department and of the poverty of the liberal arts as well. More than one colleague worried that Ray, so to speak, wore the defective blackboard as a badge of honor, as if he had already martyred himself to a lost cause. If a request for significant funding came up in a faculty meeting, those sitting in the Heritage Auditorium would wait for the other shoe to drop, and usually Ray did not disappoint them: "Yes," he would say, acknowledging the justness of the other need, "and I'd like a new blackboard."

Ray's use of "the blackboard" as a punchline started some time in the '80s and continued into the '90s. Paul Haynie, who joined.the faculty in 1990, remembers hearing it occasionally during his first few years. Eventually he realized a parallel between Ray's preoccupation with the board and a famous historical figure's obsession with a rival. Paul explained the connection to Ray: "Dr. Muncy, you are like Cato." Ray could then guess the point as Paul went on: "To him Carthage was Rome's mortal enemy, and he always thought of ways to bring it up, you know, to his fellow senators. He would always close his speeches with the phrase, 'Carthage must be destroyed.' You are getting to be just like Cato." The analogy was apt in more than one sense, perhaps. Ray's comments were like rhetorical guerrilla warfare, and his remarks did imply an enemy, in this case the new priorities in education.

According to Paul, it was not long after his Cato analogy that Ray used the blackboard line once too often. In the spring of 1992, Cliff Ganus had been retired for five years, and David Burks, the new president, had settled comfortably into the routine of running faculty meetings. President Burks had been very aggressive in building and remodeling campus facilities, and among the latest projects was the American Studies Building, home of the history department. All this was background to whatever agenda item provoked Ray into once more saying "And by the way, we need a blackboard." Paul remembers the tall, lanky Burks showing obvious but restrained irritation and saying in his often-imitated deep nasal voice, "Ray if you don't stop mentioning that blackboard! You are going to get a whole new building this summer, so just be quiet about it."

To be fair, not everyone noticed any degree of true frustration in Dr. Burks' voice, and I don't recall Ray saying he was chastised by anyone. If the remark did irritate the president, maybe Ray learned a needed lesson. He may have realized his humor had worn out its welcome, or if he had intended to make a point, the exchange let him know he had been heard. If the incident rose to the level of a confrontation, it was a minor one, and quickly forgotten. The American Studies Building did get its facelift, and the department enjoyed new blackboards. Ray retired the following year from his chairmanship but without seeing Carthage destroyed.

As for Ray's relationship with Dr. Burks, it was no more or no less than professional. Coming from the School of Business as he did, David Burks represented some of the new trends in education making Ray uneasy. It was not that Ray mistrusted him or that Dr. Burks ever said or did anything personally offensive to Ray. More than the ascendancy of the new president, it was the retirement of the old one that left Ray feeling a little adrift. Like the blackboard, Cliff Ganus had achieved the status of icon in Ray's mind. As a fixture in the leadership for almost the entire breadth of Ray's career, he represented the older, simpler Harding first loved by Ray. Working in such different domains, the two men did not spend much time together professionally, yet Ray respected the person who had been one of his first colleagues and mentors. In the spring of 1987, after Cliff officially announced his retirement in a faculty meeting, Ray quickly stood to make a motion. The faculty secretary paraphrased his words and their effect: "Ray Muncy proposed that the minutes show a warm expression of gratitude to President Ganus for his distinguished service to Harding. The faculty responded with loud and sustained applause."

For Ray, the issue was never personal. He could disagree strongly with something, in this case the relaxing of liberal arts requirements, without blaming anyone. If he resented anything, it was the force of history itself, his old discipline reminding him that change is inevitable, even if he didn't like it. His jokes and speeches in faculty meetings were almost a rote defense against this inevitability. If some did tire of Ray's posturing, they also realized that without a curmudgeon to remind us of priorities, those important things might truly be in danger of slipping from our memory—and values.

THE GREAT TONER RAID

Historians talk about the "Spirit of the Age," the Age of Reason, or the Romantic Period. However useful such labels may be, they often partake of myth rather than reality. The American 1950s cannot really be reduced to a combination of *Happy Days* and the Red Scare, but somehow it is more fun to remember the decade as the "conformist '50s." Everyone knows the cynical advice associated with journalists: If legend conflicts with truth, print the legend.

Ray's role as defender of the liberal arts, his complaints about the budget, and his unease with new trends in higher education seemed to create an aura, a kind of spirit of the age in the history department in the late 1980s. The unusable blackboard became part of the myth of the beleaguered humanists fighting the system, and so did the Great Toner Raid. The Great Toner Raid is an interesting case of fact being obscured by legend. The "raid" happened in some form; I don't doubt that. Though I do not recall Ray ever mentioning it, all his colleagues in the department swear it occurred. Unfortunately, none of them was an eyewitness. Equally unfortunately, the other organization on campus involved in the raid, the business office, has no one who can remember anything like it taking place. If I were a historian, I would either dig deeper for the truth or throw in the towel on a story that cannot be verified. Since I am not a historian, or a journalist for that matter, I will instead print the legend.

It perhaps started this way in the spring of 1990. Lott Tucker saw that cash flow was not good, so he told Buddy Rowan to tighten the belts of as many budget managers as possible. In turn. Buddy told his secretary to do a quick phone inventory of the campus offices. He may have asked her to target those offices which had gone over budget already for the year. The secretary made approximately thirty-four calls with the same few questions: "Do you have any unused supplies that could be saved until after July 1?" Then the secretary reported back to Mr. Rowan, who dispatched an employee to offices around the campus to execute the confiscation. It may be the case that of all the departments on campus, history alone had managed to over-spend and was therefore the only target.

Meanwhile, Dr. Raymond Muncy, chairman of the history department, was ending an especially stimulating class in American History. He had dis-cussed with his majors several contrarian theories for the cause of the American Revolution. As he walked the short distance from Room 211 to his office, not even the irritation of an almost useless chalk board could spoil the lingering pleasure of speculating on historical cause and effect. What if, instead of the widely accepted opinion that the colonies rebelled for eco-nomic reasons, the major factor was—

As Ray entered the door to the history offices, his reverie was inter-rupted by the sight of someone plundering the department's copier. This person had thrown open the small gray doors to the storage area and was extracting something. No one else was in the office. "What are you doing?" Ray asked the nameless minion, who replied cheerfully, "I'm here to take back a box of toner."

"Why are you taking the toner?"

"You'll have to speak to the business office about that."

"I certainly will."

By the time Rachel returned to the office, Ray sat there stunned. The look on his face said, "How could they do this to me?" He had been informed when he called that the supplies were taken as a precautionary measure to guard against future overspending. One by one the department members heard about it. At first they were angry, then amused, then in awe. It was as if Ray's dire pleas for more money had visited a bureaucratic plague upon them. At some point a biblical parallel was offered: It was the judg-ment upon the unprofitable servant for not using his talents wisely: "Whoever does not have, even what he has will be taken from him." No, Fred Jewell said, "Doing that to Ray is more like Boaz coming back and snatching the gleanings from the hands of Ruth and her people. It just vio-lates the spirit of the thing."

Taking the toner was unfair and humiliating, but it was, everyone had to admit, also funny. That particular item was about as low on the scale of budget items as you could get. The next step might be to lock the bathrooms on the second floor. What else could be done to punish them? Soon the incident became a byword in the office, a cautionary allusion. If you want-ed to warn someone about a contemplated course of action, you might say, "Better watch it; they might take away your toner." The Great Toner Raid came to stand for the little guy against the heartless bureaucracy. It was the perfect comic fulfillment of Ray's fears: vocationalism treading on the vulnerable neck of the humanities.

Did it happen? Not as I just described; remember, I'm printing the legend. Remember too that legends exaggerate to express the hopes and fears of those who make them. This history department legend is somewhere lower on the scale of seriousness than, say, the legend of the Holy Grail. It takes a kernel of reality—the battle between the bean-counters and the faculty— and plants it in the collective imagination. As far as I know, Ray was the only witness to what actually happened that fateful day, and the truth died with him. Of course, any distress he felt over the incident died long before he did. The Great Toner Raid gave him one more story to tell and embellish for the amusement of his Harding colleagues.

I have said that Ray never made budget or curriculum issues personal. Of all the incidents that occurred late in Ray's career, the most bothersome one had nothing to do with the administration or "issues." This single, isolated case hit Ray hard because it did seem so personal. It could affect him so much in part because it too was symbolic, representing in one violent instant all the things his precious liberal arts tried to overcome.

One morning in the spring of 1991, Mark Elrod decided to go into campus early. He was struggling to get interested enough to do serious work on his dissertation and thought maybe an early morning session would be productive. Once the day heated up with students, classes and club activities, the research got harder to do.

The American Studies building at 5:30 A.M. is eerily deserted, outside and in. Mark shut the door of his faithful Jeep and walked to the south end of the building, past the chain link trash receptacle, and through the double glass doors. He took the stairs two steps at a time. His office was on the south end of the second floor, but before he turned off the main hallway to the little cul de sac where he and Joe Segraves had their nooks, he noticed that on the other end of the hall the history department office door was open and a light was on.

Seeing no maintenance personnel, he decided to check. In the mini-lobby where Rachel's desk sat, papers lay scattered on the floor. Her computer monitor lay on its side on the carpet, trailing cables ripped from wall sockets. Ray's office door was open, something not unusual in itself, except that the light was on. Mark stepped hesitantly through that open door. Ray's papers and many of his books had been torn from folders or shelves and scattered all over the office. Items on his desk had been ripped away, leaving a clear space in the center, where Mark saw something that caused him to stare in disbelief.

It was human excrement.

Mark doesn't remember whether Ray actually saw the ugly sight or not. He remembers calling Security and calling Ray, but he thinks maybe Campus Security arrived before Ray and cleaned it up.

When Rachel got there, Ray was still clearing the floor of its paper mess, shock lingering on his face. By mid-morning, Fred Jewell had talked with him. His colleagues all saw that he was shaken by the incident, hurt by it. Mark was there when Ray first saw the mess.

"Oh my, oh my," Ray repeated several times as he surveyed the office. Fred recalls Ray's stunned manner as almost like that of a rape victim. After all, a teacher's office is a sanctuary of sorts, the center of his intellectual world and the hub of his contact with students. Ray kept asking, "If someone was this upset about something, why didn't he just come to me?" He was hurt to think that the rage reflected in the havoc wreaked in his office could be directed at him. And without his awareness of what he might have done to cause it.

To all of the history staff, the vandalism was obviously the work of a student. Mark recalls his frustration with the questions being asked by Security early on: "Do you have any disgruntled former employees?" "Who is the secretary?" The idea of any former faculty member doing this struck Mark as ludicrous and a waste of time. Only someone who had not worked with Ray, who did not know him as a person, could do what had been done.

Eventually the mess was cleaned up and departmental life went on. The culprit was never found, but stories surfaced of a student trying to find a copy of a test who, when unsuccessful, either as a cover for the attempted cheating or out of frustration, defecated on the desk. When told this theory, Ray had to laugh: "The test he would have been looking for was right on the desk. He probably had to move it to do his business." Though he could joke about it, Ray carried the shadow of the event in his heart for a while. I think he hoped it was an attempt to pass a test. He could live with that response to his difficult course, just as he could with budget cutbacks and the triumph of vocationalism. It was the other possibility—sheer spiteful revenge—that shook his peace of mind.

CURRICULUM MATTERS

If Ray did fall into the role of grumpy old man in meetings or lament too often the state of things, he never stopped working to promote his beloved liberal arts where it mattered most to him—in the classroom.

Dating back to the 1970s, Ray had been involved in cooperative efforts to instill the liberal arts ideals of broad knowledge and critical thinking into general education courses. Along with Winfred Wright and Bill Verkler, he taught a Global Issues course. He worked with Evan Ulrey and others in a consortium of Arkansas colleges to develop a humanities course. Although Harding never instituted the course that emerged from these efforts, the research done by Evan and Ray laid the foundation for the course later used by the International Programs. Ray may have lost most of the battles to preserve general education curriculum, but he won a victory in that case.

Ray also had significant input on the last major overhaul of the general education curriculum at Harding before his death. Dennis Organ of the English department chaired the effort to evaluate the basic courses for freshmen and sophomores. Ray was instrumental in keeping history as a requirement when some wanted it reduced to one of several choices in the general education menu.

The most exciting opportunity to preserve the influence of the liberal arts came with the advent of an Honors Program at Harding. A nationwide movement, honors programs were conceived to provide gifted students with challenging courses marked by critical thinking. Ray was chosen to be on the steering committee for the Honors Program in 1987. As Larry Long, eventual director of the program, remembers it, Ray was brought on board for his "academic excellence." While Larry traveled to other schools to investigate their programs, Ray, as the humanities representative on the committee, helped insure high standards. According to Larry, Ray constantly said, "No window dressing. Do it right. Find the best possible program and adapt it." Larry credits Ray with "shaping the sense of what was important."

Beyond setting general guidelines, Ray designed one of the program's first courses: Honors 203: The Big Questions. The idea came from Ray's own reading, a book in which the author posed a series of "meaning-of-life" kinds of questions. Ray said, "I'm going to structure my class around those." He did, and it became the touchstone course in the fledgling program, which finally held its first classes in the fall of 1989.

Based on six "Big Questions," the course was very simple: answer them, getting help from the world's great thinkers past and present. The questions:

What is the meaning of life?
Why do you believe (or not believe) in God?
Does the universe have a purpose?
What is truth?
What is being a human being?
Is freedom always good?

In the Big Questions class, Ray got to put into practice all he believed about liberal arts. His other courses applied the principles too, but with the nineteen members of the first Honors group, there was no specific body of facts to cover, no immature resistance to learning to fight against. Counting Ray, the class was made up of twenty people who loved to think and to see where their conversation led them. Actually, more than twenty voices took part once the writers from the course anthology were added: Lao-Tzu, Machiavelli, Marx, Keynes, Lucretius, Plato, Sontag, Leibniz, Skinner, Jung, et al.

Ray loved to dramatize the importance of men and women of ideas throughout history. One of his best chapel presentations ever, and he made several chapel talks, commemorated the 200th anniversary of the signing of the United States Constitution. Ray's speech invoked the drama of the event, down to the 4 P.M. signing by George Washington. As I listened to a tape of Ray's performance, however, it was his description of the intellectual credentials of the framers and signers that seemed to ignite his verbal energy the most:

> This was a most remarkable body of men. Almost every one of them had sat in some famous assembly, signed some important document, occupied some high place, or distinguished himself for scholarship, or for signal service in the cause of liberty. These men knew Plato, Aristotle, Hobbes, Locke, Montesquieu, Rousseau, Voltaire— like the backs of their hands!

The rising excitement in his voice as he names them is contagious. His tone says to his audience: "Realize that what we have in the American Constitution is more than the fruit of warfare. Before freedom was born on the battlefield and in the assembly hall, it gestated in great ideas."

Ray refused to allow the great array of secular, or even religious, thinkers have the floor to themselves. Every one of the Big Questions was put into the context of biblical thought. Ray typically tested his Honors students by having them compare and contrast a secular perspective with a biblical one.

For example, students might choose to contrast John Maynard Keynes' idea of the government's agenda for population control with Genesis 9:1: "Be fruitful and multiply." At Harding, everything is considered with the Bible in mind, but in the Honors marketplace of ideas every student was completely free—Ray did not want to tell them what to think. He wanted the Bible to compete equally with other explanations so that students discovered for themselves the value of its perspective and realized that secular perspectives did not always contradict the Word of God.

Far from passive, though, he led students through discussions. He might come to class and pull rocks from his coat pockets, setting them down on a table or window sill. He would then start naming their place of origin, expanding to a discussion of why an educated person needed to know that place. By the end of class, he had taken them on a world and historical tour. Ray would come out of those classes excited about the future. He envisioned nineteen very bright people infiltrating the work force in nineteen different jobs, all of them bringing a deep humanity to their professions, a Christian humanism recalling the highest ideals of the Renaissance movement of that name: men and women who could leaven the world with their mixture of knowledge and dedication to Christ.

In spite of whatever sense of disappointment he felt for the changing times, Ray was an idealist to the end. Only once did he even consider leaving Harding, when he was quietly offered a deanship at Arkansas State University. Though such a position would allow his crusade for liberal arts to move to a broader, perhaps more powerful, theater, he wanted to fight his battles at Harding, now too much a part of his very being to make severance possible. Besides, the disappointments of academia were not Ray's biggest problem. Curriculum and budget battles were a minor stress compared to the events of his personal life. Kandy's suicide in 1983 was followed by other family problems that lingered until his death in 1994. The cumulative strain showed little by little, so that perhaps Harding's polite academic strife was a welcome relief.

THE WOE OF DIVORCE

I remember fixing my eyes on a flaw in the curtains behind the platform. In the background Ray's voice intoned biblical truths about marriage. Behind me hundreds of people sat in the cushioned pews of the Downtown Searcy Church of Christ. To my left my oldest son, David, dressed in a dark tuxedo, stood alongside his bride, Candy Cleveland, who wore a long white gown.

They were facing Ray as he talked. This was our first wedding as parents, Ray's and mine, and that little flaw in the curtain was saving me from breaking into sobs.

I silently berated myself for being on the verge of tears. "After all," I thought, "my son is happy; he's marrying a Christian girl of whom we are fond." He would be graduating in a few weeks and she would soon have a degree as well. I knew that all this was part of God's natural order of things. Parents eventually let their children go. I would bubble with joy at this momentous new phase in all our lives. Then sadness at our loss of David overwhelmed me. Our first child! So half the time I sat staring at that flaw, for as long as I concentrated on it I would not cry. And I did not want to cause a scene in this setting. I could imagine Ray and Candy and David turning to look for the source of uncontrollable sobbing, while the other guests wondered what in the world was wrong with the mother of the groom.

I wasn't the only one battling such feelings. Ray woke up that Thursday morning, March 25, 1971, to the sight of snow-covered ground, and the unseasonable cold reflected his mood. For him too this was new territory. He purposely avoided any personal references in the ceremony he used that evening. If he kept it by the book, he would not break down. As I listened in my state of semi-detachment on the front pew, I realized he was pulling it off. He sounded good, professional and biblical, enthusiastic without choking up. Before he ended with the presentation of Mr. and Mrs. David Muncy to the congregation, I allowed the flaw to merge back into the vast folds of the velvet curtains and gazed on the smiling couple with true joy.

Our family's first wedding became history, part of the whirlwind of our lives that spring, during which Ray finished his doctorate, David graduated from college, Marc from high school, and Kandy from the sixth grade. When David and Candy left Searcy for Virginia, where a job awaited him, Ray and I were as happy as we ever had been. Inevitably, we had anguished over David, the oldest child, more than our younger children. Although talented and blessed with a great personality, he had seemed the most fragile in some ways. He made mistakes in high school and in college, but had been ready to try again when he failed. In this regard he was our most hopeful child. His marriage and graduation seemed to certify his survival of adolescence and readiness to assume his place in the world.

Geographically that place would be Virginia Beach, and professionally a company called Mill-End Carpet. By the time we visited in August of 1971, David and Candy lived in a nice apartment, he was successful in his work, and she was almost ready to get her first teaching job. David's degree in art, his second choice after calculus and extracurricular pursuits made architecture an impossibility, had served him well in his job. He was excited about the prospect of using the major even more in doing graphic advertising layouts. After a pleasant first visit, we soon fell into the routine common to parents with married children. They came on Christmas and Easter; we visited them in August; we talked often by phone. Our lives in Searcy commanded our attention, and David and Candy built their lives a thousand miles away. As we raised our two youngest and watched Marc succeed in college, the far-away life of our oldest son served as pleasant background music to our workaday world.

On February 7, 1975, students in Ray's Western Civilization class walked in to see the usual array of dates and names filling the board. They sat down and took notes at the usual furious pace, as he brought up in his lecture each word on the board, filling in details about the place or the name: John Calvin, John Knox, Counter Reformation, Ignatius Loyola, Council of Trent, Jesuits, Ericka Michelle. As time wound down and it became clear that professor Muncy had discussed all the terms except one, a student raised her hand, anxious to make sure she hadn't missed anything.

"Dr. Muncy, What are we supposed to know about, uh, Ericka Michelle?"

Ray smiled broadly, "I thought you'd never ask. You are supposed to know that Ericka Michelle Muncy is the first grandchild of Ray and Eloise Muncy, of Searcy, Arkansas, born this morning at 6:34 A.M." The bell rang with perfect timing, closing another chapter in world history. Ray never lost his sense of delight in Ericka, so special in part because she was his first grandchild. He loved slipping her name or information about her into conversations in sly, indirect ways as he had done with the history class. Christmases became brighter with Ericka as part of the celebration, and then two years later, in 1977, Ami Danielle was born to David and Candy. By this time, David was a deacon and Candy was teaching Bible classes for their congregation in Norfolk. Ray and I thought all was well.

At some point in the next four years, things changed.

To describe the trouble that soon erupted puts me in the difficult position of trying to narrate details not only painful to me but also embarrassing to the people who were involved, people whose emotional well-being is important to me. In what follows, I am constrained by a desire not to hurt them but compelled by my goal of telling the truth in love. I can tell this story at all only because, though not every issue has been resolved, David and Candy, and others, have become better people in the process of coping with their mistakes. For me, the story becomes instructive in both human weakness and in Divine providence, the two elements at work in all personal histories.

After our return from Italy in 1981, Ray and I began to notice serious financial problems in David's family. A new home in Virginia Beach and a failed business venture led to indebtedness, which in turn put new strains on the family. David had not leveled with Candy about financial matters, and she had failed to recognize the signs. With trust eroding in the deluge of problems, they sought counseling from the minister and elders at their congregation. Hundreds of miles away and helpless, we thought they were working it out.

When we saw them on the occasion of Kandy's death in 1983, we knew tension still existed, but the tunnel vision of our grief made it impossible to respond fully. We watched them drive back to Virginia in Kandy's used Volkswagen, praying that their marriage could be saved. Later that summer, when they came to Zac's wedding, we were encouraged by their apparent happiness. During our Christmas visit in the last week of 1983, however, the tide had turned away from happiness.

The split came in 1984. When we arrived for our August visit, David lived and worked in a motel on the beach. Candy and the girls shared an apartment in Norfolk. For the first time in a while, however, David seemed optimistic and direct. He felt good about a reconciliation, and as a result, we spent time with Ericka and Ami in the motel while he and Candy went out for long talks. Sometimes Candy accompanied us and the girls on outings, making Ray and me feel better about David's hopes. Both husband and wife seemed to be trying to resuscitate their marriage. When Candy invited us over to her apartment, we were delighted. At some point during that visit, David asked us to take Ericka and Ami out for a drive so that he could talk to Candy alone. When we returned, the glimmers of hope that had brightened this visit were extinguished. Neither David nor Candy said much, and David's somber mood continued in the car on the way back to the motel. His red eyes said with sad eloquence what he made official after the girls were out of earshot. He took Ray aside and told him, "It's over."

It took more than a year for the divorce to be final, and it was one of the worst years of our lives. Complicated details and confusing accusations left us all devastated at the end. When the dust had settled, Candy lived in Florida, where she made a new life as a teacher and where Ericka and Ami grew up. David stayed in Norfolk but traveled a million miles from his values. His wild ways reflected a bewilderment at Candy's rejection of him and a sense of failure at life.

Divorce leaves scars on everyone. As an elder Ray had counseled many estranged couples, and he was what some people might describe as conservative on the issue of divorce and remarriage. He never wavered from the principle of Matthew 19: marriage is forever unless spouses are unfaithful. He believed that Christians ought to take such teaching seriously and that elders should require prospective Christians to do the same. On the other hand, no eldership, he believed, should play policeman; forgiveness could untangle knots that no law could. Once David's marriage had become a statistic, Ray tried to practice with his son what he preached in classes: a combination of adherence to scripture and mercy to the afflicted. David would always be our son. Our concern was to help rehabilitate him. To our dismay, immediately after the divorce he remained aloof from our attempts. He knew we could not approve of his life, so he said little when we called. Those phone calls typified the agony of trying to reach someone who did not yet want to be reached. The smallest child can hold a telephone in its hand, but at times our phone would have been too heavy for either of us to lift alone. Together we made the calls, suffered through the silence, and prayed after the click of a dead receiver.

By early 1988 our hopes for David's rehabilitation dimmed. He had hit rock bottom and had no place to go but back home. Ray was as frustrated as I'd ever seen him. I'm not sure I can convey my husband's feelings because I'm not sure I understood them completely. He was angry, yes, but his chief emotion was a deep perplexity. He was bewildered in the presence of his unfocused, drifting son. For his part, David was contrite, having arrived in Searcy exhausted on every level from a series of failures. He found employment again, this time in Little Rock, living with us until he could get back on his feet.

Almost lost in the personal turmoil was one of Ray's proudest moments professionally. In the spring of 1988 he was awarded his third Distinguished Teacher prize. According to college policy, the third award removed him from future competition and earned him the permanent title of Distinguished Professor, rarefied air breathed by very few Harding professors. Although Ray tried to separate his professional and personal life, he accepted the award with little pleasure that year.

During the summer of 1988, we logged thousands of miles in travel while David tried to rebuild his life in Arkansas. Amidst plans for our return trip to Italy in September as part of the HUF program, Ray and I had to help my father arrange full-time care for my mother, who for some years had been a victim of Alzheimer's disease.

In September we took our second group of students to Europe. Back in Florence, we tried to recapture the excitement of seven years earlier. This time around things were not quite as much fun; a few students not quite as cooperative, the visits less thrilling. Though we wouldn't have traded the experience for anything, this second trip proved that first times make the greatest impressions. The best thing that happened was a phone call from Zac and Connie on September 27, telling us that Bradley Raymond, their first child, had arrived. Ray and I both screamed in delight as a crowd of HUF students surrounded us. We rode the crest of this good news for the rest of our stay in Europe.

Back home news was not so good. Like a yo-yo, David's life had been jerked downward again by temptation. In the months following our return from Europe, he was a lonely, confused, unfulfilled young man, once again needing to rebuild his life without material assets. We decided that providing David with anything more than necessities was no longer the best way to reach him. In order to hang on to his soul, we forced ourselves to let go of him for a time. Some people call it tough love, and the name is deserved. The burden on Ray was palpable, and thank God we had close friends to whom we could turn when our sorrow became too heavy to bear alone.

Tom Formby owned a cabin on Greer's Ferry Lake. We had spent the night there several times, and Ray always enjoyed swimming in the cold lake water, grilling steaks afterward, and talking into the night while the water lapped against the shore and the insects chattered in the background. When Tom offered the place again in the middle of all the mess with David, Ray gladly accepted.

He wanted to swim as soon as we arrived, so Tom joined him. I watched them go through their routine. At the dock Tom strapped on his life preserver. He always wore one and insisted his guests do the same. Ray had always refused, as he did on this occasion. His macho attitude went back to his days on the Kanawha, I suppose; he was always proud of his skill as a swimmer, always wanting to be the first in the water. He often executed a noisy cannonball as his preferred method of entry. On this occasion he slipped into the water and struck out for a point about one hundred yards away, the turnaround spot. Tom struggled to keep up, fearing that with Ray's recent blood pressure problems, he might overdo it. The water was at least thirty feet deep—beautiful swimming but dangerous. Ray swam strongly, though, and pulled himself up on the dock laughing.

That night after supper we prayed for a long time with Tom and Mary about our son. Safe for a moment in God's natural world, we felt closer to

Him too, and we needed His power. Some currents are just too strong to risk without a life preserver.

We didn't confide in many of our friends because the problem was so personal, and even though one part of us knew that Christian sympathy would always manifest itself, our sense of privacy dictated limits on what and with whom we shared. Of course, in the small town of Searcy and the smaller community of Harding, many people would find out. But Searcy and Harding do not fit the profile of the judgmental, finger-pointing small town citizens often seen in fiction or movies. Even when things went unspoken, we knew that others were praying for us. Still, the shame of divorce and the other problems made it very hard to be open. All we knew to do was carry on with as much dignity as possible. Ray never missed a day's work during David's problems. I too fulfilled my job responsibilities and maintained my church and social commitments. But it wasn't easy. On one especially tough day, I suddenly remembered a conversation Ray and I had years before.

It took place in the late 1970s, in the days when statistics about divorce showed up everywhere—in newspapers and magazines, in church periodicals, and in the pulpit. On this day, as usual, Ray had been reading something that made him get up from his Archie Bunker chair in the family room and look for me. I was in the kitchen when he came in, magazine in one hand.

"Sit down for a minute, please; I want to ask you something." When we were seated at the table, he said, "Eloise, you know all the talk these days about divorce. Now, we have four children." He paused, uncomfortable with the subject even though he had brought it up. "I hate to say this, but with four children, our family is a likely candidate to have divorce before things finish up."

"Promise me something, Weezie. Let's promise each other this: that if it happens—and we're going to try like crazy to see that it doesn't—but if it happens, we're not going to let it ruin our later years. We're not going to blame ourselves into a depression." I promised him, moved by the intensity of his feeling. More than ten years had passed since that short conversation at our kitchen table. In the meantime Kandy's death tested us, strengthened us I would have said, to withstand the pain of a child's divorce.

But as I remembered the long-ago promise Ray extracted from me, I said, "It's harder than we both thought, dear Ray." A lament from another victim echoed in my mind: Death is temporary; divorce is forever. I thought, "I'm afraid my promise is null. I don't have the strength to keep it."

Our struggle to cope left Ray worried about his role as elder. Would it be compromised by the situation? More than anything else in his life, he wanted to honor that position.

One Wednesday night at a regular elder's meeting, Ray stood up and asked for a little time. He summarized our recent family problems and offered to resign from the eldership. He made the offer to a room full of men who, like him, scrutinized the Bible for what it said about qualifications for elders, men who knew the list by chapter and verse: without reproach, married and monogamous, able to teach, temperate, self-controlled, hospitable, non-materialistic, spiritually mature, humble. Ray stood before these men fulfilling all those requirements. Even in his own mind, Ray knew he met all criteria, with the possible exception of one; the list included the need for an elder to manage his family well and elicit obedience and respect from his children. One question posed by the Apostle Paul in his description of qualified elders haunted Ray: "If anyone does not know how to manage his own family, how can he take care of God's church?"

In the wake of David's actions, Ray no longer felt confident of his own answer to that question. So he put it before fellow elders of seventeen years.

When he came through our door that night, Ray was close to tears. He told me about his offer to resign. His voice almost broke as he described their response: the elders, to a man, rejected his offer. They told him the same thing I had heard him say before: "God does not expect fathers to guarantee the obedience of children who are beyond the bounds of home and therefore beyond parental control." They said to Ray that as parent or elder, he could not be held accountable for the decisions of another adult, even if the adult was his child. Ray almost cried because his brothers had given him a vote of confidence at one of his darkest hours. That night Ray girded his loins for struggles to come, reaffirmed in who he was and ready to help his son by extending the grace of God to him no matter what.

David seemed to get his life together again, but not overnight and not without some problems. Continuing to work in Little Rock, he met Paula Vint at a divorce recovery class in 1989. A year later they married, David accepting the care of three sons from her first marriage and becoming a good stepfather to them. He has learned through counseling to better deal with his weaknesses. The saddest legacy of his first marriage is an estranged relationship with his two daughters, Ericka and Ami. Over the years communication has been infrequent, but God has given us some moments of joyful contact.

The most memorable of those came in 1993, the year David's older daughter, Ericka, graduated from high school. At first, David did not plan to go, but he came along after Ray and I asked him. The three of us drove together to West Palm Beach, Florida, for the occasion. It was an ordeal for David in many ways, but he wanted to take part in this milestone in Ericka's life. For Ray and me, it was a sweet reunion with two greatly missed granddaughters. It gratified us to know that in the sometimes bitter days since we had been part of their lives, these beautiful, intelligent girls had lost none of their affection for us. The short time we spent with them—spent in touring malls, shopping, and eating—was precious. It would be the last time Ray saw them.

Among the bittersweet experiences of the trip, Ray had a typical adventure in our hotel in Jupiter (near West Palm Beach) that provided comic relief for David and me. Ericka's graduation was on Sunday afternoon, so we awakened early to attend church before heading to her commencement. Ray and I had already finished one cup of coffee from the hotel's complimentary breakfast bar when David came by our third floor room to say he was going downstairs to find the luggage carrier. Since we were heading home after graduation, he wanted to pack right away.

"I'll get it," Ray said. "I want to get us more coffee anyway." Happy to avoid the task of finding and pushing the bulky carrier in and out of the elevator, David needed no persuading: "Thanks, Dad! The one we used coming in is three-tiered with more than enough luggage space." Ray said, "I'll be right back." Well, he wasn't right back. His absence stretched to about fifteen minutes and David was on the point of looking for him when we heard a knock on the door. It was Ray, with the luggage carrier, which held in the center of its lowest tier two styrofoam cups of coffee. He looked sheepish enough that I had to ask: "What took you so long?" His story was pure Ray Muncy.

Ray had found the luggage carrier with no problem and set the two cups of coffee in the center of that lowest tier. After a smooth elevator ride, he found himself at the door of what he thought was our room in no time. What he didn't realize was that he had gotten off on the fourth floor, not the third where we were staying. He knocked. A woman, a complete stranger, opened the door. Ray realized his mistake instantly, but before he could apologize and exit gracefully, she surveyed the luggage carrier, the coffee resting on it, and my husband's uniform of black pants and white shirt, and exclaimed: "Why, thank you! This is such great service." As she took the coffee—Ray felt obliged to hand it to her given the situation—she called to someone back in the room, "Dear, the hotel has sent us up some coffee. Isn't that thoughtful? Then she turned back to Ray and cooed, "Oh, thank you, too. This is so very nice!"

Ray hesitated a moment before deciding that an explanation wasn't worth it. "Thank you, ma'am," he said, suppressing a sudden desire to bow from the waist. He got back in the elevator, went down to the first floor, poured two more cups of coffee, and came back upstairs, this time to the right floor. In retrospect, I wish I had asked if the woman offered him a tip. Regardless, David and I laughed at our woeful bellboy as he finished his story.

The trip was good for us on a more serious level too; we spent time with David without any of the usual pressures or problems. We talked and laughed in the car. When we stopped for gas the first time going down, I was overcome with nostalgia to see David buy a Pepsi. As a child, he had never been able to stop without wanting something to drink. It became a family ritual to battle over how many soft drinks were allowed on a long trip. Memory is a strange thing; the most trivial image from the past can knock you over like a truck. Watching David sipping from a Pepsi can almost reduced me to tears. Near the end of our journey, we dropped David off at his house in Little Rock and said our goodbyes, knowing as we drove away that all of life's promises had not come true for our son. Heading back up Highway 67 toward Searcy, Ray, with quavering voice, said, "You know, he's still a sweet old boy."

Ray poses with his sons Zac, Marc, and David in 1989.

ZAC

Zac was the baby of the family. He usually managed to be the center of attention, loving to dance maniacally for anyone who would watch. He did a great imitation of a whirling dervish. He came into Ray's life at a time when fatherhood was easier. From the time Zac was old enough to have a personality, he and Ray seemed to be comfortable with each other.

When he was seven, Zac remembers Ray getting home at 5 P.M., putting on an apron, and helping me get supper. At 5:30, though, Ray would head to the family room to watch the evening news, either CBS or ABC. Zac would sometimes slip into the easy chair beside Ray and watch with him. While the filmed reports flickered in front of them, Ray would stroke Zac's head and talk to him occasionally. This routine planted seeds for Zac's own love of history and political science.

None of our boys gave us much trouble in their childhoods and teen years, but Zac was the model child. He was sweet tempered and cooperative. In return, he probably had more freedom than either of the other two, including use of our cars. One of my favorite mental pictures of Ray is also part of Zac's repertoire of stories about him. Imagine a warm spring day in Searcy in the late 1970s. The fellows at Donnie Bolding's Exxon station on Race, open for a couple of hours now, are pulling another car onto the rack for a lube job. They spot Professor Muncy from Harding, walking toward Race on his way to campus. They know him well because he brings his car in regularly. They also know why he is walking, but they wait for him to say it. He sees them and waves, shouting as he goes by, "Hey, boys, know what the definition of a pedestrian is? A father with two cars and two teenage drivers!" He grins and waves "so long." Kandy had one car and Zac the other, and one or both of them would hear about Ray's joke the next time they pulled in for gas.

Zac was a good little brother to Kandy. Only two years apart, they were inseparable for most of their childhoods. Further, he seemed to relish leadership roles. When he enrolled at Harding in 1979, he continued to excel. He was elected president of the Student Association his junior year. He married Connie and entered law school in Little Rock, earning his degree in 1986. We were proud of him. Rightly or wrongly, we parents depend on our children to furnish part of our own self-worth. And it's not wrong, really. But it is one of the devil's great traps for us. He takes our love of the child and turns it ever so slightly into a prop for our own egos, our own happiness.

And we had a right to be proud of Zac, of course, just as we had of Kandy, Marc, and David, for their accomplishments. Life has a way of teaching you, though, that true happiness does not rest in such things because they can be taken away.

After Zac's graduation from the University of Arkansas Law School at Little Rock in 1986, he had an opportunity to work in the Arkansas Supreme Court office, where he earned invaluable experience. After a year he and Connie moved from Beebe to Searcy for the opening of his law office. We were delighted to have him in town, but Ray regretted that he had to strike out on his own instead of finding a position in a local firm. Our depression-era mentality left us cautious when it came to the expenses involved in such a move, and we couldn't help our fears—though we kept them silent. When Brad was born in 1988, however, we turned our worry over to the Lord and enjoyed the closeness of another grandchild.

In 1992 Zac and Connie got bad news. Their son Brad, age three, was diagnosed with a benign brain tumor. They were devastated. For Zac, who like most men saw himself as the "breadwinner," even when the wife worked too, the emergency meant a new financial burden resting largely on his shoulders. Thankfully the surgery was successful and little Brad was all right.

But some time that year things started to go wrong for Zac in his law office.

In a September faculty meeting in 1993, Ray asked to speak to the group. He wanted them to hear his news, he said, before they saw it in the evening *Citizen*: "Our son Zac," Ray began, "is facing charges that could result in disbarment. The hearing will be later in the month. You know, Eloise and I never had any trouble out of Zac—" Ray could not go on for a moment. When he resumed, he asked for prayers on his son's behalf. Then he added, "It would mean a lot to Zac if some of you could come to the hearing—if it's possible."

Except for the days after Kandy's death, I had never seen Ray so low. But he did his best to help Zac, who was struck down emotionally too. To summarize a tangled process in simple terms, he had mishandled a client's funds. As his mother, I felt such pity for him, trying to understand the immense pressure of his career. It was the very pressure Ray feared in his speech at Tahkodah, a decade before, now haunting his son.

Ray knew the reasons for Zac's fall came down to choices he made, and he talked to him long and hard before the hearing. Then Ray went into the courtroom and issued a passionate defense of his son's integrity. He pled with the judge to give Zac leniency. Connie spoke up too, with the eloquence of a wife who loved her husband. She was followed by several of Zac's fellow lawyers. They made their pleas in a courtroom packed with friends and church members, those who had heard Ray's faculty meeting request and those who had learned later of the hearing. If ever a courtroom could be a haven for the accused, this one was. And the judge *was* lenient. He suspended Zac's license to practice law for only one year. As I heard the decision, I thought, "Thank God he has a chance to redeem himself." The worst had not happened.

After a wave of relief and fatigue, Ray and I were forced once again to question ourselves as parents. Intellectually, we knew that we had done our best—mistakes and all—to instill Christian values in Zac, and we felt in our hearts that he was a good person. In addition to what we knew about our personal situation, we knew that God understood his sinful children far better than we could know ourselves, and He still loved us. Forgiveness was a reality. We told Zac and each other this. Such knowledge, however, threatened to sink in the waves of doubt and guilt. It took prayer and the comfort of our dearest friends to keep us afloat.

Within six months Ray would suffer a heart attack. He would not live to see Zac have to sink lower before he could really rise. In retrospect, I feel relief that Ray was spared the agony of this second ordeal. My son lost his license for good when another past violation of professional ethics surfaced. Without a job and estranged from his colleagues in law, he was blessed with a strong wife and supportive brothers and sisters in Christ who stood by him. It took a few years, but he recovered the old Zac, more at peace with what life has to offer and more secure in the knowledge of true success. Connie, who never wavered in her support for my son, blessed me more than she knew when once during those dark days she said of her husband, "Zac is a better man now."

When Ray died he was proud of Zac; had he lived to see his son's further struggle and victory, he would have been even prouder. But Ray would have been quicker still to give the glory to God and to temper his earthly pride in his children with a humility born of suffering.

FATHERS AND SONS

In 1987, while he was helping with the Honors program and heading toward his third and final Distinguished Teacher award, Ray continued to work with the Barristers, a club for pre-law majors that he had sponsored for over twenty years. Ray managed to take the half-dozen or so members on an annual trip to a law school where the students met graduate faculty and administrators, learning the ropes of what lay beyond Harding. On the 1987 trip, he also happened to be looking for a new political science teacher and met a young man who would become an important part of the last seven years of his life.

Mark Elrod was in graduate school at Vanderbilt when Ray brought the Barristers to Nashville in the spring. Mark delighted Ray from the first. In their impromptu interview at Vanderbilt, Ray told him, "I want teachers who are good thinkers as well as good teachers," and he sensed that if Mark was anything, he was a good thinker. Mark wanted the job immediately, so in the fall of 1987, Harding's history department hired itself a new political science teacher.

Mark, a Democrat, felt a bit of culture shock at Harding in general, with its heavily Republican population, but colleagues in his own department seemed less doctrinaire. Mark recalls that Ray described himself as a "Reagan Democrat," and the two soon developed a routine of teasing each other about politics. One day Ray hung a picture of Reagan on the glass partition forming a wall between his office and Mark's. Mark countered with a Democratic poster for Michael Dukakis.

Mark also teased Ray about his attitude toward computers. By 1987, when Mark was hired, they were already common in the workplace, yet Ray never really used one.

"I know the problem," Mark said. "You think computers are a fad."

"Listen," Ray replied, "I lay out ten sharpened number two pencils when I write and I do just fine. In fact, I bet I can write faster with a number two pencil than you can with a computer. When I wear one to the nub, I'll just grab a fresh one."

The age difference in the two became a source of humor but also formed the basis of a father-son relationship that came to mean a lot to both men. In Mark's first year Ray protected the new faculty member from a vindictive student who, upset about a grade, threatened to leave Harding because of Mark. Ray read the student as emotionally unstable and quickly calmed any fears in the administration about Mark's competence. Ray's rather standard intervention was for Mark a needed vote of confidence. I'd like to think it as a small step in his rapid progress into a very effective teacher.

Despite the strong relationship Mark forged with Ray, every son feels the burden of a father's expectations, and Mark was no exception. He bore the weight of an unfinished dissertation on his back for the entire time he served under Ray. As time went on, Ray felt compelled to say something about the delay. Yet he "never made a big deal of it," according to Mark. He would encourage, but it was not in him to deliver any ultimatums or to impose a rigid set of requirements. Knowing Ray was frustrated by the lack of progress, Mark put his chairman's photograph on his office wall above, of all things, the computer—for motivation.

The picture did motivate Mark, but not enough to get the Ph.D. before Ray's retirement. At that point, Ray sent Mark a note apologizing for failing to help him finish the project. When Ray died a year later, Mark was six months away from his goal. Mark's first thought on hearing the bad news was, "He won't be here to see it." In the completed dissertation, he included Ray in the acknowledgements as "my first chairman and my second father." When I attended the victory party in honor of the history department's newest Ph.D., I told Mark that Ray was close by, celebrating, probably with a very wide grin on his face.

The motivational photograph of Ray hung over the computer in Mark's office until many years later when the history department changed buildings. Mark liked the idea, he said, of Ray having to look at a hated computer. He remembered Ray's challenge to a contest of who could write faster, the man with the computer or the man with ten pencils. He had never taken Ray up on that bet but it lingered in his memory. Consequently, after Ray's funeral, when we invited colleagues to take mementos from his office, Mark knew what he wanted. He opened the desk drawer, where among the debris he saw a number two pencil. It now occupies a niche in his own desk drawer, sharpened and ready to go.

Mark Elrod has a son of his own, and like all good fathers will try to instruct, inspire, prod, and pull the boy into manhood. Likely, both of them will survive the disappointments inevitable during the process and emerge better for the struggle. Like Ray, Mark may choose to have other children, or find one unexpectedly in his old age. If he does, I suspect he will discover an irresistible urge to assume the role again. Fatherhood, though it teaches humility, also instills dogged hope of a next, better generation who can learn from past mistakes and bring the world closer to the biblical model of filiation: a perfect father whose image is perfectly reflected in his son. Like our dreams of the perfect church, this view of fatherhood is bittersweet, but more sweet than bitter when fathers and sons do not give up.

MOTHER'S PIANO

"In this world," Jesus told his apostles, "you will have trouble," and in the last ten years of Ray's life, our family learned the truth of His words. For every heartbreak, though, God has sent solace. Who can divine all the ways in which His providence works for the good of those who love Him? We can only appreciate what else Jesus said to his followers: "Fear not, I have over-come the world." I'd like to think that Ray and I both learned to rely on this promise as we coped with what the world inflicted on our family in the 1980s and early 1990s. Even in the absurd decay of our bodies, we can have peace, for, as the next two stories illustrate, a joy of the soul survives even the inevitable decline of our physical powers.

Back in 1984, while we were still grieving for Kandy and beginning to realize the magnitude of David's marital problems, we also had a needy loved one in Alabama. My mother, Elizabeth, had shown signs of Alzheimer's disease as early as 1982, and though we still had not identified her symptoms, they were getting worse. That summer I accompanied Daddy and Mother on what would be her last trip, visiting in Oklahoma and attending a family reunion in Texas. I went to help Daddy drive and to help him cope with Mother's uncontrollable behavior. This trip meant a lot to him, but he simply could not stand the thought of traveling with her alone.

For those who have experienced Alzheimer's, Elizabeth's story will be sadly familiar. She got confused, then afraid of her own confusion. In the intervals between her memory losses, she realized she was losing her self, her identity as a human. She flew into rages. At some level Daddy knew that this nostalgic vacation would be her last. They picked me up in Searcy and we made the journey, which proved a good one for Daddy. By the time we left Texas for Arkansas, however, all three of us were worn down.

Mother did not travel well; she was uncomfortable and disoriented. On this last leg of the journey, she merely complained at first; then she started screaming. I don't mean raising her voice—I mean real screaming. It was nerve-wracking. As we drove into Arkansas, I was beside myself with frus-tration. No matter what I said to soothe her, she insisted on being very loud in her unhappiness. We must have made a beautiful sight riding down the road, Mother sitting between Daddy and me, her arms waving, mouth wide open as she screeched at us for imprisoning her. The three hours from Texarkana to Searcy never seemed longer.

In those days Zac and Connie lived in Beebe, and suddenly their apart-ment beckoned like shelter in the storm. The town was only about thirty minutes from our destination, but neither Daddy nor I could take anymore. "Mother," I said, "would you like to stop and see Zac?" Keep in mind that we had gotten nothing coherent out of her for three hundred miles. But now she snapped at me with complete clarity, as if I had asked the stupidest question in the world: "Of course I want to stop and see Zac!"

I couldn't wait to share my grief with Connie and the others, so as soon as we pulled into Zac's driveway and Mother had been helped out of the car, I began the litany of her transgressions: the cruel remarks, the sniping without cause, and most of all the screaming. Connie listened patiently as I indicted Mother, but I noticed that she seemed a bit distracted. Actually, she was looking at Mother, who had been transformed since our arrival. She was cooing pleasantly to Zac and Daddy. When we paused, she came over and announced to Connie how good it was to see them, complimenting her on the way the apartment looked. She sat down in the living room as if she had reached heaven—the look on her face was positively beatific. When we finished observing this performance, Connie waited for me to continue. Of course, I had nothing else to say, except to whisper quickly that it really had been horrible. Connie smiled politely.

A half hour later we were on the road. Mother did not scream for those last few miles into Searcy, but her restlessness increased as we drove down Race Street, onto Hayes, and finally, into the Muncy driveway. Ray welcomed us grandly, embracing Mother and practically pulling her into the house. It felt good to be home, and if Mother had seemed happy to be in Zac's house, she was suddenly ecstatic to be in our family room. Ray and I had expected this reaction for one reason: our spinet piano. Mother had always loved it and now almost babbled in her excitement. As tired as Daddy was, he smiled at the sight of the instrument. Immediately she sat down and played—I don't remember what. Ray was pleased with himself for steering her to the piano, and when she finished her tune, he whispered to me his latest plan: "I want to tape her on the piano," he said.

And sure enough, the next morning, he produced an upright microphone recorder—courtesy of the Harding Media Center. Mother needed no persuasion to play several tunes, among them "And the Band Played On" and "The Battle Hymn of the Republic." Maybe it was the occasion, but I thought she never sounded better. That tape has meant a lot to me following Mother's death in 1991. Daddy cherished his copy of it too. She couldn't read music but her ear was unfailing. As long as she had her powers of concentration, she could play her entire repertoire. No matter how incoherent her speech became, she could speak through her instrument. On several occasions I have listened to those pieces with great pleasure, for there did come a time when her piano would remain silent, when even the voice in her fingers would go mute.

During that brief time in Searcy in 1984, Alzheimer's relaxed its iron grip. Mother played and Ray recorded and Daddy and I forgot that screaming creature in the car, enjoying a visit with the old, the real, Elizabeth Griffin.

I remember once not long before her death when the family was gathered around Mother down in Alabama. We were all tired and tense, and Mother was not able to communicate very much at all. In desperation we asked her to play the piano, thinking that it would relax her and us. To our relief, she did not argue but went immediately to the piano and pounded out a rousing rendition of "Old MacDonald." We applauded. She smiled. "That was wonderful, Mama," we all said; then someone requested another song: "Please play 'Bill Bailey.'" Though she said nothing, we read compliance in her face and in the great relish with which she turned to the keyboard. With little hesitation she played once more—"Old MacDonald"! We tried again, asking for "The Missouri Waltz," and again getting "Old MacDonald." After the third try produced the same song, we decided it was better to laugh than cry, so along with applause, Mother got a generous accompaniment of chortles, guffaws, and giggles every time she repeated her one tune of the day.

To no one's surprise, she died not long after this episode. Long bereft of her mental or physical capacity, she was released at last from her sad condition. When I listen to Ray's tape, I can experience her talent before its decline, and I can remember again the story of my father's courtship of Elizabeth Legg. At our house in 1984, when Ray rescued us from her tantrum by guiding her to the piano, she said as she prepared to play another tune, "This was my Daddy's favorite." She then began playing the old drinking song "Show Me the Way to Go Home." I looked at Daddy, who was sitting behind his wife in Ray's chair, listening. He must be remembering those tumultuous days when he was eighteen, I thought. How she played for him in her home when they were courting and how her drunken father humiliated her and how he vowed to save her from that and did—taking her out of the humiliation by marrying her when she was only sixteen. Like Daddy, I cannot think of Mother at the piano without a flood of memories about their lifetime together. It wasn't always easy, but it was a beautiful kind of music.

REMOVABLE PARTS

One day in the late 1970s, perhaps, two men in suits showed up at our front door, asking for Ray. Since it was a weekday, he was on campus. I asked the nature of their business.

"We're here in response to his request for a hearing aid, ma'am. We're from the Acme Hearing Aid Company."

"Are you sure?" I asked. Ray had been deaf in one ear for many years, but he had resisted any talk of a hearing aid, so I found it hard to believe that he had initiated any contact with their company. Nevertheless, I sent them to his office. Poor Ray, I thought, he was getting older—and in this case suffering the result of a childhood condition, a problem with his mastoid requiring two surgeries long ago in West Virginia. The operations could not prevent a gradual hearing loss that became complete before he was fifty.

Ray could joke about this disability; he could joke about anything related to his problems. He liked to offer this comic complaint about his hearing: "If someone is blind and starts across the street, what happens? People break their necks to help. Everybody feels for the poor guy in danger from a car. But if someone can't hear, and asks that a statement be repeated, all he gets is 'What?' Some handicaps bring sympathy; hearing problems bring irritation."

At any rate, if Ray had finally decided to attend to his hearing problem, I was glad. I wondered how the salesmen would fare with him, and I didn't have to wait long to find out. About thirty minutes after I sent them over to campus, Ray called. He had heard them out. Their sales pitch almost convinced him until one of them said, "You know, Dr. Muncy, we have another client on campus, a Mr. Smith in the maintenance department. He seems quite satisfied with our product." Ray didn't have anything against Mr. Smith, but he did not want to become the next poster boy for hearing loss. He could imagine a future sales pitch to his colleagues: "We have other clients on campus, Mr. Smith and Dr. Muncy." He politely declined and showed the gentlemen out.

"Well, if you are so worried about things like that, why did you respond to their ad?"

"I didn't send anything in," Ray said. Suddenly, the image of our two jokesters, Kandy and Zac, appeared in my mind. I could see them giggling as they dropped the coupon in the mail. Sure enough, they later confirmed that they had seen an ad beginning with something like, "Does someone in your family suffer from hearing loss?" and decided to get dear old Dad the help he had long promised to seek himself. Ray laughed at their boldness and appreciated their concern. But the timing was not yet right. Isn't it strange how our egos work? Ray knew he needed the hearing aid and even considered it until he realized that other people would know about it. He might have to live with hearing loss, but he wasn't ready to advertise it.

And his stubbornness persisted despite the inconvenience of the condition. Mark Elrod, on board the history faculty by 1987, claims that in some meeting he got caught between Ray and Virgil Lawyer, another aging history teacher with poor hearing. Since each man sat with his bad ear turned in the direction of the other, Mark had to endure their shouting through him to make their points.

Maybe the most embarrassing incident concerning Ray's hearing occurred when he performed the wedding of Joe Segraves' daughter Beth. She had been a history major, and our families enjoyed a long and close relationship. Beth's love and respect for Ray made him a natural choice to perform the ceremony. Ray did not know her fiancé, Andy Holder, as well, but was happy to do the wedding. The ceremony went smoothly until the time came for Ray's introduction of the married couple to the audience. He said, "Ladies and gentlemen, I present to you Mr. and Mrs.—"

Then he went completely blank on the husband's name. Becky Segraves, Beth's sister and maid of honor, whispered in Ray's ear, "Andy Holder." Unfortunately, she was whispering into his bad ear, so he continued to stand there with his mouth open, trying to get the name off the tip of his tongue. The audience grew amused as the silence lengthened, punctuated by Becky's desperate whisper. Finally, Ray remembered, and the honeymoon could begin.

Even before his hearing loss became severe, Ray was forced to compromise with aging. He had partial dentures by the 1970s, and had worn glasses for many years. Eventually his pride submitted to necessity. About the time of his sixtieth birthday, he shopped for a hearing aid. He was impressed by Miracle Ear products and bought a model we thought we could afford. Sadly it did more to remind him—and others—of the insults of aging than it did to help his hearing. Mark Elrod recalls the day Ray got the aid. Its purchase coincided with some work on his dentures and a new prescription for his glasses, all coming in a week's time. As Ray lamented the expense of maintaining his teeth and eyes, and then described his encounter with the Miracle Ear salesman, Mark broke in, "If the guy had been selling toupees, you would really be set for life."

All in all, my husband did not brood over the aging process. Even the inefficient hearing aid brought some pleasure when his first grandson, Brad, discovered that by pressing on it, he could make it emit a whistling sound. If it meant fun for Brad, G-Pa Muncy didn't mind wearing it. With his beloved grandchild in his lap, making it whistle, he did not need the hearing aid. He was close enough to hear Brad's laughter and to hug him for it. Age takes things away but compensates in some delightful ways. Ray took the conversion of his hearing aid into a toy for his grandchild as a lesson about life. "You know," he would tell our friends, "Eloise will be able to make money when I die—from all the removable parts."

Thankfully, the best of Ray—his mind and heart—were going to stay with him until the end.

THIRTEEN

Overcoming the World

Ray's Last Years (1990-93)

EVEN OLD MEN WILL BE BOYS

If Ray sometimes felt beleaguered in the twilight of his career, he also began to enjoy the respect and honors that come with long and distinguished service. He was chosen by students in the Alpha Chi Honor Society as the first recipient of their Faculty Scholar award in 1992, presented to a teacher who has inspired them to greater scholarship. Don England, sponsor of the organization and fellow elder, claims that Ray was the logical first winner of the award. He likes to tell of the year, sometime in the late 1980s, when Ray approached him about sitting in on his Organic Chemistry class. Ray wanted to learn more about how scientists approach problems. For two semesters he came faithfully to the class and was among the most curious, interested students in the room. It was a love of learning to which so many of his students had responded.

By this time, with a third Distinguished Teacher Award under his belt, Ray had formed his own ideas on what made an outstanding teacher. In 1991 he presented a talk called "The Distinguished Teacher." It was about Jesus. Ray may have seen similar treatments of Christ, who has long been called the "master teacher" by a variety of people. His own tribute is brief, one page, and I'm sure was offered as an ideal for himself and others. At the same time, it is possible to read the tribute as a list of qualities that Ray valued most in himself, even if he didn't possess them in the same measure as his Lord. In the essay he praises Jesus' knowledge, authority, and incentive as a teacher. He goes on to say this:

> Never a teacher had such RAPPORT with students. He was "gentle and lowly in heart" and his students learned from him. He used ordinary things and events like lamps, salt shakers, sowers and reapers, lost sheep and coins, and a young boy kicking up his heels, running off and getting into trouble...things students could identify with.
>
> His examinations were killers because each question called on the student to examine his own life within the context of the principles clearly taught in class.
>
> Many failed, went back home and "walked no more with him." Even his 12 majors checked out before the end of the semester. Yet thousands thronged to enroll, with one little fellow willing to sit up in a tree just so he could see the teacher.
>
> Scholars have come and gone, and sages have philosophized about the meaning of life and the purpose of the universe, but all must agree that "never a man spoke like this" Distinguished Teacher from Galilee.

It is beautiful in its simplicity. I enjoy the parallels between what he admired in Jesus as a teacher and what his own reputation was among students. For example, he may have included the phrase "killer tests" in part to suggest, with irony, that maybe his exams were not the hardest in the universe after all. His possible sly references to himself aside, the speech reflects Ray's spiritual maturity. It reminds us that no matter how many earthly honors pile up, they must pale before the attributes of Jesus. When Ray stepped down as sponsor of the social club, Sigma Tau Sigma, after almost twenty years, the men of the club gave Ray a plaque engraved with the text of this speech, below which are the words: "Written and lived by Dr. Raymond Muncy." It now hangs in the History Department's office.

As an older man, Ray took the opportunity to revisit his youth in the form of social club sponsorship. Early in his career he declined to be a sponsor, preferring to concentrate on his graduate work and chairmanship. Besides, I became a sponsor of the Zeta Rho women's club, and we agreed that one of us at a time was enough. When I "retired" from Zeta Rho in 1980, he took on the role for Sigma Tau Sigma men's club and loved it. As sponsor, he came to meetings but let the students run things unless they needed him. Former club president Phillip Tucker assured me that Ray's opinion was sought many times, guiding Phillip and other club officers through traumas ranging from crooked shirt companies to the deepest personal problems.

Ray supervised the initiations and attended as many functions as he could. I had little first-hand knowledge of what went on in Sigma Tau, but according to his co-sponsors, Ray let his hair down to an extent that surprised the students, and sometimes his co-sponsors, Rowan McLeod and Paul Haynie. For instance, the club held "gator nights" at Harding's in-door pool. The game was a rough version of water polo, a mixture of swimming and wrestling that took agility and endurance. Paul and Ray would be on different teams, and Paul could not believe how aggressive Ray became once the game started. He had no problem elbowing a student out of the way to get to the ball. The first time Ray went on his rampage—dunking, shoving, and grabbing—students were reluctant to retaliate, but finally two guys got fed up and joined in dunking Ray almost head first. He came up sputtering and laughing. He gave no quarter and wanted none, an attitude Paul kept in mind when he dunked his chairman a few times.

Ray loved the so-called "rough night" of initiation. At Harding, rough night never reached the level of humiliation found at some universities, but pledges were forced to endure marching, being blindfolded, getting yelled at, and maybe being doused with food or other unpleasant substances. Despite school restrictions, rough night was more fun if the pledge masters could at least scare the new guys a little. When Sigma Tau Sigma pledges lined up for the last few hours of initiation, they faced an interrogation called "Kangaroo Court" and the ominous presence of a robed figure with torch in hand. If some of the suddenly unblindfolded pledges thought they saw a dignitary of the feared Ku Klux Klan, they were right.

Actually they were half right. The robed and hooded figure before them was Ray, wearing a genuine Klan outfit found in an old trunk by friend Jeff Taylor and given to Ray as an historical artifact. The scarlet and white colors practically blazed in the light of the fire around which club members gathered, and the ARKANSAS insignia embroidered on the back completed the authentic effect. The club president announced to the pledges, who had no idea where they were (they were near the creek behind our house), that Kangaroo Court, the final test of their fitness for Sigma Tau Sigma, was now in session. He strolled up and down the line of uneasy boys, once again blindfolded and worn down by a week of harassment, asking questions. "Pledge Mike, recite the club fight song!" "Pledge Roy, what year did the great club of Sigma Tau Sigma first grace the campus of Harding University?" After the pledge attempted an answer, the president turned to the robed figure. "O, man of wisdom, do you have words of guidance for this pledge?"

From behind the hood, Ray's stentorian voice uttered something like this: "Remember well, woeful pledge, and know that the bastions of learning that are Sigma Tau Sigma will exact from you the credit of this knowledge—know well the Chinese proverb in which the crow said to the llama: 'The road of life is pockmarked with the wasted lives of those whose candles have burned too closely to their hair, and were forced to take the fork in the road that led to expedience.' This warning will be required of you soon, oh pledge. Guard it well."

If pledge Mike could make any sense of Ray's bogus proverb, he might have been denied membership. After several other pledges took sharp questioning and listened to the man of wisdom's blathering, the president declared the Kangaroo Court over and membership decisions about to be announced. During the questioning, pledges did not know whether their answers were right or wrong, so in spite of their sense of the fun behind the "test," they were anxious when the president said dramatically, "Those pledges deemed worthy of membership will find a club t-shirt behind them on the ground. Those not worthy will find nothing and are banished immediately. You may remove your blindfolds!" Of course, each pledge found the t-shirt and was declared a member in good standing. Membership was confirmed by the dubbing of each pledge with the club sword.

Before Ray stepped down as sponsor, the university tightened its rules against hazing. At a Christian college the whole issue of conduct during initiation was a source of constant debate. As I said, over the years the worst kinds of behavior had been banned, but the school was still nervous about the potential for harm (not to mention possible lawsuits). One of the things outlawed was the Kangaroo Court. Ray did not take kindly to this prohibition. He saw nothing harmful about the court at all. He never seemed to think about the possibility of being sued by a student failing to see any humor in the silly Klan outfit. Fortunately, the only African-American who joined the club saw no problem with the display when he was warned about it beforehand. Those kinds of precautions seemed more than enough to Ray. Essentially he ignored the new ban. When he was asked if Sig Tau had a kangaroo court, he blithely said no. What he didn't say was that the club now had a "Roo Woo" court, Ray's code name for Kangaroo Court. The "Roo" came from the last syllable in Kangaroo, and the "Woo" derived from a pun on "court." To court (as in romance) is to woo; therefore a Roo Woo is a KangaROO court (WOO), a new name for an old activity.

Ray's impulsive, childish side, which he never completely outgrew, erupted every now and then. I don't defend it except to say that if he had ever thought some student might take the wrong example from his antics, he would have stopped immediately. So much of what he did—in the classroom, at church—called upon him to demonstrate responsibility and decorum. I'll forgive him for reverting to adolescence a few times a year at those club activities. I'm sure roughhousing with the students or engaging in blunt humor took him back to the days at Freed-Hardeman, or even further back to his pals on the Kanawha River, so wild and free looking out on the wide water.

GOING DOWN THE HALL

At Harding, department chairmen must step down at age sixty-five, so the spring of 1993 was Ray's last as head of the history department. In an unusual move his colleagues petitioned the administration for a dinner, something reserved for retirement from the college itself. The request was granted and in April about twenty of us gathered in the Heritage Cafeteria to eat and share stories about Ray. It proved to be an emotional evening for him. Among the faculty members paying respects were former students and protégées of his: Joe Segraves, his first colleague in the department and one of his oldest Harding friends; Tom Statom, a quiet, steady presence in the department for almost as long as Ray had been chairman; Fred Jewell, whose growth as teacher and as church elder justified Ray's early persistence in luring him to Harding; Paul Haynie, of the huge stature and tender heart; and Mark Elrod, the new blood who had energized the department—men whom Ray had brought to Harding and who considered him in various ways their mentor. And finally Tom Howard, another former student and long-time member of the department who would be taking over for Ray.

Ray enjoyed special relationships with all of them, but perhaps his most complex relationship had been with Tom Howard. Tom was very different from Ray in many ways; I've already alluded to their different leadership styles. The younger man was more aggressive, more attuned to the internal politics of Harding, yet he considered Ray a father-figure and hated the thought of disappointing him. As an elder, Ray became Tom's chief confidante. He knocked on Ray's door many times to discuss spiritual matters. In their twenty-five years of working together, Tom remembers only two tiffs with Ray. I have already described the first, the misunderstanding over Tom's hunting expedition in the early 1970s. The other came in the last year of Ray's chairmanship.

The slight breach in harmony involved Rachel, the department secretary. Since Ray had never written an official job description, and since he was very protective of her time, the other faculty grew a little frustrated with not knowing exactly what they could expect her to do for them. The whole thing was a convergence of a series of small differences into one misunderstanding. When Ray discovered that some members of the department had been discussing the issue among themselves and that Tom had told one of the deans about the problem, he was hurt and angry. He told Tom bluntly, "I don't like finding things out after the fact." Maybe Ray was feeling vulnerable at that point, because he felt betrayed by the other faculty members too. He perceived their talk among themselves as covert activity. After twenty-five years of open and congenial discussions, the thought of any secret unrest hit him hard.

Tom and the other teachers were surprised by the vehemence of Ray's feelings. True, the tension over Rachel's responsibilities had been discussed, but informally. Paul Haynie remembers Ray calling the sessions "secret meetings," which was a characterization that never occurred to Paul. To him it was typical grousing among friends, the topic of a few bull sessions. They explained all this to Ray, who seemed appeased. Tom Howard, who had taken the lead in bringing the matter out in the open, wanted to clear the air completely. Three or four days after Ray confronted him, Tom once again knocked on his chairman's door. He sat down and got to the point: "Ray, I don't want you to be upset with me. I just can't have it." Ray started laughing. Tom says it was one of those big Ray Muncy laughs. "Why Tom, I haven't thought a thing about that since. Has it been bothering you? Please don't worry about it."

Ray provided his faculty members with a job description of Rachel's duties, and all was well again. Ironically, she left shortly thereafter. I think working for Ray spoiled her, in a sense. She insists that she never felt pressure from anyone in the department and that her departure was for other reasons. With Ray's retirement imminent, she felt it was time for her to move on as well. The others describe this brief furor as nothing more than a momentary frustration. I mention it for that reason; momentary frustrations were the best these men (and woman) could do to live up to academia's reputation for assertive egos and constant bickering. Those outside Harding, maybe those outside the department, may scoff at the notion that no greater conflict arose. To them I say, consult the witnesses and see if they tell you differently.

As for the relationship between Ray and Tom Howard, it too survived. At the retirement dinner, I was surprised by the depth of Ray's emotion.

Ray speaking to the Arkansas Association of History Teachers, October 1993.

Only colleagues from history had been invited, and you would think that facing this small group, people he had seen almost every day for twenty-five years and would see the next Monday at work, would not choke him up. After all, he was not retiring permanently, not yet. Nevertheless, he fought back tears all night because of the words spoken by his colleagues. The quips and stories amused him, but the heartfelt tributes touched him more than he ever would have thought. The final, perhaps most memorable event was the presentation of a sketch to Ray. Done by talented high school student Isaac Alexander, it was a caricature of all members of the department, with Ray as the "king" wearing a lopsided crown and Mark Elrod as the baby at the foot of the throne (holding a rattle no less). Ray loved it.

The evening, so much like hundreds of dinners we attended over the years, had special poignancy, captured in Ray's joke when he took the podium to speak as guest of honor: "Usually all these nice things are said about somebody after he dies." We all laughed at the obligatory line, not realizing that Ray would never live to see his official retirement dinner.

As things turned out, Ray taught for less than a year after stepping down from the chairmanship. At first he occupied a small office in the suite with the chairman's office. He came to Tom, however, and told him he wanted to take an open office down the hall: "I don't want to appear to be looking over your shoulder," he said. "It's your show now and I'll feel more at ease letting you run it without me at command center." Tom understood, I think, and to me it was Ray at his humble best. His desire to move had nothing to do with his own ego. He was thinking of the department and of Tom, who by no means lacked confidence but who did deserve to supervise the department in his own way, without direct reminders of previous leadership styles beside him. After Ray's death, when Tom won his third Distinguished Teacher Award, putting him in Ray's elite company, he sent a beautiful letter to me expressing his love and respect for Ray as mentor and example.

IN THE GARDEN

Ray and I both grew up in families who gardened. We kept a small garden in Lancaster, Kentucky and a few tomato plants in Bloomington, but never really had time and equipment to do more than dabble. Our first house in Searcy had no space at all, so we took advantage of Harding's invitation to faculty and staff to use some of its land off Park Avenue. Cultivated by several families, the spot came to be known as "Radish Ridge," but Ray nicknamed the several adjacent gardens "Harding's communist plots," in parody of the school's aversion to collectives in the Red-baiting days of Benson. For two or three years we grew beans and other food there, right next to plots worked by Shirley and Joe Segraves and Marcie and Ted Lloyd, among other comrades.

When we moved to 1002 Hayes Street in 1967, our back yard was large enough for a small garden plot. Then later we purchased more land so that we owned property all the way to Gin Creek. From 1967 until the mid-1970s Ray cleared the land a little at a time until the garden occupied almost 2,000 square feet. Beginning as early as February for some crops, Ray would till the soil, working evenings and Saturdays during the school year. Preparing soil, planting, weeding, spraying, and gathering took so much of his leisure time that he gave up golf, turning over use of our membership at the old Searcy Golf Club to the boys. He said, "I'm just going to garden. I don't have enough time to garden and play golf, and golfing yields no harvest."

Ray took our new hobby seriously, fixing his bean poles permanently in concrete and lining up his rows with string. Wearing a broad-brimmed straw hat, he plowed the ground himself with our Sears tiller and used a push plow to work within rows. I helped plant by "hilling the rows," that is, hoeing the clods and raking up the dirt over the seeds into a continuous ridge. Our friends made fun of this time-consuming flourish, but the elevated rows looked better to us and also made weeding much easier.

We grew more than forty different vegetables and fruits at one time or another. It took water and work to bring that much to harvest each year. Strong rains blew over the corn one year and coons ate it the next. Searcy's many dry spells ruined our output regularly. Ray used to say that for everything you grow there are ten enemies to its survival. Yet our garden proved to be one of those quiet blessings during the last two decades of my life with Ray. It served as refuge for us both, a place to unwind, a place to make precious small talk, a place to watch grandchildren discover nature. In the early mornings or late evenings, Ray and I would sit in the swing, content to be surrounded by the silent life of plants. Of all the places we spent time, this little plot of ground nourished most our sense of God's presence.

On one such evening, both of us bone-tired from our gardening, Ray said to me as we rocked in the swing, "Weezie, I feel like Jonah tonight."

"You feel like who?" I asked, thinking of the unwilling servant who ran away from God's call.

"Jonah."

"Does that mean you refused to do something for the president and got fired?"

"No. It was hot out here tonight. That little bit of hoeing I did wore me out. And the drought. I've been thinking about how dry it is around Arkansas. It's just one of those days—I feel like I've been rode hard and hung up wet."

"But at least you didn't ride in the belly of a whale. And that reminds me; I want to take some squash and tomatoes to the Kellars before they leave for West Virginia. While we're at it, we ought to drop some beans off for Joe and Shirley."

"Yes. I can take some to Joe. But I was thinking of Jonah on that hot day after he preached to Nineveh. Remember how God caused the vine to grow up overnight to shade him?"

"But Jonah was angry at God. You're not mad at God, are you?"

"OK, maybe I don't feel completely like Jonah. In fact, I was just thinking of how that vine was an expression of God's lovingkindness. I believe the Bible says it eased Jonah's discomfort and made him happy. That's the part that made me identify with him. It feels good to sit here. Only we have lots of vines."

We said nothing for a minute, considering how growing things made us think of God's infinite care. Then Ray recalled verses from Psalm 104 (27-30), which he paraphrased and I will quote:

These all look to you
   to give them their food at the proper time.
When you give it to them
   they gather it up;
when you open your hand
   they are satisfied with good things.
When you hide your face
   they are terrified;
when you take away their breath,
   they die and return to the dust.
When you send your spirit,
   they are created,
   and you renew the face of the earth.

Ours was a small garden, just a hobby really, wonderful therapy, but sitting there beside it somehow put us in touch with the very rhythm of life—and the Life behind the life. The power of God is often pictured in the Bible in terms of majestic mountains and crashing seas, but in the only glimpse of the intimacy meant to exist between God and man before sin spoiled it, the setting is a garden. Ray and I were too old to feel like Adam and Eve, but felt we could imagine what it was like to hear God walking in Eden, surveying his handiwork and visiting the creatures made in His image, glad that they had no reason to fear His approach.

WEEZE, COME HERE

Ray loved his grandchildren. The transition from bachelorhood to fatherhood took a while for him, but he had no trouble at all moving into the state of grandparenthood. Actually, Ray may have learned some things from Woody Stogsdill in Bloomington because, like Woody, he loved to play with the small children of others—even before his boys and their wives supplied him with his own. Rachel Roberson's daughter, Lydia, now grown, still remembers Ray coming by one day as she sat near her Mom's desk in the history office, patiently drawing while Rachel worked. On the way in, Ray stooped down to see what she was sketching. It was a cow. "Oh," Ray said, "I love your cow, but let me show you another one." He took the pencil and drew a cartoon bovine with those big round eyes, the kind that make the animal look almost cute. Ray was really quite a good cartoonist and some of his sermons at Pine View came illustrated with drawings on the church's

1989 family picture. Standing, left to right: Ami, Ericka, David, Tina (holding Ragan), and Mark. Seated, Eloise, Ray, Zac, Connie (holding Brad).

blackboard. He showed Lydia how to form the circles and fill in details until she could do a passable imitation. It was only a few moments but it gave the child pleasure. So you see, Ray qualified as a grandfather.

In all we had five grandchildren: David and Candy's two girls, Ericka and Ami; Zac's two boys, Brad and Blake; and Marc's girl, Ragan. David's second wife, Paula, had three children from her previous marriage, and they—Gabriel, Zachary, and Eli—took to Ray in the brief time he was able to spend with them. When Ericka, our first grandchild, was born in distant Virginia, Ray said that Congress ought to make a law declaring it illegal for parents to move more than two hours from grandparents. Since David's two girls did not come as often after the divorce, Ray did most of his grandfathering of them in the late 1970s and early 1980s. Back then he said to me, "This place [1002 Hayes] is the place for grandchildren to come." And when the girls did come, they loved it. Ray was right. Something about the grandparents' house reassures children. It promises that family survives and that home is permanent.

By the 1990s Brad and Blake, living in Searcy, and Ragan, a two-hour drive away in Clarksville, occupied G-Pa Muncy—and me, Nonna. To Ericka and Ami I had been Me-Maw, but with the family's experience in Italy, the newer grandchildren came to call me by the Italian name for grandma—Nonna. Ray was always G-Pa for all the grandkids.

Ray loved his grandchildren. He would have created many memories with all of them. I think to do so was an ambition of his along with writing his next book. He felt very much as if this phase of his life was the next logical step in his walk with God. He saw himself in the stands, cheering for them in Little League. Telling them how wonderful they were when maybe circumstances told them something different. Being there to mark their rites of passage. Perfecting his role as elder by mentoring them as they grew. In a life that he felt had been blessed at almost every turn, why would he not expect to have another decade to enjoy the next stage of blessing and of growth?

Ray kept his pain from me. As early as September of 1993 he felt it in his fingers and then later in his chest. He said very little. In the whirlwind of life at that point, I did not notice. The months of Zac's troubles went by slowly, and by the end of the semester, Ray was ready to get out of town, literally. And head for Eureka Springs.

At his request I had reserved a room for December 17, 1993, at the Crescent Hotel in this northern Arkansas resort town. Ray had told me the 17th was graduation, so we planned to leave that Saturday afternoon after the commencement exercises. It turned out he was off on his dates; graduation was on the 18th, which meant that he had to call Neale Pryor to ask permission to be excused. At his age and with his length of service, Ray was still scrupulous about such things. Neale granted permission and Ray came home at noon, ready to go two hours earlier than planned. I threw my things together and off we went on the scenic, tortuous drive north to Eureka Springs for sightseeing, food, and a musical program. If I had any hint at all that things were not right, it was in the haste of Ray's departure. It had been some time since "full-steam-ahead Muncy" had been so impulsive.

Once on the road, however, Ray laughed and sang with the fervor of a man whose muteness has been healed. He enjoyed every minute of the drive. We picked up our tickets for the night's show on the way to the Crescent, then ate our dinner there. Later, still energetic, Ray practically pushed me out our hotel room door to head for the show. In light of what happened at the theater, I'll always remember the drive in on Route 62 for one thing: a neon sign for the Eureka Springs Hospital.

As we walked from the parking lot to the theater, he first complained of pain in his fingers: "My hands are hurting." In the light of the lobby, I saw his face clearly for the first time since the hotel—it was ashen. I was shocked at how sick he looked.

"Ray, let's go back right now. I know where the hospital is."

He protested that he felt better after sitting in a rocking chair and going to the bathroom, so we found our seats. I could tell that Ray was enduring, not enjoying, the program. At intermission I again begged him to leave. "No, the Christmas songs are next and you wanted to hear them." He did agree to sit in the back for the second half of the show, and about three songs into it, he leaned over: "Go get the car," he whispered.

At the little Eureka Springs hospital, the doctors, diagnosing an angina attack, administered oxygen, leaving Ray a lot better. They seemed confident that he could travel back to Searcy the following day. After a quiet night beside Ray in the room, I awakened to the bad news that his heart rate failed to achieve a discernible pattern.

"That means blockage. I'm afraid you cannot move him yet."

The day settled into a busy one for me as I went back and forth from Ray's room to various errands. Returning from one such jaunt, I found Ray reading to a fellow patient from a Garrison Keillor book. Both men were enjoying the dry wit of the Prairie Home Companion, but Ray stopped reading suddenly and motioned for me to take the book. His face was ash gray again.

The next few hours were hectic. We rang the bell, and the doctors gave him three nitroglycerin pills and then some morphine to handle the pain. Quickly they decided Ray would have to be airlifted to Springdale for further observation. No one used the expression, but I felt sure Ray was in the middle of a heart attack. It hurt to see him jammed inside the small helicopter with one nurse squeezed in beside him and the inevitable IV's running from his body. I phoned Marc, the closest child, and headed to Springdale, forty miles away over the winding local roads. On Monday morning, a catheterization revealed severe blockage requiring quadruple bypass surgery. After breaking the news, the cardiologist took me aside.

"Mrs. Muncy, I have to tell you that we lost your husband during the procedure."

I could not believe it at first: I forced him to repeat it. "We lost him. He had to be resuscitated." I don't know what alarmed me more—the fact that Ray had stopped breathing or that, knowing his condition, they were still going to operate. But the doctor assured me his arrhythmia had subsided. "He's probably better now than when he arrived on the weekend. Don't worry, he won't remember anything about it." A deep foreboding persisted in me, but I really had no choice. With a groggy Ray nodding in agreement, I signed the permission forms. The operation was set for the first available room.

While Tina waited with me, the surgery went well, doctors said, but Ray stayed in the Springdale hospital until December 30. They were waiting for a prolonged drainage of lymph fluid and protein to stop. The source of the drainage was a damaged lymph gland, nipped by a doctor during the surgery. Only when the residue reached a certain low level could we fly Ray home.

In the meantime Ray convalesced, at first in cardiac care then in a regular room. Needless to say, it was the worst Christmas since our fire in 1974. As December 25 approached, Ray recovered enough to desire company. He was also very emotional, often crying when he tried to talk. Tears usually came when a visitor expressed concern or affection for him. Kind words seemed wired to the most vulnerable spot on his bruised heart. The loss of control frustrated and amused him all at once.

Early on in the convalescence, I broached the subject of his symptoms: "You kept them from me, didn't you?" He admitted it. "Why?"

"I wanted to finish the semester." Something in his answer, hindsight on my part perhaps, signaled that his delay had been as much about his fear of finding out the truth about his health as about doing his duty.

"I wish you had told me, Ray."

"I didn't want to worry you."

"Well, now I am worried—and for good reason. But at least the surgery came in time."

He said softly, "You know, Weezie, they thought they lost me in that surgery."

The doctor in Springdale had assured me that Ray would not remember his momentary heart failure; here he was confusing the operations but knowing all too well that he had died a little. "Yeah, those men in the white coats came unglued; they were saying, 'We lost him! We lost him!'"

"Ray, darling, it wasn't during the bypass. It happened during catheterization. But they told me you would never remember it!"

"Well, I do."

And so things went. We lived a bizarre life in the Springdale hospital, sleeping in chairs, half waking to the sounds of nurses talking, rousing ourselves two at a time to visit Ray for five minutes in recovery, crying at the sight of his emaciated chest with its deep scar. We watched him sleep forever it seemed, and saw him awake under the veil of painkiller, calling with thick tongue for water. We made friends with orderlies and soft drink machines. We read every last item in the Fayetteville newspaper each day. We endured long stretches of boredom, short bursts of anxiety, and the odor of medicine and sickness that got into our pores. Our minds and bodies wanted to take on the sluggishness of the diseased who surrounded us. We prayed through the fog of jumbled nights and days. Ray was growing stronger, the doctors said, and the drainage had reached almost acceptable levels, but time seeped toward the day of release like the slow drip of his milky protein through the tube.

I never left Springdale from December 17 until Ray was discharged on the 30th. It helped to have Zac's and Marc's families come by regularly, and we did have a Christmas celebration of sorts in the hospital—a few decorations and well-wishing. To survive emotionally during the two weeks, I also escaped on occasion to run errands or to eat lunch with Tina or Connie. When Connie and I returned from a little post-Christmas shopping one day, Ray was well enough to be eager to hear about it.

"Eloise saw a beautiful sweater on sale," Connie said. "It has an old-world Santa on the front, with a beautiful blue background."

"Yes," I admitted, "it's what I've been wanting."

"Well, did you get it?" Ray asked.

"No, it was too expensive, even at thirty percent off. If it ever comes down I'll get it." Ray's reaction surprised me. "Why, if you want it, go back there and get it."

I resisted at first, but over the next few days Ray became obsessed with the idea of my having the sweater. Maybe it was his way of giving me something when he was powerless to do anything else. He seemed offended that I thought we had to economize so much. "If you want the sweater, buy it," he kept saying. "I'll have the nurses put it on my bill here!" To appease him I promised to call but nothing came of it; the sweater was the least of my worries.

At last December 30 arrived. We were almost packed and ready to go when he asked again: "Have you called about the sweater yet?" Afraid he might refuse to leave unless I did, I called the store. No, the clerk said, there had been no sale yet, but, taking my address, she promised to send the sweater if it ever went on sale.

"Are you satisfied? Can we go home now? I've slept in this hospital too many nights." He was laughing. I was trying to focus on matters of life and death and all he could think of was a blue sweater with a Santa face on it. "Let's go home," he said.

Harding sent its plane for Ray, and after a smooth flight he was soon back in his easy chair in our family room, protein tube sticking out of his chest, looking fragile but content. For an hour on Thursday, he rested comfortably in his belief that he was going to get well. In the wee hours of Friday morning, he began to chill and run a high fever. Leon Blue, our cardiologist, diagnosed pericarditis, inflammation of the heart lining.

By Monday, the third of January, Ray was more miserable than ever. Even a few days earlier, the belated Muncy gift exchange on New Year's Eve had been muted by our awareness of his feeble condition. He developed a violent cough. The myriad of pills I administered did not relieve any of the new symptoms. As I dressed his wounds twice a day, I could almost see the upheaval below skin level as the cough shook his insides. On Tuesday he asked me to call the doctor. By Wednesday Leon had prescribed a stronger cough medicine.

"It's helping," Ray said. "I think I'll walk some." His color returned by the afternoon, and that night he watched an Arkansas basketball game on television. By bedtime he felt good enough to walk the stairs to our bedroom instead of sleeping downstairs. It was about 11. How illness changes the way we live. On that day, life for Ray was the ability to take a few steps without coughing. It was watching television. Taking large pills without choking. Climbing stairs. Brushing teeth.

"I want to brush my teeth," he said, sitting on the bed. He sat there in his fleece jogging suit, his pajamas laid out beside him. "Ray! You are out of breath." I hadn't noticed it while I fluffed up his pillows. His labored breathing alarmed me. "Why don't you just sleep in your jogging outfit; it's soft." He was trying to stand in order to undo the jogging pants. "Let's just get you to bed since you're so out of breath."

"OK, but I do want to brush my teeth." The next thing I knew he was getting out of his suit anyway, so I helped him into his pajamas. His breathing was less strenuous. He suddenly remembered Bobby Lowery, someone we had visited the summer before. "You know, I wish you'd call Bobby and tell him about my operation." It was a strange request, coming when it did, but I sat down at the desk to find the number as Ray went on into the bathroom. Before I had thumbed through to the L's in our address book, I heard Ray.

"Weeze, come here."

When I entered the small half-bathroom off the bedroom, Ray was slumped in the corner; the space was too narrow for him to fall completely. He raised his head slowly and looked at me as if I was on a distant shore. His calm brown eyes seemed to reflect the swirling waters of the Kanawha River finally come to rest as they claimed another worn-out swimmer. By the time I put my arms around him, the light in those eyes had gone out.

Along with a rising panic, I felt gratitude in my heart as I held his lifeless body. I somehow knew that he had felt no pain. I took this blessing with me into the frenzied numbness that followed. The ambulances arrived and paramedics tried to revive him. Friends and family traveled with us to the hospital for the last attempts to put life back in his body. Zac and Connie came, of course. Tom and Mary Formby. Cliff and Louise Ganus. Many others. I felt the support buoying me up, but the ocean on this night was rough, very rough. Shortly after midnight, on January 6, Ray was pronounced dead.

Hearing the news in the waiting room at White County Hospital, Zac and Connie and I simply cried. Ray had come back from the dead in Springdale. He had survived the surgery. He had made it home. He wasn't supposed to die a second time. The grief was overwhelming. It relented only when a nurse took us in to see the body. Standing there with Zac and Connie, I calmed down some. I began to accept the reality of Ray's death. As I gazed on his inert form, I recalled with bittersweet anguish the man I had known for so long, but I also could say to myself that my husband had escaped his lifeless flesh.

Ray did not lie on the table; he was gone, headed upward. I saw him among the throng of witnesses on the other side of the river, invisible but more real than we can know until we join them, watching over me. When my dear husband became accessible again in this way, so did God. I can only describe my feelings as intense sweetness mingled with gall. I breathed a prayer of thanksgiving for him, and, as Connie and Zac held me close, the forty-six years of pleasure rushed back into my being to soothe this one night of awful pain. Those few minutes of viewing my husband's body began my healing.

I left Zac to sign organ donor papers and other forms. I had no reason to stay.

The next day visitors began ringing my bell at 6 A.M. Margaret Blue, Leon's wife, insisted on staying all day, clearing away some of the Christmas decorations and clutter, washing dishes. I don't know what I would have done without her. Talking to her kept the worst grief at bay. Relying on her keen organizational powers gave me a sense of some control over things, but the aftermath of Kandy's death taught me that the grieving process has surprises both bad and good. Knowing that the bad days will come, you accept the good ones with joy and humility. Every unexpected gift helps. Margaret was one of those blessings, and she brought me yet another when she retrieved my mail.

In one hand she held a few letters. In the other was a package. "It's from Springdale," she said. I took it with both hands; the heavy brown paper covered something soft and pliable. After looking at it a moment, I set it on a shelf in the closet and shut the door. I could not open the package until weeks later. But as soon as Margaret handed it to me I knew what I would find inside: the blue sweater, Santa's face smiling up at me, as if to say, "You got what Ray wanted you to have after all."

MEMORIES OF RAY

For the next few weeks I existed on willpower and the grace of God. What I did seemed to occur in a dream, not the same unreality I felt at Kandy's death, less raw shock and more numbness. In the earlier loss my being pounded with the question "Why?" With Ray's death I kept asking "Why now?" I don't know if that distinction makes sense to anyone else. Perhaps any such distinctions mean little. In both cases, life becomes unreal until God grants you enough healing to cross back over the border.

I attended Ray's funeral at the College Church building, packed with more than a thousand mourners and brimming with praise for his life. I went through his books and papers, parceling them out to others in some cases and storing them in others. I remember handing Ray's Western Civilization notes to Kevin Klein, a former student who had been hired to take Ray's place. Except for his lighter hair, Kevin's youthful qualities—a mild face, glasses, and commanding voice—reminded me of Ray when he first preached back in Belle. Like Ray, Kevin had taken a while to get serious as a student. After leaving Harding, he wrote to Ray, who advised and encouraged him. A recipient of Ray's guidance years before, Kevin confided that in no way did he think he could replace Ray. He thanked me very much for the notes. "I can't think of a better use for them," I said.

I remember the unveiling of Ray's portrait on campus. Familiar faces dotted the room in American Studies Auditorium as we gathered for a memorial service, a celebration of Ray's scholarly work.

I put out the garden that spring.

When Ray died, people suggested that I cut back on the size of the garden. I would not hear of it. It was important that it be the same, so I worked harder and hired help for the heavier labor. A little more than three months after his funeral, a complete garden had been planted. For the next seven years our garden went on just as it was when Ray lived. Only when caring for my father became a priority did I reduce the size.

Friends may have worried to see me out there in the garden, thinking the work too much for a woman alone. They would have been wrong. I was not alone. Shortly after Ray's death, a friend gave me a tape featuring a recitation of a letter received by the widow of a Civil War soldier after he died in battle. In part it says, "I will be with you always, always. When you feel the soft breeze it will be my breath." I've cherished the image ever since. In our garden I still plant and hoe and harvest, knowing that eventually a breeze will come up and I can stop to let it touch my cheek.

I answered hundreds of condolence letters. I heard from Freed-Hardeman classmates, former students, colleagues, and readers of his books. The most unusual letter came from Gaius Hardaway, who had been Ray's roommate at Ole Miss in 1967. This fellow graduate student wrote of his very different background: he was worldly and pleasure-seeking, as opposed to how he saw Ray: godly and responsible. He finally figured Ray out, he says in the letter:

> Muncie [sic] totally trusted everyone, including those…striving for more prestige and not really concerned with who they hurt or how they get it. Muncie believed so strongly about all those around him that he never developed any defense or any strategies to become a part of their world, and that made Muncie the one person that stood out over all the others I've known, including myself.

Mr. Hardaway's colorful life and writing style made his tribute to Ray all the more meaningful, and it reinforced what I believe about my husband with all my heart.

In my life without Ray, as in those letters, I kept meeting memories of him. Most of them arose in my own mind. When I worked in the garden, his presence was almost palpable at times, as if in the next second he would speak: "Eloise, we've got to get rid of those groundhogs. The cantaloupes are ruined." He appeared in corners of the house, in his chair, at the breakfast table, residual images of him getting ready for church on Sunday morning, wearing what Zac called his "wife-beater" undershirt and long black socks. I often saw him near water, doing a cannonball into the lake ahead of everyone else. I saw him on a river boat at night, framed against the lights of Little Rock, regaling banquet guests with stories. The power of memory is wonderful in its ability to recapture unbidden the texture of everyday life, but the glimpses are so fleeting that they leave a bittersweet taste. In those first months I lived in a house and world crowded with memories of Ray.

At first each past scene cut like a shard of our life together, as if in the act of remembering I could feel my sense of wholeness breaking apart one memory at a time.

Over the years I keep encountering other people who share memories, some old, some new. I heard, for example, from a former student of Ray's, Darlene Rivas, who now teaches at Pepperdine University. Ray had scribbled on one of her papers that she ought to be a history teacher. The note came at exactly the right moment in her life, and she followed his suggestion to her Ph.D. and to a scholarly book that, when we talked, was soon to be published. But what really stuck in my mind was a memory of hers from student days: sitting in Dr. Muncy's office, listening to classical music, neither she nor Ray speaking.

There came a time in the process of grieving when the images no longer stripped away my being; now each memory restores my sense of Ray's presence and therefore of my wholeness.

So many of the correspondents defined Ray's presence in terms of talking. It was Ray's gift. I don't mean the mere act of vocalizing, or his eloquence, or his mellifluous voice. I mean it in the full sense of engaging another human being as a human being. Maybe what I mean is that Ray's gift was for listening. Students said he made them feel their opinion would be valued. The good old boys felt comfortable "chewing the rag" with Ray on the street corner. People in need of advice got his full attention and often what they considered wisdom.

These visitors and correspondents also remind me of another abiding legacy of Ray's. An "aura of gladness"—that's how one former student put it. So many well-wishers mention Ray's smile or his chuckle or his laugh. It seems that his personality ran on those three forward gears—no frowning speed in the transmission. One day in Honors class, Ray began by asking students to complete the statement, "Life is like—." He went around the room getting the responses. Some students attempted to be serious; others tried for laughs. The point was to stimulate thinking about the "big questions," of course. Ray enjoyed the completed similes but offered only mild reaction until one boy said, "Life is like—a tire." Several students chuckled politely at this non sequiter, but Ray started laughing and could not stop. According to Laura Rice Shero, he went on for five minutes. The class, at first mystified at why the line was so funny to him, gradually became infected by his laughter until the whole room rocked with it—Ray at the analogy and the students at his hilarity.

That's an image I cherish when I think of Ray's impact on the world—inducing a room full of people to laugh. The man that Ray had become never let the troubles of life take away his joy. He had grown more sensitive to others over the years. He had learned to serve others more than himself and in the process had grown to better understand the nature of his God. This maturity echoed in his laugh. Laughter is not the same thing as joy. In fact, some laughter is desperation given voice. But Ray communicated in his robust laugh not only self-deprecation but contentment. Knowledge with joy. After sixty-five years he had learned the truth and the truth had set him free.

I am free, too, of grief's first terrible intensity. I will not lie and say that my life can ever regain the fervor it had, but compensations abound. Eight years after Ray's death, my life is blessed with friends and meaningful work, the latter proving to be my best therapy. In addition to gardening, I spend time each week as a "Pink Lady" volunteer at the White County Memorial Hospital. I serve as vice president of the Auxiliary. I have assumed Ray's position as cultural heritage chair for the Arts Council. I think he would be pleased at the progress we have made in preserving our local heritage. It has been comforting to serve as a contact person for families of suicide victims. It helps them to know that they are not alone and that despite the permanent emotional scars, survival is possible. I read a good deal, emulating Ray by having several books under way in different parts of the house.

My greatest joy is my grandchildren—whether having them over for play in my house and yard or trudging to the various fields and courts to watch them play baseball, softball, basketball, or soccer. Although nothing compares to being with them, I obtain much delight in selecting special gifts for birthdays and holidays. And I share in their scholastic honors with as much pride as I did as a parent. Most of all, I am blessed to see them grow. As I watch the trials and joys of my children in their childrearing from the relative peace of Nonna's chair, I cannot believe that my days as a wife and young parent flew by so quickly.

Old age is a mixed blessing, to be sure, but it does have its wisdom, its view from the mountaintop. Maybe more often than not it is experience, not great wisdom, that I feel calming me down in the midst of some family trouble. I haven't seen it all, but it is comforting to know that I have seen a lot of it. Thus maybe I can help my children and theirs weather their storms, even fight the good fights. Grandparents are a little like those ex-soldiers or politicians who get called back in to help the new administrations as advisors. We get to go back to what made life so exciting and wonderful but without the pressure. It's not that my children run to me for advice all the time, but if and when they do, I'm ready to give it. "What should I do? What should I do?"

Why, as someone once urged me to do, you simply rise above it.

ANOTHER BAPTISM

One day Brad telephoned me with something on his mind: "Nonna," he said, "I need help. I want to be baptized because I don't want to go to hell if I die. But Mom and Dad want me to be sure." I said, "Your Mom and Dad want you to go to heaven too, honey. If you're ready they will help you be baptized. Don't worry." By the time we said goodbye, my words seemed to reassure him. I had been expecting the call because Connie had forewarned me about her son's announcement. It all had a very familiar ring to me, old grandma that I was.

Before the week was out I gathered with about twenty-five close friends of Zac's and Connie's at the College Church auditorium. Elder Larry Long and Educational Minister Sam Billingsly were there, and several of Brad's Bible teachers. Among the other invitees, Connie's parents, Verna and Ralph Mansell, watched with the rest of us from the front pews as Zac sat in one of two chairs at the front.

Zac welcomed everyone, explaining that instead of waiting until Sunday and a crowd of 1,000, the family wanted to grant his son Brad's wish to be baptized right away, and perform the act in front of a few cherished friends and family members. Then we sang songs selected by Brad himself, with help from little brother Blake. Following the songs and a prayer led by Ralph, Zac asked Brad to join him up front.

At first Brad crawled into Zac's lap. As his dad talked to him, he eventually slipped into the other chair. The two talked about this important step of becoming a Christian. Then Zac pointed at us in the pews and said, "Brad, look out there and tell me who you see." Brad hesitated like a student not sure of what the teacher wanted: "I don't know."

Zac pointed directly at me: "Well, who's that?

Brad brightened, "Nonna."

"And who's that?"

"It's Papaw and Mamaw."

He pointed out a few others and then swept his hand over the entire group: "Brad, they are your support group. I know you are going to try to live for Jesus, and I think you will succeed. But son, you will fall sometimes. I know because I have. These folks have been my support group. I want you to know that you can count on them. They are one of God's gifts to you."

Zac struggled against tears as he talked. I did too but not hard enough. My tears might have been tinged with regret at the pain my son had gone through, but they were composed mainly of joy for the forgiveness he was passing on to his son. I stayed misty eyed as Zac took Brad's confession and as he baptized Brad. Our small group burst into applause and song, followed up by a round of rejoicing and hugging.

I gave my biggest hugs to my grandson and son. Funny, but I don't remember anything I said to them. I'm sure I mouthed only clichés—heartfelt but unmemorable. After all, who could be eloquent or original at a time like this?

"Ah!" I caught myself thinking, "Ray Muncy could have been eloquent." As soon as I thought his name, his presence surrounded me almost like an embrace. But, I realized, he had been here all along. He was on that little stage with Zac and Brad. He had been beside me watching Brad come up out of the water. Like the guardian angel Zac said he was, he presided over the welcoming of a fourth generation Muncy into the Lord's body. It was 1939 when little Raymond with the musical feet was baptized, not long after John D's and Flara's immersions, to complete the first two generations. Zac had been the last of the third generation.

How many baptisms had I witnessed down through the years? This ritual, fixed and familiar to me, shone gloriously as I imagined Ray standing there in a line, not just of Muncys, but of all believers, a long bead of souls stretching back to the first century and ahead to the grandchildren of Brad Muncy's grandchildren, a string as long as eternity circling ahead and back to God.

I admit that I am putting into words an inarticulate joy that pervaded me when I sensed Ray in the church building. But I felt as though he were conducting a last lesson in history, wordlessly conveying his—our—place in the flow of time. There are wars and rumors of wars. Great men and events act out their drama on the television of life while we watch and call it history. Meanwhile God's story moves forward one new birth at a time.

I am grateful to God for granting me this awareness. I miss Ray, terribly sometimes. I am lonely but never alone. This comfort of knowing our souls can transcend time and distance reminds me of one more image of Ray, an occasion for which I was absent, but one that assures me our family can never be separated from each other, or from the love of God.

It's David's story actually. David our prodigal, the child who moved away to Virginia and beyond, and who came back in stages from his far country. Living in Little Rock with his new family in the early 1990s, he seemed fine but kept a barely noticeable polite distance, as if his official return and repentance could not dissolve all the old estrangement. Ray loved David across this narrow divide, feeling as we all did that something more perhaps ought to be said, but believing the words would come to the right person at the right time.

Then Ray died. Together less often since David's college days, the boys joined in Searcy to say goodbye to their father. At some point in the public ritual of grief I secured a moment of privacy for the four of us. We stood in the small room of the funeral home where Ray's body lay in its mahogany casket. With the funeral moments away and all of us in the room alone, gazing at Ray's calm face, I said, "I want you boys to honor your dad with your lives." As soon as my unplanned words escaped, David sank to his knees, crying. When I leaned close to put my hand on his shoulder, he whispered so that only I could hear, "But I'm the one who has let him down the most!" I could only stand there touching him, part of me wishing the other two boys could have heard his words. I wanted them to believe what I did—that with those words David had come all the way home.

"And don't think for a minute," I said silently to no one in particular and to everyone, "the words came too late for Ray!"

Anyway, this is David's story. He likes to tell of a getaway with his dad sometime when he was in college. Ray took all the children to a spot on the Buffalo River where they floated down in two canoes. Marc was with David in one canoe. Kandy and Zac manned the paddles stern and bow in the other, with Ray between them. The trip got off to a bad start when David and Marc accidentally dumped the cooler containing lunch into the river. They salvaged enough food to keep everyone happy and off they went, paddling lazily, wisecracking. At some point David looked over at the other canoe, where Ray, in the inevitable white t-shirt and dark pants, sat with arms folded on his chest. His head, adorned by a handkerchief, leaned back as he surveyed the water, sky and shore while his two rowers carried him downstream. David nudged Marc. The two older brothers watched their father, completely relaxed, silent, smiling benignly on nature's beauty. Zac and Kandy soon caught on to the joke, and they all laughed at the sight. As shabbily as he was dressed, Ray's manner suggested a Near Eastern monarch traveling on a grand barge to meet other royalty.

Dad—always too funny for words.

I wonder what Ray was thinking as they all regarded him in his regal pose. Maybe he was saying to himself, "If Weezie were here, I wouldn't mind sailing down this river forever."

SOURCES

Chapter 1, Little Raymond with the Musical Feet

1. Information on the battle between union and company men was obtained from two sources: *World Book Encyclopedia*, volume 19 (Chicago: Field Enterprises Educational Corporation), 182-83, and Malcolm Keir, *Labor's Search for More* (New York: Ronald Press, 1937), 433-34.

2. Background on Ray's brief career as "Little Raymond with the Musical Feet" comes from Ivan M. Tribe, *Mountaineer Jamboree: Country Music in West Virginia* (Lexington: University of Kentucky Press, 1984): Buddy Starcher as protest singer and auditioner of amateur talent, 80-81; "Bonus Blues" lyrics, 81; Frank Welling (Uncle Si), 81-83; Orville Q. Miller, 78; Powatan, 87; Slim Clere/Nimrod, 84; Welling's fiddling contest, 83.

3. Background information on Cowboy Copas came from two sources: Richard Carlin, *The Big Book of Country Music*; and Linnell Gentry, *A History and Encyclopedia of Country and Western Music*.

Chapter 4, The Arch of Experience

1. The quote from Adron Doran is taken from his article, "A Teacher Come from God," *Gospel Advocate* 15.7 (1953), 90.

2. The churches fear of premillennialism evidenced in A. K. Gardner, "Fruits of Premillennialism," *Gospel Advocate* 24 April (1952), 266-67.

3. The background on J.N. Armstrong's battle with premillennialism comes from L. C. Sears, *For Freedom: The Biography of John Nelson Armstrong* (Austin, TX: Sweet, 1969), 275-99. (The quote comes from page 276.)

Chapter 5, The Indiana Preacher

1. Background on the "anti" movement found in Richard T. Hughes, *Reviving the Ancient Faith: The Story of Churches of Christ in America* (Grand Rapids: Erdmans, 1996), 228-235. The quote from Benjamin Franklin is found on page 228.

2. Information about John Clayton's private struggles taken from his pamphlet and used with his permission. John N. Clayton, *Why I Left Atheism* (1971). 15 pp.

3. The material comparing Clayton to Thomas inspired by John N. Clayton, "How Scientific Method Led Me to Believe in God," in *Evidences of God: Selected Articles from Monthly Newsletter 1972-1976* (Mentone, Indiana: John N. Clayton, 1977), 182-84.

Chapter 6, Passing the Tests: Early Years at Harding

1. Some of the background on George Benson was taken from John C. Stevens, *Before Any Were Willing: The Story of George S. Benson* (Abilene, TX: ACU Press, 1991), 128-35.

Chapter 7, Graduation Day: the Graduate School of Life

1. Materials on the James Attebury incident courtesy of Tom Formby.

Chapter 8, The Scholar Gypsy: Ray Speaks to the World

1. The sermon excerpts were taken from Thomas D. Clark, *The Rampaging Frontier: Manners and Humors of Pioneer Days in the South and the Middle West* (Bloomington, IN: Indiana University Press, 1939; reprint ed., 1964), 157, 159.

2. The question posed by a communitarian leader is paraphrased from Ray Muncy, *Sex and Marriage in Utopian Communities: 19th Century America* (Bloomington, IN: Indiana University Press, 1973), 13.

Chapter 11, Where There is Vision: Ray's Life as Elder

1. The story of Jody Wood is used by permission of his parents.

2. The video of Jody singing "The Blind Plower" courtesy of Tom Formby.

3. Ray's article on elders: Raymond Muncy, "Thermostats or Thermometers," *Gospel Advocate* 3 September (1981), 517.

Chapter 12, Overcoming the World

1. The epigraph for this chapter comes from Ray's Western Civilization notes.